PRAISE FOR *SUPPLY CHAIN 5.0*

"The evolution from Supply Chain 4.0 to Supply Chain 5.0 has been increasingly rapid. Supply Chain 5.0's emphasis on sustainability, resilience, and human-centricity is being identified as a key source of competitive advantage. This is a timely and practical guide that will both challenge and inspire business professionals as supply chains continue to evolve."
Richard Wilding OBE, Emeritus Professor, Supply Chain Strategy, Cranfield University

"Janeth Gabaldon and Daniel Stanton make a compelling case that the future of supply chains isn't just digital—it must also be deeply human. This book is a must-read for leaders who want to harness advanced technologies while keeping people, purpose, and performance at the center of transformation."
Lisa Morales-Hellebo, Co-Founder and General Partner, REFASHIOND Ventures

"The essential blueprint for moving beyond the digital-first era toward a future of resilient, sustainable, and human-centric orchestration. By blending academic rigor with deep consulting expertise, Daniel Stanton and Janeth Gabaldon provide the definitive playbook for leaders who recognize that people remain the ultimate engine of global supply chain excellence."
Knut Alicke, Senior Advisor and Partner Emeritus, McKinsey & Company, and co-author of *From Source to Sold*

"Spanning important concepts such as antifragility and regenerative supply chains and orchestrating rather than leading, this book provides holistic principles for successful supply chain management in an age where being human-centric is critical, and change and technology are moving faster than ever. Read this book and don't be left behind."
Lisa Ellram, University Distinguished Professor, Miami University

"An essential roadmap for your people and technologies to achieve Supply Chain 5.0. This book is a must-read for every supply chain executive and manager."
Steven Brown, supply chain educator, LinkedIn Learning

"Delivers what our field urgently needs: a practical, human-centered roadmap that moves leaders beyond technology hype and into the real work of building supply chains that are sustainable, resilient, and designed for people. This is essential reading for anyone serious about leading the next era of transformation."
Sheri Hinish, Founder, Supply Chain Revolution Global LLC (Supply Chain Queen®)

"*Supply Chain 5.0* arrives at a critical time for global supply chains and society as a whole. It offers a clear, well-researched roadmap for a future in which supply chains are deeply entwined with the success of companies and communities. A must-read, not just for supply chain managers but for anyone who wants to better understand the world around them and what needs to change."
David Shillingford, entrepreneur and investor

"Supply Chain 5.0 is here, and this incisive, comprehensive, and carefully documented book is the one practitioners and leaders cannot afford to miss."
Hannah Kain, President and CEO, ALOM

"I firmly believe that supply chain and operations leaders who will thrive in the future will be those who make the shift from 'chief of execution' to 'chief of adaptability,' being fluent in operational excellence and strategic orchestration, data and culture. *Supply Chain 5.0* is the perfect guide for leaders who are ready to make the shift. A must-read!"
Bonnie Fetch, EVP and President, Global Operations, Cummins Inc.

"*Supply Chain 5.0* does something rare: It reframes the underlying logic of supply chain management, showing how inventory, forecasting, and fulfilment are converging into a single data science problem that demands a fundamentally different kind of leadership."
Matthew Waller, William Dillard II Endowed Leadership Chair, Sam M. Walton College of Business, University of Arkansas

"In increasingly uncertain times, *Supply Chain 5.0* plots the path to improved supply chain resiliency."
Jeffrey Luft, Portfolio Development Leader, Siemens Digital Industries Software

"Managing disruptions while integrating AI is now reality for supply chain practitioners. Daniel Stanton and Janeth Gabaldon deliver valuable frameworks for practitioners to respond to the new normal and deliver sustainably for their customers."
Tim Kachur, Vice President, Genpact

"At a time when supply chain management is defined by cost pressures and geopolitical uncertainty, Daniel Stanton and Janeth Gabaldon bring a refreshing sense of possibility. They show not only what a better future could look like, but also how organizations can start moving toward it today. A genuinely inspiring read."
Janice Scully, former Senior Vice President, Supply Chain and Operations, Perrigo International

Supply Chain 5.0

Driving Human-Centric Technology in Supply Chain Operations

Daniel Stanton
Janeth Gabaldon

KoganPage

Publisher's note
Every possible effort has been made to ensure that the information contained in this book is accurate at the time of going to press, and the publishers and authors cannot accept responsibility for any errors or omissions, however caused. No responsibility for loss or damage occasioned to any person acting, or refraining from action, as a result of the material in this publication can be accepted by the editor, the publisher or the authors.

First published in Great Britain and the United States in 2026 by Kogan Page Limited

Kogan Page
Kogan Page Ltd, 2nd Floor, 45 Gee Street, London EC1V 3RS, United Kingdom
Kogan Page Inc, 8 W 38th Street, Suite 902, New York, NY 10018, USA
www.koganpage.com

EU Representative (GPSR)
eucomply OÜ, Pärnu mnt 139b–14 11317, Tallinn, Estonia
www.eucompliancepartner.com

Kogan Page books are printed on paper from sustainable forests.

ISBNs
Hardback 978 1 3986 2630 0
Paperback 978 1 3986 2629 4
Ebook 978 1 3986 2631 7

British Library Cataloguing-in-Publication Data
A CIP record for this book is available from the British Library.

Library of Congress Control Number
2026935684

Typeset by Integra Software Services, Pondicherry
Printed and bound by CPI Group (UK) Ltd, Croydon CR0 4YY

CONTENTS

ABOUT THE AUTHORS

Daniel Stanton, DBA, MBA, PMP, SCPro 1, CSCP, CBAP

Daniel Stanton, DBA, widely known as Mr. Supply Chain®, is a globally recognized expert in supply chain management, project management, and digital transformation. He is the author of *Supply Chain Management For Dummies* and *Project Management with AI For Dummies*, and he is a leading LinkedIn Learning instructor whose courses have reached more than three million learners worldwide. Stanton began his logistics career serving with a US Navy F/A-18 squadron, an experience that sparked a lifelong interest in the systems, people, and technologies that make global operations work. For more than 30 years, he has led supply chain initiatives and taught courses in technology, operations, and supply chain management, helping students and professionals understand how to design, manage, and improve complex networks. He is also a limited partner in REFASHIOND Ventures: The Industrial Transformation Fund, supporting early-stage companies that are redefining the future of supply chains. His work continues to bridge academic research, industry practice, and emerging technologies for a new generation of supply chain leaders.

You can find out more at www.danielstanton.com

Janeth Gabaldon, PhD, MBA

Janeth Gabaldon, PhD, is an Assistant Professor of Supply Chain at the J.B. Hunt Transport Department of Supply Chain Management, University of Arkansas in Fayetteville, Arkansas. She also serves as Director of Sponsored Research for the Sam M. Walton College of Business's Supply Chain Management Research Center (SCMRC). The center bridges the academia–industry-government collaboration for advancing its research enterprise. In addition, she serves on the Board of Directors for the Council of Scientific Advisors at the Global Cold Chain Foundation.

Dr. Gabaldon earned her PhD in Logistics Systems. Her research focuses on the human, technological, and supply chain systems dimensions of supply chain management, particularly in areas such as safety distribution, cold supply chain, defense logistics, and transportation systems.

Her scholarly work has been published in leading peer-reviewed journals in supply chain, logistics, and transportation, and she has secured multiple research grants at the federal, state, and foundation levels. At the University of Arkansas, she teaches both undergraduate and graduate courses in supply chain management.

Through a dual lens of rigorous academic research and active industry engagement, Dr. Gabaldon helps frame Supply Chain 5.0 not merely as a technological evolution but as a transformation centered on people, systems, and shared values.

FOREWORD

Supply chains today face pressures unlike anything we have seen in previous generations. Technology is advancing faster than organizations can absorb it. Regulations are increasing in scope and complexity. Disruptions arrive with little warning and demand responses that are both immediate and strategic. Leaders are working hard to modernize their systems and develop their people, yet many feel that progress is incremental while the world around them is changing exponentially.

This is the environment in which Supply Chain 5.0 becomes essential. The ideas in this book speak directly to the challenges facing companies, governments, and communities that depend on resilient and responsible supply chains. Daniel Stanton, DBA and Janeth Gabaldon, PhD bring together academic insight, industry experience, and practical frameworks to help leaders understand what the next era requires and how to prepare for it.

The Council of Supply Chain Management Professionals (CSCMP) has long served as a gathering place for supply chain professionals who are navigating these kinds of transitions. For more than 60 years, we have supported practitioners and academics as they develop their capabilities, share knowledge, and strengthen the supply chains that underpin global commerce. The issues explored in this book are the same ones our members confront every day. The perspectives offered here matter not only to CSCMP, but to the broader profession.

Supply Chain 5.0 challenges all of us to think differently about how we design, manage, and lead supply chains in a world that will only continue to increase in complexity. I am confident that this book will help guide that journey and support the leaders who are shaping what comes next.

Mark Baxa
President and CEO
Council of Supply Chain Management Professionals (CSCMP)

PREFACE

The need for a book about Supply Chain 5.0 emerged from a growing trend. Over the past decade, previously unseen operations have come into the global spotlight as the world has discovered, often painfully, that they are our lifelines. A pandemic, geopolitical fragmentation, climate volatility, labor shortages, cyberattacks, emerging technologies, and government interventions exposed a truth we could no longer ignore: The supply chains we built are not designed for the world we now live in.

This book began as an inquiry to understand what comes next. How will new technologies reshape sourcing, planning, production, logistics, and customer experience? And, more importantly, what is the role of people in this evolution? We quickly discovered that many organizations are struggling with similar challenges: limited visibility, technology adoption challenges, fragmented decision-making, and a workforce expected to adapt faster than ever. The deeper we looked, the clearer the pattern became.

Technology has advanced exponentially, while organizations have evolved incrementally. And uncertainty is rising.

A wave of new technologies, coupled with rapidly evolving regulations and customer expectations, is reshaping every aspect of supply chain design, implementation, and management. They are changing not only how goods and services move, but how supply chain networks are structured, how talent is developed, and how business decisions are made. Throughout our research for this book, one consistent pattern emerged: Leaders are making progress, but it feels incremental compared to the speed of change. Many worry that they are not moving fast enough to keep pace. Adopting these innovations responsibly, strategically, and at scale will require more than technical knowledge. It will require a new mindset.

We learned that Supply Chain 5.0 is not simply about upgrading hardware or software; it is an evolution toward systems that are sustainable, human-centric, and resilient by design. The future of supply chains will not be decided by technological capabilities alone, but by whether leaders choose to apply them with purpose.

Our goal is to frame Supply Chain 5.0 through the experience of real organization leaders who are already building it, one initiative at a time. Throughout this book, you will find insights drawn from academic research, industry cases, and real-world projects from companies around the world. We also provide practical frameworks for evaluating technologies, assessing risks, and preparing the workforce for the human-tech partnerships ahead.

The transition to a Supply Chain 5.0 mindset has already begun. We hope this book serves as both a guide and a catalyst to accelerating the transformation, and that you will accept our invitation to design a new generation of supply chains that are not only smarter but more humane; not only more efficient but more secure and sustainable; not only reactive but strategically future-ready.

Thank you for joining us on this journey.

ACKNOWLEDGMENTS

This book is the product of countless conversations, collaborations, challenges, and shared aspirations. We are deeply grateful to everyone who played a role in bringing this work to life.

We are indebted to the scholars whose foundational research underpins the field. Their contributions provide the groundwork for modern supply chain practice and for the ideas developed in this book.

We also want to thank our students and colleagues who continually challenge us to think more deeply, communicate more clearly, and question more boldly. Your curiosity, skepticism, and enthusiasm sharpened our thinking and strengthened this book in ways that only an engaged learning community can.

Next, we want to thank the leaders and innovators across the supply chain community who opened their doors, shared their insights, challenged assumptions, and trusted us with their experiences. Your candid reflections on the opportunities and obstacles shaping today's supply chains added depth and clarity that academic frameworks could not achieve on their own.

Finally, to every reader. Whether you are a practitioner, researcher, entrepreneur, student, policymaker, or future innovator, thank you for choosing to spend your time with this work. We hope the ideas within these pages empower you to build supply chains that are not only profitable, efficient, and effective but also more human-centered, resilient, and sustainable.

Thank you. This book exists because of you.

Introduction

The Evolution Toward Supply Chain 5.0

The industrial revolution has two phases: one material, the other social; one concerning the making of things, the other concerning the making of men.

CHARLES A. BEARD

Why We Wrote This Book

We wrote this book because we believe the future of supply chains is about far more than adopting the latest technologies or chasing the next wave of automation. Technology alone is not a solution. When implemented without a deep understanding of the broader systems it influences, technology can magnify existing problems, or worse, solve one issue while creating another, even more complex challenge.

What truly matters is not the technology itself, but how we choose to harness it—this time—to confront the most pressing issues facing business, society, and the planet. As we enter the next industrial revolution, we believe that the future of our world and the well-being of every living being will be profoundly shaped by how we manage our supply chains.

Every product we make, every service we deliver, every resource we consume, and every waste stream we generate flows through these networks. Our collective impact on the world, for better or worse, will be determined by how thoughtfully and intentionally we design and manage our supply chains. Thus, at this pivotal moment, supply chain leadership is not just about efficiency; it is about responsibility, resilience, and reimagining what is possible.

In preparing this book, we undertook a research process designed to balance academic rigor with practical insight. We reviewed a wide range of academic literature to ground our arguments in established theory and emerging research. We analyzed trade publications and industry reports to capture the latest trends, case studies, and operational realities. Most importantly, we conducted interviews with over 40 active supply chain and technology leaders across multiple industries and geographies. Their experiences and perspectives deepended our understanding of the challenges organizations face today as well as the strategies already shaping the next generation of supply chains. We also analyzed patterns across both successful and unsuccessful initiatives, extracting lessons that go beyond single-company narratives. We examined evidence systematically and attempted to translate it into a forecast of the trends shaping Supply Chain 5.0, while also developing practical recommendations that leaders can act on today.

This process allowed us to combine our distinct yet complementary perspectives in shaping the conversation around Supply Chain 5.0. Janeth approaches the topic as a researcher, guided by curiosity and a commitment to uncovering the patterns, principles, and systemic shifts that define the future of supply chains. She believes applied research can help decision makers make more informed and impactful choices. Daniel approaches the field as both a practitioner and an educator in global supply chains, drawing on years of experience working within complex networks and observing their challenges and opportunities firsthand. Together, this book brings these perspectives into dialogue, blending analytical insight with practical application, theoretical understanding with hands-on experience, and the rigor of research with lessons drawn directly from the real world.

This book is both a reflection of what we have learned so far and an open invitation to join the conversation. Supply Chain 5.0 is not a fixed destination; it is an evolving journey we are all undertaking, shaped by every decision we make and every design choice we implement.

Tracing the Journey from 1.0 to 5.0

Industrial revolutions are more than technological breakthroughs; they are inflection points for society. Each wave of innovation has transformed how we live, work, and produce, reshaping the very foundations of supply chains. As the backbone of commerce, supply chains have evolved in tandem with these broader industrial shifts, adopting new tools, capabilities, and roles. To date, four major industrial revolutions have redefined the global landscape, each marking a significant shift in technology, production systems, and social organization. We are now entering the fifth. To understand the rise of the Fifth Industrial Revolution, we must first examine the technological and societal milestones that brought us to this point.

Industry 1.0: The Age of Machines

The First Industrial Revolution began in the late 18th century and continued into the mid-19th century. Driven by industries such as textiles, iron, and coal, it gave rise to factories and established the foundation for large-scale industrial production. Its defining shift was the transition from manual labor to machine-powered processes, accelerated by the introduction of steam engines that enabled mass production on a scale never seen before. Supply chains were transformed as production centralized within factories, creating new demands for sourcing raw materials and distributing finished goods in organized ways. The societal effects were equally significant: Rural populations migrated to cities in search of factory employment, and the concept of "work" shifted from agricultural labor and home-based craftsmanship to structured industrial labor in urban settings.

Industry 2.0: The Age of Standardization

The rise of standardization and the division of labor transformed supply chains again, enabling levels of productivity and scale that had never been seen before. Manufacturing became faster, more affordable, and more consistent, opening the door to mass production and the growth of global commerce. Steamships, railways, and telegraphs compressed distance and time, turning local supply chains into international networks.

During World War I and World War II, these industrial capabilities became critical to military success, as efficient logistics meant the difference between victory and defeat. After the wars, the same systems that mobilized armies and equipment across continents were adapted for civilian use, driving a postwar surge in manufacturing, transportation, and trade.

The social impact was equally profound. As factories expanded and workforces grew, labor laws and time management systems emerged to bring structure to industrial life, highlighting the increasing importance of the industrial worker. Cities swelled as rural populations migrated in search of steady wages and urban opportunities. This rapid urbanization fueled demand for housing, transit, and infrastructure, forcing cities to expand and adapt. Behind the scenes, supply chains evolved from basic mechanization into the early foundations of manufacturing resource planning, laying the groundwork for today's interconnected global economy.

Industry 3.0: The Age of Computers

The late 20th century marked a decisive shift as analog systems gave way to digital technology, launching the Third Industrial Revolution. Advances in computing power were at the heart of this transformation. Electronics, information technology, and automation reshaped the factory floor, delivering unprecedented levels of control, precision, and efficiency. Programmable logic controllers (PLCs), computer networks, and digital sensors provided real-time visibility into production, fundamentally changing how work was managed.

Computers also broke down barriers within organizations. Enterprise resource planning (ERP) systems and barcoding created tighter connections between design, production, inventory, and logistics, enabling faster decisions, tighter coordination, and shorter lead times. These digital tools laid the groundwork for more integrated operations.

Supply chains further transformed the ability to collect, process, and analyze data at scale. Companies could forecast demand with greater accuracy, optimize inventory, and coordinate logistics in ways that were previously unimaginable. This ushered in more agile, data-driven supply chains. This era also brought a digital awakening to the workforce: As computers became essential tools, digital literacy became a core skill across every level of the enterprise. With computing power enabling global sourcing and just-in-time (JIT) production, this period established the foundations for today's lean and interconnected global supply networks.

Industry 4.0: The Age of Connectivity

The Fourth Industrial Revolution has been unfolding around us, transforming the way industries operate by integrating physical, digital, and biological technologies. Advances in artificial intelligence, robotics, the Internet of Things, additive manufacturing, and biotechnology are no longer separate developments; they are being combined into tightly connected systems that enable new levels of automation and intelligence across industries and value chains.

For supply chains, this integration is redefining the rules. Building on decades of digitalization, Industry 4.0 is shifting supply chains from linear, reactive models to dynamic, predictive networks. Real-time data, end-to-end system integration, and advanced analytics are enabling faster and more accurate decisions than traditional human-led processes alone could achieve.

As customer expectations for speed, customization, and transparency continue to rise, companies are turning to these integrated technologies to remain competitive. This shift is creating a demand for supply chain professionals who can manage complex digital ecosystems, making continuous upskilling and reskilling essential.

However, Industry 4.0 also presents challenges. The push for automation can displace skilled labor and prioritize cost efficiency over resilience, leaving supply chains more exposed to disruption. The rapid integration of new technologies also accelerates energy use and resource consumption, raising critical questions about long-term sustainability and environmental impact.

Industry 5.0: Human-centricity, Resilience, and Sustainability

We are entering Industry 5.0, a new era in which human creativity and advanced technologies are integrated in more intentional and meaningful ways. This era brings together multiple streams of innovation while also aligning technological progress with human values, environmental sustainability, and social well-being.

Building on the foundations of Industry 4.0, this phase is shifting the focus from pure automation to collaboration between people and machines. Rather than replacing humans, technology is positioned to amplify human strengths, combining machine-level efficiency with human insight and adaptability.

For supply chains, this convergence is transformative. Productivity and profitability are no longer pursued in isolation; they are balanced with resilience, sustainability, and human-centric objectives. Human-robot collaboration on the factory floor, circular supply chain models, and ethically guided AI applications are early signs of this shift. Supply chains are becoming human-centric ecosystems where people, performance, and planetary health are integrated priorities supported by advanced technologies (see Figure 0.1).

Industry 5.0 represents more than just another wave of technology. It signals a systemic transformation aimed at fostering long-term prosperity for people, organizations, and the planet. At its core, it is about harnessing innovation responsibly, ensuring that progress generates shared value and aligns economic growth with social equity and environmental stewardship.

The Drivers of Supply Chain 5.0

In the evolving landscape of Industry 5.0, where human–machine collaboration, sustainability, and resilience are paramount, the fundamental requirement for profitability remains unchanged. No supply chain, regardless of its technological sophistication or ethical or environmental aspirations, can

Figure 0.1 Timeline of the Five Industrial Revolutions

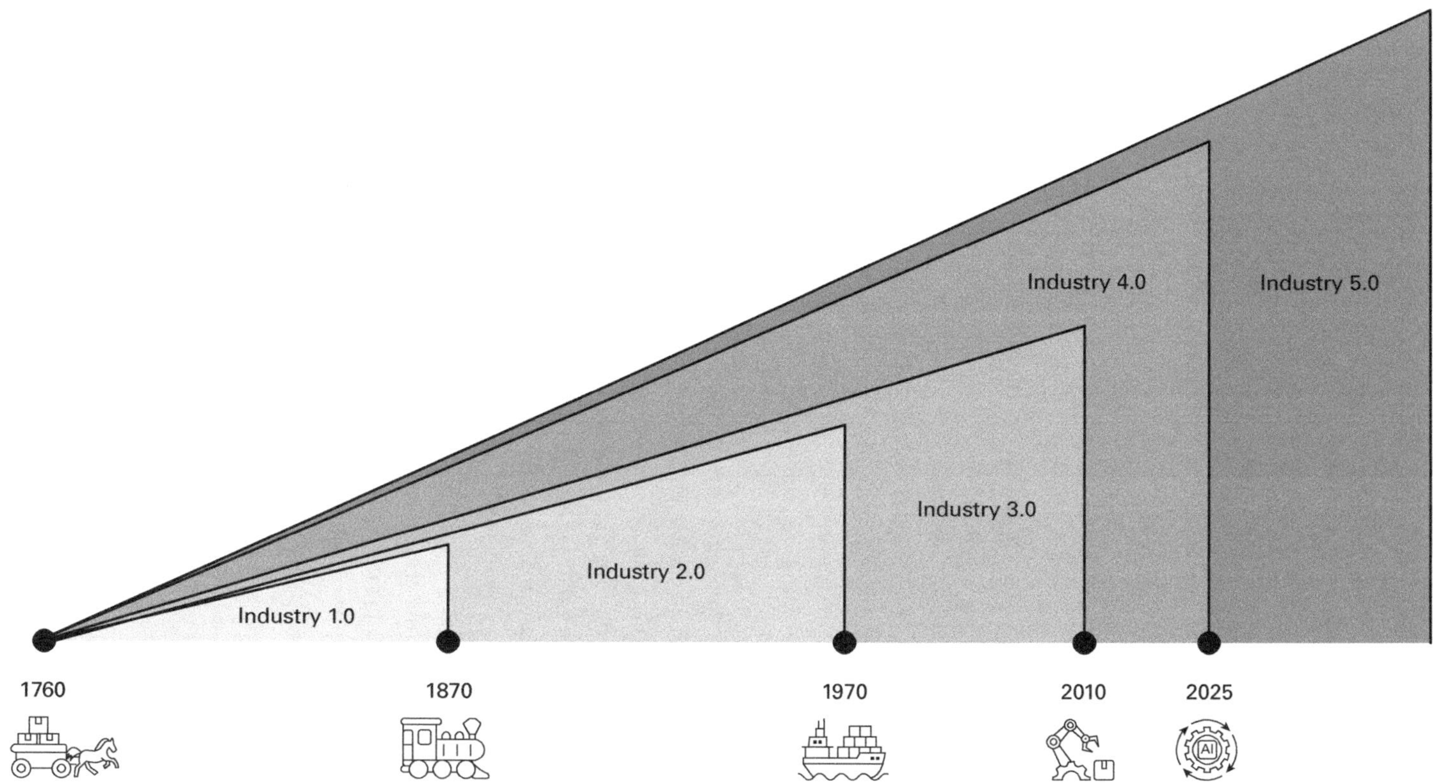

endure without generating economic returns. Profitability is not merely a financial metric; it is the lifeblood that fuels innovation, supports workforce development, and enables long-term investments in environmental and social responsibility. This economic viability underpins the ability to invest in resilience, sustainability, and human-centric design.

Supply Chain 5.0 must therefore strike a delicate balance: Leveraging advanced technologies while ensuring that the network contributes to and benefits from economic viability. This chapter examines the intersection of profitability and the principles of Industry 5.0, and how organizations can design supply chains that are not only intelligent and sustainable but also economically sound. Figure 0.2 illustrates the core drivers of Supply Chain 5.0.

Building on that foundation, three strategic principles define how modern supply chains create competitive advantage. Resilience protects profitability by ensuring continuity and enabling quick adaptation in the face of disruption. Sustainability aligns operational performance with long-term value creation and environmental responsibility. Human-centricity drives efficiency and innovation by placing people and their needs at the center of decision-making. Together, these principles provide a framework for building stronger, more adaptable, and future-ready supply chains, and each deserves a closer look.

Resilience in supply chains refers to the ability to absorb shocks, adapt quickly to disruptions, and emerge stronger than before (Wieland and Durach, 2021). A supply chain that is optimized only for efficiency and cost is fragile and will break under stress. A truly resilient supply chain goes further; it can sense early signals of change, shift capacity, reconfigure networks, and maintain continuity of service and value creation under a wide range of conditions. Perhaps the most advanced form of resilience is antifragility, in which the system improves when stressed. Antifragile supply chains utilize disruptions as feedback, learning from shocks to evolve their capabilities and strengthen the network over time (Taleb, 2012).

Sustainability involves designing and operating supply chains to meet present needs without compromising the ability of future generations to meet their own. It encompasses reducing environmental impact, utilizing resources responsibly, promoting social equity, and ensuring long-term economic stability. A central pillar of sustainable supply chains is circularity, which focuses on extending the life of materials and products through reuse, remanufacturing, and recycling, rather than relying on a linear “take, make, dispose” model (Ellen MacArthur Foundation, 2019). Circular supply chains are supported by life cycle analysis, which evaluates the environmental and social impact of

Figure 0.2 Drivers of Supply Chain 5.0

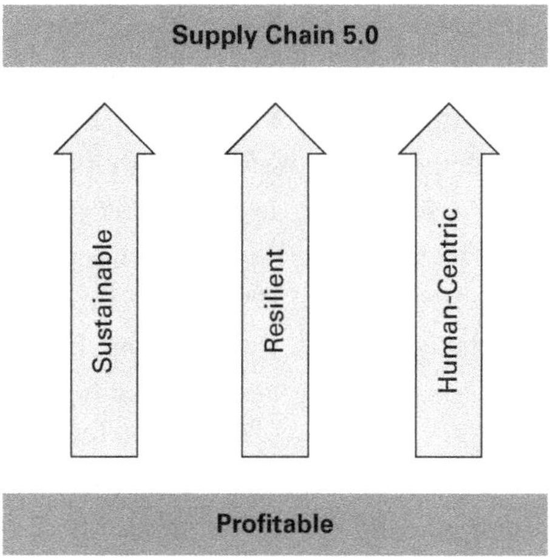

NOTE Adapted from the authors' analysis

a product or process across its entire lifespan from raw material extraction to end-of-life recovery (International Organization for Standardization, 2018). Together, these approaches enable supply chains to create enduring value for business, society, and the planet.

Human-centricity is the principle of placing people at the heart of design and decision-making. It begins with the workforce, using technology to augment human capability rather than replace it, fostering safe and inclusive workplaces, and empowering employees through meaningful work and continuous learning. Human-centricity also extends to customers by deeply understanding what they value, which includes not only price and speed but also trust, transparency, personalization, and ethical practices. Supply chains built on this principle engage customers as active participants in shaping value, so that they can deliver products and services that reflect both their needs and their values. Ultimately, human-centricity creates value not only for shareholders but also for employees, customers, suppliers, and the communities they serve.

These three principles are not independent goals but mutually reinforcing foundations. A human-centric supply chain becomes more resilient because it engages people as problem solvers and collaborators. A sustainable supply chain protects its ability to operate over time, creating the stability that resilience requires. A resilient network provides the flexibility to adopt sustainable practices and to keep people at the center of design.

Understanding resilience, sustainability, and human-centricity in this integrated way sets the stage for the concepts, frameworks, and examples that follow in the book.

Shifting from Optimization to Orchestration

A supply chain is more than a series of steps for moving goods from one place to another. Supply chains are "the complex systems made of people, processes, and technologies that we engineer and manage to deliver the goods and services customer value" (Stanton, 2023, p.8). This dynamic, interconnected network spans organizations, platforms, and resources, working in concert to move goods and services from raw materials to final delivery and sometimes back again. At its core, the supply chain encompasses planning, sourcing, manufacturing, distribution, storage, and servicing of everything we consume. It connects global suppliers, local warehouses, transportation networks, digital platforms, and customer touchpoints, while increasingly integrating return flows and sustainability practices. It underpins daily operations while also serving as a critical engine for long-term strategic growth and competitiveness.

To help supply chain leaders navigate this complexity, the Supply Chain Operations Reference (SCOR) model was introduced in 1996 by the global consulting firm Pittiglio, Rabin, Todd, and McGrath (PRTM) (River Logic, n.d.) and AMR Research. PRTM was acquired by PwC and AMR was acquired by Gartner. Before the acquisitions, the SCOR model was transferred to the Supply Chain Council (SCC), which expanded and refined it before merging with the American Production and Inventory Control Society (APICS). APICS eventually became the Association for Supply Chain Management (ASCM), which now maintains and continues to evolve the SCOR model. Since its creation, SCOR has become a widely adopted framework for standardizing supply chain processes, defining performance metrics, and identifying best practices. It provides a common language and a structured method for analyzing, improving, and aligning supply chain performance across industries.

SCOR 12.0 (APICS, 2017) defined six core processes that represented the building blocks of supply chain operations:

- Plan: Align supply and demand, develop strategies, and manage resources.
- Source: Procure goods and services to meet demand.

- Make: Transform raw materials into finished products.
- Deliver: Manage orders, transportation, and distribution to customers.
- Return: Handle the return of products due to defects, excess, or end-of-life.
- Enable: Support the above processes through data management, compliance, infrastructure, and other enabling functions.

In 2022 ASCM replaced SCOR 12.0 with the SCOR Digital Standard (SCOR DS) (ASCM, 2022). This updated model was designed to support modern, digital-first supply chains. The "Make" process was renamed Transform to reflect its relevance to both service and physical supply chains, and "Deliver" was split into two distinct components: Order and Fulfill.

So SCOR DS organizes supply chain activities into a set of seven integrated processes which align operations with strategic business goals:

- Plan: Develop integrated strategies that balance demand with resources across all supply chain functions (Order, Source, Transform, Fulfill, Return).
- Source: Procure goods and services, including supplier selection, purchase order management, delivery, and receiving.
- Transform: Convert raw materials or components into finished products or services, including assembly, disassembly, and maintenance.
- Order: Manage customer order details, including pricing, payment, location, and fulfillment status.
- Fulfill: Handle order execution activities, including picking, packing, shipping, installation, and invoicing.
- Return: Manage the reverse flow of goods or services, including inspection, disposition, reuse, and reintegration of inventory.
- Orchestrate: Govern the overall value chain by integrating people, processes, and technologies to create aligned, resilient, and sustainable operations.

Within this updated structure, the process formerly known as "Enable" has been replaced with "Orchestrate," marking a fundamental change in how supply chains are managed. While Enable focused on providing the tools, systems, and infrastructure to support operations, Orchestrate describes a strategic leadership role. It is about guiding the entire supply chain by aligning people, data, and technology to drive coordinated action and deliver organizational objectives. Orchestrate encompasses performance and risk management, environmental and social governance, digital oversight, talent and contract governance, circular economy strategies, and network design. It positions the supply chain as a central driver of business success and a catalyst for building sustainable, resilient ecosystems.

SCOR DS also introduces four core concepts that define effective supply chain: Supply, demand, synchronize, and regenerate. Each is enabled by the Orchestrate process, which provides strategic alignment across all functions:

- Supply ensures reliable sourcing, production, and delivery of goods and services, supported by the Source and Transform processes.
- Demand focuses on anticipating and meeting customer needs through the Order and Fulfill processes.
- Synchronize emphasizes coordination across all functions, partners, and technologies, embodied in the Plan process.
- Regenerate addresses sustainability and resilience by restoring resources, reducing waste, and managing reverse flows through the Return process.

This updated structure reflects the reality that modern supply chains are not a series of one-way steps but continuous, interconnected systems that adapt and evolve over time.

Aligning Strategy with Execution

To thrive in this new era, supply chain leaders need both a strategic vision and a practical framework for execution. Industry 5.0 sets the direction with its emphasis on resilience, sustainability, and human-centricity. Frameworks like the SCOR Digital Standard provide the operational roadmap, defining the processes required to translate these priorities into coordinated action.

Supply Chain 5.0 serves as the execution layer, where processes connect Industry 5.0's strategic horizon to daily execution.

For leaders, this integration means moving beyond viewing resilience, sustainability, and human-centricity as trade-offs or add-ons to cost and efficiency. Instead, Supply Chain 5.0 incorporates them as fundamental design parameters. SCOR DS provides a structure to operationalize these goals, ensuring that strategic priorities are translated into measurable results across the network.

Industry 5.0 identifies the outcomes supply chains must achieve, while SCOR DS provides the structured path to reach them. At the center are the four essential results: Resilience, sustainability, human-centricity, and profitability. Surrounding them are the SCOR DS processes, which translate strategic priorities into coordinated daily execution across the value chain. Enclosing both is Supply Chain 5.0, which integrates purpose, process, and performance into networks designed for adaptability and long-term success.

This approach reorients supply chain management from a focus on short-term efficiency to the development of purpose-driven systems. It encourages leaders to view their supply networks as dynamic ecosystems, where technology, people, and resilient strategy align in pursuit of a shared vision and benefit. Embracing this perspective can help organizations effectively meet immediate operational demands while strategically navigating toward the future of Supply Chain 5.0 (see Figure 0.3).

Figure 0.3 Supply Chain 5.0: Blending the SCOR DS processes with Industry 5.0 goals

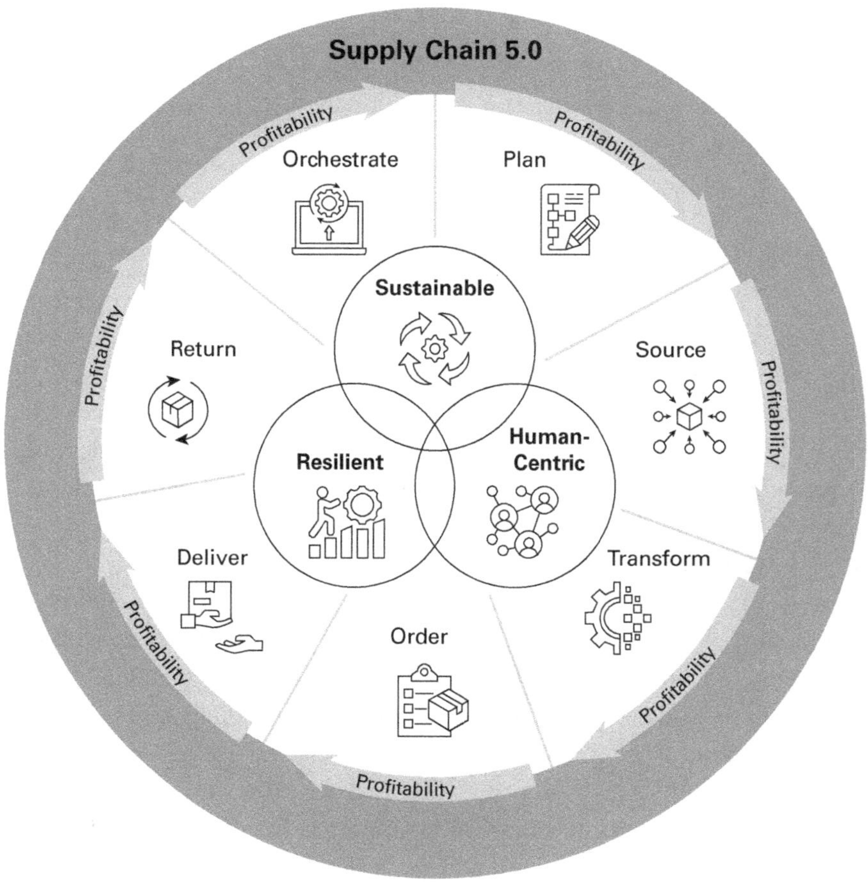

This resulting shift lays the foundation for what lies ahead. This book is organized into four parts, each designed to guide you through the evolving landscape of Supply Chain 5.0. Part One introduces the foundational principles. Part Two explores each stage of the supply chain in terms of the SCOR DS processes. Part Three addresses the challenges and barriers that organizations may face when adopting Supply Chain 5.0. Finally, Part Four looks ahead to the trends that will shape the future of supply chains. We conclude with a forward-looking reflection in Shaping What's Next: The Road Ahead for Supply Chain 5.0.

In other words, supply chain processes and Industry 5.0 combine to form Supply Chain 5.0:

- Strategic Horizon: Establishes the overarching goals of resilience, sustainability, human-centricity, and long-term value creation.
- Operational Roadmap: Defines the core processes (Plan, Source, Transform, Order, Fulfill, Return, Orchestrate) and provides the structure for daily execution and alignment.
- Integration: Aligns the operational roadmap strategic horizon to create purpose-driven networks.

KEY TAKEAWAYS

- Supply Chain 5.0 requires aligning technology innovation with environmental responsibility, resilience, and societal impact.
- The journey from Industry 1.0 to 5.0 shows a shift from mechanization to human–machine collaboration, sustainability, and purpose-driven design.
- Industry 5.0 uses advanced technologies to amplify rather than replace human capability.
- Profitability remains essential, but must be balanced with resilience, sustainability, and human-centric value.
- Supply Chain 5.0 integrates Industry 5.0's strategic goals with execution discipline to create adaptive, ethical, and purpose-driven networks.
- Resilience, sustainability, and human-centricity form the three reinforcing pillars of competitive advantage in Supply Chain 5.0.
- The shift from optimization to orchestration reframes supply chains as dynamic ecosystems rather than linear processes.
- Frameworks enable leaders to operationalize Industry 5.0 principles across planning, sourcing, production, fulfillment, and returns.

References

APICS (2017) Supply chain operations reference model (SCOR), version 12.0. APICS. www.apics.org/docs/default-source/scor-training/scor-v12-0-framework-introduction.pdf?sfvrsn=2 (archived at https://perma.cc/M8SV-CUGV)

ASCM (2022) Supply chain operations reference model: SCOR digital standard. ASCM. www.ascm.org/globalassets/ascm_website_assets/docs/intro-and-front-matter-scor-digital-standard2.pdf (archived at https://perma.cc/JAA5-HNFE)

Association for Supply Chain Management (2022, August 23) ASCM releases new SCOR Digital Standard. *PR Newswire*. www.prnewswire.com/news-releases/ascm-releases-new-scor-digital-standard-301626710.html (archived at https://perma.cc/49A2-UHCE)

Beard, C. A. (2013) *Industrial Revolution*. Routledge.

Ellen MacArthur Foundation (2019) Completing the picture: How the circular economy tackles climate change. Ellen MacArthur Foundation. www.ellenmacarthurfoundation.org/completing-the-picture (archived at https://perma.cc/CRZ2-BF3T)

International Organization for Standardization (2018) Environmental management — Life cycle assessment — Principles and framework (ISO 14040:2018). ISO.

River Logic, Inc. (n.d.) The ultimate SCOR model for supply chain decisions. River Logic. https://riverlogic.com/?blog=the-ultimate-scor-model-for-supply-chain-decisions (archived at https://perma.cc/6AB2-X39X)

Stanton, D. (2023) *Supply Chain Management For Dummies*. John Wiley & Sons

Taleb, N. N (2012) *Antifragile: Things that gain from disorder*. Random House.

Wieland, A. and Durach, C. F. (2021) Two perspectives on supply chain resilience. *Journal of Business Logistics*, 42(3), 315–22

PART ONE
Understanding Supply Chain 5.0

Defining the Shift: What makes Supply Chain 5.0 Different?

01

As machines get better at being machines, humans have to get better at being more human.

ANDREW J. SCOTT

Reframing the Mission of Supply Chains

What if supply chains were no longer seen merely as engines of efficiency and profit but as platforms for generating shared value across economies, societies, and ecosystems? In earlier industrial revolutions, the focus was on productivity, automation, and scale, often at the expense of human well-being and environmental sustainability. But as we move from Industry 4.0 into Industry 5.0, the mission of supply chains is being fundamentally redefined.

This chapter explores what it means to lead in this new environment. It examines the principles of Supply Chain 5.0 and show how we can align technology, values, and strategy to create a smarter, more sustainable future.

This transition is not only aspirational; it is becoming essential. Today's supply chains must operate in a world shaped by climate change, demographic shifts, geopolitical instability, and rising expectations for fairness, transparency, and sustainability. Traditional models that prioritize speed and cost alone are no longer sufficient. The seven rights of supply chain management—the right product, quantity, condition, place, time, customer, and cost—remain important, but they must now be considered alongside broader responsibilities. If supply chains are defined by processes, then the way that we transform them is through projects. To help organizations manage this transition effectively, we developed the Supply Chain 5.0 Adoption Model (see Figure 1.1). At the center of the model are Supply Chain 5.0 projects. These are the initiatives that bring the transformation to life. On the left side of the model are the technological capabilities developed during Industry 4.0, including automation, artificial intelligence, and advanced analytics. These tools enable progress and feed into the design of new projects. Above the projects are structural business goals such as profitability, regulatory compliance, and brand reputation. These goals influence how supply chain initiatives are selected and prioritized. Below the projects is the broader business environment, which includes government policy, shifting customer expectations, and disruptive events such as natural disasters or pandemics. These forces continually influence and challenge supply chain decisions.

To the right of the model are the goals of Supply Chain 5.0, which include sustainability, resilience, and human-centricity. These values represent the outcomes that organizations are striving to achieve through their projects. Arrows in the model show the flow of influence. Technology, strategy, and external conditions shape the projects, and those projects serve as the means for delivering on the values of Supply Chain 5.0. The entire framework is enclosed within the context of VUCA (Volatility, Uncertainty, Complexity, Ambiguity) (US Army, 2010) which defines the conditions in which supply chains must now operate.

This model allows supply chain leaders to begin asking different questions:

- How do our sourcing and production choices affect communities and the environment?
- Are our labor and procurement practices fair and sustainable?
- Can we build resilience without increasing waste or inequality?
- Are we empowering people through technology or displacing them without a plan?
- Are we designing supply chains that can adapt and evolve or simply react to disruptions?
- Are we using technology to enhance human insight or to automate decisions without reflection?

Figure 1.1 Supply Chain 5.0 Adoption Model

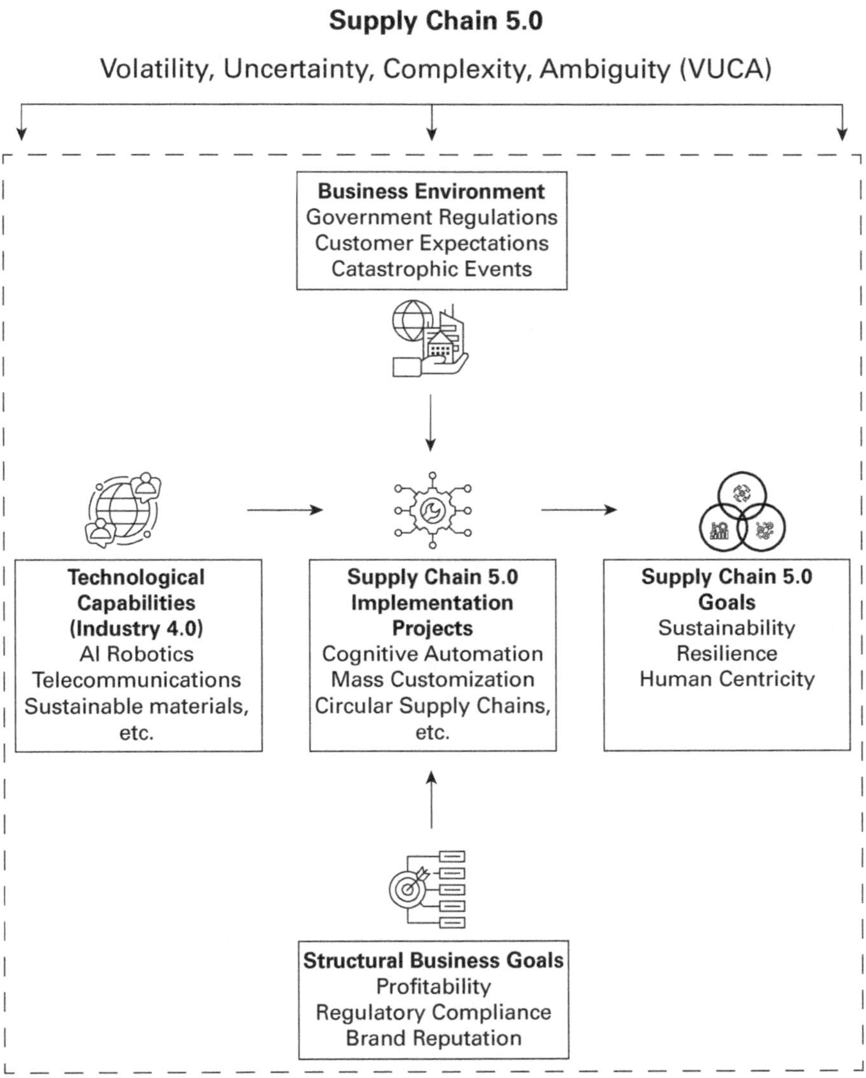

Supply Chain 5.0 calls for a fundamental shift in leadership mindset. Technology is no longer just a tool for efficiency. It becomes a means to strengthen human capabilities and enable professionals to focus on long-term planning, innovation, stakeholder trust, and building systems that meet both business needs and social expectations. Organizations that resist this shift may face increased risk, from regulatory penalties and reputational damage to difficulty attracting and retaining talent. More importantly, they may lose the trust of customers, employees, and partners. However, those that embrace this evolution will be better prepared to lead in a world where performance, purpose, and people are all part of the same equation.

Why Now?

Throughout history, pivotal moments have reshaped industries, societies, and economies. What sets the present moment apart is not simply the presence of change, but the extraordinary speed and scale at which it is unfolding. In the past, industrial revolutions evolved over decades, allowing institutions time to adapt. As we look around today, digital and technological change is often outpacing the capacity of organizations, governments, and global systems to respond.

Each industrial revolution has emerged from a combination of new capabilities and urgent needs. Industry 1.0 harnessed mechanical power and steam, which allowed production to move beyond the limits of manual labor. Industry 2.0 introduced electricity and mass production, meeting the need to scale goods for rapidly urbanizing populations and expanding global trade. Industry 3.0 introduced digitalization and early automation to manage growing complexity and the flow of information. Industry 4.0 brought robotics, the Internet of Things, and real-time analytics, addressing the demands of a highly connected and global economy.

We now stand at another critical inflection point in the evolution of supply chains, shaped by both technological change and mounting pressures on the planet and society. Climate change, resource constraints, geopolitical uncertainty, and rising social expectations are putting unprecedented stress on supply networks. At the same time, advances in artificial intelligence, robotics, and collaborative technologies are producing systems capable of surpassing human performance in speed, scale, and precision. This makes it essential to plan not only for how humans and intelligent machines will work together in supply chains, but also for whether those supply chains will help create a more sustainable and equitable world or amplify harm on a global scale. The result of these forces is the emergence of Industry 5.0.

Supply Chain 5.0 is not about abandoning optimization but about balancing it with orchestration. Leaders must understand the tradeoffs and adopt a more strategic, values-driven approach to decision-making. Supply

Chain 5.0 prioritizes adaptability, transparency, and human impact alongside performance and efficiency. It shifts the focus from maximizing output and minimizing cost to creating supply chains that are resilient, sustainable, and centered on long-term value.

This shift is already underway in many industries. Companies that once focused narrowly on cost reduction and lean efficiency are now redesigning their operations to support circular models, ethical labor practices, and community impact. Technology investments are being evaluated not just by return on investment but by how they strengthen human capability, increase visibility, and align with environmental and social objectives.

The real risk isn't in embracing innovation but in clinging to outdated assumptions. Continuing to optimize legacy systems might provide short-term gains, but it won't prepare supply chains to succeed amid increasing complexity and disruption. The challenges we face today, including climate emergencies, geopolitical shocks, and rapidly changing consumer expectations, are too systemic and interconnected for incremental fixes.

Supply Chain 5.0 is not just a wishful vision. It is a strategic necessity because it offers a framework for supply chains that are efficient, adaptive, regenerative, and aligned with broader societal needs. The path forward is becoming clearer each day. Supply chain leaders will achieve optimization through orchestration. Leading with both purpose and performance will not only build a competitive edge but will shape the future of global supply chains and deliver lasting value for all of the stakeholders in an interconnected and rapidly changing world.

The Impact of Supply Chain 5.0 on Leadership

While researching this book, one insight stood out: The rules of supply chain management are shifting. Profitability is still essential but leaders must now balance it with additional priorities that carry equal significant weight. In a landscape defined by volatility, demand for transparency, and rising stakeholder expectations, supply chains are expected to deliver more than products and services. They must also embody values such as agility, sustainability, and trust.

This shift requires more than upgrading tools or digitizing workflows. It calls for a redefinition of what it means to lead a supply chain today. Leaders face high-stakes decisions about technology adoption, balancing innovation with responsibility, and aligning operational goals with broader societal impact.

Organizations face profound changes within and around their supply chains, requiring leaders to make better decisions and guide their teams through successful transformation. Meaningful progress happens when technology, people, and purpose align to create measurable impact. Supply chain leaders who navigate this transition effectively can position their organizations to generate lasting value for the business, society, and the planet.

Today's supply chain leaders must evolve from managing isolated, streamlined processes to orchestrating interconnected ecosystems. They must move beyond efficiency alone and embrace the role of human-centered strategists. This transformation requires new capabilities: The courage to challenge legacy systems, the vision to connect purpose with performance, and the discipline to adopt technology in ways that enhance human potential rather than replace it.

The question is no longer "What should we do?" but "Who do we need to become as leaders?"

Leadership Archetypes at a Crossroads

As supply chains transitioned through Industry 4.0, leadership approaches centered on control, standardization, and efficiency proved highly effective. Centralized leadership, transactional management, and Lean philosophy enabled organizations to digitize traditionally siloed and linear flows while maintaining consistency across increasingly complex networks. However, the move toward Supply Chain 5.0 is exposing the limits of these approaches. The new era demands agility, collaboration across ecosystems, and a human-centric approach that balances technological power with social and environmental responsibility. To understand why the leadership styles that worked so well in Industry 4.0 now need to evolve, it is important to examine their foundations, their strengths, and where they fall short in the face of Supply Chain 5.0's emerging challenges.

Centralized leadership is a concept that evolved over time through the contributions of various scholars and practitioners. Rather than attributing it to a single individual, it is more accurate to trace its roots to classical management thinkers like Frederick W. Taylor and Max Weber.

Taylor's work on scientific management focused on the engineering of processes and emphasized improving economic efficiency through the systematic analysis of tasks (Wienclaw, n.d.). Taylor proposed that leaders need to train workers in standardized, optimized methods and establish clear performance benchmarks, with the belief that greater productivity would generate financial benefits for both employers and employees.

Similarly, sociologist and organizational theorist Max Weber highlighted the value of a well-defined hierarchy, clear roles and responsibilities, and formal rules and procedures. His model of bureaucracy established the idea of a pyramid-like structure with layers of authority designed to ensure order, consistency, and accountability (Lutzker, 1982).

Over time, these foundational theories shaped the familiar organizational pyramid structure and the centralized leadership style that many companies still use today. Centralized leadership is a structural approach in which nearly all planning, resource allocation, and policy decisions rest with a single leader or a small, top-tier group. Authority flows downward through a clear chain of command, with lower levels focused on execution rather than decision-making.

In practice, this creates a top-down decision flow with limited lateral or upward input, uniform policies and KPIs across sites or business units, and fast crisis response: One voice, one plan, but often at the cost of slower local adaptation (Zannetos, 1965). Centralized leadership, when used strategically, can help coordinate complex operations, align teams around clear goals, and maintain quality standards, especially in large, distributed supply chains where consistency and efficiency are critical. However, while this model can deliver clarity, brand consistency, and tight risk control, its rigidity can clash with the agility, generality, and cross-ecosystem collaboration that are required for Supply Chain 5.0.

Transactional leadership theory is commonly attributed to the work of German sociologist Max Weber (1947) and was later expanded by American political scientist James McGregor Burns in 1978 (Thien, 2018). Burns' theory suggests that social change occurs between leaders and followers. The fundamental premise is that leaders negotiate with their subordinates regarding the quantity and quality of work to be accomplished in exchange for compliance with the leader's wishes, so each derives something of value. Consequently, this approach is founded on formal and informal contractual agreements established between the leader and their subordinates. (Avolio and Yammarino, 2013). Because of this cost-benefit exchange process, transactional leaders are more goal-oriented than people-oriented (Dartey-Baah, 2015).

Transactional leadership is effective for predictable, linear systems where efficiency and control are the primary drivers of success. It relies on clearly defined roles, standardized processes, and performance tied to rewards and penalties, creating a system optimized for stability and repeatability. This approach worked well in environments where supply chains operated like finely tuned machines with limited variability. However, today's supply chains need to be adaptable and responsive to changes in consumer demands, supply constraints, regulatory changes, and workforce expectations (see Table 1.1). Industry 5.0 requires leaders who can inspire, empower, and orchestrate, skills that transcend the quota-and-bonus paradigm. Servant leadership in particular shifts the focus from commanding to enabling. It places the needs of employees, partners, and customers first, with the expectation that by serving and empowering others, the organization becomes stronger and more resilient as a whole. This approach aligns with the human-centric foundation of Supply Chain 5.0, where technology and process are designed to enhance human capability rather than constrain it.

Lean is an operations philosophy that focuses on maximizing customer value by eliminating waste throughout the production process. It originated from the Toyota Production System, developed by Taiichi Ohno, which shifted attention away from individual machine efficiency toward improving the overall flow of products through the system. The term "Lean" was later introduced by MIT researcher John Krafcik (1988) and its core principles were formalized by Jim Womack and Dan Jones in their book *Lean Thinking* (2003). These principles include defining value, mapping the value

Table 1.1 Limitations of Industry 4.0 leadership styles

Supply Chain 5.0 characteristics	Where centralized leadership breaks down	Where transactional leadership breaks down	Where Lean leadership breaks down
Human-centric, purpose-driven ecosystems: Workers co-create with cobots and generative AI agents; engagement and meaning drive productivity and innovation.	Decisions, resources, and problem-solving authority stay at headquarters. Local talent become task-takers rather than co-creators, resulting in low engagement, muted innovation, and higher attrition.	Transactional leadership relies on extrinsic rewards (bonuses, compliance metrics) but rarely taps intrinsic motivation or shared purpose. As a result, it struggles to unleash the creativity and ethical judgment that Supply Chain 5.0 demands.	The relentless cadence of takt time and standardized work can limit autonomy and crowd out reflective, creative tasks if not balanced carefully.

(continued)

Table 1.1 (Continued)

Supply Chain 5.0 characteristics	Where centralized leadership breaks down	Where transactional leadership breaks down	Where Lean leadership breaks down
Continuous innovation at the edge: Frontline teams must experiment, learn, and pivot in real time, using rapid prototyping and fail-fast learning.	Central KPIs are typically cost-focused; voices at the edge who experience externalities often have little influence. Creativity gets stifled, and the best ideas remain buried in local notes or never surface at all. Bureaucratic approval cycles and rigid budgets delay experiments and penalize failure.	Command-and-control contracts ("do X, get Y") discourage risk-taking. People protect their KPIs instead of testing bold ideas that may fail before they succeed.	Tight KPI targets and zero-defect cultures can discourage the risk-taking and iterative experimentation that digital twins, additive manufacturing, and AI analytics make possible.
Distributed, cross-company value webs: Data, talent, and intellectual property flow across multiple suppliers, customers, NGOs, and regulators.	Centralized logic reinforces pyramid structures where a select group defines purpose and guardrails, but day-to-day sensing, learning, and innovating must shift to the network's edge, where data originates, talent thrives, and value is created collaboratively.	Transactional logic reinforces firm-centric silos: "my bonus, my metrics." It offers no mechanism for building the trust and shared accountability needed to govern multi-party platforms or circular loops.	Lean emerged in vertically integrated settings; its metrics can reinforce firm-centric optimization rather than enabling platform-level, multi-party value creation.

(continued)

Table 1.1 (Continued)

Supply Chain 5.0 characteristics	Where centralized leadership breaks down	Where transactional leadership breaks down	Where Lean leadership breaks down
Resilience and efficiency: Redundancy, optionality, and social impact matter as much as unit cost; supply networks must absorb shocks, reroute, or switch capacity quickly.	Escalating decisions up a chain of command slows reaction speed and creates single points of failure, resulting in longer recovery times during disruptions and reputational damage.	Transactional KPIs (throughput, OEE, cost per unit) push leaders to squeeze buffers and ignore externalities, often at the expense of flexibility, sustainability, and stakeholder well-being.	Lean's drive to cut buffers and "excess" capacity leaves systems brittle when facing pandemics, climate events, or geopolitical shocks.
Ethical AI and sustainability mandates: Decisions must balance profit with privacy, emissions, and equity.	A small core team may push rapid rollouts while under-resourcing ethics reviews or stakeholder dialogue, increasing the risk of regulatory fines, community backlash, or brand damage.	Rules-and-rewards schemes ensure compliance but do not nurture principled judgment. They leave little room for reflective dialogue on ethics, biases, or planetary boundaries.	Lean toolkits focus on process waste, not algorithmic bias, data ethics, or stakeholder transparency. Classic Lean measures waste inside the factory gate (scrap, motion, overproduction) but often overlooks product life-cycle externalities and ecosystem regeneration.
Multi-party ecosystems: multi-generational, multicultural, and multi-geographic teams collaborate virtually.	Top-down governance optimizes the focal firm but cannot align incentives or enable seamless data sharing across partners. The risks include data silos, trust gaps, and stalled platform projects.	A carrot-and-stick style is interpreted differently across cultures and generations, risking disengagement or backlash where autonomy and inclusion are highly valued.	Lean's relentless focus on incremental waste reduction may crowd out open-ended exploration and design thinking, areas where diverse perspectives can truly shine.

stream, creating flow, establishing pull, and pursuing perfection. Lean aims to reduce lead times, minimize inventory, and eliminate defects. These outcomes closely align with Industry 4.0 efforts to digitize and optimize production flows.

However, Industry 5.0 introduces a broader definition of success that incorporates human well-being, system resilience, and regenerative impact alongside efficiency. Lean remains highly relevant, but within the context of Supply Chain 5.0, it needs to be extended. Instead of focusing solely on eliminating waste within a single facility, leaders must consider how to create net-positive value across the entire supply chain ecosystem. This shift calls for a more holistic approach that integrates Lean principles with goals related to sustainability, inclusivity, and long-term adaptability.

Redefining Leadership for Supply Chain 5.0

Supply Chain 5.0 raises a critical question: Who must we become as leaders to meet its demands? Traditional leadership models, designed for linear, efficiency-driven systems, tend to over-centralize decision-making, place technology ahead of people, and trade resilience for cost savings. These characteristics are increasingly misaligned with the needs of today's dynamic, ecosystem-based supply networks. The era ahead requires a departure from rigid, top-down control toward decentralized, distributed, and adaptive approaches capable of managing complexity and rapid change.

Decentralized Leadership

Decentralized leadership emerged as a response to these limitations. Henri Fayol (1916/2016) described centralization and decentralization as a continuum, emphasizing that managers must balance authority based on the situation. Chester Barnard (1938) highlighted that authority is sustained not only through hierarchy but also through cooperation and informal networks, establishing the importance of shared decision-making. Peter Drucker (1992) demonstrated how moving decision-making closer to business units enabled large companies such as General Motors to stay flexible and innovative as they scaled. More recently, distributed leadership and agile management approaches have extended these principles, empowering teams at every level to collaborate, experiment, and adapt in real time (Spillane, 2005).

Rather than concentrating authority at a single headquarters, this model shifts decision-making and problem-solving closer to where expertise and customer interactions occur. Authority and resources are intentionally distributed across multiple nodes, including regional hubs, business units, cross-functional teams, and individual contributors, while the center provides strategic direction and guardrails. This balance of clear purpose with local autonomy enables faster responses, cross-functional collaboration, and innovation, all of which are critical in Supply Chain 5.0 environments.

In the context of Industry 5.0, decentralized leadership aligns closely with the complexity, speed, and human-centered demands of modern supply chains. Some of the key benefits include:

- Faster response times: Local teams can sense disruptions, make decisions, and solve problems without waiting for approvals to climb a long chain of command—a critical advantage when resilience and agility are priorities.
- Greater innovation: When people at the edge have the autonomy and resources to test ideas, experiment, and learn, they're more likely to surface creative solutions and share best practices across the network.
- Higher engagement and retention: Distributed leadership empowers teams to take ownership of outcomes, making work more meaningful and motivating, which supports the human-centric goals of Industry 5.0.
- Better alignment with ecosystems: Modern supply chains increasingly operate as value networks spanning multiple companies and stakeholders. Decentralized decision-making helps different players collaborate, share data, and adapt in real time.

In short, decentralized leadership balances clear strategic direction with the local flexibility needed to handle complexity, co-create with partners, and adapt quickly, all essential capabilities for supply chains to stay competitive in the Industry 5.0 era.

Yet, this approach comes with real challenges, especially in the context of managing end-to-end supply chains:

- Coordination complexity: Shifting decisions to multiple nodes can create silos or duplicate efforts if teams are not aligned around shared goals, standards, or data. Without strong coordination, decentralized structures can easily drift in different directions.
- Inconsistent execution: Granting local autonomy can lead to variations in how policies, standards, or customer experiences are implemented across sites or partners, which may hurt quality, compliance, or brand reputation.

- Leadership skill demands: Empowering decision-making at many levels requires leaders throughout the organization to be capable, trusted, and aligned with its purpose. If local leaders are not adequately trained or supported, decentralized structures can result in confusion and uneven performance.

Distributed Leadership

As an extension of decentralization, distributed leadership spreads leadership functions across multiple individuals or teams instead of concentrating them in a single leader or focal point (Spillane, 2005). Decentralized leadership focuses on where authority and decision-making reside, while distributed leadership focuses on how leadership is shared and practiced. It treats leadership as a collective social process rather than a structural hierarchy (Spillane, 2005; Gronn, 2002).

Distributed leadership emerged from studies of real organizations where leadership responsibilities were shared across levels. James P. Spillane's early 2000s work framed it as a way to understand leadership as shared practice rather than the responsibility of a single role (Spillane, 2005). Peter Gronn advanced the concept of "concertive action," showing how leadership emerges from interactions among people rather than formal authority structures (Gronn, 2002).

In Supply Chain 5.0, this approach supports the complexity, speed, and human-centered demands of modern supply chains. Sharing leadership enables faster responses, encourages innovation, and drives higher engagement and ownership. It also fosters stronger collaboration across partners and value networks.

Some of the key benefits include:

- Faster response and adaptability: Decision-making happens closer to where problems and opportunities arise, allowing teams to act quickly without waiting for top-down approvals.
- Greater innovation: When leadership is shared, teams at every level are encouraged to experiment, learn, and share new ideas—driving continuous improvement and creative problem-solving.
- Higher engagement and ownership: Distributed leadership gives employees more autonomy and a stronger sense of responsibility, which increases motivation, retention, and overall job satisfaction.

- Stronger cross-company collaboration: This approach makes it easier to work with partners, suppliers, and stakeholders across the value network by enabling shared problem-solving and data exchange where value is created.

Distributed leadership blends strong strategic alignment with local decision-making flexibility, creating a balance that helps supply chains stay competitive, resilient, and people-focused in Industry 5.0. However, it also introduces specific challenges for supply chain leaders:

- Coordination and alignment risks: When authority is shared across many teams or partners, maintaining a consistent purpose and direction can be difficult. Without strong communication and clear guardrails, local decisions may conflict or drift apart.
- Technology and data gaps: This approach relies on real-time data, collaboration tools, and network-wide visibility. Any breakdown in systems or data sharing can slow problem-solving and weaken decision quality.
- Leadership capability demands: Success depends on leaders at all levels having the skills, mindset, and trust to make sound decisions and take ownership. Without proper training and support, uneven capability can create confusion and inconsistent performance.

A key takeaway from this leadership style is that distributed leadership in Supply Chain 5.0 brings advantages, but requires guardrails, strong knowledge-sharing, robust training, and the right digital infrastructure to unlock its full potential without sacrificing coordination and control.

Adaptive Leadership

A third leadership style well suited to the demands of Supply Chain 5.0 is adaptive leadership. Developed in the 1990s by Harvard Kennedy School professor Ronald Heifetz, adaptive leadership provides a framework for addressing complex challenges that lack straightforward solutions. In *Leadership Without Easy Answers* (1994) and later *The Practice of Adaptive Leadership* (with Marty Linsky and Alexander Grashow, 2009), Heifetz distinguished between "technical problems," which can be solved through existing expertise, and "adaptive challenges," which require people to confront difficult realities, learn new ways of working, and adapt together over time.

Adaptive leadership focuses on helping organizations to respond effectively to uncertainty and rapid change. It emphasizes learning, experimentation, and the willingness to rethink established habits, often requiring teams to step outside their comfort zones. These principles make it especially relevant to supply chain leaders navigating the complexity and evolving demands of Supply Chain 5.0. The core principles of adaptive leadership can guide supply chain leaders as they navigate the challenges and opportunities of Supply Chain 5.0:

- Distinguish technical and adaptive challenges: Technical challenges can be solved with established expertise and existing procedures. Adaptive challenges require new learning, shifts in mindset, and shared experimentation. They demand change from everyone involved, not just the leader.
- Get on the balcony: Leaders need to step back from daily operations, the "dance floor," to view the bigger picture from the "balcony." This perspective helps them spot patterns, diagnose root issues, and understand how people are responding.
- Regulate distress: Change creates discomfort. Effective adaptive leaders help teams face tough realities without becoming overwhelmed, keeping tension productive rather than paralyzing.
- Give the work back to the people: Leaders cannot solve adaptive challenges on their own. They must create safe spaces and processes that allow teams to take ownership, collaborate, and develop solutions together.
- Protect voices of dissent: Honest feedback and new ideas often come from those challenging the status quo. Adaptive leaders safeguard these voices and foster open debate and learning.
- Maintain disciplined attention: Teams often avoid difficult issues. Adaptive leaders keep focus on the most critical challenges, even when the conversations are uncomfortable.

In complex, fast-moving supply chain environments such as global disruptions, technology shifts, sustainability mandates, or governmental policy changes, many problems are adaptive. There's no single playbook. Supply chain leaders must help people learn, adjust, and co-create new ways forward together, particularly in the Supply Chain 5.0. However, there are key challenges supply chain leaders may face when using adaptive leadership:

- Overcoming resistance to change: Adaptive leadership asks people to question longstanding habits, assumptions, or processes, but in supply chains, where standardization and efficiency are deeply embedded, this can trigger strong resistance from teams, partners, or even customers.
- Balancing stability with experimentation: Supply Chain 5.0 relies on consistent operations and efficiency, yet adaptive leadership demands

experimentation, learning, and iteration. Leaders must balance the need for reliable day-to-day performance with encouraging safe-to-fail trials and new ideas.

- Navigating complex stakeholder networks: Modern supply chains are global, multi-tiered, and interdependent. Adaptive challenges often cross organizational and even national boundaries, so leaders must align diverse partners who may have different incentives, priorities, or cultures.
- Managing uncertainty without clear solutions: Adaptive leadership is about tackling problems that don't have straightforward answers. In supply chains, this can feel uncomfortable for teams used to clear metrics, SOPs, and fixed KPIs. Leaders must help people stay focused and motivated despite ambiguity.
- Developing new skills at all levels: Adaptive leadership pushes decision-making and problem-solving responsibility down the hierarchy, but frontline managers and teams may not have the experience, tools, or confidence to take on this new role without training and support.

Adaptive leadership is a powerful approach for navigating Supply Chain 5.0, but leaders must intentionally build the culture, skills, and systems that help teams tackle complex, evolving challenges together.

All of this suggests that Supply Chain 5.0 calls for a new kind of leadership; one that is deeply human-centric, ethically grounded, and strategically adaptive. Today's leaders must go beyond managing efficiency and operations; they must orchestrate complex ecosystems while placing people and purpose at the center of decision-making. This means leading with empathy and emotional intelligence, creating blended environments where human creativity and machine intelligence can thrive together. Leaders must be systems thinkers, capable of seeing the bigger picture across functions, partners, and geographies, while proactively building resilience into their supply chains. They must embrace digital fluency, not just to adopt technologies, but to guide their ethical and profitable implementation. Purpose-driven decision-making becomes critical, where environmental stewardship, social responsibility, and transparent governance are embedded into strategy without forgetting the business profitability. In a world of disruption, successful leaders will also need agility, learning mindsets, and the ability to rapidly pivot through feedback loops and pilot innovation. Above all, Supply Chain 5.0 demands leaders who can integrate performance with principles: Those who understand that long-term value is created not only through optimization but through collaboration, sustainability, and the empowerment of people with technology across the entire supply chain network.

The HUMANS Leadership Framework

To lead effectively in the Supply Chain 5.0 era, executives need more than high-level principles. They need practical roles that define how leadership should function in real-world settings. Supply Chain 5.0 introduces leadership demands that are as complex and adaptive as the environments they operate in.

Dynamic Capabilities Theory (DCT) offers a useful way to understand what makes organizations successful in volatile and uncertain conditions (Teece et al., 1997). DTC highlights three core abilities: Sensing opportunities and threats, seizing them through strategic action, and transforming internal capabilities to remain competitive over time. For supply chain leaders moving into Supply Chain 5.0, this perspective is critical. As supply chains become more human-centered, digitally connected, and sustainability-driven, the ability to adapt continuously is no longer optional; it is a strategic requirement. DCT reframes transformation as an ongoing set of capabilities that must be developed across technology, people, and partnerships rather than as a one-time project.

To make these ideas easier to apply in practice, we adapted DCT into a framework designed specifically for supply chain leaders. The result is the HUMANS Leadership Framework, illustrated in Figure 1.2, which defines six skill areas essential to Supply Chain 5.0. These capabilities include scanning the horizon and interpreting trends as a Horizon Scanner, evaluating and deploying technology for strategic advantage as a Utility Architect, using modeling and analytics for better decisions as a Modeling Advocate, building agile and responsive supply networks as an Agility Enabler, developing trust-based relationships across ecosystems as a Network Orchestrator, and integrating people, processes, and systems to drive execution as a Systems Integrator.

Hypothetical Example: Applying the HUMANS Leadership Framework

Imagine a global consumer goods company facing simultaneous pressures from extreme weather disrupting supply routes, growing consumer demand for sustainable sourcing, and rapid advances in AI-enabled planning tools. Leadership realizes that traditional supply chain strategies are no longer sufficient and decides to adopt the HUMANS Leadership Framework to guide its transformation into Supply Chain 5.0.

Figure 1.2 The HUMANS Leadership Framework for Supply Chain 5.0

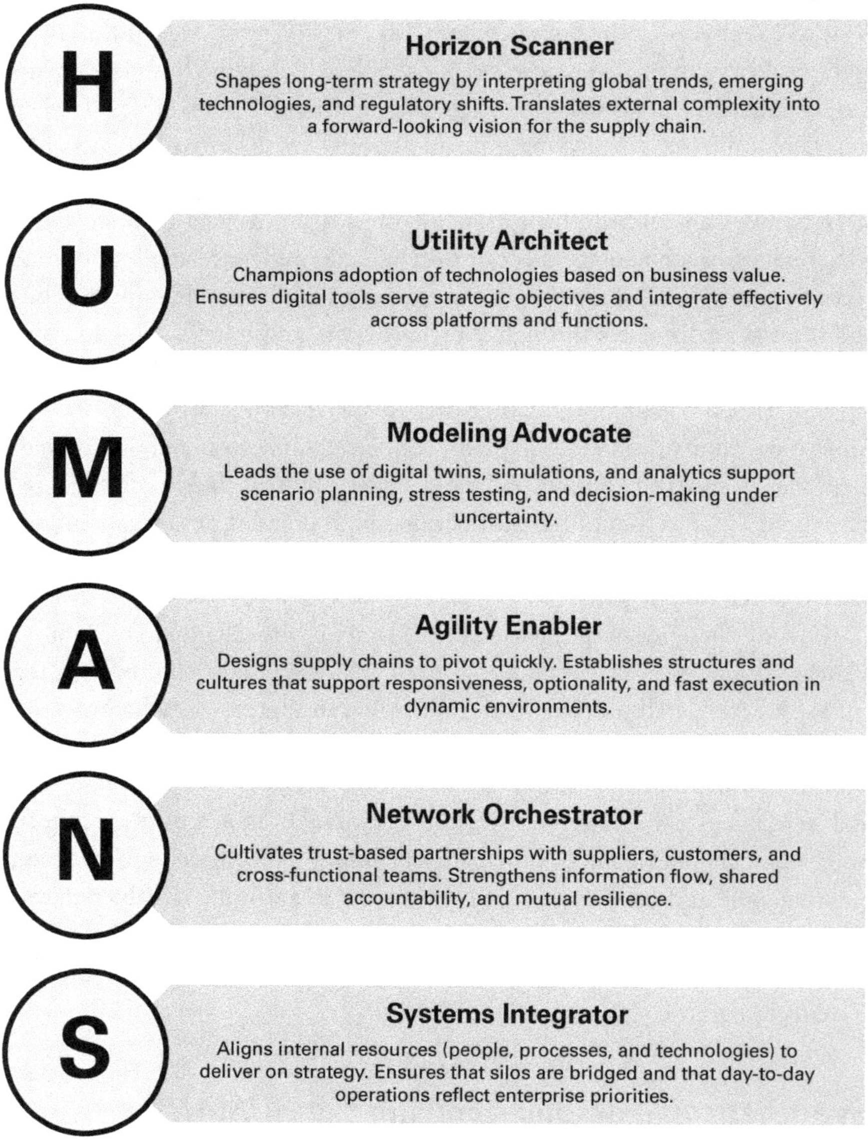

In this scenario, executives begin to take on multiple roles at once. Acting as Horizon Scanners, they develop an early-warning system that combines climate risk data and consumer sentiment analytics to anticipate disruptions and demand shifts. As Utility Architects, they deploy AI-based planning and robotic process automation, aiming not only to reduce costs but also to enable human teams to focus on complex problem-solving and innovation. In the Modeling Advocate role, they build digital twins to simulate different scenarios, balancing cost, service levels, and environmental impact.

As Agility Enablers, they reconfigure their supplier network to establish flexible, regionalized production hubs capable of responding quickly to geopolitical or environmental shocks. In the Network Orchestrator role, they foster trust-based partnerships with suppliers, NGOs, and even competitors to share logistics capacity and minimize environmental impact. Finally, as Systems Integrators, they focus on aligning people, processes, and technology to ensure the entire supply chain operates as a cohesive system rather than as isolated initiatives.

In this hypothetical example, the company is building a supply chain that is not only more resilient and adaptive but also more sustainable and trusted by stakeholders. It underscores a central lesson of Supply Chain 5.0: The way leaders design the collaboration between people and technology will determine whether future supply chains contribute to a more sustainable and equitable world or amplify existing risks and harm.

The HUMANS Framework provides a structured way to define the evolving leadership roles required in Supply Chain 5.0. These are not fixed job titles but adaptable approaches that can be applied in different combinations depending on an organization's context and strategic priorities. Effective leaders often need to draw on several of these roles at once, anticipating disruptions, enabling agile decision-making, and fostering collaboration across ecosystems. The framework also serves as a tool for assessing existing capabilities, identifying gaps, and aligning leadership development with enterprise goals. As supply chains face increasing technological complexity and rising stakeholder expectations, structured models like HUMANS can help clarify what effective leadership looks like and provide guidance for developing it across the organization.

Leading Through Disruption

Disruption is no longer an outlier. It is now the prevailing context in which supply chains operate. Supply chain disruptions are unplanned and unanticipated events that disrupt the normal flow of goods and materials within a supply chain, and as a consequence expose firms within the supply chain operations and financial risk (Craighead et al., 2007, p.132).

Unlike routine variability, disruptions are non-routine, high-impact events that challenge existing operational models and assumptions. They can be classified by cause (e.g., supply-side, demand-side, or contextual) or by onset pattern (e.g., sudden versus slow-building). These typologies help leaders craft targeted response strategies aligned with the disruption's nature and origin.

Disruptions may result from external shocks such as pandemics, natural disasters, or geopolitical conflict. They can also stem from internal or systemic changes, such as technological adoption, evolving regulations, labor unrest, and changing social or environmental expectations. Their distinguishing characteristics, such as scale, unpredictability, and the ability to cascade across networks, expose underlying vulnerabilities and call for decisive leadership.

The global supply chain environment has become defined by VUCA: Volatility, Uncertainty, Complexity, and Ambiguity (US Army, 2010). In this environment, risk management is no longer sufficient. Leaders must also drive transformative change in response to broader technological, societal, and environmental shifts. Within the framework of Supply Chain 5.0, disruption is reframed not merely as a threat, but as an inflection point. Disruptions become an opportunity for reinvention, value creation, and competitive differentiation.

To meet these challenges, supply chain organizations must do more than deploy new tools. They must adopt new ways of thinking. This includes investing in digital infrastructure and workforce capabilities, cultivating adaptive leadership, and designing business models that emphasize flexibility, innovation, and long-term resilience.

Quantitative frameworks have emerged to help organizations assess and prepare for disruption. For instance, Simchi-Levi et al's Time-to-Survive (TTS) and Time-to-Recover (TTR) metrics provide a structured way to evaluate the resilience of supply chain nodes and identify critical vulnerabilities (Simchi-Levi, et al, 2015). Some scholars have also distinguished between two modes of resilience: Reactive and proactive. Reactive resilience, or absorptive capacity, enables an organization to withstand shocks; proactive resilience, or adaptive capacity, allows for evolution and transformation in response to changing conditions (Wieland and Durach, 2021).

The leadership challenge in this context reflects what Clayton Christensen described in *The Innovator's Dilemma* (Christensen, 2016). He distinguished between sustaining innovations, which improve existing systems and performance, and disruptive innovations, which introduce new solutions that may appear inferior initially but ultimately redefine industries. Historically, many successful firms have failed to embrace disruptive innovation because it threatened their existing profit models and operational structures. In the supply chain context, this dynamic is increasingly visible. Organizations that concentrate solely on cost control and incremental gains risk being overtaken by more agile competitors better suited to a volatile and fast-changing environment.

To succeed in this environment, leaders must adopt a mindset that is rooted in speed, adaptability, and situational awareness. The OODA loop, developed by US Air Force Colonel John Boyd (Richards, 2004), is one example of a practical mental model for making better decisions more quickly. OODA stands for Observe, Orient, Decide, and Act. The cycle emphasizes a leader's ability to gather information from the environment, interpret it in context, make timely decisions, and take decisive action. In rapidly changing scenarios such as supply chain disruptions, the ability to iterate through this loop faster and more accurately than competitors enables organizations to respond with agility, maintain strategic coherence, and outmaneuver more rigid rivals. The OODA loop shifts leadership focus from perfect planning toward dynamic execution, making it especially relevant in VUCA conditions.

Another critical concept for modern supply chain leaders is the idea of Black Swan events, introduced by Nassim Nicholas Taleb (Taleb, 2007). Black Swans are rare, high-impact events that are difficult to predict but, in hindsight, appear obvious. The COVID-19 pandemic is often cited as a Black Swan, though Taleb himself has argued it was a "white swan" because it was foreseeable. Regardless, the concept draws attention to the limits of forecasting and the illusion of stability. Black Swans challenge risk models, undermine traditional planning assumptions, and reveal deep fragilities in systems. For supply chains, this underscores the importance of building resilience not just to known risks, but also to unpredictable and systemic shocks. Leaders must therefore design for flexibility, maintain optionality, and cultivate cultures capable of adapting under uncertainty.

Disruptive forces such as climate change, shifting regulations, labor market transformation, and rapid digital acceleration are redefining what supply chains must deliver. Disruption is no longer an occasional challenge but a constant feature of the global supply chain landscape, influencing daily operations as well as long-term strategy, organizational design, and stakeholder priorities.

Leaders who cling to legacy systems and outdated strategies risk losing relevance. Those who view disruption as a catalyst for reinvention rather than a threat will be better positioned to create supply chains that are resilient, adaptive, and strategically differentiated. This shift requires questioning entrenched assumptions and pursuing business models that prioritize innovation and agility.

Frameworks such as Blue Ocean Strategy, developed by W. Chan Kim and Renée Mauborgne (2015), encourage organizations to move beyond saturated, highly competitive markets and create uncontested spaces where competition becomes irrelevant. Another approach, Bend the Curve (Razeghi, 2016), emphasizes accelerating performance improvement through systemic redesign rather than incremental change. Both models offer structured ways to turn disruption into opportunity, enabling leaders to drive transformation instead of merely reacting to change.

As disruptive forces grow more frequent and complex, they will continue to reshape investment priorities, leadership practices, talent strategies, and the architecture of global supply chains. The following analysis examines how these dynamics are influencing supply chain strategy in the context of Industry 5.0:

- Disruptions expose systemic weaknesses. Global supply chains face overlapping shocks from climate change, cyberattacks, labor shortages, and geopolitical unrest. Static contingency plans are no longer enough. These events reveal overreliance on single suppliers, lack of visibility, outdated technology, and rigid processes. The 2021 Ever Given blockage of the Suez Canal, which halted global trade for six days and cost an estimated $6–10 billion (Reuters, 2021), underscored the fragility of just-in-time models and the need for diversified routes and digital visibility. Leaders must use such crises to redesign supply chains for adaptability and resilience.
- Disruptions require human-centered leadership. In Supply Chain 5.0, the human elements of safety, fairness, and equity are central. During disruption, leaders must act with integrity, protecting workers, ensuring sourcing transparency, and managing operations ethically. These actions safeguard long-term brand reputation and stakeholder trust.
- Disruptions accelerate technology adoption. Disruption often drives rapid innovation by highlighting the shortcomings of the status quo. Every disruption should be considered an opportunity to apply technology to reinforce the capabilities of resilience, sustainability, and human-centricity.
- Disruptions expand leadership responsibilities. Leaders must align people, processes, and technology across traditionally separated silos while embedding ESG principles and guiding ethical digital transformation.
- Disruptions impact brand trust. How companies respond shapes long-term credibility. Transparent communication, strategic clarity, and a focus on shared value build trust and define industry leadership, while missteps can erode reputation quickly.

- Disruptions reshape financial models. Volatile rates, costs, and contract changes challenge the limits of traditional cost-optimization models. Companies need dynamic costing, flexible working capital strategies, and risk-adjusted planning to stay financially resilient.
- Disruptions transform workforce dynamics. Labor shortages, evolving regulations, and shifting worker expectations require new talent strategies. Responses vary by region: Japan's aging population drives automation while Europe and North America are investing in workforce development. Addressing these dynamics in regionally appropriate ways is critical for continuity and growth.

In an era of constant disruption, the ability to lead through uncertainty defines supply chain leadership. When leaders are prepared, disruption is not only a test but also a prime opportunity to redesign systems, embrace innovation, and position supply chains as engines of long-term value.

Toward Resilience and Regeneration

For many years, supply chain management was primarily focused on optimization, aiming to increase speed, reduce costs, and improve efficiency. These objectives continue to be important; however, current conditions characterized by frequent disruptions, rising stakeholder expectations, and increasing environmental concerns require a broader perspective. Supply chains are evolving to encompass not only operational excellence but also resilience and regeneration.

Supply chain resilience can be understood through two complementary lenses. The first, often referred to as engineering resilience or absorptive capacity, is the ability of a supply chain to resist disruptions and recover quickly to its original state. The second, ecological resilience or adaptive capacity, emphasizes the ability of the supply chain to transform in response to disruptions, potentially altering its structure or function to better cope with future challenges (Wieland and Durach, 2021).

Resilient supply chains cultivate strategies that increase absorptive and adaptive capacity. Although these strategies may involve initial investments, they can reduce downtime and improve service levels over time. Digital technologies, including real-time visibility tools, artificial intelligence, and digital twins, facilitate proactive risk management and enable agile decision-making. These capabilities allow organizations to maintain performance in uncertain environments, demonstrating that resilience and optimization can coexist and support each other (see Figure 1.3).

Figure 1.3 Supply Chain Resilience

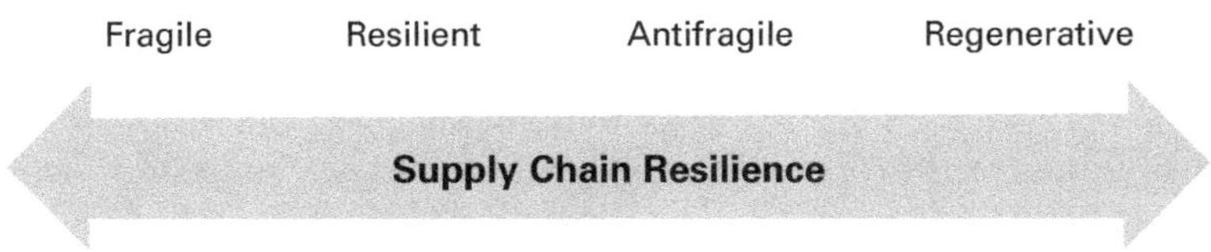

You can often assess the maturity of a supply chain by examining its resilience. Supply chain maturity progresses through stages that reflect how deeply adaptability and long-term thinking are embedded into operations. At the earliest stage, organizations operate in a reactive mode, responding to disruptions only after they occur. This stage typically relies on contingency plans and rapid-response teams, but it lacks the proactive systems required to prevent recurring vulnerabilities.

As organizations mature, they become more resilient. This stage focuses on anticipating risks and building the ability to absorb shocks without major disruptions to operations. Strategies such as diversified sourcing, redundant capacity, and scenario planning become more prominent. The emphasis shifts from recovery to continuity, ensuring that the system can maintain essential functionality under stress.

Beyond this lies antifragility, a concept introduced by Nassim Nicholas Taleb (2012), where supply chains are not only resistant to disruption but actively improve when exposed to it. At this stage, disruptions are treated as opportunities to test, learn, and refine. Organizations develop adaptive feedback loops and leverage advanced analytics and digital twins to model responses and optimize performance based on real-world stressors.

The most advanced stage is regeneration, where supply chains move beyond merely surviving or adapting to actively restoring and renewing the resources and systems they depend on. This involves designing networks that contribute positively to the environment, society, and the broader economic ecosystem. Regenerative supply chains integrate circular economy principles, restore natural and social capital, and create long-term value that benefits both the business and the communities they serve. At this level, resilience and sustainability are no longer separate goals but deeply intertwined.

Regeneration occurs all around us in ecosystems that rely on natural cycles such as nutrient recycling, plant growth, and decomposition to restore resources, repair damage, and maintain balance over time. These processes ensure that ecosystems can recover from disturbances and continue supporting life by renewing soil fertility, purifying water, and sustaining biodiversity.

Just as ecosystems restore and renew themselves through interconnected cycles, a regenerative supply chain is designed to restore, renew, and enhance resources rather than simply minimizing harm. This expanded view redefines resilience to include the capacity to adapt, recover, and generate sustainable value throughout the entire supply network.

Resilience and regeneration work alongside optimization and orchestration in supply chains by combining operational efficiency with environmental and social considerations. This balanced approach helps organizations achieve performance goals while building supply chains capable of adapting to change, sustaining resources, and delivering long-term value. These issues are central to Supply Chain 5.0 and will be explored in greater depth throughout the book.

Early Movers and Lessons Learned

As the transition to Supply Chain 5.0 accelerates, understanding the framework is only the first step. It is equally important to study the leaders and organizations already applying these principles in real-world operations. The experiences of these early adopters demonstrate what can be achieved when technology is used to strengthen human capability, enable ethical decision-making, and deliver lasting value.

We can see these concepts being applied by organizations that are already moving toward regenerative supply chain models. Companies like Redwood Materials and Caterpillar are already demonstrating that purpose, resilience, and innovation can work together across supply chains to create competitive advantage when driven with clear intent. Examining their strategies, challenges, and results provides practical insight into leading transformation at scale. Their approaches to sourcing, data orchestration, and circular logistics show that Supply Chain 5.0 is not a future concept but a present reality. Learning from these examples equips us to shape the future with greater clarity and impact.

REAL-WORLD EXAMPLE Redwood Materials: Circular Supply Chains for EV Batteries

Tesla began its battery journey using essential virgin materials like lithium, cobalt, nickel, and copper. Recognizing the unsustainable nature of traditional mining and supply dependencies, Tesla partnered with Redwood Materials, founded by ex-Tesla CTO JB Straubel, to start transforming used batteries into high-value feedstock. Redwood Materials now works with multiple automakers including BMW, Isuzu, Toyota, Ford, Volkswagen, Panasonic, Lyft, and more to collect and recycle batteries and production scrap (Redwood Materials, n.d.; de la Garza, 2024). Their recycling system captures more than 95 percent of the critical minerals in a spent battery including lithium, nickel, cobalt, and copper, yet does so with a far lighter footprint than conventional mining and refining. Lifecycle analysis shows these recycling processes use about 80 percent less energy, emit 70 percent less carbon dioxide, and require 80 percent less water (Thomas, 2024).

As recycled material volumes grow, automakers can significantly reduce their reliance on mined inputs. This shift promises cost reductions, less exposure to global commodity volatility, and greater supply chain control. Manufacturers can also shorten lead times and build localized resilience

Many companies are finding that batteries deemed unsuitable for vehicle use often still retain substantial capacity for secondary applications. Tesla is reusing these batteries in grid-connected storage systems before recycling them with Redwood Materials to maximize lifespan and resource use. Nissan is also active in this space: Its Battery Energy Storage Solution at its Franklin, Tennessee, headquarters uses retired Leaf batteries to reduce peak electricity use and cut emissions by approximately 3.7 tons per year (Nissan, 2024). These initiatives extend both the economic and environmental value of EV batteries, help stabilize energy systems, and delay the demand for recycling, reinforcing the tiered, circular lifecycle model.

Redwood's model illustrates how circular design can extend well beyond a single company. By partnering with diverse automakers and supporting multiple lifecycle stages such as vehicle use, grid storage, and recycling, it creates a scalable, regenerative battery supply chain. This approach lowers costs, enhances strategic autonomy, and positions the industry to deliver long-term sustainable impact.

REAL-WORLD EXAMPLE Caterpillar: How CAT Reman Reduces Costs, Resource Use, and Environmental Impact

Caterpillar Inc. is one of the world's largest manufacturers of construction and mining equipment, diesel and natural gas engines, industrial gas turbines, and locomotives. Operating in more than 190 countries through a vast network of dealers and manufacturing facilities, the company supports industries ranging from heavy construction and energy to transportation and resource extraction.

Within this global footprint, Caterpillar's Reman program plays a critical role in reducing environmental impact while maintaining performance standards. The program restores worn engine components and other parts to like-new condition, significantly lowering the demand for virgin raw materials. Instead of casting and machining new parts, CAT Reman dismantles returned components, cleans and inspects them, applies engineering updates, and reassembles them to original specifications. This process extends part lifecycles, conserves energy and resources, and minimizes the need for newly mined materials (Caterpillar, 2023).

Compared to manufacturing new parts, this system requires approximately 85 percent less energy, uses 85 percent less water, emits 61 percent fewer greenhouse gases, and conserves a similar amount of raw materials. The result is a substantially lower environmental footprint and leaner production costs for Caterpillar (Circular X, 2023).

Customers benefit from this approach with high-quality remanufactured parts at roughly 60 percent of the cost of new components, while maintaining performance and warranty coverage. A global core exchange model encourages customers to return used parts, which ensures a steady supply of materials and minimizes dependence on raw material markets

CAT Reman's international network of facilities and dealerships allows localized remanufacturing and service. That reduces transportation emissions and improves turnaround time, further enhancing efficiency and customer satisfaction

By combining profitability, customer value, and sustainability, the CAT Reman program exemplifies how industrial leaders can leverage regeneration to strengthen resilience, reduce costs, and build competitive differentiation.

Policy-Driven Transformation

From Europe to Asia, forward-looking governments are already accelerating the shift from automation-first (Industry 4.0) to human-centric, sustainable and resilient supply chain ecosystems. Tracking and aligning with these policies gives supply chain leaders an early advantage on the operational and compliance playbook of the coming decade.

The European Union (EU), which consists of 28 member states, published a report in January 2021 through its Directorate-General for Research and Innovation. The report describes a paradigm that complements Industry 4.0 by positioning research and innovation as key drivers for the transition to a sustainable, human-centric, and resilient European industry. This approach shifts the focus from shareholder value to stakeholder value, generating benefits for all involved. EU Industry 5.0 aims to harness the potential of new technologies to deliver prosperity beyond jobs and economic growth, while respecting planetary boundaries and placing the well-being of workers at the center of the production process (Breque et al., 2021). The approach seeks to position European industry as a key driver of economic and societal transitions. The Commission's priorities include ensuring that industry contributes by adopting a human-centric approach, proposing AI regulations; supporting the upskilling and reskilling of European workers through a Digital Education Action Plan; and promoting resource-efficient and sustainable industries through the Green Deal and Industry Strategy policy initiatives (European Commission, 2021). For supply chain leaders, the report suggests several policy pathways to make industry 5.0 actionable: Invest in research and innovation, skills and workforce development, regulations and incentives, collaboration and partnerships, and resilient supply chains.

Japan, through its cabinet office, has proposed a policy vehicle called "Society 5.0" (Government of Japan, n.d.). Society 5.0 is Japan's vision for a future super-smart society that builds on the digital transformation of Industry 4.0 but expands it beyond industry to all aspects of society. It aims to solve social challenges by integrating advanced technologies, such as AI, IoT, big data, and robotics, into every sector, creating a people-centered society that balances economic growth with solutions to social problems like an aging population and sustainability. The concept envisions seamless connections between cyberspace and the physical world, fostering innovation, enhancing quality of life, and driving inclusive growth that benefits all citizens. In Industry 5.0, supply chain leaders are expected to harness advanced technologies like AI, IoT, and big data—the same core technologies behind

Society 5.0—but not just for efficiency. They must also create resilient, adaptive, and transparent supply networks that address broader societal challenges such as environmental sustainability, aging workforces, and changing consumer needs. Society 5.0 emphasizes integrating cyberspace and the physical world to solve social issues, which means supply chain leaders will need to design systems that use real-time data and automation to balance efficiency with flexibility and human well-being.

The policy vehicle for Industry 5.0 in the Netherlands is called Smart Industry 5.0, part of the Dutch Research Agenda (NWA). This initiative funds consortia to pilot human-centric, circular, and resilient manufacturing, aligning with the Netherlands' goal of achieving a circular economy by 2050. The Smart Industry 5.0 theme focuses on enabling the transition to a more human-centered, resilient, and sustainable industrial sector. It calls for research that integrates technological innovation, such as digitalization, automation, and AI, with social and organizational aspects to build industrial systems that empower workers, strengthen resilience, and tackle pressing societal challenges like sustainability and labor market shifts. The program promotes interdisciplinary collaboration among academic, public, and private partners, aiming for practical solutions that keep Dutch industry globally competitive while advancing climate neutrality and inclusive growth.

For supply chain leaders, Smart Industry 5.0 is highly relevant because it makes clear that the next generation of industrial innovation must go beyond efficiency and automation. It must actively embed human factors, resilience, and sustainability into operations and supply networks. This requires leaders to rethink how technologies like AI and IoT are deployed, not just to optimize costs and speed, but to create supply chains that are more adaptable to disruptions, more circular and resource-efficient, and better aligned with workforce well-being. Moreover, the program's emphasis on collaboration between academia, government, and industry means supply chain leaders have both an opportunity and an expectation to co-create solutions that deliver economic, environmental, and social value simultaneously.

These three initiatives stand out because they include explicit policy language referencing Industry 5.0 (EU and Netherlands) or its close counterpart Society 5.0 (Japan) and back it with targeted funding and regulatory frameworks. All three prioritize human-centric metrics such as worker well-being, meaningful employment, and safe human-robot collaboration, expanding performance measures beyond efficiency and throughput. Sustainability and resilience are treated as core mandates, with carbon neutrality, circularity, and shock preparedness embedded in grant requirements and national industrial strategies. Each program also emphasizes public–private execution, combining government funding with industry pilots and testbeds to ensure policy objectives are translated into practical, scalable results rather than remaining theoretical.

KEY TAKEAWAYS

- Supply Chain 5.0 expands the mission of supply chains from cost and efficiency to creating shared value for businesses, society, and the environment.
- Leaders need to balance speed and optimization with resilience, sustainability, and human-centricity.
- Technology can be a tool for augmenting human judgment and creativity rather than replacing people outright.
- Disruption is a constant condition and an opportunity for reinvention, not a temporary anomaly.
- Leadership shifts from centralized and transactional approaches to decentralized, distributed, and adaptive models suited for complexity.
- Resilience and regeneration emerge as strategic priorities, moving supply chains beyond shock absorption toward long-term renewal.
- The HUMANS Leadership Framework outlines six capabilities leaders need to navigate Supply Chain 5.0 with purpose and agility.
- Long-term competitiveness increases when organizations align performance with ethical, social, and environmental commitments.
- Examples from Tesla, Caterpillar, and others show that circularity and regenerative practices can create both economic and ecological advantage.
- Government initiatives in the EU, Japan, and the Netherlands demonstrate that policy is accelerating the shift toward human-centered, sustainable, and resilient supply chains.

References

Avolio, B. J. and Yammarino, F. J. (Eds.) (2013) *Transformational and Charismatic Leadership: The road ahead*. Emerald Group Publishing.

Barnard, C. I. (1938) *The Functions of the Executive*. Harvard University Press.

Beard, C. A. (2013) *Industrial Revolution*. Routledge.

Breque, M., De Nul, L. and Petridis, A. (2021) Industry 5.0: *Towards a sustainable, human-centric and resilient European industry*. Luxembourg, LU: European Commission, Directorate-General for Research and Innovation, 46.

Government of Japan (n.d.) Society 5.0: A human-centered society integrating cyberspace and physical space. Council for Science, Technology and Innovation. www8.cao.go.jp/cstp/english/society5_0/index.html (archived at https://perma.cc/5Q8G-XAER)

Caterpillar Inc. (2023, May 16) Cat® Reman process: Recycling while remanufacturing. Caterpillar Inc. www.cat.com/en_US/blog/recycling-while-remanufacturing.html (archived at https://perma.cc/YK79-SX93)

Christensen, C. M. (2016) *The Innovator's Dilemma*. Harvard Business Review Press.

Chui, M. and Bush, J. (2023, July 26) Forward thinking on how to live our longer lives with Andrew J. Scott [Audio podcast episode]. McKinsey Global Institute. www.mckinsey.com/mgi/forward-thinking/forward-thinking-on-how-to-live-our-longer-lives-with-andrew-j-scott (archived at https://perma.cc/GU29-D25R)

Circular X (2023) Case study: CAT - Reman Hub. www.circularx.eu (archived at https://perma.cc/Z8ZE-BLK8)

Craighead, C. W., Blackhurst, J., Rungtusanatham, M. J., and Handfield, R. B. (2007) The severity of supply chain disruptions: design characteristics and mitigation capabilities. *Decision Sciences*, 38(1), 131–156.

Dartey-Baah, K. and Ampofo, E. Y. (2015) Examining the influence of transformational and transactional leadership styles on perceived job stress among Ghanaian banking employees. *International Journal of Business and Management*, 10(8), 161–70. https://doi.org/10.5539/ijbm.v10n8p161 (archived at https://perma.cc/6NUD-KXQP)

de la Garza, A. (2024, May 30) Redwood Materials: Creating a circular battery economy. *Time*. www.time.com/6979982/redwood-materials (archived at https://perma.cc/2EKT-P73Y)

Drucker, P. F. (1992) Organizations. *Harvard Business Review*, 20(7), 281–93.

European Commission, Directorate-General for Research and Innovation. (2021, January 7) Industry 5.0: Towards more sustainable, resilient and human-centric industry. https://research-and-innovation.ec.europa.eu/research-area/industrial-research-and-innovation/industry-50_en (archived at https://perma.cc/767J-BUDV)

Fayol, H. (1916/2016) *General and Industrial Management*. Ravenio Books.

Gronn, P. (2002) Distributed leadership as a unit of analysis. *The Leadership Quarterly*, 13(4), 423–51.

Heifetz, R. A. (1994) *Leadership Without Easy Answers*. Harvard University Press.

Heifetz, R. A., Grashow, A. and Linsky, M. (2009) *The Practice of Adaptive Leadership: Tools and tactics for changing your organization and the world*. Harvard Business Press.

Kim, W. C. and Mauborgne, R. (2015) *Blue Ocean Strategy: How to create uncontested market space and make the competition irrelevant*. Expanded edition. Harvard Business Review Press.

Krafcik, J. F. (1988) Triumph of the lean production system. *MIT Sloan Management Review*, 30(1), 41.

Lutzker, M. A. (1982) Max Weber and the analysis of modern bureaucratic organization: Notes toward a theory of appraisal. *The American Archivist*, 45(2), 119–30.

Nissan Americas (2024, October 3) Pioneering sustainability: Nissan LEAF batteries get a second life. *Business Wire*. www.businesswire.com/news/home/20241003937341/en/Pioneering-Sustainability-Nissan-LEAF-Batteries-Get-a-Second-Life (archived at https://perma.cc/E7MV-VRSY)

Razeghi, A. (2016) *Bend the Curve: Accelerating your startup's success*. The Techstars Series.

Redwood Materials, Inc. (n.d.) About. www.redwoodmaterials.com/about/ (archived at https://perma.cc/5Q8G-XAER)

Reuters. (2021, March 26) Suez Canal blockage could cost $6 billion to $10 billion in lost trade – allianz. *Reuters*. www.reuters.com/article/business/suez-canal-blockage-could-cost-6-billion-to-10-billion-in-lost-trade-allianz-idUSKBN2BI25Y/ (archived at https://perma.cc/34DA-VLEX)

Richards, C. (2004) *Certain to Win: The strategy of John Boyd, applied to business*. Xlibris Corporation.

Simchi-Levi, D., Schmidt, W. Wei, Y., Yun Zhang, P., Combs, K., Ge, Y., Gusikhin, O., Sanders, M. and Zhang, D. (2015) Identifying risks and mitigating disruptions in the automotive supply chain. *Interfaces*, 45(5), 375–90.

Spillane, J. P. (2005, June) Distributed leadership. *The Educational Forum*, 69(2), 143–50. Taylor & Francis Group.

Taleb, N. N. (2007) *The Black Swan: The impact of the highly improbable*. Random House.

Taleb, N. N. (2012) *Antifragile: Things that gain from disorder*. Random House.

Teece, D. J., Pisano, G. and Shuen, A. (1997), Dynamic capabilities and strategic management. *Strategic Management Journal*, 18(7), 509–33.

Thien, L. M. (2018) Transactional leadership: What do we know? In D. Adams (Ed.), *Mastering Theories of Educational Leadership and Management* (pp. xx–xx) University of Malaya Press.

Thomas, J. (2024, September 19) BMW, Redwood Materials partner on electric vehicle battery recycling initiative. *Charleston Business*. https://charlestonbusiness.com/bmw-redwood-materials-partner-on-electric-vehicle-battery-recycling-initiative/ (archived at https://perma.cc/FYB8-SBUS)

US Army War College Press. (2010) *Strategic Leadership Primer for Senior Leaders* (3rd ed.) [PDF]. US Army War College. www.govinfo.gov/content/pkg/GOVPUB-D101-PURL-gpo128928/pdf/GOVPUB-D101-PURL-gpo128928.pdf (archived at https://perma.cc/F3HS-79W6)

Wienclaw, R. A. (n.d.) Scientific management in organizations. *Research Starters*. EBSCO.

Wieland, A. and Durach, C.F. (2021), Two perspectives on supply chain resilience. Journal of Business Logistics, 42: 315–22. https://doi.org/10.1111/jbl.12271 (archived at https://perma.cc/BG38-8MF6)

Womack, J. P. and Jones, D. T. (2003) *Lean Thinking: Banish waste and create wealth in your corporation* (2nd ed.). Free Press.

Zannetos, Z. S. (1965) On the theory of divisional structures: Some aspects of centralization and decentralization of control and decision making. *Management Science*, 12(4), B-49.

02

Human and Machine: Designing Collaborative Supply Chains

We shape our tools and thereafter our tools shape us.

MARSHALL MCLUHAN

As supply chains become more intelligent, interconnected, and increasingly autonomous, a profound shift is underway. Technologies such as Artificial Intelligence (AI), machine learning (ML), and machine vision are no longer confined to isolated tasks; they are now embedded deep within the daily flow of planning, production, and logistics. These systems excel at parsing massive datasets, detecting patterns, and automating routine decisions at speeds that no human can match.

Yet the more capable these systems become, the clearer one truth stands out: Humans are not becoming less important; they are becoming differently important. Supply Chain 5.0 reframes the conversation. The objective is not to design systems that replace people, but to design systems that enhance and elevate human capability.

Where Industry 4.0 focused on digitization and automation, Supply Chain 5.0 introduces a human-centric lens: Machines provide scale and speed, while people bring innovation, judgment, creativity, and ethical discernment. This is not a tug-of-war between humans and machines, but a collaboration that benefits both through intentional design.

In this chapter, we examine what that collaboration entails in practice. How do we build supply chains where algorithms and human insight do not compete for control, but instead work in synergy? How do we design workflows, governance models, and physical environments that make the most of both? And most critically, how do we ensure that technology doesn't erode the human experience of work, but enhances it?

Supply Chain 5.0 is not about choosing sides; the future of supply chains is about the quality of collaboration between humans and machines. It is about building systems that combine human intelligence and machine intelligence to create supply chains that are not only faster and more efficient but also more resilient, sustainable, and human-centered.

The Information Value Chain

Advanced technologies do not define Supply Chain 5.0, but rather by how people and machines work together to create value. AI, robotics, and automation are expanding their roles across supply chains, but their most significant potential is realized when combined with human expertise. To understand this interaction, the Information Value Chain (IVC) provides a framework for mapping where machines excel, where humans add unique value, and where the two must collaborate (see Figure 2.1).

The IVC organizes supply chain tasks into four categories based on task complexity:

- Data: Collecting and processing raw data, such as sensor readings or serial number assignments.
- Information: Organizing data into usable formats, like warehouse inventory tracking or order status updates.
- Knowledge: Analyzing information to support decisions, such as selecting suppliers or optimizing transportation routes.
- Wisdom: Applying judgment, intuition, and strategic thinking—for example, negotiating contracts or designing a supply network.

Computers and AI are particularly strong on the data and information side of the chain, where repetitive, high-volume tasks benefit from automation and pattern recognition. Humans, by contrast, excel at wisdom-level tasks that require judgment, empathy, and an ethical understanding of context. Between these lies the knowledge layer where AI and people collaborate, with machines providing insights and options, and humans weighing trade-offs and making final decisions.

Figure 2.1 The Information Value Chain Adapted for AI

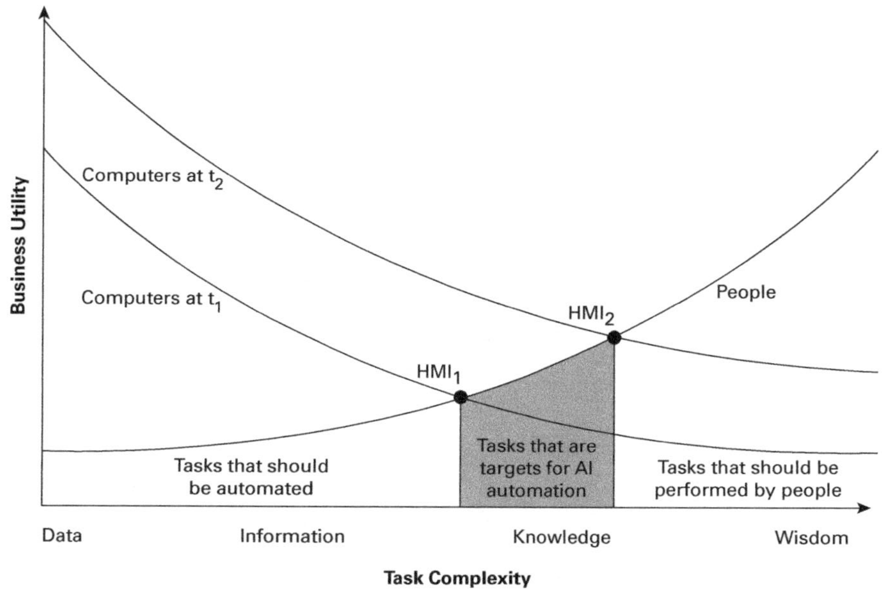

Where the roles of humans and machines overlap lies the human–machine interface (HMI). This is where information must flow seamlessly between information systems and supply chain practitioners. Today, tasks at the HMI include demand planning, supplier evaluation, and scenario modeling. AI aggregates and analyzes large datasets, while people apply business acumen and strategic priorities to interpret the results.

As AI capabilities advance, the HMI shifts to the right on the IVC. Tasks that currently require human judgment will increasingly be augmented, or even automated, by AI. For example, dynamic pricing and real-time inventory balancing, once the domain of experienced planners, are becoming machine-assisted functions. However, this shift does not eliminate the need for humans. Instead, it elevates their roles toward the wisdom end of the chain: Shaping strategy, managing exceptions, and ensuring ethical and sustainable decisions.

The IVC illustrates that Supply Chain 5.0 is not "man vs. machine" but "man with machine." AI-powered forecasting can suggest production plans but humans refine them to align with corporate strategy and social responsibility goals. Predictive maintenance systems can flag equipment failures but human operators determine how to balance cost, safety, and service commitments. This partnership between humans and machines enables organizations to achieve all four critical outcomes for Supply Chain 5.0:

- Profitability: Automating data-heavy, repetitive tasks allows supply chain teams to focus on high-value decisions that drive revenue growth and cost efficiency, unlocking greater returns on assets and operations.
- Resilience: Real-time machine insights combined with human judgment create a more adaptive supply chain, enabling faster responses to disruptions and maintaining continuity under pressure.
- Sustainability: AI systems can optimize for energy use, emissions, and waste reduction, while people ensure that environmental and social considerations are embedded into strategic decisions.
- Human-centricity: By offloading routine work to AI, employees are empowered to focus on creativity, collaboration, and problem-solving, building a more engaged workforce and ensuring technology serves people.

Understanding the IVC makes one thing clear: The highest-value work in Supply Chain 5.0 occurs where ambiguity and judgment intersect. Nowhere is this more visible than in exception handling. Disruptions and anomalies expose the limits of both machine precision and human intuition in isolation. They are the stress tests for any human–machine system, revealing whether collaboration has been intentionally designed or left to chance.

The Role of Humans in an Automated Supply Chain

As supply chains become increasingly intelligent and autonomous, it can be tempting to assume that technology will eventually replace human decision-making. AI systems are already outperforming people in processing vast datasets, detecting patterns, and executing routine, rule-based tasks at scale. These capabilities are transforming core functions such as demand forecasting, inventory optimization, and supplier performance monitoring (Everstream Analytics, 2025; Resilinc, 2025).

Despite these advances, humans judgment remain indispensable. The defining strength of human operators lies in their ability to navigate ambiguity, make trade-offs under uncertainty, and apply creativity when facing unstructured or novel situations that fall outside the parameters of algorithms. These are the conditions that dominate the most critical moments in supply chain management, including disruptions, exceptions, and strategic pivots.

Exception Handling

Exception handling is the structured detection, prioritization, and resolution of unplanned events (Xu et al., 2003). Xu et al. classify supply chain exceptions into three categories: Input, such as supplier shortages; process, including machine failures or cyberattacks; and output, including last-minute order changes. AI excels at flagging anomalies and surfacing patterns across these domains, but data alone cannot resolve the situation. Decisions often involve conflicting priorities, ethical considerations, and downstream impacts that require contextual awareness and human judgment.

In Chapter 1, we introduced the OODA loop (Observe, Orient, Decide, Act) as a framework for making rapid decisions under uncertainty. Exception handling in supply chains follows this exact pattern. AI systems excel at the "observe" phase by scanning massive data sets for anomalies. Humans bring value in the "orient" and "decide" phases, where context, trade-offs, and creativity shape the appropriate course of action before execution in the "act" stage. Supply Chain 5.0 leverages this division of labor, utilizing machines to compress the time it takes to detect and model scenarios while keeping humans central to orientation and decision-making in complex, ambiguous situations.

For example, a delayed shipment detected by an AI-driven control tower may present multiple corrective options, such as rerouting freight at a premium, delaying orders, or reallocating inventory from another market. The algorithm can rank these choices based on cost and lead time. However, only a human can weigh the strategic trade-offs, such as protecting a key customer relationship, maintaining regulatory compliance, or balancing short-term margin erosion against long-term market share. This ability to integrate context, nuance, and strategy into choices is uniquely human and remains irreplaceable (Gartner, 2023).

Ambiguity, Trade-Offs, and Creativity

AI models are trained on historical patterns and defined parameters. When they encounter scenarios outside their training data or where goals are not strictly quantifiable, they often fail to produce reliable results. Humans, in contrast, excel at reconciling incomplete information, synthesizing conflicting objectives, and generating creative solutions.

This is not a weakness of AI but an example of complementarity. Intelligent systems provide rapid situational awareness and data-driven recommendations, while people supply the interpretive, ethical, and strategic layer that ensures decisions align with broader organizational and societal goals. The most advanced supply chains are not those with the least human involvement but those that design technology and talent to function as co-architects of value creation (Busse, 2024; Natarajan et al., 2025).

Recognizing the role of human judgment naturally leads to the question of how to structure collaboration between people and intelligent systems. Governance models such as human-in-the-loop and human-on-the-loop provide a framework for defining where and how humans remain engaged in decision-making. These approaches ensure that automation remains fast and efficient while preserving human oversight for exceptions, ethical trade-offs, and strategic alignment. The next section explores how these governance models translate the balance between intelligent systems and human authority into operational practice within Supply Chain 5.0.

The Automation Continuum

Designing collaborative supply chains requires more than simply layering automation onto existing workflows. It demands a clear framework for how humans and intelligent systems share authority. One way to conceptualize this balance is as a continuum that stretches from fully manual operations at one end to fully autonomous, agentic systems at the other. Between these poles are hybrid modes where humans and machines interact: Human-in-the-loop (HITL) and human-on-the-loop (HOTL).

As shown in Figure 2.2, the interaction between people and intelligent systems in Supply Chain 5.0 can be visualized as a continuum with four distinct steps: manual operation, HITL, HOTL, and fully automated agentic systems.

At the first step, manual operation, humans perform the entire decision cycle without machine assistance. This mode offers maximum contextual judgment but is slow and prone to error in data-heavy environments.

The second step, HITL, embeds people directly inside the decision cycle. The machine can process data, generate recommendations, or even propose actions, but a human validates, approves, or overrides the outcome before execution. HITL emphasizes control and contextual awareness, though often at the cost of speed and scalability.

Figure 2.2 The Automation Continuum

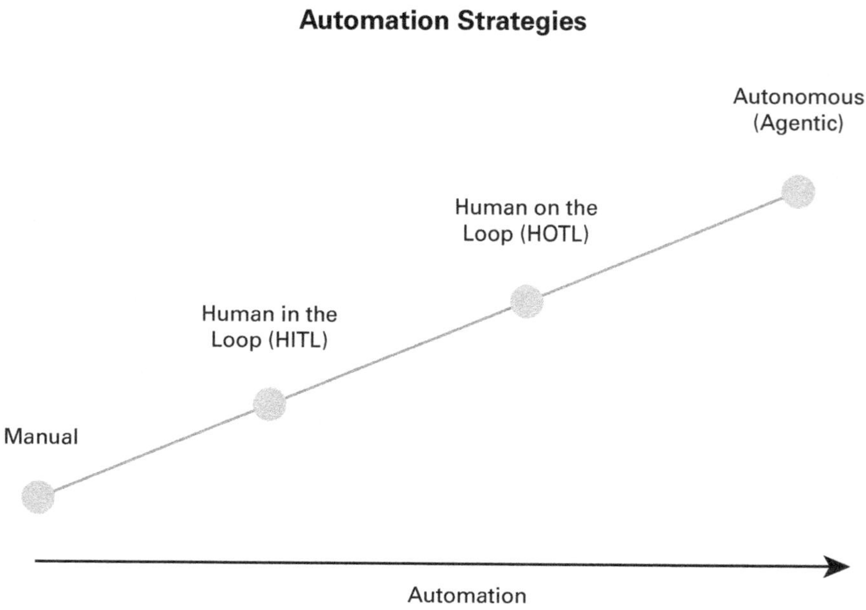

The third step, HOTL, shifts more authority to the machine. Automation executes decisions independently under normal conditions, while humans supervise at a higher level and intervene only when an anomaly, ethical concern, or edge case arises. HOTL prioritizes speed and scalability while retaining a safeguard for oversight.

At the far right of the continuum lies fully automated agentic systems, where the machine acts without human intervention, making and executing decisions autonomously. This mode promises maximum efficiency but it also carries the highest risk of error propagation, ethical blind spots, and loss of accountability if not carefully governed (Natarajan et al., 2025).

The continuum from manual to fully agentic automation can also be seen as a spectrum of how the OODA loop is allocated. Manual processes keep all four stages with human operators. HITL systems automate "observe" and sometimes "act," while humans still "orient" and "decide." HOTL pushes "observe" and "decide" into machine territory under normal conditions, reserving human intervention for high-risk or anomalous cases. Fully agentic systems attempt to automate the entire OODA loop, which is why they demand the highest level of governance and ethical guardrails.

The shift toward HITL and HOTL models is not just an operational choice but is increasingly becoming a regulatory requirement. The European Union's Artificial Intelligence Act classifies many supply chain applications as "high-risk" systems and mandates that AI-generated recommendations must be explainable, traceable, and overseen by humans who can understand and override automated outputs (European Commission, 2024). In the United States, the National Institute of Standards and Technology's AI Risk Management Framework (AI RMF 1.0) emphasizes similar principles, requiring organizations to document AI-generated recommendations, maintain audit trails, and ensure that humans retain meaningful authority over critical decisions (NIST, 2023). Together, these frameworks underscore that effective HITL and HOTL governance is not only good practice but also foundational for compliance, safety, and trust in intelligent supply chain systems.

Designing collaborative supply chains is not only a technical or operational challenge; it is also an ethical one. Systems that grant excessive authority to machines risk amplifying bias, eroding trust, and making decisions that prioritize efficiency over human well-being or environmental impact. Conversely, systems that rely too heavily on human intuition may sacrifice speed and consistency in ways that harm customers and the communities they serve. The balance between human and machine is therefore not neutral;

it carries profound consequences for workers, partners, and society. Supply Chain 5.0 calls on leaders to design this balance consciously, ensuring that technology serves people and the planet, rather than the other way around.

Choosing the right governance model depends on the specific task at hand. For highly sensitive or ambiguous activities, manual or HITL approaches may be most appropriate. For routine, high-volume tasks, HOTL or even fully automated systems can unlock significant efficiency. As technologies mature, tasks often migrate along this continuum. What begins as manual or HITL may evolve into HOTL as algorithms improve accuracy and trust, and eventually shift toward agentic automation when the business case, risk tolerance, and ethical guardrails align.

This dynamic movement is a key feature of Supply Chain 5.0. Instead of limiting processes to one mode, leaders must continually reassess where each task fits on the spectrum and adjust governance as technology and organizational priorities evolve.

Examples of the Automation Continuum

Avatar Robotics approaches the shift from manual work to higher levels of automation with the understanding that progress will be gradual. As Colin Webb noted in a 2025 interview for this book, we will not move from zero to general-purpose robotic automation overnight, and the ongoing automation process is likely to create more jobs than it displaces. This perspective shapes the company's strategy of deploying flexible, wheeled humanoid robots in industrial facilities to address labor shortages and logistical challenges. Their human-in-the-loop model uses remote operators, sometimes located internationally, to control robots and handle tasks that current AI cannot yet perform reliably. The approach improves adaptability, safety, and cost efficiency while keeping human judgment at the center of operations. Avatar plans to increase autonomous capabilities as the technology matures while maintaining human oversight for work that requires dexterity or situational awareness, strengthening resilience across supply chain operations.

Tele-driving provides another compelling example of an HITL approach. In Dr. Saif Benjaafar's 2024 study, remote human drivers operated vehicles at a distance using advanced connectivity and control interfaces. The AI system handled basic navigation and safety protocols, but a human operator made every critical driving decision. This model enabled fleets to scale with fewer drivers while maintaining human oversight for complex, unpredictable events, demonstrating the resilience benefits of keeping people closely involved (Benjaafar, Wang, and Yang, 2025).

Maersk's AI-powered vessel delay predictions illustrate a transition toward HOTL. Satellite AIS data feeds a machine-learning engine that forecasts delays up to seven days in advance (Kalamatas, 2025). Planners may receive automated recommendations for reallocating equipment or rebooking capacity, but typically they retain the final authority to implement which option (Maersk 2025). For example, their customized control towers quickly flag issues and propose solutions, while humans supervise and contextualize actions to align with broader strategic goals (Maersk, 2024).

DHL's control tower "risk cockpit" leans further toward HOTL. When a typhoon threatens Shenzhen, the system autonomously generates a heat map of at-risk SKUs and proposes mode shifts. Human network managers review the plan and sign off before carriers are re-tendered. Most decisions are executed automatically, with human oversight preserved for escalation thresholds and ethical trade-offs such as customer prioritization or regulatory compliance (Straight, 2023).

Navigating Automation Trade-Offs

Moving along this continuum involves balancing competing priorities. HITL offers the highest degree of human control and ethical oversight but can slow decision-making in fast-moving environments. HOTL and agentic models offer greater speed and scalability, but increase the risk of algorithmic overreach and the erosion of human accountability.

Dr. Sriraam Natarajan's research warns that many so-called HITL systems actually function as "AI-in-the-loop," where human authority is nominal and algorithms effectively drive outcomes. Without deliberate governance, organizations may slip into overreliance on machine recommendations, mistakenly assuming neutrality where biases and data quality issues persist (Natarajan et al., 2025).

Similarly, Dr. Maria De-Arteaga's work on algorithmic decision support highlights the dangers of misplaced trust. In her study of child welfare screening tools, she found that human operators often adapted their behavior based on algorithmic scores, sometimes deferring to the machine even when it was wrong. Crucially, the research also showed that when humans recognized flawed recommendations, they were willing to override them, underscoring the need for explainability and clear channels for human veto power in automated systems (De-Arteaga, Fogliato, and Chouldechova, 2020).

For supply chain leaders, the lesson is clear: HITL and HOTL are not simply technical configurations but governance choices that define the relationship between people and machines. Effective hybrid systems explicitly codify when and how human authority enters the loop, which escalation thresholds trigger oversight, and how to preserve ethical and strategic alignment as automation scales.

Supply Chain 5.0 is not about replacing people with algorithms. It is about designing socio-technical systems that combine the speed and scale of machines with the judgment, creativity, and accountability of humans. Navigating the continuum from manual to hybrid to fully autonomous operation requires deliberate choices about architecture and constant calibration to ensure that technology remains a tool for human-centered resilience, profitability, and sustainability.

Building Hybrid Work Environments

Supply Chain 5.0 is not about automating existing processes in isolation. It is about designing workflows where people and intelligent systems operate as co-architects of value creation. This requires building hybrid work environments that explicitly define the roles of humans and machines and structure the hand-offs between them.

Some of the most advanced supply chain organizations are already demonstrating how hybrid models can unlock productivity and resilience. At Amazon's 2024 mega fulfillment center, more than 1,000 mobile robots handle storage and transport tasks. Still, over 1,400 human associates remain essential for managing irregular items, handling exceptions, and ensuring quality control (Dresser, 2025). Kroger's high-speed fulfillment hubs employ a similar approach, with 1,000 bots supporting 400 associates who specialize in resolving anomalies and upholding the customer promise. DHL reports productivity gains of up to 70 percent in sites where collaborative robots, or cobots, handle repetitive motions while human workers focus on value-added analysis and exception resolution (Straight, 2023).

These examples illustrate that the highest-performing environments are not "all machine" or "all human," but carefully designed blends where each actor contributes its strengths.

A key component of this approach is the hybrid work cell. In these environments, every task within a value stream is explicitly assigned to either a machine, a human, or a shared "hand-off" zone. Escalation triggers are defined in advance, making it clear when a process should shift from machine to human control. For example, a cobot might pick and place items until a weight anomaly is detected, at which point a human operator steps in to inspect and make a judgment call.

This explicit mapping eliminates ambiguity during disruptions and ensures that exception handling is integrated into the workflow, rather than added after the fact. It also provides a foundation for scaling automation responsibly, allowing new technologies to be introduced into a structure where human oversight and accountability are already in place.

Operationalizing hybrid work requires a socio-technological design mindset (Sailer et al., 2023). Overall, we identified three design cues that stand out, which can also be seen in Figure 2.3:

- Value stream mapping: Start by mapping core value streams and flagging every decision point that still requires human context. This helps determine where HITL and HOTL models should be deployed.
- Escalation matrices: Define cost, customer, and compliance thresholds that route issues to the right human quickly. These matrices prevent delays and ensure accountability when exceptions occur.
- Digital twins: Build digital twins early to simulate human–machine hand-offs and stress-test workflows under disruption. This allows leaders to refine hybrid designs before deployment and adapt quickly as technologies mature.

At its core, this approach embodies the socio-technological design philosophy of Supply Chain 5.0. Technology is not layered on top of legacy processes; instead, people and intelligent systems are designed to work together from the ground up. Machines handle sensing, computation, and repetitive motion. Humans focus on judgment, creativity, and balancing stakeholder trade-offs. The result is a supply chain that is not only more efficient and resilient but also more sustainable and human-centric.

By building hybrid work environments with clear roles, defined hand-offs, and continuous feedback loops, organizations can operationalize human–machine synergy and turn it into a competitive advantage.

From Dashboards to Control Towers

Decision support systems in supply chain management are undergoing a profound evolution. What began as static dashboards displaying historical

Figure 2.3 Operationalizing Hybrid Work Through Socio-Technological Design

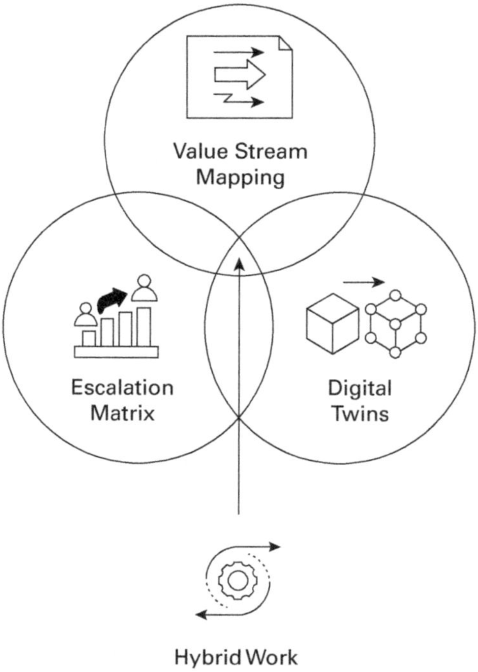

metrics is rapidly transforming into dynamic, predictive control towers that can orchestrate real-time operations. In some organizations these systems are referred to as command centers because they serve as the central nervous system of supply chain decision-making. This shift marks a critical stage in the development of Supply Chain 5.0.

Traditional dashboards were designed to provide visibility. They consolidated data from enterprise systems into static reports and charts, offering snapshots of key performance indicators such as inventory levels, order status, and supplier performance. Although valuable, these dashboards were descriptive and reactive. They depended on human users to interpret the data, identify patterns, and decide on the appropriate actions.

Control towers (or command centers, as we will discuss in Chapter 11) represent the next stage in this evolution. Instead of passively reporting past events, they integrate multiple data streams in real time, detect anomalies, simulate potential responses, and can recommend or initiate corrective actions. These systems combine structured enterprise data with unstructured signals such as weather alerts, port disruptions, and social sentiment to create a multi-layered, predictive view of the supply chain.

Control towers are operational embodiments of the OODA loop. They integrate streams of real-time data to observe, use AI-driven analytics to orient and predict, provide decision options for human operators to decide, and trigger rapid actions across the network. The most advanced systems shorten the OODA cycle dramatically, enabling supply chains to respond to disruptions in minutes rather than days while still embedding human judgment where it matters most.

Unilever's global ocean control tower illustrates this transformation. Before it was implemented, regional planners used dashboards that showed lagging indicators like stockouts, late shipments, and interventions were largely reactive. The new control tower utilizes AI and ML to predict disruptions caused by weather, supplier risks, or port congestion, and provides real-time mitigation strategies. Human planners use the system to focus on scenario selection, customer prioritization, and relationship management. The initiative improved on-time delivery by 10 percent and reduced response time to disruptions by more than 50 percent (Unilever, 2021).

FourKites also demonstrates how command centers redefine supply chain visibility. Many of its clients previously relied on siloed transportation management data and static dashboards that reported delays only after they occurred. The FourKites Intelligent Control Tower now provides real-time predictive estimated times of arrival, proactive disruption alerts, and AI-generated risk mitigation recommendations. Human planners evaluate the risk levels flagged by the system, select among pre-simulated resolution options, and coordinate with internal stakeholders to protect customer orders. This combination of predictive analytics and human oversight has achieved dynamic estimated time of arrival predictions with over 90 percent accuracy and has significantly reduced decision latency.

Control towers are more than a technical enhancement. They reflect the core philosophy of Supply Chain 5.0 by shifting beyond visibility into real-time orchestration. Traditional dashboards ask what happened. Control towers ask, "What should we do now?" and increasingly "What will happen next?" and "How can we shape it?"

The value of these systems lies in their ability to combine machine capabilities with human expertise. Control towers use AI for sensing, prediction, and simulation, while humans supply strategic alignment, ethical oversight, and creative problem-solving. They are practical embodiments of the socio-technological design that defines Supply Chain 5.0, creating supply chains that are faster, more adaptive, and more human-centric.

Building an Augmented Workforce

The conversation about automation in supply chains often starts with cost reduction, but the real opportunity lies in capability amplification. This perspective is supported by the World Economic Forum's Future of Jobs 2025 report, which finds that organizations adopting augmentation strategies rather than full replacement expect net employment to grow by eight percent, with the fastest-growing roles focused on human–machine orchestration and data-driven decision-making (WEF, 2025).

An augmented workforce can also create a competitive advantage. Companies that effectively blend human judgment with machine speed can respond to disruptions more quickly, innovate faster, and deliver superior customer experiences compared to their peers, who rely on either manual labor or full automation alone. This advantage compounds over time: Organizations that capture and institutionalize human–machine learning loops build proprietary capabilities that are difficult for competitors to replicate. In a volatile market environment, the ability to combine algorithmic prediction with human adaptability becomes not just operationally valuable but strategically differentiating.

Examples from across various industries demonstrate how pairing people with intelligent systems creates a workforce that is both more productive and more adaptable. At BMW's Dingolfing plant, collaborative robots, or cobots, assist technicians in installing heavy drive shafts with millimeter precision. The machines handle the physical strain, while humans perform the fine assembly tasks and quality checks. The result has been greater precision, fewer injuries, and sustainable productivity over time (BMW, 2017; BMW, 2019).

Avatar Robotics applies the same principle in warehouse operations. The company is developing fleets of robots that human operators can guide remotely. One way that they are using this technology is with a human-in-the-loop model which combines robotic precision with human adaptability, allowing warehouses to handle irregular items, adjust to changing workflows, and maintain productivity even during labor shortages. Operators can work from anywhere, creating a distributed labor pool while improving safety by removing people from hazardous environments (Avatar Robotics, 2025).

Tokyo-based Avatarin extends this model into service industries with telepresence robots. A single operator can supervise and control multiple robots that provide remote customer interaction in museums, retail, and healthcare settings. During the COVID-19 pandemic, Avatarin's systems maintained over 95 percent of pre-pandemic service levels in some sites while creating new revenue streams through remote access programs. This model demonstrates how human-supervised automation can provide resilience and flexibility while maintaining the human touch (ANA Holdings, 2021).

While the augmented workforce offers compelling benefits, it is not without challenges. Integrating human–machine systems requires significant investment in software, data integration, and workforce training. Poor data quality can undermine machine recommendations, amplifying biases or producing suboptimal outcomes. Accountability can also become blurred when decisions are co-produced by algorithms and people, raising questions about liability when things go wrong. These friction points underscore the need for disciplined data governance, transparent model design, and clearly defined decision rights to ensure that augmentation enhances both performance and trust.

The augmented workforce highlights a central truth about Supply Chain 5.0: The goal is not to minimize human involvement but to maximize human value. By shifting routine, dangerous, or physically demanding work to machines, organizations can allow people to focus on judgment, creativity, and relationship-building.

Shifting from automation to true human–machine collaboration changes more than workflows; it reframes what supply chains are designed to achieve. Success in Supply Chain 5.0 depends on more than efficiency or speed. It is defined by whether systems advance three core pillars: Sustainability, resilience, and human-centricity. The next chapter explores these pillars in depth and shows how they serve as the foundation for designing supply chains that create lasting value for businesses, people, and the planet.

KEY TAKEAWAYS

- Map the human–machine boundary using the Information Value Chain to identify each task's level and assign what AI should handle and where humans should stay involved.
- Design workflows for collaboration by letting machines manage sensing and repetition while humans focus on judgment and creativity.

- Make exception handling a human domain by using AI for detection and modeling but keeping people responsible for ambiguous or high-stakes decisions.
- Choose HITL or HOTL at the task level by defining where humans validate, supervise, or step back, and adjusting as systems improve.
- Create clear escalation matrices by defining triggers that move control from machines to humans during disruptions.
- Use digital twins to simulate workflows and stress-test hand-offs before deploying automation.
- Shift from dashboards to control towers by enabling real-time sensing, prediction, and recommendations while keeping humans aligned to strategy.
- Prioritize workforce augmentation by using automation to reduce strain and routine work so people can focus on higher-value tasks.
- Embed ethics and trust in every system by ensuring explainability, usability, and human override capabilities.

References

ANA Holdings (2021, September 3) Avatarin continues its commitment to improve global mobility. www.anahd.co.jp/ana_news/en/2021/09/03/20210903-1.html (archived at https://perma.cc/492T-K6RU)

Avatar Robotics (2025) Avatar Robotics. www.avatarrobotics.com (archived at https://perma.cc/B6ZZ-WGDZ)

Benjaafar, S., Wang, Z. and Yang, X. (2025) Human-in-the-loop automation: Ride-hailing with remote (tele-) drivers. *Management Science*, 71(3), 2527–43. https://papers.ssrn.com/sol3/papers.cfm?abstract_id=4130757 (archived at https://perma.cc/8ALU-33UK)

BMW (2017) Human-robot collaboration in the axle drive assembly: BMW Group Plant Dingolfing. www.press.bmwgroup.com/global/photo/detail/P90249739/human-robot-collaboration-in-the-axle-drive-assembly-bmw-group-plant-dingolfing-02/2017 (archived at https://perma.cc/9HZL-ACA4)

BMW (2019) BMW Group invests 400 million euros in Plant Dingolfing for BMW iNEXT. www.press.bmwgroup.com/global/article/detail/T0303346EN/bmw-group-invests-400-million-euros-in-plant-dingolfing-for-bmw-inext (archived at https://perma.cc/2KRL-7EQ5)

Busse, C. (2024, August 6) The secret to successful enterprise AI? 'Human-in-the-loop' design. *Forbes Innovation*. www.forbes.com/councils/forbestechcouncil/2024/08/06/the-secret-to-successful-enterprise-ai-human-in-the-loop-design/ (archived at https://perma.cc/2GG4-HE8B)

De-Arteaga, M., Fogliato, R. and Chouldechova, A. (2020) A case for humans-in-the-loop: Decisions in the presence of erroneous algorithmic scores. In *Proceedings of the 2020 CHI Conference on Human Factors in Computing Systems* (pp. 1–12) https://doi.org/10.1145/3313831.3376369 (archived at https://perma.cc/SW6Z-SDM5)

Dresser, S. (2025, January 15) Amazon launches a new AI foundation model to power its robotic fleet and deploys its 1 millionth robot. *Amazon News*. www.aboutamazon.com/news/operations/amazon-million-robots-ai-foundation-model (archived at https://perma.cc/ZH6Z-XPMQ)

European Commission (2024) Proposal for a regulation laying down harmonised rules on artificial intelligence (Artificial Intelligence Act) *Official Journal of the European Union*. https://digital-strategy.ec.europa.eu/en/library/proposal-regulation-laying-down-harmonised-rules-artificial-intelligence (archived at https://perma.cc/P9MS-BPX5)

Everstream Analytics (2025) Real-time risk intelligence for resilient supply chains. www.everstream.ai (archived at https://perma.cc/38NS-9YSW)

FourKites (2025) FourKites Intelligent Control Tower. www.fourkites.com (archived at https://perma.cc/QF2V-84S2)

Gartner (2023) Supply chain technology user wants and needs survey. Gartner Research.

Kalamatas, M. (2025) Maersk unveils AI-powered port delay forecasting tool for global clients. EAN Networks. https://ean-network.com/maersk-unveils-ai-powered-port-delay-forecasting-tool-for-global-clients/ (archived at https://perma.cc/43X9-KV2Q)

Maersk (2024) Customs control tower. www.maersk.com/supply-chain-logistics/customs-services/customs-control-tower (archived at https://perma.cc/W2U7-NHGR)

Maersk (2025) The Logistics Trend Map. www.maersk.com/insights/logistics-trend-map (archived at https://perma.cc/7DX6-E4HR)

McLuhan, M. (1964) *Understanding Media: The Extensions of Man*. MIT Press.

Natarajan, S., Mathur, S., Sidheekh, S., Stammer, W. and Kersting, K. (2025, April) Human-in-the-loop or AI-in-the-loop? Automate or collaborate? In *Proceedings of the AAAI Conference on Artificial Intelligence*, 39(27), 28594–28600. https://doi.org/10.1609/aaai.v39i27.35083 (archived at https://perma.cc/M7WT-R4VF)

NIST (National Institute of Standards and Technology) (2023) Artificial Intelligence Risk Management Framework (AI RMF 1.0) US Department of Commerce. https://nvlpubs.nist.gov/nistpubs/ai/nist.ai.100-1.pdf (archived at https://perma.cc/J8FY-NLDS)

Resilinc (2025) EventWatch: Multi-tier supply chain risk monitoring. www.resilinc.com (archived at https://perma.cc/FMR5-XJEZ)

Sailer, K., Thomas, M. and Pachilova, R. (2023) The challenges of hybrid work: an architectural sociology perspective. *Buildings and Cities*, 4(1), 650–68.

Straight, B. (2023, September 15) DHL Supply Chain facility is showcasing how automation and humans can coexist. *Supply Chain Management Review*. www.scmr.com/article/dhl_supply_chain_facility_is_showcasing_how_automation_humans_can_coexist (archived at https://perma.cc/MQT4-CJJY)

Unilever (2021) What happens when machine learning meets ocean shipping? *Unilever News*. www.unilever.com/news/news-search/2021/what-happens-when-machine-learning-meets-ocean-shipping/ (archived at https://perma.cc/2TZS-CDPC)

WEF (2025) The future of jobs report 2025. World Economic Forum. www.weforum.org/publications/the-future-of-jobs-report-2025/ (archived at https://perma.cc/9T4N-ABCT)

Xu, H. Q., Besant, C. B. and Ristic, M. (2003) System for enhancing supply chain agility through exception handling. *International Journal of Production Research*, 41(6), 1099–1114. DOI: 10.1080/0020754021000049826

03 The Three Pillars of Supply Chain 5.0

Modern supply chains are the only wonders of the world... These are the systems that make everything else.

BRIAN LAUNG AOAEH

Supply Chain 5.0 represents a decisive shift in how we design, manage, and measure the networks that drive the global economy. In earlier industrial eras, supply chains were primarily defined by their ability to cut costs, increase speed, and maximize efficiency. While these priorities remain essential, they are no longer sufficient. The demands of the 21st century require supply chains that deliver lasting value not only to businesses but also to society and the planet.

This new paradigm rests on three interconnected pillars: sustainability, resiliency, and human-centricity. Each addresses a distinct aspect of what modern supply chains must accomplish. Sustainability anchors operations within environmental and social boundaries, transforming responsible resource stewardship into a source of innovation and competitive advantage. Resilience ensures that these systems can absorb shocks and adapt to constant disruption, moving beyond reactive risk management to proactive, designed-in stability. Human-centricity keeps people at the center, ensuring that technology amplifies human judgment and creativity rather than replacing it.

Climate change is forcing companies to reassess their sourcing, production, and logistics strategies. Geopolitical tensions and trade disruptions are testing the limits of global networks. Automation and AI are redefining the relationship between people and machines across every stage of the value chain. At the same time, customers, employees, and regulators are demanding greater transparency, ethical practices, and measurable impact. Together, these pressures are pushing supply chains beyond the automation and digitization of Industry 4.0 into the adaptive, regenerative, and people-centered systems that define Supply Chain 5.0.

This chapter explores the three pillars that underpin this evolution. It examines why they matter now, how they reinforce each other, and what practical steps organizations can take to embed them into their networks. By integrating sustainability, resilience, and human-centricity into a single operating model, leaders can build supply chains that are not just designed to withstand change but positioned to thrive in it.

Designing Products and Services for the Three Pillars

Many of the defining characteristics of a Supply Chain 5.0 network are determined long before a product reaches production. The ability to build sustainability, resilience, and human-centricity into operations is effectively established during the design phase. Decisions about materials, sourcing models, manufacturing processes, and end-of-life management set the parameters for everything that follows in the supply chain (Braungart et al., 2007; Hsu et al., 2024).

From a sustainability perspective, product design influences resource intensity, recyclability, and environmental impact throughout the life cycle. Choosing renewable or recycled inputs, designing for disassembly, and minimizing hazardous substances create downstream supply chains that can operate within ecological boundaries. Products engineered for modular repair or longer lifespans inherently support circular supply chains and reduce waste streams, enabling a regenerative model rather than a linear one (Ellen MacArthur Foundation, 2023).

Resilience is also rooted in upstream decisions. When design teams select materials that allow for substitution, adopt component standardization, or incorporate multiple sourcing options into the bill of materials, they create networks that can adapt to disruptions. A product designed with interchangeable parts or embedded digital traceability is inherently more robust in the face of shocks such as raw material shortages or supplier failures. These design choices establish adaptive capacity into the network before a single order is placed (Ivanov, 2023).

Human-centricity is shaped in the same early stages. Ethical sourcing requirements, ergonomic considerations for assembly and packaging, and transparency mechanisms for labor standards are established during design. Even consumer-facing features, such as products that are easier to repair or reuse, tie back to human-centric values by empowering both workers and end-users. These decisions influence not only the working conditions throughout the supply chain but also the way people interact with products across their lifecycle (Tóth et al., 2023).

Because these foundational choices cascade through sourcing, production, logistics, and end-of-life systems, integrating the three pillars during design creates a multiplier effect across the entire network. Organizations that embed sustainability, resilience, and human-centricity into their design governance are not only building more adaptive and responsible supply chains, but also laying the groundwork for long-term value creation and strategic advantage in a Supply Chain 5.0 environment.

Sustainability as a Core Principle

In traditional supply chain models, sustainability was often treated as an external requirement. Companies viewed environmental and social initiatives as responses to regulation or consumer pressure, secondary to cost reduction and operational efficiency. Within the Supply Chain 5.0 framework, sustainability shifts from being a compliance obligation to becoming a central strategic driver. Instead of existing at the margins, it becomes embedded in planning and execution, fueling innovation and competitive advantage (Henrich et al., 2022; McKinsey Technology Council, 2023).

Why Sustainability Matters Now

Sustainability is no longer a secondary consideration or a marketing differentiator. It has become a core strategic requirement for supply chains operating in an environment shaped by climate change, resource scarcity, and rising regulatory and consumer expectations. Global networks are being measured not just on efficiency and cost, but on their ability to minimize environmental impact and contribute to social value creation. Organizations that fail to embed sustainability risk supply disruptions from climate events, loss of market access due to evolving regulations, and reputational damage from stakeholders demanding transparency (Dacre et al., 2024).

At the same time, sustainability is emerging as a powerful driver of innovation and resilience. Companies that invest in regenerative practices, circular systems, and renewable inputs are discovering new value streams while reducing dependency on volatile raw materials. Integrating sustainability early in design and sourcing decisions allows businesses to future-proof operations against environmental and social risks, positioning them to thrive in a rapidly changing global landscape (PwC, 2025).

REAL-WORLD EXAMPLE McDonald's and Regenerative Agriculture

McDonald's is integrating regenerative agriculture into its supply network as a way to both cut emissions and enhance resilience. Led by Chief Sustainability Officer Beth Hart, the company committed to reducing agriculture-related emissions by 16 percent by 2030 compared to a 2018 baseline (Balch, 2025). Rather than imposing prescriptive requirements on suppliers, McDonald's co-invests with farmers, funding pilot programs and sharing data on practices such as cover cropping, reduced tillage, enzyme-enhanced cattle feed, and rotational grazing.

By positioning itself as a partner and incubator rather than a top-down enforcer, McDonald's created a platform where sustainability initiatives become both scalable and economically viable. Farmers benefit from improved yields and soil health, while McDonald's gains a more stable and regenerative supply base. This approach illustrates how embedding sustainability upstream can simultaneously address climate goals and operational resilience.

REAL-WORLD EXAMPLE Patagonia and Traceable Supply Chains

Patagonia has long been a leader in embedding environmental and social responsibility into its supply chain. Since 1996, all of its cotton has been organic, and the company now leads industry initiatives in regenerative organic agriculture (Patagonia, 2025a). Patagonia's Supply Chain Environmental Responsibility Program tracks impacts at supplier factories, while its Material Traceability Program ensures transparency across upstream sourcing (Patagonia, 2025b).

By combining internal governance with third-party certifications such as the Forest Stewardship Council and Fair Trade USA, Patagonia demonstrates how sustainability can be institutionalized. The company's integration of environmental stewardship with labor transparency shows that sustainability is most effective when environmental and social dimensions are pursued together. The result is not only reduced ecological impact but also stronger brand equity and customer loyalty.

Circular Economy Integration

A central driver of sustainability in Supply Chain 5.0 is the adoption of circular economy principles. In contrast to the traditional linear "take-make-dispose" model, circular supply chains are designed to keep products, components, and materials circulating at their highest possible value for as long as they can be used (Ellen MacArthur Foundation, 2023). This approach reduces waste, regenerates natural systems, and creates new avenues of value creation for businesses.

Circular supply chains bring the broader goals of the circular economy into operational practice. They focus on three essential principles. The first is eliminating waste and pollution through intentional product design and process innovation. The second is circulating materials through strategies such as repair, reuse, refurbishment, and remanufacturing. The third is regenerating nature by using renewable inputs and embedding restorative practices into sourcing and production (PwC, 2025).

Supply Chain 5.0 is accelerating this shift from theory to execution. Digital twins allow organizations to simulate product lifecycles and design for durability and end-of-life recovery. IoT sensors track materials in real time, making reverse logistics and recycling more efficient. Blockchain creates verifiable records of material provenance, supporting transparency and compliance across complex, multi-tier supply networks (Rejeb et al., 2025).

At the core of circular systems is a series of interconnected "loops" that keep resources moving through the value chain. These loops provide a practical blueprint for turning circularity into a daily operational reality. When integrated into product design, manufacturing, and logistics, they enable companies to minimize waste, unlock new revenue streams, and build resilience against resource constraints. The 10 loops below represent the core practices that allow supply chains to evolve from linear systems into regenerative ecosystems.

- Reduce: Minimize material and energy use in production and consumption.
- Reuse: Extend the life of products without significant processing.

- Recycle: Convert used materials into new products to avoid waste.
- Refuse: Avoid non-essential or unsustainable products and packaging.
- Repair: Fix damaged goods to extend their lifecycle.
- Refurbish: Restore older products with updated components.
- Remanufacture: Rebuild products using recovered parts for the original function.
- Repurpose: Adapt products or components for new uses.
- Recover: Extract useful energy or materials from non-recyclable waste.
- Rethink: Innovate business models and product design to eliminate waste entirely.

Integrating these loops is not a one-time initiative but a fundamental shift in how supply chains are conceived and managed. Each loop reinforces the others, creating a network where materials, value, and knowledge flow continuously, rather than being lost at the end of a product's life. Organizations that embed these practices early in the design stage and carry them through production and distribution position themselves to meet sustainability goals while building adaptive and future-ready networks. In Supply Chain 5.0, circularity is not only an environmental imperative but also a strategic pathway to resilience, innovation, and long-term competitive advantage.

Strategic Role and Benefits

Embedding sustainability into Supply Chain 5.0 generates value across multiple dimensions, as we saw in the real-world examples above. On an operational level, it reduces resource dependency and optimizes energy use, allowing companies to build leaner, more efficient systems that are less vulnerable to fluctuations in supply and cost. Strategically, it acts as a safeguard against regulatory changes and reputational risks, enabling organizations to stay ahead of evolving compliance requirements and consumer expectations. Financially, sustainability initiatives can lower costs through waste reduction and improved resource efficiency, while also opening entirely new revenue streams through circular business models and sustainable product lines. Socially, they strengthen trust and credibility with a wide range of stakeholders, including suppliers, employees, customers, and the communities in which companies operate (Dacre et al., 2024).

However, the shift from treating sustainability as a compliance requirement to positioning it as a core strategic capability demands a different kind of governance and investment. Organizations must adopt metrics that weigh environmental and social performance alongside traditional measures such as cost and speed. This requires integrating sustainability into decision-making at every stage, from product design to supplier selection and logistics planning. Supplier relationships need to evolve into partnerships grounded in shared sustainability objectives, ensuring that environmental and social goals are embedded throughout the network rather than isolated at the top tier.

Technology also plays a critical enabling role. Investments in digital twins, IoT, and advanced analytics should be evaluated not only for their potential to drive efficiency but also for their ability to minimize environmental impact and support social responsibility initiatives. For example, a predictive analytics tool that reduces excess inventory not only cuts costs but also reduces waste and the carbon footprint associated with storage and transportation. Similarly, traceability platforms do more than ensure compliance; they create a foundation for ethical sourcing, transparent reporting, and more substantial stakeholder confidence.

Actionable Principles for Sustainable Supply Chains

- Select suppliers with strong sustainability practices by evaluating environmental certifications, labor standards, and alignment with circular economy goals.
- Source from nearby suppliers when possible, to reduce transportation emissions and improve responsiveness.
- Build flexibility into product specifications by considering alternative materials and finishes that reduce environmental impact without decreasing customer value.
- Choose manufacturing strategies that balance efficiency and sustainability, such as make-to-stock (MTS), make-to-order (MTO), or engineer-to-order (ETO).
- Explore innovative manufacturing techniques like 3D printing to enable on-demand production, reduce lead times, and minimize waste.
- Design for circularity by embedding sustainability at the product and process design stage, selecting renewable materials, engineering for disassembly, and planning for reuse and recycling.
- Measure more than cost and speed by including carbon emissions, water usage, and social impact in key performance indicators.

- Collaborate across networks by building partnerships with suppliers, logistics providers, and customers to achieve shared sustainability goals and unlock efficiencies.
- Integrate technology for transparency by using digital twins, IoT, and traceability platforms to monitor environmental performance in real time and drive continuous improvement.
- Balance short-term and long-term value by developing governance systems that align immediate operational priorities with long-term sustainability objectives.

Resilience in a World of Constant Disruption

Resilience in Supply Chain 5.0 is not a reactionary measure, but a capability built into the system from the outset. Traditional supply chains often approached resilience as an emergency response mechanism that activated only after a disruption occurred. In the Supply Chain 5.0 paradigm, resilience is a proactive and continuous design principle. It enables networks to anticipate shocks, absorb impacts, adapt operations in real time, and recover to a stable state with minimal loss of function. This represents a fundamental shift away from building buffers and toward creating supply chains that can dynamically reconfigure themselves in response to fluctuations in demand and supply.

Why It Matters Now

Resilience has moved from being an optional safeguard to a fundamental capability for modern supply chains. In a world defined by volatility, uncertainty, complexity, and ambiguity (VUCA), disruptions are no longer rare anomalies but ongoing conditions that continually test the limits of global networks. Companies that fail to build resilience face cascading failures, extended recovery times, and loss of market share when competitors recover faster or adapt more effectively (Ivanov, 2023).

Resilience in Supply Chain 5.0 is not just about bouncing back after a crisis. It is about designing networks that can anticipate shocks, absorb impacts, and adapt in real time. It is also about moving beyond survival to building systems that become stronger when put to the test. Organizations that embrace this proactive and adaptive approach are discovering that resilience does more than protect operations; it creates competitive advantage by enabling agility, protecting brand reputation, and maintaining customer trust even in the face of disruption (McKinsey Technology Council, 2023).

From Fragility to Antifragility: Designing Resilient Supply Chains

Resilience can be understood as part of a continuum that moves from fragility to resilience and ultimately to antifragility. Fragile systems break under stress because they are optimized for efficiency at the expense of adaptability. Resilient systems are designed to absorb shocks and return to a stable state. Antifragile systems go one step further by becoming stronger through disruption, using stress as a trigger for innovation and improvement (Taleb, 2012). In the context of Supply Chain 5.0, this means creating networks that not only survive crises but learn from them in real time, integrating feedback loops, modular architectures, and adaptive decision frameworks to evolve under pressure. Several studies suggest that antifragile supply chains can transform disruption into a strategic advantage, enabling organizations to capture market opportunities more quickly than competitors when conditions change (Christopher and Peck, 2020; Ivanov and Dolgui, 2021). Moving from resilience to anti-fragility requires deliberate design choices, including decentralized control, real-time sensing, and organizational cultures that treat disruption as a source of insight rather than purely as a threat.

A brief illustration captures this reality. Imagine a company preparing to launch its new "Gluten-Free Avocado Toast Kit." Marketing campaigns are live, social media is buzzing, and distribution is synchronized across channels. Then a volcanic eruption shuts down the sole supplier of avocados, a cyberattack locks a major logistics partner's warehouse management system, and a critical shipment is delayed due to a port closure. Within hours, a perfectly optimized just-in-time network becomes a network in crisis. In a traditional model, recovery might take weeks. In the Supply Chain 5.0 network built for resilience, digital twins model alternative sourcing scenarios, enabling supply chain leaders to evaluate and select the most effective options; AI-driven control towers reconfigure production plans in real time; and distributed micro-fulfillment centers begin assembling substitute kits from available inventory within hours. Customers still receive their product, and the disruption becomes a test of capability rather than a point of failure.

REAL-WORLD EXAMPLE Siemens

This shift from reaction to design is illustrated by Siemens, which faced severe global supply chain disruptions during the COVID-19 pandemic. To maintain operations, Siemens deployed a combination of digital twins, AI, and IoT sensors to simulate and optimize production flows in real time. Digital twins provided a dynamic model of the company's factories and supply network, enabling planners to test multiple disruption scenarios and evaluate the impact of alternative responses before implementing them. AI-driven predictive analytics helped forecast demand fluctuations and identify bottlenecks, while IoT devices monitored equipment and inventory levels across facilities to provide accurate, up-to-the-minute data. As a result, Siemens was able to reconfigure production remotely, reroute logistics, and minimize downtime, demonstrating how Supply Chain 5.0 tools can make resilience a designed-in feature rather than an afterthought (Villar et al., 2023).

REAL-WORLD EXAMPLE AgriDigital

A different example of resilience through technology can be found in agriculture. AgriDigital launched a blockchain pilot to digitize transactions and automate grain supply chain processes in Australia. The platform provided end-to-end traceability, automated smart contracts, and improved visibility for all participants. By linking shipment events to payment triggers, the system reduced administrative overhead and significantly cut dispute resolution times. During regional transport disruptions, the blockchain platform enabled faster coordination among farmers, traders, and logistics providers, ensuring that grain deliveries continued with minimal interruption. The project demonstrated that even in resource-based industries, digital solutions can provide the transparency and trust required to maintain operations during disruption (Mudditt, 2022)

Resilience also depends on understanding and managing the structure of supplier networks. Many vulnerabilities in global supply chains are hidden several tiers upstream. Tier 1 suppliers may be well monitored, but disruptions often originate with Tier 2 or Tier 3 suppliers who provide critical subcomponents or raw materials. Supply Chain 5.0 emphasizes end-to-end visibility, using technologies such as supplier mapping, blockchain, and collaborative platforms to extend insight beyond immediate partners. Table 3.1 illustrates the role of different supplier tiers and an example of how resilience strategies can be applied.

Designing resilience into Supply Chain 5.0 involves more than technology deployment; it requires a structured approach. A practical framework consists of four interconnected capabilities. The first is anticipation, which uses predictive analytics, scenario planning, and market intelligence to identify potential shocks before they occur. The second is absorption, which focuses on building flexible capacity and buffers that can take the initial impact without halting operations. The third is adaptation, which relies on real-time visibility and agile decision-making to reconfigure operations as disruptions unfold. The fourth is recovery, which emphasizes returning the network to a stable state while capturing lessons learned to strengthen future performance (Ponomarov and Holcomb, 2009).

Integrating this framework into Supply Chain 5.0 requires aligning people, processes, and technology around resilience as a strategic objective. AI and ML enable the modeling of scenarios and the detection of anomalies earlier than traditional systems. Digital twins and IoT sensors create a living picture of the supply chain, making it easier to test and execute contingency plans quickly. However, human judgment remains critical. While algorithms can suggest optimal reconfiguration strategies, it is supply chain professionals who evaluate trade-offs, prioritize outcomes, and ensure that responses align with broader organizational goals.

Table 3.1 Different Supplier Tiers and Resilience Strategies

Supplier Tier	Role	Example Resilience Strategy
Tier 1	Direct suppliers of finished components or services	Establish joint digital twins with manufacturers to simulate disruption scenarios
Tier 2	Suppliers of sub-components or processed materials	Integrate AI-driven forecasting to align with Tier 1 demand and reduce variability
Tier 3	Providers of basic raw materials	Use blockchain to ensure traceability and ethical sourcing, reducing hidden risks

Actionable Principles for Building Resilient Supply Chains

- Embed flexibility and redundancy into networks during the design stage. Use modular production, regional diversification, and multi-sourcing strategies to reduce dependency on single nodes and critical points of failure.
- Deploy IoT sensors, digital twins, and control towers to monitor supply chain conditions continuously. Real-time data allows earlier detection of disruptions and faster, more informed response strategies.
- Move beyond minor variances in scenario planning. Model "black swan" events and stretch assumptions to identify vulnerabilities and create adaptive strategies that can handle worst-case scenarios.
- Combine AI-driven predictive analytics with human judgment to create a balanced approach. Machines excel at pattern recognition and speed, while humans bring context and strategic thinking to bear in uncertain situations.
- Aim to create antifragile systems that improve when disrupted. Incorporate feedback loops, modular structures, and adaptive processes that allow the network to learn, innovate, and become stronger after every shock (Taleb, 2012).

Human-Centric Supply Chains

Supply Chain 5.0 represents a decisive shift away from the machine-dominated focus of Industry 4.0 and toward a people-centered model that integrates advanced technology with human judgment, creativity, and values. In Industry 4.0, automation and digitization were often deployed with the primary aim of reducing labor costs and increasing efficiency. Industry 5.0 reframes this approach by recognizing that the long-term success of supply chains depends on systems designed to empower people rather than displace them (European Commission, 2021). Human-centric supply chains balance technological capability with ethical responsibility and social value creation, making people co-creators in innovation rather than passive operators.

This shift is particularly urgent as supply chains face simultaneous pressures to digitize, decarbonize, and respond to social expectations around fair labor and transparency. Workforce transformation is at the center of this challenge. Jobs are being redefined as automation takes over repetitive tasks, while digital fluency and problem-solving become essential skills across all tiers of the supply network. At the same time, ethical sourcing and worker well-being are no longer peripheral concerns. Investors, regulators, and consumers are demanding proof of fair labor practices and measurable social impact across global supply chains (Ivanov, 2023). Human-centric approaches not only meet these expectations but also build more adaptive and resilient networks by leveraging the unique strengths of people in decision-making, creativity, and collaboration with artificial intelligence.

Why It Matters Now

Human-centricity is not a soft value-add; it is emerging as a strategic driver. Supply chains that prioritize worker engagement and well-being demonstrate higher adaptability during disruptions, reduced turnover, and stronger innovation outcomes (Sariisik and Demir, 2025). Co-creation with AI amplifies this potential. When designed for collaboration rather than substitution, human–AI teams can outperform either working alone, combining the speed and scale of machine intelligence with human contextual awareness and ethical judgment (Longo et al., 2017).

Human-centricity also extends beyond direct employees to include suppliers, contractors, and even informal labor across extended networks. Ethical sourcing frameworks, such as the OECD Due Diligence Guidance and ESG reporting requirements, are prompting companies to assess labor conditions across their entire value chain (OECD, 2021). This approach aligns with a growing recognition that supply chain performance is inseparable from the human systems that support it. Ensuring safe, fair, and empowering working conditions is not just a moral obligation; it is a practical necessity for maintaining operational continuity and trust.

REAL-WORLD EXAMPLE Veja and the Catadores Cooperatives

Veja, a sustainable footwear company, provides a compelling example of human-centric supply chain design. In 2023, Veja partnered with the Catadores network, a cooperative of waste pickers in Minas Gerais, Brazil, to build a fully traceable supply chain for recycled polyester sourced from post-consumer plastic bottles (Nugent, 2024). The partnership addressed a key challenge for Veja: Ensuring transparency in its recycled materials while creating social value.

Through this collaboration, Catadores workers earned three to four times the local market rate, and the cooperative received over $160,000 in bonuses for the six million bottles collected that year.

The initiative demonstrates several dimensions of human-centricity. It enhances worker livelihoods, integrates informal labor into the formal economy, and creates traceable, sustainable inputs that strengthen brand credibility. It also reflects a co-creation model where business and community work together to design mutually beneficial systems. By embedding social value into material sourcing, Veja illustrates how human-centric practices can simultaneously advance environmental goals, strengthen resilience, and create competitive advantage. This approach aligns with Supply Chain 5.0's vision of networks designed not only for efficiency but for shared value creation across all stakeholders.

Human-Centric Design Framework

Creating human-centric supply chains requires deliberate design choices that prioritize the human experience at every level of the network. Four core pillars can guide this process: Usability, trust, ergonomics, and empowerment.

Usability focuses on making tools and processes intuitive and accessible. Employees should spend their time solving problems, not wrestling with complex systems. For example, DHL has invested in AI-powered analytics with user-friendly interfaces to help warehouse workers optimize picking routes, reducing both fatigue and errors (Phipps, 2025).

Trust ensures that people can rely on the systems that support their decisions. Transparency and explainability are critical when deploying AI and automation. Siemens has implemented protocols requiring AI-generated recommendations to include confidence levels and rationale, allowing employees to make informed choices and maintain oversight (World Economic Forum, 2023).

Ergonomics addresses both physical and cognitive well-being. Technologies such as collaborative robots and augmented reality systems are designed to reduce strain and mental load, thereby creating safer and more sustainable working environments. Amazon's ergonomic improvements in fulfillment centers illustrate how physical design can minimize injury risk and support long-term workforce health (Yaniz, 2024).

Empowerment is the ultimate goal. When technology enhances human capability rather than replacing it, adoption rates rise and performance improves. Empowerment also fosters adaptability, as workers who feel confident and informed are more capable of responding to disruptions and contributing to innovation.

Actionable Principles for Human-Centric Supply Chains

Integrating human-centricity into Supply Chain 5.0 can be guided by five actionable principles:

- Deploy AI, robotics, and digital tools to enhance decision-making and creativity rather than eliminate roles. For example, Maersk's internal academies train staff to use digital logistics platforms, turning automation into a tool for empowerment rather than displacement (Dagar et al., 2024).
- Foster cross-functional and cross-organizational collaboration. Unilever's joint sustainability planning with suppliers demonstrates how co-creating solutions can reduce waste and build transparency across complex networks (Villar et al., 2023).
- Integrate fair labor and social responsibility into sourcing and production. Patagonia's supplier audits and prioritization of socially responsible vendors show how ethical practices can be embedded into operational systems (Patagonia, 2025b).
- Prioritize the creation of safe, flexible, and meaningful work environments. Investing in mental health programs, ergonomic design, and participatory decision-making fosters loyalty and operational stability.
- Support ongoing workforce development to adapt to evolving roles and technologies. Continuous learning programs ensure employees remain capable contributors in increasingly digital and automated supply chains.

Integrating the Triple Imperative

Supply Chain 5.0 is not defined by sustainability, resilience, or human-centricity as separate objectives. Its true power emerges when these three priorities are designed as a unified operating model. When they are integrated, they create exponential value because they reinforce one another.

Sustainable sourcing practices can reduce risk exposure by diversifying inputs and ensuring long-term resource availability, which in turn supports resilience. Empowered and engaged workforces enhance operational stability, thereby improving both adaptability and innovation in sustainable practices. When technology is used to connect all three, supply chains become dynamic ecosystems capable of thriving under constant change rather than merely surviving (Ivanov, 2023).

Integration also transforms these principles from compliance-driven initiatives into strategic advantages. Companies that align environmental stewardship, operational adaptability, and human empowerment build supply networks that are trusted by stakeholders, flexible under pressure, and capable of delivering long-term value. This alignment is becoming a hallmark of forward-thinking organizations that recognize supply chains not as cost centers but as strategic assets shaping the future of business and society (McKinsey Technology Council, 2023).

Technology as an Enabler

Technological integration is what makes this balancing act scalable. Modern digital tools provide the infrastructure to connect sustainability, resilience, and human-centricity into one cohesive system (see Table 3.2).

When deployed together, these technologies do more than digitize operations. They act as connective tissue, linking environmental performance, adaptive capacity, and human well-being in a single operating system.

Trade-Offs and Synergies

Balancing the three pillars requires navigating both synergies and tensions because each priority brings its own set of operational requirements and strategic trade-offs. When sustainability, resilience, and human-centricity are pursued together, they sometimes reinforce one another in powerful ways. For example, sustainable sourcing practices reduce long-term dependency on volatile resources, which directly supports resilience by making supply chains less vulnerable to disruption. At the same time, ethical labor practices and investment in workforce well-being strengthen human capital, which improves the adaptive capacity of networks during periods of change. These synergies demonstrate how aligning the three pillars can create a multiplier effect that enhances overall performance and long-term value creation.

However, the integration of these pillars also introduces inevitable tensions that require careful governance. Building redundancy to increase

Table 3.2 Main Technologies and Their Role in the Three Pillars

Technology	Role in Sustainability	Role in Resilience	Role in Human-Centricity
Artificial Intelligence (AI)	Optimizes energy use, reduces waste, supports sustainable sourcing decisions	Predicts disruptions, models risk scenarios, and supports adaptive planning	Provides decision support that augments human judgment and reduces cognitive load
Digital Twins	Simulate product life cycles and optimize designs for circularity	Stress-test supply chain configurations under disruption scenarios	Provide safe training environments and ergonomic process design
Internet of Things (IoT)	Tracks resource use and enables closed-loop material flows	Offers real-time visibility across the network for faster disruption response	Monitors working conditions and enhances safety for frontline employees
Blockchain	Verifies sustainable sourcing and creates transparent ESG data	Secures transactions and improves trust in multi-tier networks	Builds trust with workers and partners by ensuring data integrity and accountability

resilience can lead to higher resource consumption, which may conflict with sustainability objectives if not managed thoughtfully. Prioritizing human-centric production methods may initially reduce short-term cost efficiency compared to fully automated systems, creating pressure in industries that operate on tight margins. Similarly, rapid-response protocols intended to enhance resilience can inadvertently increase cognitive load and stress on workers unless they are implemented with human-centric design principles in mind.

Effectively balancing these dynamics requires moving beyond a one-size-fits-all approach. Organizations must evaluate decisions not only based on immediate operational impact but also for their long-term systemic impact. Scenario planning, cross-functional governance, and integrated performance metrics can help navigate these intersections by identifying where synergies can be amplified and where trade-offs must be mitigated. The ability to manage these relationships with nuance and foresight is what distinguishes organizations that make incremental improvement from those that build truly adaptive, regenerative, and human-centered supply networks. Table 3.3 highlights these synergies and trade-offs.

Table 3.3 Main Synergies and Trade-Offs Among the Three Pillars of Supply Chain 5.0

Combination	Synergies	Trade-Offs
Sustainability + Resilience	Regenerative practices ensure long-term resource security while resilient networks protect those practices during disruption	Building redundancy to enhance resilience can increase resource use if not carefully designed
Sustainability + Human-Centricity	Ethical labor practices strengthen sustainable sourcing and improve social outcomes	Human-centered production methods can initially reduce cost efficiency compared to fully automated systems
Resilience + Human-Centricity	Skilled, empowered workers improve adaptive responses during crises and help balance competing priorities	Rapid response strategies can create stress on workers if not designed with ergonomic and psychological support
All Three Combined	Integrated systems create adaptive, regenerative supply chains that align with societal and environmental needs while empowering people	Requires careful governance to avoid overemphasizing one pillar at the expense of the others

REAL-WORLD EXAMPLE Schneider Electric

Schneider Electric provides an example of how the triple imperative can be integrated into a single operating model. The company has embedded sustainability into every aspect of its supply chain strategy, from sourcing renewable materials to leveraging circular economy principles in product design. Its EcoStruxure™ platform uses IoT, AI, and predictive analytics to reduce energy use, track emissions, and optimize resource allocation in real time. These practices have helped Schneider Electric consistently rank among the most sustainable corporations globally (Corporate Knights, 2024).

Resilience is built into Schneider Electric's operations through advanced digital twins and scenario planning tools that simulate disruptions and enable rapid reconfiguration of production and logistics. During supply chain shocks, these capabilities allowed the company to reroute flows and maintain service levels without compromising sustainability goals.

Human-centricity is embedded through workforce training and inclusion initiatives. Schneider Electric invests heavily in upskilling employees to manage digital systems while maintaining a focus on safe and ergonomic workplaces. Programs such as Access to Energy extend this philosophy beyond internal operations, supporting underserved communities and emphasizing that supply chain innovation must also serve social equity (Fuchet, 2024).

This combination of environmental stewardship, operational adaptability, and human empowerment has allowed Schneider Electric to create a supply chain that is not only efficient but also trusted, resilient, and strategically aligned with long-term societal needs.

Actionable Principles for Integrating the Three Pillars

- Start with governance by establishing an integrated framework that evaluates every supply chain decision against sustainability, resilience, and human-centric criteria.
- Use AI, IoT, blockchain, and digital twins not as isolated tools but as part of a unified data architecture that supports all three pillars.
- Incorporate environmental, social, and resilience indicators into core performance dashboards alongside cost and efficiency.
- Make human-centricity the foundation for adoption. Involve employees in co-designing systems and prioritize technologies that empower rather than displace.
- When testing new initiatives, measure their impact on all three pillars. Successful pilots should have a clear roadmap for rapid scaling across the enterprise.
- Use scenario planning to identify potential conflicts between pillars early and design strategies that optimize for long-term systemic value rather than short-term gains.

Building Adaptive, Regenerative, Human-Centric Supply Chains

Supply Chain 5.0 is not defined by any single technology or initiative. Its true power lies in the convergence of sustainability, resilience, and human-centricity into a unified operating model. When these pillars work together, they create supply networks that do more than deliver products. They become systems capable of adapting to volatility, regenerating resources and communities, and placing people at the center of technological progress. This is not a theoretical vision. It is a practical mandate for organizations seeking to remain competitive and relevant in a world defined by complexity and constant change (European Commission, 2021; Dacre et al., 2024).

Designing for this future requires moving beyond compliance-driven strategies and short-term cost optimization. While meeting regulatory requirements and improving efficiency remain essential, Supply Chain 5.0 asks leaders to aim higher. It demands innovation that transforms environmental responsibility into competitive advantage, resilience into a core capability rather than a reactive response, and human-centricity into a source of operational strength and creativity. Organizations that view these pillars as strategic levers rather than checkboxes will be better positioned to shape markets, influence industries, and create enduring value for stakeholders.

The journey toward this integrated model will not unfold uniformly across industries or regions. Each organization must adapt the principles of Supply Chain 5.0 to its unique context, resources, and constraints. Yet the overarching goal remains the same: To build supply chains that are not only efficient but also adaptive, regenerative, and human-centered. These systems will define the next generation of global commerce, influencing environmental outcomes, economic resilience, and social equity at a scale few other business functions can match (Henrich et al., 2022; Ivanov, 2023).

As we transition into the next chapter, the focus shifts from vision to execution. The Supply Chain 5.0 Playbook in the next chapter outlines a roadmap for translating these principles into concrete strategies and operational systems. It explores how to assess organizational readiness, prioritize investments, and design scalable transformations that embed sustainability, resilience, and human-centricity into the core of supply chain operations. The work ahead is not simply about implementing new technologies or processes. It is about cultivating a living, evolving system that can meet the needs of both today and tomorrow.

KEY TAKEAWAYS

- Supply Chain 5.0 redefines value creation by moving beyond cost and efficiency to integrate environmental stewardship, adaptive capacity, and human empowerment as core strategic drivers.
- The three pillars of sustainability, resilience, and human-centricity are interconnected, and their true impact comes from being designed as one unified operating model rather than pursued as separate initiatives.
- Sustainability has shifted from compliance to strategy, with circular economy practices, regenerative sourcing, and technology-enabled transparency creating both ecological and financial value.
- Resilience is now a designed-in capability, not an emergency response. Supply Chain 5.0 networks anticipate, absorb, adapt, and recover from disruption while moving toward anti-fragility, where systems become stronger under stress.
- Human-centricity balances technological innovation with social responsibility, ensuring AI and automation amplify human judgment, creativity, and well-being rather than displacing people from the value chain.
- Design decisions upstream set the trajectory for all three pillars. Materials, sourcing models, and product architectures made early in the lifecycle create multiplier effects across sustainability, resilience, and human impact.
- Technology acts as the connective tissue linking the pillars. AI, digital twins, IoT, and blockchain enable real-time visibility, traceability, and co-creation between people and systems, making integration scalable.
- Balancing the pillars requires navigating synergies and trade-offs. Aligning them creates exponential value, but governance and scenario planning are needed to avoid over-optimizing one pillar at the expense of the others.
- Real-world examples like Schneider Electric, McDonald's, and Patagonia show that integration is practical and profitable, demonstrating that sustainability, resilience, and human-centricity can coexist without compromising operational performance.
- Supply Chain 5.0 is a strategic mandate, not a future concept. Climate change, technological disruption, and shifting stakeholder expectations are accelerating the need for adaptive, regenerative, and people-centered networks today.

References

Aoaeh, Brian Laung, Cofounder, REFASHIOND Ventures (Stanton, 2025) In-person interview for this book.

Balch, O. (2025) "No lettuce, no Big Mac": Why Beth Hart is steering McDonald's towards regenerative agriculture. *Reuters*. www.reuters.com/sustainability/land-use-biodiversity/no-lettuce-no-big-mac-why-beth-hart-is-steering-mcdonalds-towards-regenerative-2025-04-14/ (archived at https://perma.cc/S4SR-HX6D)

Braungart, M., McDonough, W. and Bollinger, A. (2007) Cradle-to-cradle design: Creating healthy emissions – A strategy for eco-effective product and system design. *Journal of Cleaner Production*, 15(13–14), 1337–1348. https://doi.org/10.1016/j.jclepro.2006.08.003 (archived at https://perma.cc/WL62-QXBZ)

Christopher, M. and Peck, H. (2020) Building the resilient supply chain. *International Journal of Logistics Management*, 31(1), 37–55. http://dx.doi.org/10.1108/09574090410700275 (archived at https://perma.cc/PXW2-5KVJ)

Corporate Knights. (2024, January 17) The 20th annual Global 100. Corporate Knights. www.corporateknights.com/rankings (archived at https://perma.cc/4YGB-DB49)

Dacre, N., Yan, J., Frei, R., Al-Mhdawi, M. K. S. and Dong, H. (2024) Advancing sustainable manufacturing: A systematic exploration of Industry 5.0 supply chains for sustainability, human-centricity, and resilience. *Production Planning & Control*, 1–30. https://doi.org/10.1080/09537287.2024.2380361 (archived at https://perma.cc/C2QT-KBP6)

Dagar, M., Tate, M. and Johnstone, D. (2024) Digital transformation at Maersk: The never-ending pace of change. *Journal of Information Technology Case and Application Research*, 26(2), 111–43. https://doi.org/10.1080/15228053.2023.2300921 (archived at https://perma.cc/FM6K-4STT)

Ellen MacArthur Foundation (2023) Building a circular supply chain: Achieving resilient operations with the circular economy. https://ellenmacarthurfoundation.org (archived at https://perma.cc/XTL5-VFN6)

European Commission (2021) Industry 5.0 – Towards a sustainable, human-centric and resilient European industry. Publications Office of the European Union. https://data.europa.eu/doi/10.2777/308407 (archived at https://perma.cc/J8EZ-H554)

Fuchet, A. (2024, September 2) Access to energy: How Schneider Electric helps light up the globe. Schneider Electric Blog. https://blog.se.com/digital-transformation/2024/09/02/access-to-energy-how-schneider-electric-helps-light-up-the-globe/ (archived at https://perma.cc/9WNC-QL2R)

Henrich, J., Li, J. D., Mazuera, C. and Perez, F. (2022) Future-proofing the supply chain. McKinsey & Company. www.mckinsey.com/capabilities/operations/our-insights/future-proofing-the-supply-chain (archived at https://perma.cc/32YQ-5ARZ)

Hsu, C. H., Li, Z. H., Zhuo, H. J. and Zhang, T. Y. (2024) Enabling Industry 5.0-driven circular economy transformation: A strategic roadmap. *Sustainability*, 16(22), 9954. https://doi.org/10.3390/su16229954 (archived at https://perma.cc/364M-RPDG)

Ivanov, D. (2023) The Industry 5.0 framework: Viability-based integration of the resilience, sustainability, and human-centricity perspectives. *International Journal of Production Research*, 61(5), 1683–1695. https://doi.org/10.1080/00207543.2022.2118892 (archived at https://perma.cc/6RFD-E8A4)

Ivanov, D. and Dolgui, A. (2021) A digital supply chain twin for managing the disruption risks and resilience in the era of Industry 4.0. *International Journal of Production Research*, 59(7), 2053–2069. https://doi.org/10.1080/09537287.2020.1768450 (archived at https://perma.cc/7RMY-PCWA)

Longo, F., Nicoletti, L. and Padovano, A. (2017) Smart operators in Industry 4.0: A human-centered approach to enhance operators' capabilities and competencies within the new smart factory context. *Computers & Industrial Engineering*, 113, 144–59. https://doi.org/10.1016/j.cie.2017.09.016 (archived at https://perma.cc/F2F3-HDFX)

McKinsey Technology Council (2023) McKinsey technology trends outlook 2023. McKinsey & Company. www.mckinsey.com/capabilities/mckinsey-digital/our-insights/the-top-trends-in-tech-2023 (archived at https://perma.cc/7AEK-89P2)

Morgner, R. and Burger, M. (2024) Siemens: Acting resiliently through hybrid process intelligence in the supply chain metaverse. In L. Reinkemeyer (Ed.), *Process intelligence in action: Taking process mining to the next level* (Chap. 19). Springer. https://doi.org/10.1007/978-3-031-61343-2_19

Mudditt, J. (2022) Grain brain: Can blockchain solve global grain supply? *Forbes Australia*. www.forbes.com.au/news/innovation/grain-brain/ (archived at https://perma.cc/7QH9-ZVM7)

Nugent, C. (2024) How Brazil's recycling co-ops are helping turn plastic waste into shoes. *TIME*. https://time.com/7198461/brazil-recycling-co-ops-helping-turn-plastic-waste-into-shoes-veja/ (archived at https://perma.cc/XYU5-3AXP)

OECD (2018), OECD Due Diligence Guidance for Responsible Business Conduct, OECD Publishing, Paris, https://doi.org/10.1787/15f5f4b3-en (archived at https://perma.cc/TF5J-BA9W)

Patagonia (2025a) Cotton for change. www.patagonia.com/our-footprint/cotton-for-change.html (archived at https://perma.cc/887M-9Z59)

Patagonia (2025b) Supply chain environmental responsibility program. www.patagonia.com/our-footprint/supply-chain-environmental-responsibility-program.html (archived at https://perma.cc/FV75-A93S)

Phipps, S. (2025) Why the future of your supply chain is human-centric. Slimstock. www.slimstock.com/blog/human-centric-supply-chain/ (archived at https://perma.cc/34T9-NN2D)

Ponomarov, S. Y. and Holcomb, M. C. (2009) Understanding the concept of supply chain resilience. *International Journal of Logistics Management*, 20(1), 124–43. https://doi.org/10.1108/09574090910954873 (archived at https://perma.cc/TPJ7-2VFF)

PwC (2025) What is the circular economy model? www.pwc.com/gr/en/advisory/grc-internal-audit/sustainability-climate-change/circular-economy-model.html (archived at https://perma.cc/8YVP-ZD2Z)

Rejeb, A., Rejeb, K., Keogh, J. G. and Süle, E. (2025) When Industry 5.0 meets the circular economy: A systematic literature review. *Circular Economy and Sustainability*, 1–32. https://doi.org/10.1007/s43615-025-00570-y (archived at https://perma.cc/H6KH-V3W8)

Sariisik, G. and Demir, S. (2025) Industry 5.0: A human-centric paradigm for sustainable and resilient industrial transformation. *Journal of Social Perspective Studies*, 2(2), 50–66.

Stanton, D. J. (2025) In-person interview with Brian Laung Aoaeh for this book [Personal communication].

Taleb, N. N. (2012) *Antifragile: Things that gain from disorder*. Random House.

Tóth, A., Nagy, L., Kennedy, R., Bohuš, B., Abonyi, J. and Ruppert, T. (2023) The human-centric Industry 5.0 collaboration architecture. MethodsX, 11, 102260. https://doi.org/10.1016/j.mex.2023.102260 (archived at https://perma.cc/5V3H-9DSA)

Villar, A., Paladini, S. and Buckley, O. (2023) Towards supply chain 5.0: Redesigning supply chains as resilient, sustainable, and human-centric systems in a post-pandemic world. *Operations Research Forum*, 4(3), 60. https://doi.org/10.1007/s43069-023-00234-3 (archived at https://perma.cc/TNB2-4LFP)

World Economic Forum (2023) Siemens: Navigating the people implications of digital transformation. Good Work Alliance. https://initiatives.weforum.org/good-work-alliance/case-study-details/siemens:-navigating-the-people-implications-of-digital-transformation/aJY68000000PAvWGAW (archived at https://perma.cc/5LRJ-5PT8)

Yaniz, R. J. (2024, December 23) Amazon will implement nationwide ergonomic safety measures following DOL settlement. *Occupational Health and Safety*. https://ohsonline.com/articles/2024/12/23/amazon-will-implement-nationwide-ergonomic-safety-measures-following-dol-settlement.aspx (archived at https://perma.cc/UC6H-JEK5)

The Supply Chain 5.0 Playbook as a Roadmap for Transformation

04

Let it be said of us—that we did not merely lead for profit, but we led for people. That we did not chase power, but we built something that would outlast us. Because in the end, the true measure of leadership is not how far we go, but how many we lift along the way.

SHEKAR NATARAJAN

Bridging the Gap: From Industry 4.0 to Supply Chain 5.0

This chapter moves from theory to action. Having explored the vision of Supply Chain 5.0 and the human and machine paradigm shift, we now focus on the practical roadmap for transformation. The goal of this playbook is to connect the digital backbone of Industry 4.0 with the human-centric design principles of Supply Chain 5.0, outlining the steps organizations can take to facilitate this transition.

To operationalize this vision, Supply Chain 5.0 reimagines the classic Observe, Orient, Decide, Act (OODA) loop, a longstanding concept used in strategy and operations, as a shared cycle between humans and machines (Boyd, 1987). In this reimagined model, AI accelerates the observe and orient phases by processing vast amounts of data and surfacing patterns in real time. At the same time, humans apply judgment, values, and contextual insight in the decision and action stages. The result is not just faster decision-making but a fundamentally different kind of collaboration, where technology amplifies human capability instead of replacing it.

To succeed, leaders must see the move from Industry 4.0 to Supply Chain 5.0 not as the replacement of one paradigm with another but as a natural evolution. Industry 4.0 provides the digital infrastructure, including cyber-physical systems, intelligent automation, and real-time data, that connected global value networks and enabled efficiency at scale. Supply Chain 5.0 builds on that foundation by emphasizing three priorities: Sustainability, resilience, and human-centricity. These principles shift technology from being a driver of efficiency to a tool for enabling adaptive, inclusive, and environmentally responsible supply chains (see Align Purpose, People, and Performance below for detailed definitions).

Table 4.1 serves as a reference point for this shift. It compares the technology-centric design principles of Industry 4.0 with the human-centered priorities of Supply Chain 5.0. By examining goals, the role of technology, workforce engagement, and performance metrics, the table highlights how organizations are redefining value creation to balance productivity and cost efficiency with resilience, sustainability, and human well-being.

Table 4.1 Shift from Industry 4.0 to Supply Chain 5.0

Dimension	Industry 4.0 (Today)	Supply Chain 5.0 (Next Stage)
Primary Goal	Operational efficiency and automation	Resilience, sustainability, and human-centricity
Technology Role	Enable machine connectivity and data collection	Harness technology to empower people
Design Principle	Technology-centric and process-driven	Human-centric and ethically aligned
Value Creation Focus	Efficiency and scalability	Purpose, adaptability, and stakeholder impact
Workforce Engagement	Upskill to operate advanced systems	Co-create with technology; empower employees
Customer Role	End-point consumer of optimized outputs	Active participant shaping personalized value

(continued)

Table 4.1 (Continued)

Dimension	Industry 4.0 (Today)	Supply Chain 5.0 (Next Stage)
Performance Metrics	Productivity, throughput, and cost reduction	Resilience, sustainability, and decision-making
Innovation Model	R&D-driven, centralized	Ecosystem-driven, collaborative
Collaboration Model	Machine-to-machine and system integration	Human–machine collaboration and machine-to-machine ecosystems

The progression from Industry 4.0 to Supply Chain 5.0 represents a fundamental redefinition of what success entails in modern supply chains. While Industry 4.0 emphasized efficiency, automation, and throughput—critical pillars that remain relevant—Supply Chain 5.0 introduces new priorities: Adaptability in the face of disruption, sustainability as a strategic imperative, and the recognition that technology should enhance, not replace, human capabilities.

Where Industry 4.0 focused on machine-to-machine integration and automation, Supply Chain 5.0 emphasizes human-to-machine collaboration. AI, robotics, and digital twins are becoming tools for augmenting human decision-making, rather than substituting for it. This requires a deliberate design mindset: Technologies must be implemented to support people, improve their work experience, and enable them to solve more complex problems.

Another defining characteristic of Supply Chain 5.0 is the expansion of value creation beyond the boundaries of the business itself. Industry 4.0 prioritized cost optimization and speed within organizational walls. Supply Chain 5.0 considers the entire ecosystem, focusing on shared value for suppliers, customers, communities, and the planet. This shift changes how organizations measure performance, moving from traditional KPIs such as cost per unit and operational equipment effectiveness (OEE) to metrics that incorporate environmental impact, resilience, and human well-being.

This evolution is not a conceptual exercise; it is a practical reality. Increasing regulatory pressure, customer expectations, and the reality of global disruptions make the shift to Supply Chain 5.0 an urgent strategic priority. Organizations that can integrate digital innovation with human-centric design are better equipped to manage uncertainty, attract and retain talent, and build trust with stakeholders across the value chain.

Align Purpose, People, and Performance

Defining a clear and actionable strategic vision is the essential first step for any organization pursuing Supply Chain 5.0 transformation. Without a guiding vision, efforts to modernize processes or adopt new technologies risk becoming fragmented and disconnected from broader business objectives. In Supply Chain 5.0, this vision rests on three priorities that shape both operational decisions and long-term strategy. Sustainability focuses on reducing environmental impact and advancing circular economy practices that benefit society as a whole. Resilience emphasizes building systems that can anticipate and adapt to disruption caused by events such as geopolitical instability, extreme weather, or shifting customer demand. Human centricity ensures that people remain at the center of decision-making so that technology enhances human capabilities rather than replacing them.

To translate these principles into an actionable strategy, leaders need to develop a vision that balances three critical elements: Purpose, people, and performance (see Figure 4.1).

"Purpose" describes why the organization's supply chain exists beyond meeting immediate business objectives. Some companies define purpose by setting science-based carbon reduction targets or by committing to international standards such as the UN Sustainable Development Goals (United Nations, n.d.). Others use frameworks like LEED certification for sustainable facilities or pursue carbon neutrality standards such as PAS 2060. Defining purpose in these concrete terms connects day-to-day operations with larger societal and environmental outcomes, creating a narrative that engages employees, customers, and stakeholders.

"People" emphasizes the recognition that supply chains are fundamentally human systems. While advanced technologies such as AI, robotics, and automation play a critical role, a human-centric supply chain focuses on enhancing employee skills, protecting workforce well-being, and enabling collaboration across the value chain. Organizations may set goals aligned with workforce engagement benchmarks or ISO 45001 (International Organization for Standardization, 2018) standards for occupational health and safety, while also fostering a culture of innovation and inclusion. Placing people at the center of supply chain design ensures that technology adoption strengthens human capabilities and relationships rather than diminishing them.

"Performance" encompasses the metrics by which the supply chain measures its success. In Supply Chain 5.0, performance extends beyond traditional efficiency and cost targets to include environmental, social, and resilience outcomes. Organizations can adopt industry frameworks such as the GRI (Global Reporting Initiative, n.d.) for sustainability reporting, ISO 14001 (International Organization for Standardization, 2015) for environmental management systems, or technology convergence models such as those from the World Economic Forum (Medikepura, 2025). Measuring performance through these broader terms allows leaders to balance operational excellence with long-term impact.

Example: Operationalizing Purpose, People, and Performance

When a global packaged goods manufacturer began a major digital transformation of its supply chain, leadership recognized that technology alone would not ensure success. The executive team sought to design a Supply Chain 5.0 network that would deliver efficiency while also building resilience, advancing sustainability, and strengthening the connection to the workforce.

The process began with a series of cross-functional workshops that brought together leaders from operations, procurement, sustainability, and human resources. The goal was to create a shared supply chain purpose that extended beyond operational efficiency. The group aligned its objectives with the Science-Based Targets initiative (SBTi) and the United Nations Sustainable Development Goals (UN SDGs) to establish measurable commitments to reducing carbon emissions, supporting ethical sourcing, and delivering social impact. This collaborative effort shifted the focus from moving products at the lowest cost to delivering goods in a way that created value for both communities and employees.

With automation, artificial intelligence forecasting, and new digital platforms on the horizon, the organization conducted a workforce impact assessment to understand how roles and skills would change. The findings informed a comprehensive talent strategy that emphasized reskilling, capability development, and new models of human–machine collaboration. Employees were included early in the design process, which built trust and increased engagement throughout the transition.

Figure 4.1 Aligning People, Purpose, and Performance

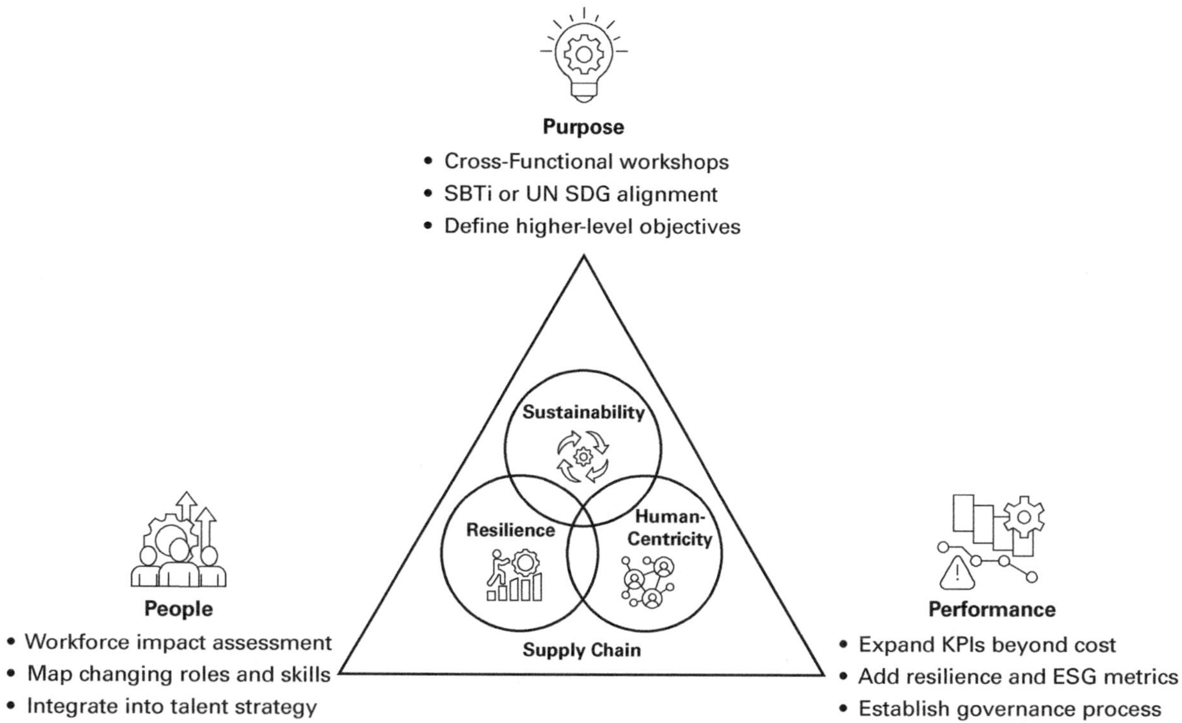

Existing measurement systems were reviewed to ensure they supported the broader vision. Traditional indicators, which focused primarily on unit cost and service levels, were expanded to include resilience, environmental and social governance outcomes, and workforce well-being. A recurring governance process was established to review progress across purpose, people, and performance, maintaining strategic balance and adjusting to changing conditions.

The principles in this case are not specific to a single organization. They illustrate an approach that can be applied to any Supply Chain 5.0 transformation. Aligning purpose with measurable sustainability goals ensures that operations create value beyond efficiency. Mapping the people impact integrates technology and human capability, strengthening workforce engagement during periods of change. Expanding performance metrics embed resilience and social responsibility alongside productivity.

When these three elements are designed and governed together, they create a unifying framework for transformation. The result is a supply chain that connects innovation with human potential and societal value, transforming isolated initiatives into a coordinated journey.

Technological Foundations of Industry 4.0

The technologies summarized in Table 4.2 form the backbone of Industry 4.0. Core digital enablers such as Industrial Internet of Things (IIoT), AI, and digital twins drive real-time visibility and predictive decision-making, while physical systems like AMRs and cobots bridge the digital–physical divide. Together, they establish the foundation on which Supply Chain 5.0 builds its human-centric vision.

These technologies create the digital and physical foundation that enables new forms of collaboration and innovation possible. However, technology alone does not deliver transformation. Its value emerges only when it is applied to solve real-world challenges that balance operational, environmental, and human needs.

The following real-world example illustrates this principle. It shows how existing Industry 4.0 tools such as IoT sensors, AI analytics, and automated control systems can be combined within a Supply Chain 5.0 mindset to achieve sustainability goals while managing operational risk.

Table 4.2 Technologies Linked to Industry 4.0

Technology	Description	References
Industrial Internet of Things (IIoT)/IoT	Industrial-scale sensor networks and connectivity for real-time monitoring and control.	(nibusinessinfo.co.uk, n.d.; SAP, n.d.; Wikipedia contributors, 2025)
Artificial Intelligence (AI) and Machine Learning (ML)	Intelligent analytics, optimization, and predictive decision-making.	(McKinsey & Company, n.d.; SAP, n.d.)
Big Data and Advanced Analytics	Processing and analyzing large-scale data for insights and predictive maintenance.	(MachineMetrics, 2023; nibusinessinfo.co.uk, n.d.)
Cloud Computing	Scalable computing and data-sharing infrastructure for connected systems.	(nibusinessinfo.co.uk, n.d.)
Edge Computing	Localized, low-latency processing near devices for real-time decisions.	(Logap, 2024)
Autonomous and Collaborative Robots (Cobots)	Smart robots that work alongside humans in flexible production environments.	(nibusinessinfo.co.uk, n.d.)
Augmented Reality (AR) and Virtual Reality (VR)	Mixed-reality tools for training, maintenance, and remote assistance.	(nibusinessinfo.co.uk, n.d.)
Simulation and Digital Twins	Virtual models of assets and processes for design, optimization, and monitoring.	(MachineMetrics, 2023)
Horizontal and Vertical System Integration	Connecting systems and data flows across departments and supply chains.	(MachineMetrics, 2023)
Cybersecurity for Industrial Systems	Securing devices, networks, and data in connected industrial environments.	(nibusinessinfo.co.uk, n.d.)

(continued)

Table 4.2 (Continued)

Technology	Description	References
Additive Manufacturing (3D Printing)	On-demand, flexible manufacturing for customized parts and components.	(Dilberoglu et al., 2017)
Human–Machine Interfaces (HMI)	Next-generation interfaces (touch, gesture, voice, AR/VR) for operator interaction.	(Wikipedia contributors, 2025; McKinsey & Company, n.d.)
Connectivity and Advanced Networks (Fiber Optics and 5G)	High-speed, low-latency communication for IIoT and smart factories.	(Wikipedia contributors, 2025; McKinsey & Company, n.d.)
Quantum Computing	Next-generation computation enabling massive optimization, simulation, and encryption capabilities beyond classical computing.	(Ahmed, 2025)
Nuclear Fusion for Energy Systems	Potential to provide abundant, clean, stable power for energy-intensive smart factories and industrial operations.	(Worland, 2025)

REAL-WORLD EXAMPLE The Move to Minus 15 °C Coalition

A strong example of collaborative innovation in pursuit of sustainability is the Move to –15°C Coalition (Move to Minus 15°C Coalition, 2024). This initiative demonstrates how coordinated action across the supply chain can simultaneously reduce emissions, safeguard food quality, and manage operational risk. The coalition unites food producers, logistics providers, technology companies, and sustainability specialists to question the long-standing cold-chain benchmark of –18°C. Studies indicate that raising storage temperatures to –15°C could lower carbon emissions by approximately 17.7 million tons per year—the equivalent of removing 3.8 million cars from the road—while maintaining food safety under normal conditions.

For certain foods like frozen berries and vegetables, slightly higher temperatures may better preserve nutritional value. Flash-freezing at peak ripeness, along with techniques such as Individual Quick Freezing (IQF), can more effectively lock in vitamins and antioxidants than long-term storage at lower temperatures. In some cases, nutrient retention in frozen produce can even surpass that of fresh alternatives.

At the same time, these sustainability improvements come with trade-offs. A shift from –18°C to –15°C increases the risk during refrigeration interruptions or power outages because products at the warmer temperature will thaw more quickly. Managing that risk requires a foundation of trust among partners and a willingness to accept controlled risk in pursuit of environmental benefits. To build that trust, participants in the Coalition acknowledge the need for transparent risk management. Retailers and brand owners must trust suppliers and logistics providers. Suppliers and carriers must ensure food safety and sustainability outcomes for customers and regulators.

Technologies can help reduce this risk. IoT sensors allow continuous temperature monitoring of cold-chain assets. AI-powered analytics can identify anomalies, forecast equipment failures, and improve container performance. Automated alert systems notify operators immediately when a temperature deviation occurs. In more advanced cases, agentic control systems may automatically trigger adjustments, such as activating backup cooling or rerouting shipments, without requiring manual input.

By integrating these technologies, the system becomes more resistant to interruptions, and stakeholders gain the confidence needed to support the higher temperature standard. The result is a cold chain that is more sustainable, transparent, and resilient at the same time.

The Move to –15°C Coalition demonstrates the Supply Chain 5.0 mindset: Aligning partner goals, managing trade-offs, and using technology to balance environmental benefit with operational safety and trust.

The Vatican's recent transition to a fully solar-powered state through agrivoltaics offers a compelling model for how Supply Chain 5.0 can embed sustainability in ways that generate multiple, interdependent benefits. Inspired by the call for environmental stewardship articulated in *Laudato Si'*, where Pope Francis urged humanity to care for its "common home" and warned of escalating ecological degradation (Environmental and Energy Study Institute, 2015), the Church moved beyond symbolic advocacy to structural action. By installing transparent, crop-friendly solar panels across key facilities and developing a large agrivoltaic installation at Santa Maria di Galeria, the Vatican demonstrated how energy infrastructure can be paired with agriculture to improve crop yields, conserve water, and strengthen climate resilience while simultaneously producing renewable power (Pearce, 2025). This integrated approach reflects the essence of Supply Chain 5.0: Designing systems that reduce environmental impact, diversify value creation, and improve long-term operational sustainability. As the first country to run entirely on solar agrivoltaics, the Vatican illustrates that sustainability need not be a trade-off; when engineered thoughtfully, it becomes a multiplier of efficiency, resilience, and social responsibility.

Assess Readiness and Prioritize Initiatives

A successful Supply Chain 5.0 transformation begins with a clear understanding of the organization's current state. This process involves two distinct but complementary steps: First, leaders assess internal readiness; second, they apply the CIMO model to evaluate the broader environment and design a strategic transformation plan.

Step One: Assess Business Readiness

Before planning interventions, leaders need a structured assessment of their current capabilities. This is where a Supply Chain 5.0 Readiness Checklist such as the one in the following section (Supply Chain 5.0 Readiness Maturity Model) can serve as a valuable tool. The checklist we are sharing is an example, not a prescriptive standard. Regardless of the version used, it should evaluate maturity across critical domains such as digital infrastructure, operational processes, workforce capabilities, supplier collaboration, and sustainability practices.

We recommend using this checklist as a starting point rather than a definitive framework. Categories and maturity descriptions may need to be adapted to fit your organization's specific industry, strategic priorities, and operational challenges. For instance, a food logistics company might prioritize cold chain integrity and traceability, while an industrial manufacturer may focus on integrating robotics and improving energy efficiency.

By systematically assessing their current state, organizations can identify capability gaps that must be addressed to advance toward Supply Chain 5.0.

Step Two: Apply the CIMO Model to Design the Transformation Plan

Once internal readiness is understood, leaders can apply the CIMO (pronounced SEE MOW) model to analyze the broader context and design a strategic transformation roadmap.

The CIMO Model (Figure 4.2) is a widely used framework in design science and evidence-based management to structure problem-solving and research (Denyer et al., 2008). CIMO stands for Context, Intervention, Mechanism, and Outcome. The model emphasizes that effective solutions are not universally applicable but depend on the context in which they are implemented. It begins by defining the Context in which a problem exists, including environmental, organizational, or market conditions. The Intervention refers to the specific actions, tools, or strategies applied to address the problem. Mechanism focuses on the underlying processes or causal pathways that explain how and why the intervention is expected to work. Finally, Outcome specifies the intended or observed results, providing a way to evaluate success and refine future actions. By explicitly linking context, interventions, mechanisms, and outcomes, the CIMO model supports rigorous analysis and helps practitioners design solutions that are both evidence-based and adaptable to specific supply chain or organizational settings.

In the case of Supply Chain 5.0, the Context is framed by the overarching objectives of sustainability, resilience, and human-centricity. These goals influence transformation priorities through three factors. First, business goals and constraints such as profitability targets, regulatory compliance, and brand reputation define the organization's strategic boundaries. Second, the broader business and social environment, including government regulations, shifting customer expectations, and external disruptions like climate events or pandemics, creates both pressures and opportunities. Third, available technological capabilities, ranging from AI and robotics to telecommunications and sustainable materials, form the operational toolkit for driving change.

The Intervention stage involves selecting and deploying capabilities that address the gaps identified in the readiness assessment and align with the context analysis. Interventions may include cognitive automation to enhance decision-making, mass customization to improve customer responsiveness, circular supply chains to reduce environmental impact, and collaborative robotics to support the workforce.

Figure 4.2 CIMO Model for Supply Chain 5.0 Deployment

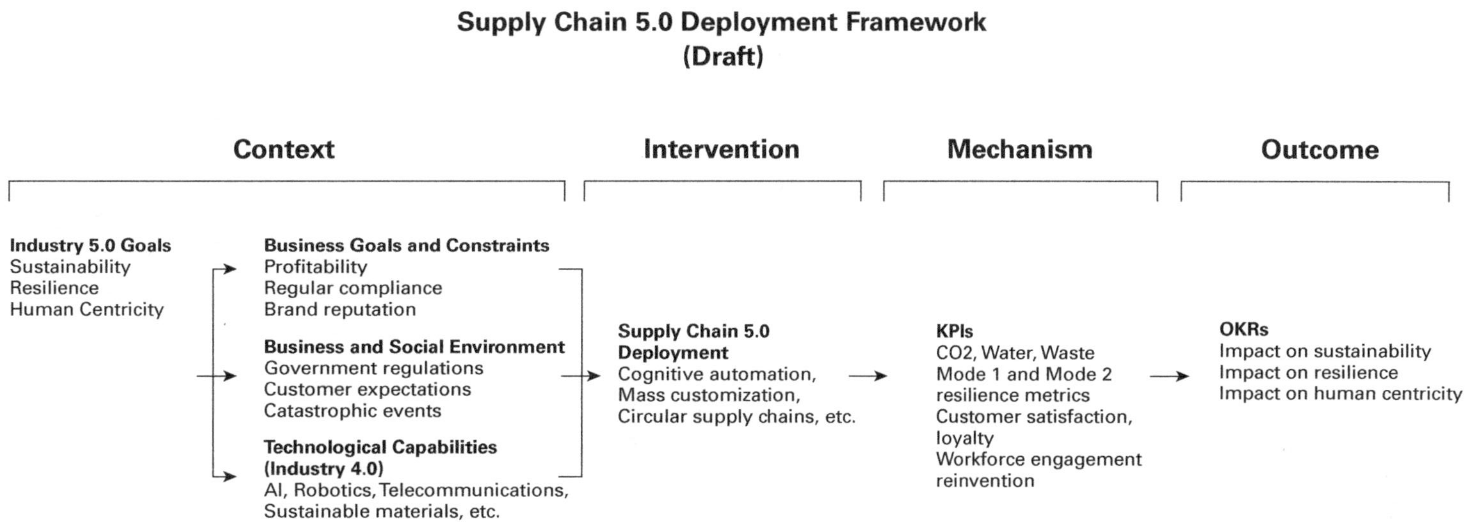

The Mechanism consists of defining clear Key Performance Indicators (KPIs) to measure the effectiveness of interventions. These metrics might track carbon emissions, water use, waste generation, supply chain recovery times, customer satisfaction, and workforce engagement. Selected KPIs should closely align with the chosen interventions and meaningful within the organization's operational context.

The Outcome is expressed through measurable Objectives and Key Results (OKRs) that reflect systemic progress toward sustainability, resilience, and human-centricity. Rather than focusing on individual project outputs, these outcomes measure the broader organizational impact of transformation initiatives.

By starting with a readiness assessment and then applying the CIMO framework, leaders can move beyond isolated improvements and design a coherent, strategically grounded transformation plan. This structured approach ensures that interventions are both context-aware and purpose-driven, aligned with the long-term vision of Supply Chain 5.0.

Supply Chain 5.0 Readiness Maturity Model

The Gartner Supply Chain Maturity Model presents a five-stage framework that helps organizations assess and improve their supply chain capabilities by progressing from reactive, siloed operations toward fully integrated, strategy-driven networks. At the early stages, companies rely heavily on manual processes, limited visibility, and functionally isolated decision-making (Cornerstone, 2019). As maturity increases, companies adopt standardized processes, expand cross-functional coordination, and integrate planning and execution across the enterprise (Cornerstone, 2019). At the highest levels, supply chains achieve end-to-end visibility, leverage advanced analytics and technology, and align operational decisions with broader business strategy to create a responsive and continuously improving network (Bodenstab, 2017). Gartner's model serves as a benchmarking tool that helps organizations identify their current stage, understand capability gaps, and prioritize investments that enhance resilience, efficiency, and long-term performance (Gartner, 2022).

For many organizations beginning their transformation journey, having a structured method to assess current capabilities can provide a helpful starting point. What follows is a representative Supply Chain 5.0 Readiness Checklist. It outlines five commonly recognized domains that many organizations consider when evaluating their readiness for transformation. This model is not intended as a universal standard, but rather as a reference point that leaders can adapt to fit their specific industry, organizational context, and strategic priorities.

1 **Strategic alignment**
In many organizations, assessing strategic alignment involves examining how explicitly sustainability, resilience, and human-centric objectives are embedded in supply chain strategy. This might include reviewing whether these principles are reflected in leadership communications, operational goals, and investment decisions. Some organizations evaluate whether ESG goals are treated as central business drivers or remain peripheral concerns.

2 **Digital and technological infrastructure**
Leaders often review the maturity of their digital infrastructure, assessing systems' interoperability, cloud adoption, and real-time data capabilities. Depending on the industry, evaluations may also focus on the integration of technologies such as AI, IoT, robotics, and digital twins. In some cases, organizations consider how these technologies support automation, mass customization, and value chain transparency.

3 **Workforce readiness and culture**
Organizations frequently assess their workforce's digital skills, adaptability, and engagement. Evaluations may cover training and development programs, cultural openness to innovation, and employee participation in change initiatives. In human-centric organizations, workforce empowerment and inclusion can be key areas of focus.

4 **Supplier and partner ecosystem**
Some organizations examine the digital maturity and sustainability practices of their suppliers and partners. This may include reviewing collaboration practices, data-sharing capabilities, ethical sourcing policies, and joint efforts in areas like circularity and shared risk management. In more advanced cases, organizations assess the extent to which their broader ecosystem contributes to innovation and transformation.

5 **Performance measurement and governance**
Many organizations review whether their metrics and governance systems extend beyond traditional financial KPIs to include environmental performance, supply chain resilience, and workforce outcomes (see Figure 4.3). Governance structures may also be evaluated based on their ability to drive cross-functional decision-making, continuous learning, and transparent progress reporting.

Using the Supply Chain 5.0 Readiness Maturity Model

This representative framework is not a prescription. Instead, it provides a structure that leadership teams can adapt, expand, or simplify according to their specific needs. The goal is not strict adherence to a generic model, but the creation of a meaningful assessment process tailored to each organization's context. For some companies, digital infrastructure may be the primary focus. For others, supplier collaboration or workforce engagement may represent the most critical starting point.

Regardless of the configuration, having a systematic method for evaluating current capabilities enables organizations to identify priority areas for

Figure 4.3 Supply Chain 5.0 Readiness Assessment

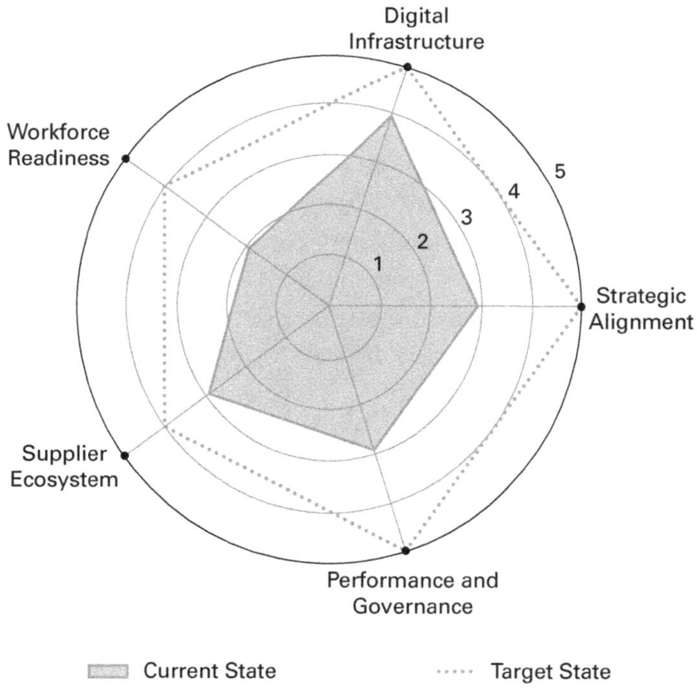

Table 4.3 Supply Chain 5.0 Readiness Maturity Model Implementation Levels

Domain	1 - Initial	2 - Emerging	3 - Developing	4 - Advanced	5 - Leading
Strategic Alignment	No strategy linking supply chain to sustainability, resilience, or human-centricity.	Early goals discussed but not operationalized.	Goals partially integrated; some initiatives reflect priorities.	Strategy embedded in operations; goals consistently drive decisions.	Vision fully embedded; ESG goals drive investment and operations.
Digital and Technological Infrastructure	Legacy systems; minimal digital adoption.	Isolated digital tools or pilot projects.	Core processes digitized; early AI/IoT/ automation.	Integrated platforms with advanced analytics and automation.	Fully connected, real-time digital network using AI, robotics, and digital twins.
Workforce Readiness and Culture	Minimal digital skills; no structured development programs.	Some upskilling efforts underway.	Structured training; employee engagement increasing.	Culture of innovation; widespread digital fluency.	Workforce co-creates innovation; continuous upskilling embedded.
Supplier and Partner Ecosystem	Transactional relationships; little transparency or collaboration.	Early digital collaboration; limited sustainability expectations.	Supplier partnerships incorporate sustainability and resilience goals.	Strategic supplier collaborations and data sharing.	Ecosystem-wide innovation and circular economy partnerships.
Performance Measurement and Governance	KPIs focus solely on cost and efficiency.	Basic ESG or resilience metrics tracked.	Balanced KPIs include ESG, resilience, and operational measures.	Governance structures monitor and drive improvements.	Continuous, cross-functional management of KPIs aligned to strategic vision.

development. These insights can then shape strategic planning and guide the design of targeted transformation initiatives aligned with their own version of Supply Chain 5.0 (see Table 4.3).

Modernize Systems While Centering on People

Supply Chain 5.0 is often associated with advanced digital technologies. However, the full scope of Industry 5.0 encompasses a much broader range of innovations. Alongside digital tools, organizations must also consider advancements in fields such as advanced materials, biological engineering, next-generation energy technologies, and quantum computing. Together, these technologies create new possibilities for designing, manufacturing, distributing, and recycling products. Modernizing systems in this context means more than digitization. It requires rethinking the entire technological foundation of the supply chain, while ensuring that people remain at the center of transformation.

Modernization often starts with digital upgrades. Organizations invest in integrated, cloud-based platforms that enable real-time data sharing, automation, and predictive analytics. AI supports demand planning and risk management. Digital twins allow organizations to simulate physical systems in virtual environments, reducing experimentation costs and improving resilience. Robotics enhances precision and throughput in warehouses and manufacturing environments. However, these tools represent only part of the modernization landscape.

In materials science, innovations such as sustainable composites, biodegradable plastics, and graphene-based materials are changing the possibilities for manufacturing and packaging.

Biological engineering is enabling the use of bio-based feedstocks, cultured materials, and new forms of sustainable agriculture. Energy innovations, including next-generation batteries, hydrogen fuels, nuclear fusion research, and grid-scale energy storage, are reshaping the energy foundations of production and logistics. Quantum computing, which is still emerging, holds the potential to transform optimization, encryption, and simulation capabilities within complex global supply chains.

Integrating these technologies into supply chains offers enormous potential for sustainability, efficiency, and innovation. However, Supply Chain 5.0

emphasizes that technology must serve human needs. Modernization is not an isolated technical project. It must be understood as part of a broader effort to create supply chains that empower people and communities, protect the environment, and deliver resilient business performance.

Centering people within this technological transformation begins by recognizing the wide range of human stakeholders who shape and are shaped by supply chains. Employees interact with supply chain systems directly, whether through operating machinery, managing digital interfaces, or making strategic decisions. Suppliers and logistics providers bring critical knowledge, materials, and services. Customers influence supply chain priorities through their expectations around sustainability, transparency, and customization. Shareholders and executives set long-term strategic direction. Regulators define the compliance landscape related to safety, labor rights, and environmental impact. Even competitors can become stakeholders through collaborative initiatives such as industry alliances or shared infrastructure projects.

Each of these groups interacts with supply chains in different ways, and each must be considered when introducing technological change. For employees, modernization must be accompanied by workforce development. Training in digital tools is essential, but so is education related to new materials, sustainable manufacturing practices, and bio-based processes. Change management efforts must address not only how employees work, but also how they perceive their roles in a rapidly evolving supply chain.

Process redesign should follow human-centric design principles. Workflows need to be reimagined not solely for efficiency, but for usability, safety, and collaboration. Inclusive innovation practices can help by involving frontline workers, suppliers, and even customers in the co-creation of solutions, ensuring that technologies are adopted effectively and meet real operational needs.

Supplier and partner collaboration also evolves with modernization. Digital platforms, material innovations, and new energy systems often require changes in supplier capabilities and relationships. Engaging suppliers in joint research, shared infrastructure development, or capacity-building initiatives strengthens collaboration and creates shared value.

Ultimately, modernizing systems while centering people means integrating advanced technologies across physical, biological, and digital domains, in ways that enhance human contributions rather than replace them. The goal is to build supply chains that are technologically advanced, environmentally sustainable, operationally resilient, and fundamentally human-centric. In

Supply Chain 5.0, technology is a tool to help people solve complex problems, create sustainable products, and build resilient global systems together.

REAL-WORLD EXAMPLE Utilizing Technology to Safeguard Crews from Fire Hazards at Sea

During a recent interview for this book, a shipping industry expert highlighted a major safety challenge in modern maritime logistics: The danger of fires caused by hazardous materials stored in shipping containers. This is not just a hypothetical concern but a recognized operational risk, especially as global shipments of lithium-ion batteries and chemical products continue to increase. Fires at sea can spread quickly, endangering the crew, the vessel, and the cargo.

The expert pointed out a common operational structure that increases this risk. Crews on cargo ships work around the clock, staying vigilant 24/7 during voyages. In contrast, the company's shore-based executives and support teams usually work regular business hours, five days a week. This creates a vulnerability when a fire hazard appears outside those hours, leaving crews to handle urgent safety issues without immediate support or guidance from safety experts or land-based management teams.

Many crews currently rely on manual checks and human observation to spot early signs of heat buildup or combustion. However, continuously monitoring all cargo, especially inside enclosed containers, is hard to maintain with manual methods alone. The expert highlighted this challenge as a clear example of where Industry 4.0 technologies could be integrated to develop a more resilient and human-centered solution.

By integrating existing technologies such as thermal sensors, automated alert systems, and fire suppression mechanisms, shipping companies can greatly reduce reliance on manual monitoring and decision-making during high-risk situations. Automated systems can identify abnormal heat levels inside containers and initiate immediate local responses, even if shore management personnel are unavailable. Automated alerts can also notify both the crew and shore-based teams simultaneously, creating a continuous feedback loop without overloading human operators.

According to the expert, such a solution would not replace human decision-making but would support and safeguard it. Automated detection and suppression systems would lower physical risks to crew members, reduce their cognitive workload, and enable prompt responses in environments where every second counts. This approach also aligns with broader principles of Supply

Chain 5.0, where technology is used to improve human safety, operational resilience, and sustainability.

This scenario illustrates how a real-world safety challenge can be addressed by integrating emerging technologies within a human-centered operating model. It is not a distant vision of the future. These technologies are available today, but are often not integrated or systematically used for this specific issue. For supply chain leaders, it offers an example of how modernization efforts can deliver immediate, practical benefits while prioritizing the people who operate and depend on these complex systems.

Managing Change Through the ADKAR Lens

Modernizing systems while centering on people is not only a design challenge but also a challenge in guiding human behavior and organizational culture. Implementing Supply Chain 5.0 often requires shifting long-established routines, redefining roles, and adopting entirely new ways of working. Technologies and processes can be deployed quickly, but meaningful adoption by people requires deliberate planning and structured support.

The ADKAR Model was developed by Prosci founder Jeff Hiatt and is grounded in empirical research across hundreds of change initiatives. It identifies Awareness, Desire, Knowledge, Ability, and Reinforcement as the outcomes individuals need to adopt new ways of working successfully. Awareness begins by helping employees understand why the change is necessary and how it aligns with the broader vision of building a sustainable, resilient, and human-centered supply chain. Desire focuses on creating personal motivation by showing how the change benefits not only the organization but also each person's role, growth, and sense of purpose. Knowledge equips employees with the information and understanding needed to navigate the new systems, while Ability develops the practical skills and confidence to apply that knowledge in daily operations. Finally, Reinforcement ensures the change is sustained over time through recognition, measurement, and continuous improvement.

Embedding frameworks like ADKAR into Supply Chain 5.0 initiatives creates a bridge between technology and culture. It ensures that investments in digital platforms, advanced materials, or collaborative robotics translate into lasting human capability rather than temporary compliance. By guiding people step by step through the emotional and practical dimensions of transformation, organizations can cultivate a workforce that is not only ready to adapt but eager to co-create the future of the supply chain.

EXAMPLE

Using ADKAR to Drive Human-Centric Supply Chain 5.0 Transformation

A global consumer goods company launched a Supply Chain 5.0 initiative to integrate digital twins, AI-based demand planning, and collaborative robotics into its regional distribution centers. While the technology stack was advanced, early pilot testing revealed a significant obstacle: Warehouse employees were hesitant to embrace the new systems. Many worried about job security and felt uncertain about their ability to adapt to more complex digital tools. Leadership quickly realized that without a deliberate focus on change management, the project's human-centric vision would not succeed.

To address this, the company adopted the ADKAR model as a framework for guiding the workforce through the transformation:

- Awareness: The project began with a clear communication effort that explained why the transformation was needed and how it supported broader goals such as sustainability, waste reduction, and safer working environments. Leadership hosted open forums where employees could ask questions and voice concerns, building trust and transparency from the outset.
- Desire: Managers worked closely with team leaders to connect the transformation to personal benefits for employees. They emphasized opportunities for skill development, safer working conditions, and the organization's commitment to retraining rather than downsizing. Employees were invited to participate in shaping aspects of the new workflows, which helped shift perceptions and generate a sense of ownership.
- Knowledge: With support beginning to grow, the company rolled out training programs designed to make the new systems approachable and relevant. Hands-on exercises and scenario-based learning helped employees connect new tools like digital twins and collaborative robotics to their day-to-day responsibilities.
- Ability: To build confidence, the company created mentorship pairs that allowed employees to practice new processes in a live environment with guidance from experienced colleagues and digital specialists. This structure helped smooth the transition and reduced anxiety about learning on the job.

- Reinforcement: The organization established regular feedback loops through surveys and team discussions to monitor progress and gather employee insights. Early successes were highlighted and recognized, reinforcing positive behavior and demonstrating that the new systems could enhance roles and create value for both the workforce and the business.

As the transformation progressed, operational accuracy improved, engagement levels rose, and employees began to view the Supply Chain 5.0 initiative not as a technology project imposed from above, but as a human-centered evolution of their workplace.

This case illustrates how the ADKAR model can bridge the gap between advanced technology and human adoption. By focusing on Awareness, Desire, Knowledge, Ability, and Reinforcement, the company established a foundation that enabled Supply Chain 5.0 to deliver both operational and cultural transformation.

The DIRECT Project Leadership Model

Supply chains can be understood as complex systems comprising people, processes, and technologies that work together to deliver value to customers. When organizations seek to improve or adapt that system, we do it through projects. Every change to a supply chain, whether it involves implementing new technology, redesigning a process, or reorganizing teams, happens as part of a project.

The DIRECT Project Leadership Model, developed by Daniel Stanton (2023), provides a framework for guiding these changes effectively. It identifies six responsibilities that every project leader must embrace (see Figure 4.4). These are not sequential steps. They are a basket of ongoing responsibilities that leaders must manage throughout the project's life cycle:

- **Define the challenge or opportunity**
  The leader ensures that the team gathers requirements and develops a clear understanding of the problem or opportunity the project addresses. This includes listening to stakeholders, clarifying objectives, and documenting what success looks like.
- **Investigate the options**
  The leader ensures the team conducts thorough due diligence to evaluate alternatives. This can include market research, benchmarking against

industry best practices, and exploring multiple approaches to ensure decisions are informed and strategic.

- **Resolve to a course of action**
  The leader guides the team in developing a realistic plan and securing the necessary approvals. This responsibility is about aligning the team and stakeholders on a clear path forward that is achievable and supported.
- **Execute the plan**
  The leader supports the team as they carry out the work defined in the plan. This involves tracking issues and risks, managing scope changes, measuring progress, and ensuring that the team has the resources and guidance they need to succeed.
- **Change over to the new process or system**
  The leader manages the critical period when the organization switches from the old way of doing things to the new one. The changeover often has many moving parts that must be monitored closely, issues that must be addressed quickly, and contingency plans that must be in place to minimize disruption.
- **Transition the people**
  The leader plans for how the change will impact every stakeholder. For employees, this may involve training or re-training to prepare them for new roles. For customers, a communication plan may be necessary to keep them informed. For the project team, it can mean supporting them in closing out the project and preparing for their next assignments.

The choice of the acronym DIRECT carries an intentional double meaning. In addition to representing the six project leadership responsibilities, it echoes the role of a movie director. A director does not perform every role on set. Instead, they bring together actors, camera operators, sound engineers, and editors, aligning their contributions to create a coherent story.

Similarly, a project leader using the DIRECT Model does not execute every task in the project. Instead, they ensure that people, processes, and technologies work together in harmony to deliver value. This perspective shifts leadership from a command-and-control approach to one of coordination and alignment, which are essential qualities in complex supply chains.

This analogy connects naturally to the concept of orchestration in Supply Chain 5.0. Modern supply chains are vast networks that depend on advanced technology, human expertise, and collaborative processes. Orchestration is about ensuring that all of these elements are synchronized, just as a conductor harmonizes different instruments in an orchestra.

The DIRECT Model provides a framework for that orchestration. By defining challenges, investigating options, developing a plan, executing effectively, managing changeovers, and supporting people through transitions, leaders ensure that every part of the system plays its role in creating value for customers.

This approach recognizes that supply chains are not simply mechanical systems. They are living networks that require vision, coordination, and a human-centered touch. A project leader using the DIRECT Model is not just managing tasks. They are directing a performance in which people, processes, and technologies work together to deliver results that are efficient, sustainable, and resilient.

Scale What Works and Sustain Momentum

In Supply Chain 5.0, transformation is not a one-time initiative but a continuous process of learning, adaptation, and scaling. Early wins—such as a successful digital pilot, a supplier partnership, or a process improvement—are only the starting point. The true challenge is converting these isolated successes into long-term, organization-wide change. To achieve this, companies require formal structures that facilitate sustained progress and expand their impact throughout the supply chain.

Figure 4.4 The DIRECT Project Leadership Model

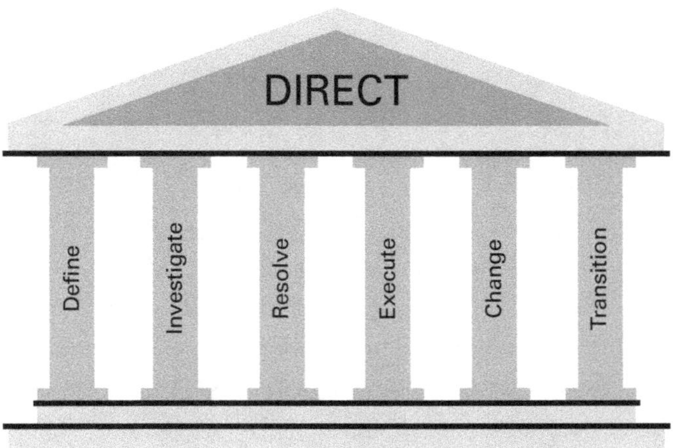

SOURCE Stanton (2016)

At this stage, the CIMO model remains a valuable guide. Having deployed interventions and identified the mechanisms through which results are measured, organizations now focus on translating those activities into meaningful outcomes. Governance, feedback, and performance management all play roles in ensuring that interventions contribute to the organization's long-term strategic objectives.

Governance structures help organizations manage complexity as they scale. This may involve setting up a dedicated transformation office, a cross-functional leadership council, or a network of working groups that monitor progress across digital adoption, sustainability, workforce development, and supplier collaboration. The purpose of governance is to maintain strategic alignment, ensuring that interventions remain connected to business priorities and that resources are allocated effectively. Governance bodies also create accountability, providing a structured forum for evaluating progress and resolving barriers that may prevent scaling.

Feedback mechanisms are equally important for sustaining momentum. Information must flow from every part of the supply chain, including employees, suppliers, logistics partners, customers, and regulators. Supplier audits, employee surveys, customer feedback, and operational performance reviews can all serve as sources of insight. By capturing data consistently from across the stakeholder network, organizations can refine their strategies, adapt interventions, and identify new opportunities for improvement.

Measuring progress requires more than tracking individual performance indicators. In the CIMO framework, mechanisms describe how interventions are assessed, often through key performance indicators. These KPIs may include metrics such as energy consumption, carbon emissions, delivery lead times, workforce retention, and supply chain recovery speed. While KPIs help monitor operational performance, they do not by themselves indicate whether the organization is moving toward its strategic goals.

For this reason, organizations must complement KPIs with objectives and key results. OKRs express the broader outcomes the organization aims to achieve, directly linked to the foundational goals of Industry 5.0: Sustainability, resilience, and human-centricity. Examples of OKRs might include achieving full supply chain transparency, reaching a defined reduction in Scope 3 emissions, improving supplier labor standards, or establishing new business models based on circular economy principles. OKRs capture the systemic impact organizations seek, providing a strategic target against which operational data can be evaluated.

As organizations scale successful interventions, both KPIs and OKRs should be integrated into a unified performance management system. Dashboards and reporting processes can help leadership monitor operational, environmental, and social indicators alongside progress toward strategic outcomes. This integration creates a shared understanding of progress across departments and encourages collaboration in solving cross-functional challenges.

Continuous learning is also essential for sustaining transformation. Successful practices and lessons learned should be shared through structured knowledge management processes, such as after-action reviews, cross-functional workshops, and communities of practice. Scaling is not simply a matter of repeating the same solution at a larger scale. It involves embedding new ways of working, new capabilities, and new mindsets across the entire supply chain.

Leadership plays a critical role in sustaining momentum. Leaders must consistently communicate how day-to-day improvements connect to long-term strategic outcomes. Recognizing the contributions of employees and partners, celebrating milestones, and reinforcing the Supply Chain 5.0 vision help sustain focus and energy as transformation progresses.

Ultimately, the goal is not isolated project success or incremental efficiency gains. The aim is to achieve systemic outcomes: Supply chains that are more sustainable, more resilient, and more human-centric. The combination of clear governance, continuous feedback, meaningful KPIs, and ambitious OKRs allows organizations to scale what works and sustain transformation over time.

REAL-WORLD EXAMPLE Using IoT Visibility to Optimize Routes and Strengthen Supply Chain 5.0 Performance

Tive is a leader in real-time shipment visibility technology. Their IoT tracking devices are small, portable sensors that attach directly to shipments or containers. These devices transmit live data on location, temperature, humidity, shock, and light exposure. Combined with cloud-based analytics, Tive devices provide end-to-end visibility for goods in transit, enabling companies to monitor conditions and respond to disruptions as they happen (Stanton and Gabaldon, 2025).

A leading global logistics provider utilized Tive's IoT tracking technology to analyze transportation routes between the Port of Los Angeles and Long Beach, and Memphis. By collecting real-time and detailed data on shipment movements, the company uncovered how route selection impacts the entire supply chain beyond just transportation efficiency.

The data revealed a surprising insight. The route that appeared shorter on traditional maps produced highly variable delivery times, fluctuating by plus or minus three days. In contrast, a slightly longer alternative route demonstrated far greater consistency, with delivery times varying by only plus or minus one day.

Further investigation revealed the driver-related factor behind this difference. The longer route had more strategically placed truck stops, which allowed drivers to better comply with hours-of-service regulations. This enabled them to plan rest periods more effectively and achieve more predictable delivery windows.

This level of delivery visibility highlights one of the biggest challenges for modern supply chains. Variability permeates every aspect of the operation. When delivery ETAs fluctuate by multiple days, the impacts cascade across multiple areas of the business:

- **Staffing:** Warehouse teams must schedule labor based on uncertain arrival times, which can lead to idle time or overtime costs.
- **Customer ETAs**: Inconsistent delivery windows reduce customer trust and can require expensive expedited shipping to compensate.
- **Production scheduling:** Manufacturers that are dependent on inbound materials often face disruptions, forcing them to make last-minute changes to production runs.
- **Inventory planning:** Unpredictable replenishment timing forces companies to increase buffer stock, which ties up capital and warehouse space.
- **Safety stock calculations:** Higher variability pushes planners to build in larger safety stock levels, which can increase carrying costs and hide underlying inefficiencies.

By applying advanced analytics to IoT tracking data, the logistics provider optimized route selection and demonstrated how Supply Chain 5.0 integrates technology, human factors, and operational strategy:

- **Resilience:** Reducing delivery time variability strengthened the network's ability to handle disruption.
- **Sustainability:** More predictable routes minimized unnecessary detention and fuel usage caused by schedule uncertainty.
- **Human-centricity:** Recognizing driver work patterns and regulatory needs ensured that solutions worked for both people and systems.

This real-world example illustrates that in a Supply Chain 5.0 environment, visibility extends beyond tracking shipments. It is about unlocking insight to coordinate every link in the chain. By using IoT data to manage variability, companies can transform operational planning from reactive to proactive and build supply networks that are more reliable, cost-effective, and human-centered.

Building the Future, One Process at a Time

With these foundations, we now move from building the vision to transforming core supply chain processes. The next chapters explore Plan, Source, Transform, Fulfill, Order, Return, and Orchestrate through the Supply Chain 5.0 lens, turning principles into everyday action.

In the chapters ahead, we will explore questions such as:

- How does planning change when resilience and adaptability become more critical than forecast accuracy?
- What does sourcing look like when supplier ecosystems are built on shared ESG goals and digital trust?
- How are we making and delivering transformed by advanced materials, human–machine collaboration, and sustainable energy systems?
- How do returns and reverse logistics evolve in a circular economy?
- And how do enabling and orchestrating processes connect these capabilities into a living, learning, and human-centered network?

The Supply Chain 5.0 Playbook is not just a guide for deploying technology. It is a guide for leading people and systems into a future where profitability, resilience, and human flourishing converge. As we move into Part 2, we shift focus from building the framework to putting it into action. The upcoming chapters are not just about upgrading individual processes—they are about reworking the entire value network to operate with resilience, sustainability, and human-centric design at its core. This is where the concepts of Supply Chain 5.0 come to life in the everyday decisions, flows, and collaborations that drive modern supply chains.

KEY TAKEAWAYS

- Supply Chain 5.0 builds on Industry 4.0 rather than replacing it. It connects digital infrastructure with human-centric design to create supply chains that are sustainable, resilient, and people-focused.
- Purpose, People, and Performance are the foundation. Aligning these three elements ensures that technology adoption serves a higher mission beyond efficiency and cost reduction.
- The OODA loop is reimagined for human–machine collaboration. AI accelerates observation and orientation, while humans provide judgment, context, and ethical decision-making.

- Technology is a means, not the end. IIoT, AI, robotics, and digital twins are powerful tools, but their true value is realized when they enhance human capability and drive ecosystem-wide value creation.
- Transformation requires readiness. Assessing digital maturity, workforce capability, supplier alignment, and governance is essential before launching large-scale initiatives.
- Change is cultural as much as technical. Using frameworks like ADKAR helps guide employees through the emotional and behavioral aspects of transformation, turning resistance into engagement.
- Collaboration drives sustainability. The Move to −15°C Coalition demonstrates how shared innovation can reduce emissions and enhance quality while mitigating operational risk.
- Scaling success needs structure. Governance, feedback loops, and integrated KPIs and OKRs ensure that early wins translate into long-term, systemic change.
- Modernization must center on people. Human-centric design prioritizes employees, partners, and communities at the heart of technological upgrades, resulting in supply chains that are inclusive and adaptable.
- Supply Chain 5.0 is a continuous journey. The goal is not isolated improvements, but building living, learning networks that deliver lasting value to businesses, society, and the planet.

References

Ahmed, H. (2025, July 4–5) Quantum computing: A new era for big data, cloud computing, AI, and IIoT in Industry 4.0. In *Proceedings of the 4th International Conference on Trends in Advanced Research (ICTAR)* (Konya, Turkey) Association for Scientific Proceedings. www.researchgate.net/publication/393683544_Quantum_Computing_A_New_Era_for_Big_Data_Cloud_Computing_AI_and_IIoT_in_Industry_40 (archived at https://perma.cc/P7GC-VCSR)

Bodenstab, J. (2017) Gartner's Five-Stage Maturity Model for Supply Chain Analytics. ToolsGroup. www.toolsgroup.com/blog/gartners-five-stage-maturity-model-for-supply-chain-analytics/ (archived at https://perma.cc/ZYS9-23BM)

Boyd, J. R. (1987) *A Discourse on Winning and Losing*. Maxwell Air Force Base: Air University Library.

Cornerstone (2019) Supply chain maturity: Is more always better? *The Brief*, Cornerstone Performance Management. www.cornerstone.com.au/thebrief/article-supply-chain-maturity-is-more-always-better/ (archived at https://perma.cc/EKL9-HZM3)

Denyer, D., Tranfield, D. and van Aken, J. E. (2008) Developing design propositions through research synthesis. *Organization Studies*, 29(3), 393–413. https://doi.org/10.1177/0170840607088020 (archived at https://perma.cc/EX2T-NYYA)

Dilberoglu, U. M., Gharehpapagh, B., Yaman, U. and Dolen, M. (2017) The role of additive manufacturing in the era of Industry 4.0. *Procedia Manufacturing*, 11, 545–54. https://doi.org/10.1016/j.promfg.2017.07.148 (archived at https://perma.cc/Z7LT-X8RQ) www.sciencedirect.com/science/article/pii/S2351978917303529 (archived at https://perma.cc/9XFZ-Z657)

Environmental and Energy Study Institute (2015) Pope Francis calls for climate action in seminal encyclical. EESI, 19 June. www.eesi.org/articles/view/pope-francis-calls-for-climate-action-in-seminal-encyclical (archived at https://perma.cc/CA6B-PUU7)

Gartner (2022) Assess supply chain logistics maturity. www.gartner.com/en/supply-chain/trends/assess-supply-chain-logistics-maturity (archived at https://perma.cc/H4RN-94PY)

Global Reporting Initiative (n.d.) Global Reporting Initiative (GRI). www.globalreporting.org/ (archived at https://perma.cc/V7WR-DUJ8)

Hiatt, J. and Hiatt, J. M. (2006) *Adkar: A model for change in business, government and our community: How to implement successful change in our personal lives and professional careers*. Prosci Research.

International Organization for Standardization (2015) Environmental management systems—Requirements with guidance for use (ISO 14001:2015) International Organization for Standardization. www.iso.org/standard/60857.html (archived at https://perma.cc/A7D6-LBPF)

International Organization for Standardization (2018) Occupational health and safety management systems—Requirements with guidance for use (ISO 45001:2018) International Organization for Standardization. www.iso.org/standard/63787.html (archived at https://perma.cc/LVT3-U3HD)

MachineMetrics (2023, October 10) Industry 4.0 technologies. www.machinemetrics.com/blog/industry-4-0-technologies (archived at https://perma.cc/XLR9-5B42)

McKinsey & Company (n.d.) What are Industry 4.0, the Fourth Industrial Revolution, and 4IR? www.mckinsey.com/featured-insights/mckinsey-explainers/what-are-industry-4-0-the-fourth-industrial-revolution-and-4ir (archived at https://perma.cc/E4YU-BW4L)

Medikepura, A. A. (2025) Technology convergence is leading the way for the fifth industrial revolution. Emerging Technologies. World Economic Forum.

Move to Minus 15 °C Coalition (2024) About the Move to Minus 15 °C. www.movetominus15.com/about-us (archived at https://perma.cc/LMJ6-NHLJ)

Natarajan, S. (2025, July) Finally found the words because there are moments that define you… [LinkedIn post]. LinkedIn. www.linkedin.com/posts/shekarnatarajan_finally-found-the-words-because-there-are-activity-7349552627552055297-F_lU/ (archived at https://perma.cc/4K7C-WR88)

nibusinessinfo.co.uk (n.d.) Industry 4.0 technologies. Invest Northern Ireland. www.nibusinessinfo.co.uk/content/what-industry-4.0 (archived at https://perma.cc/VA6V-3MYL)

Pearce, J. (2025) The Vatican is first 100% solar country via agrivoltaics: Who is next? *Forbes*. www.forbes.com/sites/joshpearce/2025/11/25/the-vatican-is-first-100-solar-country-via-agrivoltaics-who-is-next/ (archived at https://perma.cc/EE9Q-CS3B)

Prosci (n.d.) The PROSCI ADKAR® model. www.prosci.com/methodology/adkar (archived at https://perma.cc/9XGJ-GR6M)

SAP (n.d.) What is Industry 4.0? www.sap.com/products/scm/industry-4-0/what-is-industry-4-0.html (archived at https://perma.cc/N4QW-7VFR)

Stanton, D. (2016) The Direct Project Leadership Framework: Leading Projects Video tutorial, Linkedin learning, formerly Lynda.com. www.linkedin.com/learning/leading-projects/the-direct-project-leadership-framework-24026221

Stanton, D. (2023) *Supply Chain Management for Dummies* (3rd ed.) John Wiley & Sons.

Stanton, D. and Gabaldon, J. (2025) Interview with Krenar Komoni, founder of Tive. In-person interview for this book.

United Nations (n.d.) The 17 Sustainable Development Goals. https://sdgs.un.org/goals (archived at https://perma.cc/L2XH-NK2X)

Wikipedia contributors (2025, July 12) Industrial Internet of Things. *Wikipedia*. https://en.wikipedia.org/wiki/Industrial_internet_of_things (archived at https://perma.cc/R52S-ZEVW)

Worland, J. (2025, July 17) A nuclear fusion breakthrough may be closer than you think. *Time*. https://time.com/7302543/nuclear-energy-commonwealth-fusion/ (archived at https://perma.cc/PG53-B3QC)

World Economic Forum (2022) The Cyber Resilience Index: Advancing organizational cyber resilience. World Economic Forum. www.weforum.org/publications/the-cyber-resilience-index-advancing-organizational-cyber-resilience/ (archived at https://perma.cc/VEB2-HJB2)

PART TWO
End-to-End Process Management Overview

You may recall from the introduction that the Supply Chain Operations Reference (SCOR) Digital Standard, often referred to as SCOR DS, is a cross-industry framework that provides practitioners with a unified language for mapping processes, capturing best practices, measuring performance, and benchmarking against peers. The 2022 digital update by the Association for Supply Chain Management (ASCM) reimagines the model for an era defined by always-on, interconnected, data-driven supply chains, moving beyond the traditional linear approach.

In this context, we acknowledge that supply chain networks are far more than a static web of connections. They function as a dynamic, living ecosystem of companies collaborating to ensure the seamless flow of goods, services, financial resources, and information. These entities are continuously interacting, adapting, and evolving, especially as modern technologies reshape how supply chains operate.

In the following seven chapters, we will explore how Supply Chain 5.0 aligns with the seven major SCOR DS management processes across core supply chain flows, with a sharp focus on five critical dimensions: People, planet, profit, resiliency, and, above all, technology.

Think of SCOR DS as the skeleton and Supply Chain 5.0 as the muscle and nervous system. By mapping forward-looking technology to human-centric, sustainable, and resilient practices, and linking them to specific processes, metrics, and best practices, we aim to give you both the inspiration and the step-by-step blueprint needed for action. Together, these elements form the foundation of a future-ready supply chain, enabling you to enhance performance, increase adaptability, and create lasting value for all stakeholders.

While we have designed this discussion to be industry-neutral and widely applicable, it is important to recognize that certain processes will always be unique to your location, industry, and organization. Therefore, we provide a general overview that you can adapt to your specific context. Just as every human body is unique, so too is every supply chain, each defined by its own structure, environment, and purpose.

Plan: Designing for the Future 05

Plans are worthless, but planning is everything.

DWIGHT D. EISENHOWER

Plan: From Reactive to Predictive Planning

The SCOR DS framework recognizes planning as a continuous, interconnected process that integrates people, data, and systems to shape the behavior of the entire supply chain. The Plan process in SCOR DS refers to the strategic activities involved in designing roadmaps for operating the supply chain effectively (ASCM, 2022). Planning directly influences the other five core SCOR DS phases: Order, Source, Transform, Fulfill, and Return (ASCM, 2022).

In essence, planning aligns supply chain strategy with operational reality, ensuring every part of the network is prepared to meet demand with agility and precision. It functions across strategic, tactical, and operational levels, enabling organizations to coordinate resources, mitigate risk, and drive performance improvement over time. As such, planning is not merely a preliminary activity; it is a critical, ongoing capability that underpins supply chain success.

Within the framework of Supply Chain 5.0, Planning serves as the strategic backbone of the entire supply chain ecosystem. Its core purpose is to strengthen the three foundational pillars of modern supply chains—resilience, sustainability, and human-centricity—while ensuring long-term profitability.

- Resilience: By anticipating disruptions and enabling agile, scenario-based agility.
- Sustainability: By reducing excess inventory, waste, and emissions through better alignment of resources and demand.
- Human-centricity: By balancing workloads, fostering collaboration, and enhancing the quality of decision-making.

At the highest level, Plan is also executed across five core supply chain processes: Order, Source, Transform, Fulfill, and Return (ASCM, 2026). This interconnected framework enables us to reimagine how these well-established operations function in the era of Supply Chain 5.0. Table 5.1 presents a high-level overview of selected technologies that support the objectives of Supply Chain 5.0 within the Plan process. Following this, we provide a detailed explanation of each component, accompanied by a real-world example to illustrate its application.

Table 5.1 Evolution of Planning Processes: SCOR DS and Supply Chain 5.0

Plan Aspect	SCOR DS Definition	Supply Chain 5.0 Evolution
Plan-Order	Creating and implementing plans to allocate resources effectively to fulfill order requirements.	Dynamic, intelligent planning using real-time data, AI forecasts, and adaptive algorithms for responsive order fulfillment.
Plan-Source	Allocating material resources to meet sourcing requirements over specified time periods.	Predictive, collaborative sourcing with AI-driven insights, supplier transparency, and sustainability integration.
Plan-Transform	Strategic planning of production resources to meet transformation (production/service) requirements.	Real-time, adaptive planning using AI and human collaboration to optimize production and service delivery.
Plan-Fulfill	Executing actions to allocate delivery resources to meet fulfillment requirements.	Customer-centric, intelligent fulfillment with hyper-personalization, real-time responsiveness, and ecosystem integration.
Plan-Return	Allocating return resources to meet anticipated and unanticipated return requirements, including refurbishment for reissue.	Circular, predictive return planning with sustainability focus, scenario modeling, and enhanced customer experience.

Plan Order

Plan Order is the process of creating and implementing plans to allocate resources effectively in order to fulfill specific requirements within the order management system (ASCM, 2022). In the era of Supply Chain 5.0, this process evolves into a predictive, intelligent capability. It is no longer merely about meeting order requirements; it is about dynamically allocating resources based on real-time data, AI-driven forecasts, and adaptive algorithms.

This expanded role goes beyond fulfilling current demand to actively shaping future demand. By leveraging predictive insights, Plan Order enables supply chains to anticipate needs, optimize fulfillment strategies, and adapt to changing conditions with precision and agility. The outcome is faster delivery times, reduced last-mile costs, and greater resilience to demand fluctuations—key advantages in a rapidly evolving marketplace.

REAL-WORLD EXAMPLE Amazon: Anticipatory Shipping Model

A powerful example of this evolution can be seen in Amazon's use of anticipatory shipping. The company filed a patent for a "method and system for anticipatory package shipping," which describes shipping items to a general geographic area before the customer has even placed the order. The exact delivery address is determined later, sometimes while the package is already in transit (Amazon Technologies, 2013). Media coverage, including reports by the *Wall Street Journal*, explains how Amazon leverages customer browsing patterns, purchase histories, and regional demand data to forecast orders and strategically stage inventory. In some cases, products are even loaded onto vehicles bound for high-probability areas before any order is placed (Bensinger, 2014; LV Staff, 2023).

SUMMARY SNAPSHOT

Amazon's anticipatory shipping is not just a clever fulfillment strategy; it illustrates the core transformation of order planning in Supply Chain 5.0. From reactive (waiting for the order) to proactive (anticipating the order). From cost minimization to multi-pillar optimization.

- **Circular sustainable alignment:** By reducing waste in logistics through (1) predictive demand staging that minimizes long-haul transport and fuel use, and (2) positioning inventory where it is most needed, the company avoids excess stock and carbon-intense expedited shipments but also creates a leaner, greener supply chain that aligns with environmental stewardship.
- **Demand foresight, agility in fulfillment, and risk mitigation:** Anticipatory shipping demonstrates resiliency in practice by using browsing patterns, purchase histories, and regional data to forecast demand, enabling the supply chain to absorb sudden shifts in consumer behavior or disruptions, aligning with resiliency.
- **Personalization at scale:** AI-driven forecast personalizes logistics by anticipating individual or community needs before they are expressed. This makes the supply chain feel more human-aware rather than reactive.

Plan Source

This process involves designing and implementing time-phased actions to allocate material resources strategically, ensuring that sourcing activities meet projected supply chain requirements with precision and adaptability (ASCM, 2022). In Supply Chain 5.0, the development of these time-phased sourcing strategies transforms into a hyper-intelligent, technology-enabled capability. The Plan Source process evolves from a traditional, schedule-based function into an innovative, collaborative, and sustainable sourcing ecosystem.

Powered by AI-driven demand sensing, digital twins, blockchain-based traceability, and autonomous procurement platforms, sourcing decisions are dynamically optimized across global networks. IoT sensors provide real-time visibility into material availability, while machine learning algorithms continuously refine resource allocation. Combined with cloud-based planning engines and edge computing, this approach ensures sourcing is not only responsive but also predictive, resilient, and fully aligned with sustainability and human-centric goals.

REAL-WORLD EXAMPLE Nestlé: Satellite and AI-Enabled Sourcing for Coffee and Cocoa

Nestlé has developed a sourcing approach that demonstrates how the Plan Source process can evolve into a predictive, resilient, and sustainability-aligned capability under Supply Chain 5.0. The company integrates satellite monitoring, AI-driven data science, and on-the-ground supplier collaboration to anticipate material needs, manage risks, and ensure compliance with environmental and social standards.

A key component of this approach is the utilization of satellite imagery to monitor sourcing regions for coffee and cocoa. This technology enables Nestlé to identify deforestation risks, verify compliance with its Forest Positive strategy, and take prompt action when risks are detected (Nestlé, 2019; Nestlé, 2024a). As of 2024, the company reported that 93.5 percent of its primary supply chains for commodities such as coffee and cocoa were considered deforestation-free (Nestlé, 2024a).

The company also applies advanced satellite capabilities for reforestation monitoring. Through a partnership with Airbus, Nestlé utilizes Pléiades Neo satellites to monitor the growth of over 150,000 shade trees planted in coffee sourcing areas in southern Thailand. This supports the company's Global Reforestation Program, contributing to long-term carbon removal and ecosystem restoration (Nestlé, 2024b).

Beyond monitoring, Nestlé uses AI and data science to improve climate resilience in coffee production. By combining weather data, crop performance databases, and genomic information, researchers at the Nestlé Institute of Agricultural Sciences are developing new varieties of arabica coffee that are resistant to drought and disease. These innovations support more accurate yield forecasting and sourcing planning in the face of climate variability (Dominguez, 2023).

Finally, Nestlé integrates precision agriculture tools into its sourcing model. Real-time monitoring of weather, soil, and water conditions collected via satellite, drones, and IoT sensors allows farmers to optimize inputs, reduce environmental impact, and meet regenerative farming standards (SIAL Newsroom, 2023). This networked, technology-driven approach creates a sourcing system that is not only responsive but also predictive, resilient, and aligned with human-centric and sustainability objectives.

SUMMARY SNAPSHOT

Nestlé's example shows how Plan Source in Supply Chain 5.0 moves from transactional procurement toward a predictive, resilient, and sustainability-aligned system. By weaving together AI, satellites, IoT, and supplier collaboration, Nestlé demonstrates how the three pillars are reflected.

- **Forest positive strategy:** The use of satellite monitoring to identify deforestation risk and verify compliance exemplifies the prioritization of environmental stewardship to prevent deforestation and invest in reforestation initiatives.
- **Sourcing systems:** By integrating AI-driven data science, the firm builds climate resilience into its sourcing system, utilizing weather data, crop performance records, and genomic insights to protect yields against climate variability. The predictive capabilities improve forecasting and sourcing planning, while reducing disruptions and commodity price volatility. Technologies such as satellite and IoT monitoring also provide early warning systems for risks, allowing for real-time adaptation.
- **Collaboration:** The sourcing approach emphasizes collaboration with farmers and suppliers on the ground, ensuring that technology augments rather than replaces human expertise. Real-time agronomic insights from drones and IoT sensors empower farmers to make better decisions, improve yields, and reduce input costs, directly benefiting livelihoods.

Plan Transform

The process involves designing and implementing strategic actions over defined time periods to allocate production resources in a way that meets transformation requirements, whether for manufacturing or service delivery (ASCM, 2022). In the Supply Chain 5.0 framework, the traditional Plan Transform process, which has historically focused on allocating production resources over time to meet transformation requirements, evolves into a more intelligent, adaptive, and proactive capability.

Instead of relying on fixed schedules and historical data, planning becomes real-time and predictive. AI and ML models analyze vast datasets to forecast demand, identify potential disruptions, and recommend optimal resource allocation strategies. Supply Chain 5.0 emphasizes collaboration between humans and innovative technologies, with planning tools that integrate human insights, ethical considerations, and sustainability goals, while autonomous systems handle routine decisions and adjustments.

Plans are no longer one-size-fits-all; they dynamically adapt to customer-specific requirements, regional constraints, and shifting market conditions. This flexibility enables mass customization and faster response times. Advanced simulation tools allow planners to model various scenarios, such as supply disruptions or demand spikes, and prepare contingency plans in advance. The result is a transformation process that is inherently more resilient, agile, and aligned with the principles of Supply Chain 5.0. This capability not only strengthens operational performance but also delivers measurable value through reduced downtime, optimized resource utilization, and a faster path from strategy to market impact.

REAL-WORLD EXAMPLE Bosch: Predictive Quality Systems

As of 2025, Bosch is a global leader in deploying predictive quality systems as part of its Industry 4.0 strategy. By integrating AI and IoT into its manufacturing operations, Bosch enhances product quality, reduces defects, and optimizes production processes. The company utilizes predictive analytics across its global facilities to identify potential product defects early in the production cycle, enabling proactive quality control and enhancing outcomes for both customers and the environment.

This AI-powered quality monitoring system has achieved a reduction of up to 90 percent in customer complaints, along with measurable improvements in product reliability and customer loyalty.

Bosch's approach directly connects to the Plan Transform component of the Supply Chain 5.0 framework. Its predictive quality systems do more than improve inspection after the fact; they actively inform and shape upstream production planning decisions. This integration allows planners to adjust schedules, reallocate resources, and incorporate quality risk factors into strategic, tactical, and operational plans, ensuring that quality management is embedded at the earliest stages of the supply chain. As a result, planning can be elevated from a reactive to a dynamic, anticipatory capability.

SUMMARY SNAPSHOT

- **Proactive production planning:** Real-time defect insights feed into acquisition plans and resource allocation, enabling teams to adjust production schedules and material orders before quality issues escalate. This aligns with the Plan Transform and Plan Source sub-processes by facilitating agile, forward-looking planning rather than fixed scheduling.
- **Scenario modeling and resilience:** Predictive analytics enable Bosch to simulate "what-if" scenarios, such as imminent tool wear or raw-material anomalies, and respond preemptively. This reinforces strategic and tactical planning levels by embedding quality-related risk factors into master plans, enhancing operational resilience.
- **Human-centric and sustainable planning:** By preventing defects early, Bosch not only improves product outcomes but also supports worker efficiency (less rework to monitor) and environmental sustainability through reduced waste. This reinforces the Supply Chain 5.0 pillars of human-centricity, sustainability, resilience, and profitability.

Plan Fulfill

This process involves designing and executing strategic actions over defined time intervals to allocate delivery resources in a way that effectively meets fulfillment requirements (ASCM, 2022). In the Supply Chain 5.0 framework, the Plan Fulfill process undergoes a significant transformation, from traditional resource allocation into an intelligent, responsive, and customer-centric capability.

Instead of relying solely on historical data, Supply Chain 5.0 integrates AI-driven forecasting and real-time analytics to anticipate customer demand and fulfillment needs with greater precision. Delivery resources are dynamically allocated using adaptive algorithms that factor in current inventory levels, transportation constraints, and customer priorities, enabling faster, more efficient fulfillment.

While AI manages complex data processing and optimization, human planners provide strategic oversight, ethical judgment, and creative problem-solving, ensuring a balanced and resilient fulfillment strategy. Planning also extends beyond internal operations to encompass suppliers, logistics partners, and customers, fostering a synchronized and transparent fulfillment network.

By combining intelligent automation with human expertise, the transformed Plan Fulfill process drives higher customer satisfaction, reduces operational costs, and enhances competitive advantage in an increasingly dynamic marketplace.

REAL-WORLD EXAMPLE Ocado: A Robotic Grid System for Grocery Packing

Ocado, a UK-based online grocery technology provider, has redefined order fulfillment through its highly automated Customer Fulfilment Centres (CFCs). At the heart of these facilities is the "Grid," a massive storage and retrieval system populated by thousands of autonomous robots that move across a steel framework, retrieving products from bins stacked beneath them. Each robot communicates wirelessly with a central control system that orchestrates movements with millisecond precision.

The fulfillment process begins with AI-powered demand forecasting, which predicts product requirements by analyzing historical sales data, seasonal trends, and external factors like weather. These forecasts inform real-time allocation of robots, storage slots, and picking tasks. As customer orders arrive, adaptive algorithms prioritize tasks based on product availability, order deadlines, and delivery routes.

Robots deliver bins to human "pick stations," where employees assemble customer orders with minimal handling time. This hybrid human–machine workflow ensures both speed and accuracy. Machine learning models constantly adjust the allocation of robots and resources to balance workloads across the warehouse, minimize congestion on the Grid, and optimize energy use.

Ocado reports that its automation enables the picking of a 50-item grocery order in as little as five minutes, significantly reducing lead times and increasing order accuracy compared to conventional fulfillment centers. The system's scalability has allowed Ocado to license its technology to global partners, including Kroger in the United States and Sobeys in Canada.

Ocado's approach exemplifies the Plan Fulfill transformation within Supply Chain 5.0. By combining AI-driven forecasting, real-time analytics, and adaptive robotics with human oversight, Ocado creates a fulfillment process that is intelligent, responsive, and customer-centric. The system dynamically allocates resources based on shifting demand, integrates suppliers and delivery partners into the planning loop, and supports sustainability through efficient energy use and reduced waste. This synergy of advanced technology with human decision-making aligns directly with Supply Chain 5.0's pillars of resilience, sustainability, and human-centricity, delivering faster service, higher accuracy, and a competitive advantage in an increasingly dynamic market.

SUMMARY SNAPSHOT

The company's fulfillment approach illustrates how Plan Fulfill in Supply Chain 5.0 integrates intelligent automation, predictive analysis, and human oversight into a seamless system. The result is a fulfillment model that balances sustainability through efficiency, resiliency through adaptability, and human-centricity through collaboration, delivering faster, more accurate, and ethically aligned outcomes for customers and partners worldwide.

An energy-efficient grid system and machine learning-driven optimization reduce wasted movements, congestion, and excess energy use. By dynamically allocating robots and resources, the system minimizes inefficiencies, packaging waste, and unnecessary transportation, aligning fulfillment with environmentally conscious practices.

A hybrid human–machine model is kept despite its advanced automation. Robots handle repetitive retrieval tasks while human workers focus on quality control and order assembly. This division of labor not only enhances efficiency but also reduces ergonomic strain on employees. Human planners oversee strategic decisions, applying ethical judgment and creativity where AI cannot, ensuring that fulfillment remains aligned with customer expectations and societal values.

Plan Return

This strategic and tactical process involves defining and adjusting actions over designated periods to allocate return resources and assets in response to both anticipated and unanticipated return requirements (ASCM, 2022). Its scope includes planned returns of products and unplanned returns of sold merchandise. The process also covers the refurbishment and preparation of products for reissue to customers.

In the Supply Chain 5.0 framework, the Plan Return process evolves from a reactive, resource-based function into a strategic, intelligent, and circular capability. Returns are no longer treated as exceptions. AI and ML predict return volumes and timing by analyzing customer behavior, product lifecycle data, and service history, enabling proactive resource planning.

Resources and assets for handling returns are dynamically allocated using real-time data and adaptive algorithms, ensuring efficient processing of both planned and unplanned returns. Returned products are evaluated for refurbishment, reuse, or recycling, while planning incorporates remanufacturing workflows, inventory reintegration, and sustainability metrics supporting the principles of a circular supply chain. Scenario-based planning tools anticipate disruptions in reverse logistics, enabling agile responses to spikes in return volumes, shifts in customer demand, or changes in regulatory requirements.

By transforming returns into a planned, value-generating process, organizations can recover asset value, reduce waste, and strengthen customer trust, driving profitability, advancing sustainability goals, and fostering long-term loyalty.

REAL-WORLD EXAMPLE UPS: Acquires Happy Returns to Streamline Reverse Logistics

Happy Returns is a US-based reverse logistics company that offers seamless, customer-friendly return options via its Return Bars. Customers return items without packaging or labels, and the platform aggregates these returns for efficient processing and disposition. In 2023, UPS acquired Happy Returns, expanding its reach and logistical capabilities to combine innovative tech expertise within the UPS network and offer customers the ability to return items as easily as they buy them.

UPS now reimagines the Plan Return process by integrating convenience, predictability, and resource efficiency right from the planning stage of returns. After a month of automation, UPS process accuracy surged by 65 percent driving a 50 percent efficiency increase in item sorting, and customers get their refunds or exchanges approved instantly.

SUMMARY SNAPSHOT

- **Human-centric drop-off points:** By enabling consumers to return items without packaging at convenient Return Bars, Happy Returns reduces friction and increases return rate predictability.
- **Efficient logistics planning:** Returns are aggregated from various Return Bars and routed to central hubs for quality inspection and disposition, streamlining routing and capacity allocation.
- **Resource optimization:** The centralized hubs allow strategic planning for refurbishment, restocking, or recycling, ensuring reverse logistics align with broader sustainability and inventory strategies.

This approach fosters transparency, reduces waste, and simplifies coordination among retailers, logistics providers, and customers, all critical in transforming return processing from ad hoc to strategically planned operations.

Plan Orchestrate

Although the SCOR SD does not explicitly suggest a Plan Orchestrate process, we would like to highlight the importance of thinking about *plan orchestration* in the era of Supply Chain 5.0. We think of plan orchestration as the strategic process of synchronizing and coordinating multiple, interdependent supply chain plans across functions, geographies, partners, and technologies into a unified, dynamic execution framework. It goes beyond creating isolated plans for sourcing, production, fulfillment, and returns; it ensures that all these plans are harmonized, continuously aligned, and adaptable to real-time changes in demand, supply, and operational conditions.

REAL-WORLD EXAMPLE Companies Leading in Supply Chain Orchestration

Kinaxis offers the Maestro platform, an AI-enabled, end-to-end supply chain orchestration tool. It combines a unified data fabric, real-time intelligence, and seamless integration to keep data, people, and processes synchronized across the entire supply chain. The platform supports rapid scenario modeling and digital twin capabilities, enabling organizations to respond agilely to disruptions.

SUMMARY SNAPSHOT

The real-world example exemplifies how we need to start thinking on Plan Orchestration in Supply Chain 5.0 to unify siloed plans into a dynamic, end-to-end execution framework. By aligning sustainability, resilience, and human-centricity, the platform enables companies to make smarter, faster, and more ethical decisions, transforming orchestration from reactive coordination into a predictive, collaborative capability that drives competitive advantage and profitability. In summary, in the era of Supply Chain 5.0, understanding each dimension of planning is not only operationally critical but also strategically transformative.

For supply chain executives, these planning domains now represent intelligent ecosystems powered by AI, real-time data, and human–machine collaboration within embedded technologies. Planning is no longer a static exercise; it is a dynamic capability that anticipates disruptions, personalizes customer experiences, and aligns with sustainability goals. Executives who grasp the nuances of each planning function can orchestrate supply chains that are self-optimizing, resilient, and ethically driven, positioning their organizations to thrive in a hyper-connected, rapidly evolving global landscape. Mastery of these processes enables leaders to move from reactive management to proactive orchestration, where supply chains become adaptive engines of innovation and competitive advantage. The next question is, how prepared is your organization to shift from reactive planning to predictive across all supply chain domains?

Maturity Stages: Basic, Integrated, Predictive

Regardless of your applications in the planning supply chain area, and for practical purposes, we would like to introduce the stages of maturity: Basic, Integrated, and Predictive. In this book, these maturity stages represent a progression in supply chain capabilities, especially in how organizations plan, make decisions, and respond to changes. These stages are highly correlated with the adoption of emergent technologies.

These stages are not attributed to a single inventor but have evolved through the combination of various maturity models developed over time. One of the most influential models in supply chain maturity is the Supply Chain Process Maturity Model developed by Lockamy and McCormack (2004; 2013). Their model includes five levels: Ad hoc, Defined, Linked, Integrated, and Extended. The stages Basic, Integrated, and Predictive are often seen as a simplified or adapted version of this framework, especially in modern digital supply chain contexts. Cheshmberah and Beheshtikia (2020), in a comprehensive literature review, discuss various maturity models in supply chain management, including those focused on integration and visibility. They highlight how models have evolved from simple assessments to more complex frameworks incorporating digital technologies and predictive analytics. Dr. Handfield developed a Supply Chain Maturity Model that evaluates organizational capabilities across six dimensions using a progressive five-level scale. While not using the exact terms "Basic," "Integrated," and "Predictive," his model supports the conceptual evolution toward predictive capabilities.

Thus, the Basic, Integrated, Predictive framework is a modern abstraction derived from earlier models like Lockamy and McCormack's five-level maturity model that reflects the evolution of supply chain planning from manual and siloed operations to integrated systems and ultimately to intelligent, AI-driven decision-making. Since these stages are widely used in consulting, academic literature, and industry assessments, often tailored to specific domains like S&OP, demand planning, or digital transformation, we would like to apply this maturity model to the Plan section of Supply Chain 5.0. See Figure 5.1.

Basic. The Basic stage is characterized by manual processes, limited data visibility, and reactive decision-making. Planning is often siloed across departments, and decisions are based on historical data or gut instinct.

a. Key traits:
   Spreadsheet-based planning
   Minimal collaboration across functions
   Static forecasts and schedules
   Low automation and digitalization
b. Challenges:
   Inflexibility in responding to disruptions
   Poor alignment between supply and demand
   High risk of inefficiencies and stockouts

Figure 5.1 Plan Maturity Stages

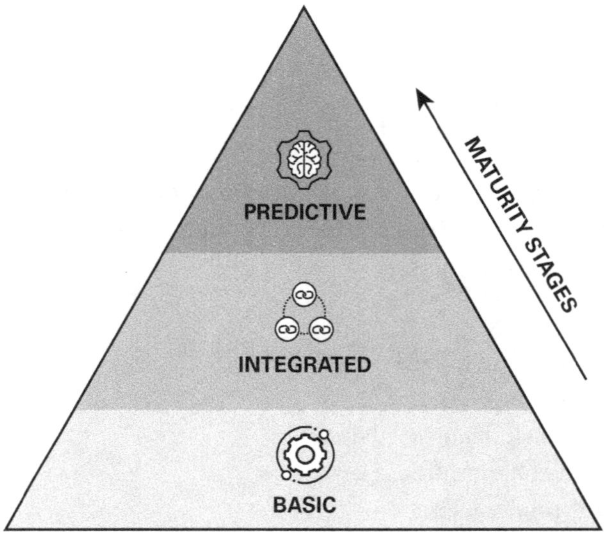

Role of technology: At this stage, technology is minimal and often limited to basic tools like spreadsheets or standalone software.

Typical technologies:

Excel or manual data entry systems
Basic ERP modules (used in silos)
Email and phone-based communication

Impact:

Low visibility and coordination
High dependency on human effort
Reactive decision-making

Example: Small and mid-sized enterprises (SMEs) relying on spreadsheets and manual planning. A mid-sized company used historical sales data and seasonal trends to manually adjust production schedules.

Integrated. The Integrated stage involves connected systems, cross-functional collaboration, and data-driven decision-making. Planning processes are standardized and supported by enterprise systems like ERP, APS, and SCM platforms.

a. Key traits:

Real-time data sharing across departments
Use of integrated planning tools (e.g., S&OP, IBP)

Enhanced visibility into supply chain nodes
Collaboration with suppliers and partners

b. Benefits:
Improved forecast accuracy
Better resource utilization
Faster response to market changes

Role of technology: Technology enables cross-functional integration and real-time data sharing. Systems begin to communicate, improving planning accuracy and responsiveness.

Typical technologies:
Full ERP systems (e.g., SAP, Oracle)
Advanced planning systems (APS)
Supply chain management platforms
Cloud-based collaboration tools
IoT for real-time tracking

Impact:
Improved visibility and coordination
Data-driven decisions
Enhanced agility and responsiveness

Example: Firms using ERP and digital twins for synchronized planning. Firms integrate lean management with simulation models to forecast and mitigate disruptions.

Predictive. The Predictive stage leverages advanced analytics, AI/ML, and digital twins to enable proactive and intelligent planning. Decisions are made based on simulations, scenario modeling, and predictive insights.

a. Key traits:
AI-driven demand sensing and forecasting
Autonomous planning systems with human oversight
Scenario-based planning and risk mitigation
Integration of sustainability and resilience metrics

b. Strategic advantages:
Anticipation of disruptions before they occur
Optimization of trade-offs (cost, service, sustainability)
Enhanced agility and innovation

Role of technology: Technology becomes a strategic enabler to anticipate disruptions, optimize decisions, and support human-centric planning.

Typical technologies:
AI/ML for demand sensing and forecasting
Digital twins for scenario simulation

Predictive analytics and prescriptive models
Autonomous planning systems
Blockchain for traceability
Human-AI collaboration platforms

Impact:

Proactive and resilient planning
Real-time optimization
Human-centric decision support
Sustainability and risk mitigation

Example: Firms using predictive analytics for route optimization and demand sensing. Companies using AI and digital twins for scenario planning and predictive maintenance.

The development from basic planning tools to connected ecosystems is ongoing, and the question is how and why we transition from connected ecosystems to intelligent ones for the benefit of people, the planet, and resilient, profitable supply chains. In the context of Industry 5.0, the most suitable maturity stage for supply chain planning is the Predictive stage, but with a crucial twist: It must be human-centric and ethically aligned.

Human-AI collaboration: AI supports planners, doesn't replace them.

Resilience: Predictive models anticipate disruptions.

Sustainability: Technologies optimize for environmental and social impact.

Customization: Systems adapt to human needs and ethical considerations.

Using SIPOC to Explore Key Activities in the Plan

SIPOC is an acronym for Suppliers, Inputs, Process, Outputs, and Customers. SIPOC analysis became popular in the 1980s with the rise of Total Quality Management (TQM), because it was a simple tool for summarizing the boundaries and flow of a process in a way that links high-level understanding to operational detail.

Key activities within each major process are chosen to illustrate how the process operates, how it creates value, and how it supports the broader goals of resilience, sustainability, and human-centricity.

Each SIPOC diagram begins by identifying a specific subprocess within the framework (see Figure 5.2). This structure clarifies where a subprocess begins and ends, what it depends on, and who it affects.

Including SIPOC diagrams in these chapters serves three key purposes:

- grounding theory in practice, showing how each part of the supply chain depends on and contributes to others;
- enabling consistent comparison by using a standardized structure to analyze different processes;
- revealing points of impact, highlighting where decisions, risks, and relationships affect people and the environment.

These diagrams are not intended to be exhaustive. Instead, they provide a focused, practical view of how selected activities function within the broader SCOR DS model. By doing so, they help readers move from abstract frameworks to tangible insights, showing how supply chains operate in reality and how they can be made stronger, more sustainable, and more people-centered.

Table 5.2 outlines the key activities found in the Plan process when mapped against SIPOC.

Figure 5.2 Plan SIPOC

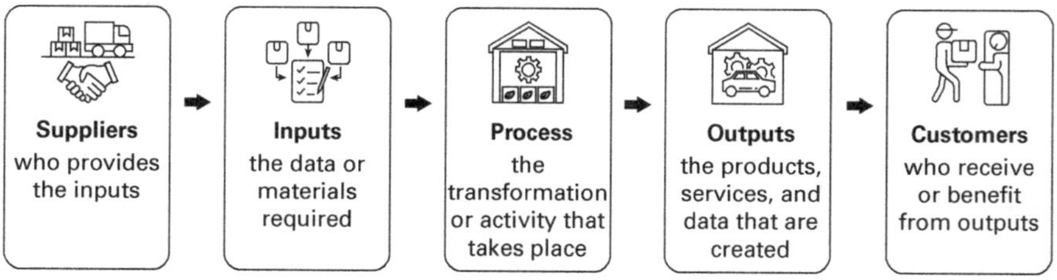

Table 5.2 Key Activities Found in the Plan Process When Mapped Against SIPOC

Subprocess	Suppliers	Inputs	Processes	Outputs	Customers
Analyze Demand	Sales, Marketing, Historical Order Data	Sales forecasts, market intelligence, historical demand data	Analyze patterns, trends, and events influencing demand	Demand plan, forecast scenarios	Master Planning, Procurement, Executive Team
Balance Supply and Demand	Manufacturing, Procurement, Logistics	Capacity data, inventory levels, supplier lead times, demand plan	Match forecasted demand with available and planned supply	Feasible supply plan, demand-supply match report	Procurement, Production Scheduling
Inventory Planning	Warehouse Management, Inventory Control	Inventory policies, carrying costs, demand variability	Determine optimal inventory targets by location and product	Inventory targets, replenishment signals	Fulfillment, Distribution, Sourcing
Capacity Planning	Production Engineering, HR, Facility Ops	Equipment availability, labor schedules, maintenance plans	Assess available capacity against projected workloads	Capacity plans, bottleneck reports	Manufacturing, Executive Leadership
Risk Identification and Scenario Planning	Finance, Legal, Global Affairs	Risk register, geopolitical data, supplier risk profiles	Model disruptions, assess vulnerabilities, test scenarios	Risk mitigation strategies, scenario-based plans	Leadership Team, Business Continuity

Technology and Innovation in Modern Planning

Today's planning processes are becoming increasingly sophisticated, leveraging intelligent technologies to handle complexity, reduce latency, and improve decision accuracy. Key enablers include:

- **Predictive analytics and ML:** These methods use statistical and AI techniques to uncover patterns in historical data and forecast future outcomes, enhancing planning precision and enabling automated detection of trends
- **Digital twins:** Digital twins are virtual replicas of physical systems that integrate real-time data to simulate scenarios and optimize responses, boosting operational efficiency, resilience, and decision-making within supply chains.
- **AI-based optimization engines:** These tools solve complex planning challenges, such as capacity allocation, inventory placement, and scheduling, in real time by automating trade-off decisions
- **Integrated business planning (IBP) platforms:** These systems align strategic and tactical planning across functions and time horizons, enabling synchronized decision-making across the enterprise
- **Control towers:** Often supported by digital twins and advanced analytics, control towers deliver real-time visibility across the supply chain and flag exceptions quickly to enable proactive planning interventions.

By integrating these technologies, supply chain planning becomes more responsive and accurate, significantly reducing errors and delays. Importantly, these tools create pathways for more sustainable and people-centered decisions by optimizing resource use and embedding resilience throughout the planning cycle.

The key difference between modern planning technologies in supply chains and Industry 5.0 lies in focus and purpose, and that difference has a big impact on how these technologies are applied. First, the focus. Technology-driven is about what tools are used, while human-driven is about why and how we use those tools, and thus leaders shift to placing humans, sustainability, and societal well-being at the center of technological deployment. Second, the purpose. Current planning tech focuses on efficiency, responsiveness, and cost optimization. Once these are integrated into the supply chains, the purpose becomes integrative:

- **Human-centricity:** Technology enhances, rather than replaces, human decision-making.

- **Sustainability:** Decisions must optimize not just for profit, but for environmental and social impact.
- **Resilience:** Processes are designed to absorb shocks without compromising people or planet.

When these modern planning technologies are applied within a Supply Chain 5.0 mindset, they're used not just to optimize operations but to align with broader values. For example:

- Predictive analytics and AI: Still used to forecast demand and balance supply, but with parameters that factor in ethical sourcing, labor well-being, or carbon impact.
- Digital twins: Simulate not only operational outcomes but also sustainability metrics (e.g., emissions) or workforce safety scenarios.
- Optimization engines: Weigh social/environmental constraints alongside cost and speed.
- Control towers and Integrated Business Planning: Integrate ESG (Environmental, Social, Governance) and human impact KPIs into planning dashboards.

Empowering Strategic Planners

As we explore the Plan section of the supply chain, our aim is to equip supply chain leaders to think strategically, emphasizing human–AI collaboration in planning and embedding ethical decision-making within the context of Supply Chain 5.0. In this new era, planning is no longer a purely technical function; it has become a strategic capability that blends human insight, technological intelligence, and ethical foresight.

We conclude this section by examining how planning evolves into a human-centric, resilient, and ethically grounded process through the integration of advanced technologies and collaborative decision-making.

Human-AI Collaboration: From Automation to Augmentation

In traditional supply chain planning, automation was primarily used to reduce manual effort and improve efficiency. In Supply Chain 5.0, the focus shifts from automation to augmentation, where AI enhances, rather than replaces, human decision-making.

Leaders should embrace two key shifts:

- **AI as a co-planner:** Digital technologies can process and analyze vast datasets to identify patterns, forecast demand, and simulate scenarios. Final decisions remain with humans, who interpret these insights in context—especially when safety, ethics, or accountability are at stake.
- **Human-in-the-loop systems:** These ensure that human judgment stays central for complex or ethically sensitive decisions. While automation optimizes certain planning activities, humans are freed to focus on higher-order problem-solving, innovation, and strategic alignment.

By adopting these principles, planning in Supply Chain 5.0 becomes a collaborative, values-driven capability that balances efficiency with responsibility. Working together, humans and intelligent systems can anticipate disruptions, adjust plans dynamically, and build the resilience needed to thrive in an increasingly complex and uncertain environment.

Ethical Decision-Making: Planning with Purpose

For the strategic thinker, ethical decision-making is as critical as operational performance. In Supply Chain 5.0, planning with purpose means aligning operational decisions with broader societal values, sustainability, fairness, and transparency.

Leaders should prioritize three shifts:

- **Sustainable trade-offs**
  Balancing cost, speed, and environmental impact. AI can model these trade-offs, but humans determine which values take precedence.
- **Bias and fairness**
  Algorithms may inherit biases from historical data. Ethical planners must review and adjust models to ensure fairness in supplier selection, labor practices, and customer service.
- **Transparency and accountability**
  Ethical planning requires clear documentation of decisions, particularly when AI is involved, so stakeholders understand the "how" and "why" behind them.

Ethical planning in Supply Chain 5.0 goes beyond efficiency; it integrates the triple bottom line, considering profit, people, and planet. Advanced technologies, especially AI, must be guided by responsible AI principles: Fairness, accountability, transparency, and privacy. Equally important is stakeholder engagement, ensuring that employees, suppliers, customers, and communities are part of the decision-making process.

The outcome is a planning approach that is both strategically effective and socially responsible. Is this possible? Absolutely, but it demands deliberate commitment, structural change, and continuous accountability. Table 5.3 is a readiness and implementation checklist that readers can utilize strategically.

Actionable Principles for Plan

- Connect long-term planning strategies with day-to-day execution so every decision advances resilience, sustainability, and human-centric goals.
- Predict and influence demand by combining AI forecasting, market intelligence, and customer sentiment analysis to shape (not just respond to) future needs.
- Plan for resilience by embedding risk signals, multi-sourcing strategies, and crisis-response protocols into every stage of the supply chain.
- Utilize technologies like scenario planning and digital twins to anticipate disruptions, demand surges, or regulatory changes, and promptly activate contingency strategies.
- Automate repetitive, data-heavy tasks with AI while empowering humans to focus on ethical decisions, creative problem-solving, and relationship building when planning your supply chains.
- Synchronize across the value network so suppliers, manufacturers, distributors, and customers operate from a single, transparent planning framework.
- Balance automation with human expertise, ensuring that AI handles data-intensive optimization while people lead in innovation, ethics, and relationship management.
- Design for agility by building flexible capacity, scalable processes, and modular systems that can pivot quickly to meet changing requirements.

Table 5.3 Readiness and Implementation Checklist

Readiness Area	Indicators to Evaluate	Quick Win or Long-Term?
Strategic Alignment	Planning processes reflect resilience, sustainability, and human-centricity in strategic goals and decision criteria. ESG and risk goals are integrated into supply chain strategy.	Long-Term
	Leadership communications and KPIs emphasize scenario readiness, emissions reduction, and workforce well-being.	
Digital and Technological Infrastructure	Forecasting tools, optimization engines, and integrated planning platforms are in place. Systems support real-time visibility, interoperability, and simulation modeling.	Long-Term
	Use of AI, IoT, or digital twins to enable agile planning and proactive response.	
Workforce Readiness and Culture	Planners are trained in analytics, scenario modeling, and cross-functional collaboration. There is a culture of innovation and participation in change initiatives.	Quick Win (training); Long-Term (culture)
	Workforce input is considered in workload planning and change management efforts.	

Supplier and Partner Ecosystem	Key suppliers and partners are involved in demand and capacity planning. Shared data and visibility tools are used to align upstream and downstream activities.	Quick Win (collaboration); Long-Term (ecosystem maturity)
	Partners are engaged in ESG and resilience planning, including circularity and joint risk modeling.	
Performance Measurement and Governance	Planning performance is tracked using a mix of financial and non-financial indicators, including emissions, responsiveness, and workforce development.	Quick Win (metrics); Long-Term (governance)
	Governance structures support cross-functional decision-making and continuous improvement in planning practices.	

- Incorporate circular economy flows into forward and reverse planning, enabling refurbishment, reuse, and recycling to protect value and reduce waste.
- Treat planning as a continuous learning loop, analyze outcomes, capture lessons, and evolve strategies to stay ahead of future challenges.

REAL-WORLD EXAMPLE Siemens: Digital twins in warehouse planning

Siemens has embraced digital twin technology to revolutionize warehouse planning and operational decision-making. This approach creates precise virtual replicas of warehouse operations, enabling the company to simulate and evaluate service provider performance, operational strategies, and automation investments before committing resources.

Through these digital twins, Siemens can model highly complex warehouse environments, accounting for varying product types, storage configurations, and workflows. Simulations include loading frequencies, staffing levels, equipment utilization, and potential bottlenecks, allowing operational risks and performance metrics to be assessed well before any physical changes are made.

Importantly, the technology also navigates real-world constraints, such as German labor regulations that restrict individual worker tracking. Digital twins deliver rich operational insights while protecting employee privacy, ensuring compliance and supporting strategic planning across multiple facilities.

Key applications include:

- validating service provider proposals before contract execution
- testing automated logistics solutions
- assessing the feasibility and ROI of Automated Guided Vehicle (AGV) deployments
- designing scalable warehouse optimization strategies

By shifting warehouse planning from a reactive, manual process to a data-driven, predictive methodology, Siemens gains the ability to test, refine, and optimize its operations virtually, significantly reducing risks, avoiding costly trial-and-error, and accelerating decision-making.

This approach reflects a growing trend in supply chain management, where digital simulation technologies are becoming integral to strategic planning and operational excellence. In the context of Supply Chain 5.0, Siemens' use of digital twins demonstrates how advanced technology can enhance resilience, boost efficiency, and enable more human-centric, sustainable decision-making.

KEY TAKEAWAYS

Planning in Supply Chain 5.0 is not a preliminary step but an ongoing, interconnected capability that underpins resilience, sustainability, and human-centricity across the supply chain, all with the use of technologies.

- The Plan function is embedded in Order, Source, Transform, Fulfill, Return, and Orchestrate, ensuring alignment of strategy with operational execution.
- Planning evolves from reactive, schedule-based practices to predictive, intelligent, and adaptive systems using AI, digital twins, and real-time analytics.
- Embed technologies into planning as a competitive advantage.
- Turn production planning into quality planning by leveraging predictive quality systems.
- Utilize orchestration tools to maintain real-time alignment among partners, geographies, and functions.
- Know your company's maturity stage and assess if you are still basic, integrated, or predictive, and plan your next move.
- Adopt the right technologies and align them with strategy; don't just focus on cost savings.
- Position AI as a co-planner; let machines crunch the data at scale while humans provide ethical judgment, creativity, and strategic oversight when planning your supply chain.
- Anticipate orders and returns; both are equally impactful.

References

Amazon Technologies, Inc. (2013) Method and system for anticipatory package shipping (US Patent No. 8,615,473) United States Patent and Trademark Office. https://patents.google.com/patent/US8615473B2 (archived at https://perma.cc/KYH5-8TLM)

Association for Supply Chain Management (2022) SCOR Digital Standard: Introduction to processes. https://scor.ascm.org/processes/introduction

Association for Supply Chain Management (ASCM) (2026). SCOR Digital Standard. Process Plan.

Bensinger, G. (2014, January 17) Amazon wants to ship your package before you buy it. *Wall Street Journal*. www.wsj.com/articles/BL-DGB-32082 (archived at https://perma.cc/64KF-9FKW)

Bosch Global (2025) Ten years of Industry 4.0. Bosch. www.bosch.com/stories/10-years-industry-4-0-at-bosch (archived at https://perma.cc/LV3X-DDYU)

Bosch SDS (2025) AI for sustainable manufacturing: Optimizing energy savings and ROI with Bosch SDS. https://bosch-sds.com/blog/ai-for-sustainable-manufacturing-optimizing-energy-savings-and-roi-with-bosch-sds (archived at https://perma.cc/3HHM-HG6L)

Cheshmberah, M. and Beheshtikia, S. (2020) Supply chain management maturity: An all-encompassing literature review on models, dimensions and approaches. *LogForum*, 16(1), 103–116.

Dominguez, L. (2023, May 25) Nestlé uses AI and data science to battle environmental challenges in coffee production. Consumer Goods Technology. https://consumergoods.com/nestle-uses-ai-and-data-science-battle-environmental-challenges-coffee-production (archived at https://perma.cc/325X-B5RT)

Eisenhower, D. (1957, November 14) A speech to the National Defense Executive Reserve Conference in Washington, D.C. In Public Papers of the Presidents of the United States (p. 818) National Archives and Records Service, Government Printing Office.

Handfield, R. and Linton, T. (2017) *The LIVING Supply chain: The evolving imperative of operating in real time*. John Wiley & Sons.

Kinaxis (2023) Maestro: The AI-powered orchestration platform. www.kinaxis.com/en/solutions/platform (archived at https://perma.cc/4ZU2-FRGQ)

Lockamy, A. and McCormack, K. (2013) The effect of on supply chain performance: An empirical study. In 1st Annual International Interdisciplinary Conference (Aiic), Azores, Portugal.

Lockamy III, A. and McCormack, K. (2004) The development of a supply chain management process maturity model using the concepts of business process orientation. *Supply Chain Management: An International Journal*, 9(4), 272–78.

LV Staff (2023, September 6) Amazon anticipatory shipping. Logistics Viewpoints. https://logisticsviewpoints.com/2023/09/06/amazon-anticipatory-shipping (archived at https://perma.cc/F8DY-ZWP3)

Nestlé (2019, September 13) Nestlé Forest Positive strategy. Nestlé. www.nestle.com/media/pressreleases/allpressreleases/nestle-forest-positive-strategy (archived at https://perma.cc/DEU5-V5ZV)

Nestlé (2024a) Deforestation-free supply chains. Nestlé. www.nestle.com/sustainability/nature-environment/forests/deforestation-supply-chains (archived at https://perma.cc/PZG6-ZJ7P)

Nestlé (2024b, May 16) Using satellite technology to increase transparency in reforestation. Nestlé. www.nestle.com/media/news/satellite-technology-reforestation-transparency (archived at https://perma.cc/8QSS-NXH4)

Ocado Group (2024) Results and presentations. www.ocadogroup.com/investors/results-and-presentations (archived at https://perma.cc/J5SJ-N44S)

Ocado Group (2025, August 14) 25 years of Ocado: From online grocer to global technology pioneer. www.ocadogroup.com/media/stories/25-years-of-ocado-from-online-grocer-to-global-technology-pioneer (archived at https://perma.cc/U4MQ-LAD3)

SIAL Newsroom (2023, October 6) Nestlé harnesses AI for precision farming. SIAL Paris Newsroom. www.sialparis.com/en/trends/News/nestle-ai (archived at https://perma.cc/FL3J-32XD)

Siemens (2022) Digital transformation of intralogistics start-up. www.siemens.com/global/en/company/stories/industry/2022/intralogistics-warehouse-digital-twin-digital-transformation-addverb-india.html (archived at https://perma.cc/U9K6-546Y)

Siemens (2023) Siemens distribution center in Nuremberg: Digital twin in intralogistics. www.siemens.com/global/en/company/stories/industry/2023/siemens-distribution-center-nuremberg-digital-twin-intralogistics-germany.html (archived at https://perma.cc/486U-SQRT)

Siemens (2023, March 20) Maximum transparency: Siemens shows the holistic digital twin of a logistics center. https://press.siemens.com/global/en/pressrelease/maximum-transparency-siemens-shows-holistic-digital-twin-logistics-center (archived at https://perma.cc/5UQ9-4WPY)

Siemens (2024) Logistics operations consulting. https://plm.sw.siemens.com/en-US/digital-logistics/consulting/logistics-operations (archived at https://perma.cc/6DM7-UWYJ)

Tiatra (2023) Siemens builds fully automated warehouse with digital twin. https://tiatra.com/siemens-builds-fully-automated-warehouse-with-digital-twin (archived at https://perma.cc/H73H-BZTG)

UPS (2023, October 25) UPS to acquire Happy Returns, a leader in reverse logistics. https://investors.ups.com/news-events/press-releases/detail/2107/ups-to-acquire-happy-returns-a-leader-in-reverse-logistics (archived at https://perma.cc/MV7S-3RLP)

UPS (2025, January 5) How we're making customer returns easy: Happy Returns x UPS. https://about.ups.com/us/en/our-stories/customer-first/how-we-re-making-customer-returns-easy--happy-returns-x-ups.html (archived at https://perma.cc/PQ9C-KEXP)

Source: Securing Inputs 06

The real competition is between supply chains, not companies.

MARTIN CHRISTOPHER, EMERITUS PROFESSOR OF MARKETING AND LOGISTICS, CRANFIELD SCHOOL OF MANAGEMENT

Ethical and Resilient Sourcing in a Connected World

The Source process in the SCOR Digital Standard (SCOR DS) includes all activities related to procuring goods and services, such as planning and scheduling orders, selecting suppliers, placing orders, coordinating deliveries, receiving and inspecting incoming materials, and transferring them to the correct location within the supply chain (ASCM, 2022). This covers both direct and indirect materials or services necessary to support manufacturing, operations, or customers' orders. Key activities involve sourcing raw materials, components, energy, packaging, and services from external or internal suppliers (ASCM, 2022).

In the Supply Chain 5.0 framework, Source serves as a strategy for the entire supply chain's ecosystem, as it directly shapes the flow, quality, and resilience of all downstream activities. Every decision made in sourcing, whether about suppliers, raw materials, or partnerships, sets the conditions for how effectively organizations can transform, fulfill, and return products. Source: Supply Chain 5.0 is predictive, collaborative, and sustainability-driven by integrating technologies in supplier ecosystems.

- Resilient: By diversifying supply options and modeling disruption scenarios
- Sustainable: By holding suppliers accountable for deforestation-free, low-carbon, and circular practices

- Human-centric: By fostering fair labor, ethical practices, and collaborative relationships with partners and producers

Source becomes more than a function; it acts as the foundation that enables every other supply chain process to operate profitably, intelligently, responsibly, and competitively in a rapidly evolving global environment.

Before examining the sourcing, we also want to highlight an equally essential and complementary process, known as Order, within the SCOR DS. Chapter 8 of this book will provide a detailed analysis of this key Order process. For now, it is essential to understand that an order encompasses all activities related to a customer's purchase of products or services, including key details such as order location, pricing, payment methods, fulfillment status, and other transactional data necessary for processing and managing the order lifecycle (ASCM, 2022). This distinction is crucial in supply chain management because Order and Source are two separate but interconnected process categories that serve different roles in the end-to-end supply chain. Table 6.1 illustrates this difference visually.

Table 6.1 Key Differences of Source and Order in SCOR DS

Process	Focus	Purpose	Key activities	Example
SOURCE	Upstream procurement (Supplier-facing)	To acquire the goods and services your organization needs to operate, whether for production, resale, or operations.	• Selecting and managing suppliers • Placing purchase orders for raw materials, components, or services • Scheduling deliveries from suppliers • Receiving and inspecting goods • Handling supplier payments • Ensuring sustainability and compliance in sourcing practices	You buy steel from a supplier to make refrigerators → That's a SOURCE process.

(continued)

Table 6.1 (Continued)

Process	Focus	Purpose	Key activities	Example
ORDER	Downstream customer interaction (Customer-facing)	To capture, manage, and fulfill customer orders for your company's products or services.	• Receiving and validating customer orders • Determining order attributes: Pricing, location, quantity, payment method • Communicating order status • Managing changes, cancellations, and exceptions • Coordinating with fulfillment, delivery, and invoicing	A customer orders a refrigerator from your website and selects home delivery → That's an ORDER process.

In the SCOR DS context, this distinction is vital because of the emphasis on modularity and digital focus. Orders underscore the increasing significance of digital commerce, real-time order fulfillment, and customer experience. Meanwhile, sourcing continues to evolve to include sustainable sourcing, supplier collaboration, and risk management, especially as digital and physical technologies, as well as sustainability, become increasingly prominent. Making a clear early distinction between the Source and Order processes is not just a matter of terminology for this book; it's a strategic imperative. Therefore, supply chain leaders can strategize effectively in their respective areas of the supply chain.

In the context of Supply Chain 5.0, these domains demand different technologies, sustainability strategies, and human–machine dynamics. Understanding their unique roles empowers organizations to design more resilient, ethical, and adaptive supply chains from end to end.

For leaders in Supply Chain 5.0, the sourcing process becomes more relevant and strategic than ever before. It shifts from a transactional activity to a core element of organizational strategy, influencing cost, continuity, ethics, innovation, and brand perception. In this era, the sourcing process is intricately linked to the three pillars of the supply chain: Resilience, sustainability, and human-centricity.

At the highest level, Source is also executed across four core supply chain processes: Strategic sourcing, direct procurement, indirect procurement, and source return (ASCM, 2022). See Table 6.2.

Table 6.2 Evolution of Sourcing Processes: SCOR DS and Supply Chain 5.0

Source Aspect	SCOR DS Definition	Supply Chain 5.0 Evolution
Strategic Source	Involves identifying and engaging key suppliers through a comprehensive analysis of total spend and supplier capabilities. The emphasis is on cultivating long-term partnerships with vendors who contribute to both profitability and customer satisfaction.	In addition to cost and efficiency, sourcing embraces resilience, ethics, and collaboration. The process becomes more dynamic, data-driven, and aligned with broader societal goals, collaborative partnerships, innovation, and shared values.
Direct Procure	Refers to the acquisition of goods and services that are integral to the final product, such as raw materials, components, and inputs used in the transformation process. These purchases have a direct impact on production outcomes and customer value, making them critical to operational efficiency and product quality.	A transactional function also becomes strategic, intelligent, and a sustainable capability that supports innovation, resilience, and customer-centricity, with an emphasis on product traceability, ethical sourcing, and end-of-life product recovery.
Indirect Procure	Encompasses the acquisition of goods and services that support an organization's operations but are not directly tied to the production of its core offerings. These purchases, including rent, utilities, maintenance, repairs, operations supplies, and professional services, enable business continuity and efficiency. Unlike direct procurement, indirect sourcing often involves a broader supplier base and more variable relationship dynamics, reflecting its diverse and decentralized nature.	It aligns with purpose-driven goals such as carbon neutrality and digital transformation, optimizing spend categories like energy, facilities, and services for impact rather than just cost. AI and automation streamline routine tasks and enhance spend visibility. Flexible supplier ecosystems and digital platforms enable agile, on-demand procurement, positioning indirect sourcing as a key contributor to innovation and adaptability.
Source Return	Return and Disposition Management involves handling goods and assets returned due to defects, excess inventory, maintenance needs, or business agreements.	In Supply Chain 5.0, this process is enhanced by predictive technologies and sustainable practices that enable refurbishment, reintegration, or responsible disposal.

Strategic Source

In Supply Chain 5.0, strategic sourcing emphasizes resilience, ethics, and collaboration alongside cost and efficiency. The process becomes more dynamic, data-driven, and aligned with broader societal goals. Supplier partnerships adopt a human-centric approach, shifting from transactional to collaborative relationships, where innovation, agility, and shared values become key metrics for evaluating suppliers. With the use of technologies, AI and ML are used to analyze spending patterns, risk factors, and supplier performance in real-time through predictive analytics that anticipate disruptions and improve sourcing strategies. Similar technologies, such as blockchain and digital twins, are building intelligent ecosystems like e-procurement platforms that learn and adapt, smart contracts to automate compliance, payments, and performance tracking, and hyper-automation to simulate scenarios. These enable proactive sourcing adjustments and help visualize the impact of decisions on cost and the circular economy potential.

REAL-WORLD EXAMPLE Digital Product Passports (DDPs)

With rising regulatory requirements and growing consumer expectations for transparency, brands face intensifying pressure to trace and disclose every stage of their supply chains. Digital product passports (DPPs) are scannable digital records that embed detailed product information and are emerging as a critical solution. The London-based fashion brand Nobody's Child (McGregor, 2025; Roberts-Islam, 2024), European Consortium LVMH (2025), and Siemens Battery Passport are early adopters (2025).

Nobody's Child has become an early mover in implementing DPPs, starting with its denim line and expanding across all product categories by Autumn/Winter 2025. The brand-initiated pilot programs in 2023, beginning with four initial pilots that covered denim, and subsequently expanded to 50 styles across seven suppliers. Plans include a full rollout, so that every new garment produced from summer 2025 will carry a scannable QR code linking to detailed product data. Implementing this program has required them to collect 110 data points per product, including fiber origins, energy usage, water footprint, care and repair instructions, and supply chain traceability down to the farms or recycling facilities supplying raw materials (i.e., Tier 5 traceability).

By 2030, DPPs will be mandatory for all garments sold in the European Union (European Commission, 2025), making them a cornerstone of supply chain accountability and compliance. The Nobody's Child example provides insight into the challenges faced by early adopters, including convincing suppliers to share more data, integrating QR codes uniquely per SKU, and ensuring the data is accurately linked and maintained across all internal systems. On the benefits side, Nobody's Child views DPPs as more than just regulatory compliance. They consider them tools for trust building, transparency, and risk management: Customers can scan the code to view carbon/water footprints, as well as sourcing details, which strengthens the brand's reputation. Additionally, deeper traceability enables the brand to identify risks (e.g., in energy sourcing or labor in water-stressed regions), establish more meaningful sustainability targets, and plan for circularity (e.g., by linking to repair, resale, or rental services).

SUMMARY SNAPSHOT

Nobody's Child demonstrates how Digital Product Passports serve as the connective tissue in a Supply Chain 5.0 network. They transform transparency into a strategic sourcing capability that links sustainability goals, resilience planning, and human-centric engagement.

- **Source traceability:** Tracing materials back to Tier 5 suppliers (farms, recycling facilities) ensures they meet deforestation-free and ethical standards. Manufacturers can access carbon and water footprints per batch, enabling cleaner production decisions. And in the end, recycling is easier at the product's end of life.
- **Resiliency readiness:** Real-time data enables the company to have faster corrective actions when sustainability risks or compliance gaps arise, but also to be more resilient against regulatory shocks.

Direct Procurement

In Supply Chain 5.0, direct procurement becomes a capability that supports innovation, resilience, and customer-centricity. In Supply Chain 5.0, direct procurement evolves into a smart, technology-enabled function that strikes a balance between efficiency, sustainability, and resilience. Material sourcing is guided by real-time data, AI-driven forecasts, and digital twins, ensuring decisions account not only for cost and quality but also for traceability, ethics, and environmental impact. Through integration with advanced manufacturing technologies such as collaborative robotics, additive manufacturing, and IoT-enabled systems, procurement enables both just-in-time and just-in-case strategies to coexist, delivering responsiveness while reducing waste and inefficiencies.

Direct procurement also becomes a strategic enabler of circular supply chains and resilience. Procurement teams collaborate with suppliers to design for reuse, remanufacturing, and recycling, thereby embedding circularity into their sourcing strategy from the outset. Human-AI collaboration strengthens procurement performance, with AI handling analytics and risk monitoring while humans lead on negotiation, strategic judgment, and ethical oversight. Supported by risk intelligence tools, procurement diversifies supply bases, applies scenario modeling, and deploys nearshoring strategies to anticipate disruptions.

REAL-WORLD EXAMPLE Siemens Battery Passport: Building Transparency and Accountability in Energy Storage

Siemens (2025) has developed the Battery Passport, a digital tracking system designed to enhance transparency and sustainability in the battery manufacturing value chain. The passport serves as a detailed digital record for each battery, documenting its entire lifecycle, from raw material sourcing through manufacturing and use to end-of-life recycling or reuse. This system enables manufacturers, suppliers, regulators, and customers to access verifiable information about battery composition, the origin of materials, environmental impact, and recycling credentials.

In practice, the Battery Passport helps Siemens (and its partners) reduce environmental and ethical risks, such as sourcing of conflict minerals or materials from environmentally sensitive regions. It also supports regulatory compliance and builds consumer trust by proving that traceable data backs sustainability claims. The technology empowers industry players to plan for circularity: Better design for disassembly, cleaner material choices, and more effective recycling. By integrating this digital record-keeping into the supply chain network, Siemens is turning what was once a compliance and reporting cost into a strategic asset, one that enhances resilience, sustainability, and transparency across the battery industry.

Although solutions like this are primarily aimed at companies involved in the battery supply chain that must comply with EU (2025) battery regulations for sustainability and traceability, they also provide additional strategic advantages for businesses, such as increased transparency, data-driven insights, and future profits from mandatory regulations.

SUMMARY SNAPSHOT

Siemens projects illustrate how direct sourcing in Supply Chain 5.0 goes beyond just cost. Instead, it becomes a data-driven, transparent, and collaborative process that uses digital twins, AI, and lifecycle traceability to create sustainable, resilient, and human-centered results.

- **Traceability as a sourcing:** Siemens' Battery Passport demonstrates how direct sourcing can embed full material traceability from mining and processing to end-of-life recovery. For procurement teams, this means supplier contracts are no longer judged only on price and delivery, but also on verified sustainability and circularity credentials.
- **Human-AI collaboration in supplier selection:** Siemens integrates AI to manage large data flows while humans provide oversight. In sourcing, AI can scan supplier networks for risk signals (e.g., regulations and changes in raw materials), while humans manage negotiations and make ethical decisions. Here, direct sourcing in Industry 5.0 strikes a balance between automation for scale and human judgment for values and strategy.
- **Building resilience through diversification:** Direct sourcing becomes a risk-intelligent discipline, where resilience is embedded into everyday procurement decisions. Applied to direct sourcing, procurement leaders can use resilience scoring and predictive analytics to design balanced supplier portfolios (global + nearshoring + on-demand suppliers).

Indirect Procurement

In Supply Chain 5.0, indirect procurement shifts from a support role to a strategic driver of resilience, sustainability, and employee well-being. Spend management is aligned with organizational values, ensuring that categories such as energy, facilities, and services contribute not only to efficiency but also to initiatives like carbon neutrality and digital transformation. AI and automation streamline transactional tasks, such as invoicing, supplier onboarding, and contract renewals, while intelligent spend analytics uncover hidden savings and compliance risks across decentralized purchasing.

At the same time, indirect procurement adopts a human-centric and sustainability-focused approach. Procurement teams collaborate with HR, IT, and facilities to co-design solutions that improve employee experience and productivity. ESG criteria also apply to non-core categories such as travel and office supplies, holding suppliers responsible for environmental and social impacts. By leveraging agile supplier networks and digital platforms, indirect procurement enables rapid adaptation, on-demand sourcing, and integration with emerging service models, transforming it into a proactive driver of organizational agility and innovation.

REAL-WORLD EXAMPLE From Support Function to Strategy: Indirect Sourcing in Industry 5.0

Because of the nature of indirect sourcing in the supply chain, we want to show that in Industry 5.0, indirect sourcing is no longer just about back-office procurement. It is now a strategic tool for sustainability (Unilever), efficiency (IBM), and employee well-being (Microsoft).

Unilever's procurement strategy integrates indirect procurement into its overall spending and manages it effectively. The company has moved away from having individual business units handle their own purchasing, instead choosing to centralize and standardize procurement across the organization through the use of procurement technology, online reverse auctions, and consolidation (Global Performance Group, 2025; Hargreaves, 2024).

IBM's AI-driven procurement platforms, including WatsonX Orchestrate, use specialized AI agents to automate tasks such as invoice processing, contract renewals, and supplier onboarding, thereby reducing manual effort. By automating repetitive tasks, this technology allows procurement staff to focus on higher-value activities, such as strategic sourcing and risk management. Routing discrepancies for human review and clearing blocked invoices are also part of reducing errors and strengthening governance (IBM, 2025; Belcic et al, 2025).

Microsoft's approach to improving the employee experience through indirect procurement for hybrid work emphasizes a comprehensive strategy that utilizes internal resources and strategic sourcing. The company sources a wide range of goods and services, not for manufacturing products, but to support daily operations and employee well-being (Boyd, 2025).

SUMMARY SNAPSHOT

In Industry 5.0, indirect sourcing evolves from a support function into a core strategic lever.

- **Embed indirect purchasing into the overall business strategy:** Indirect sourcing can amplify corporate sustainability goals when managed strategically across the enterprise.
- **Orchestrate procurement tasks:** Intelligent automation technologies can transform indirect sourcing into a driver of operational efficiency and governance excellence.
- **A tool for employee experience:** Indirect sourcing under Supply Chain 5.0 is human-centric, aligning organizational resources with employee needs and well-being.

Source Return

In Supply Chain 5.0, Source Returns evolve from reactive returns and repairs to proactive and regenerative asset management. The concept evolves as a predictive and value-generating process, rather than the management of defective or excess items. Organizations utilize AI, IoT, and digital twins to predict failures, optimize maintenance schedules, and prolong asset lifecycles. Returned products and MRO assets are not just refurbished; they are redesigned for circularity, enabling reuse, remanufacturing, or upcycling. For example, blockchain and smart contracts ensure compliant handling of warranty claims and recalls, while sustainability metrics guide disposition decisions. This evolution supports a closed-loop supply chain that minimizes waste, maximizes resource efficiency, and aligns with ethical and environmental goals.

REAL-WORLD EXAMPLE Remanufacturing as Strategic Sourcing: Lessons from Caterpillar

Caterpillar operates one of the world's most extensive remanufacturing programs, where returned engines, transmissions, and components are disassembled, rebuilt, and upgraded to "like-new" condition. As of 2025, Caterpillar's remanufacturing (Cat Reman) program remains a core part of its commitment to a circular economy (Caterpillar, 2025a).

Using predictive analytics and IoT monitoring, Caterpillar proactively identifies which parts are nearing end-of-life, allowing returns to be managed as planned value recovery rather than reactive repairs. This creates a regenerative loop where materials and energy are conserved, allowing customers to benefit from lower lifecycle costs. Some key results for the sourcing side include 80–90 percent less new materials used in many cases and 65–87 percent less energy used in remanufacturing compared to new manufacturing. In this program, sourcing is critical for ensuring the supply of "cores" (used parts returned by customers) maintains the health of the supply chain (Caterpillar, 2025b). Reliable sourcing of cores is crucial for maintaining a stable supply chain and minimizing reliance on new materials. In 2025, promotions such as complimentary extended service coverage for customers purchasing a remanufactured engine incentivize core returns, thereby strengthening this supply (Caterpillar, 2025c).

SUMMARY SNAPSHOT

The Caterpillar example is an excellent fit with the framed Source Return in Supply Chain 5.0. Let us map some of its principles directly.

- **From reactive repairs to regenerative management:** Returns evolve from "defective/excess items" to a predictive, value-generating process, utilizing technologies to anticipate parts nearing end-of-life.
- **Transparency and governance in returns:** Technologies can also be leveraged to enhance governance mechanisms, securing sourcing flows and aligning the incentives of suppliers, customers, and the company.
- **Source can be an incentive:** Returns are critical inputs that sustain the supply chain. Without reliable returns, the loop breaks and dependence on raw materials increases. These incentive programs strengthen this upstream sourcing channel, showing how returns become a strategic input, not a liability.

Technology and Innovation in Sourcing

Back in 2003, Linder and colleagues published a foundational article that, although not directly referencing Industry 5.0, underscored the deliberate importance of a strategic sourcing approach, an approach now being advanced through Industry 5.0 technologies. Much of the early literature emphasized broad implications for supply chains rather than examining the specific strategic shifts within the sourcing function. More recent contributions from 2024 and 2025, particularly by McKinsey and Forbes, have begun to focus directly on the evolving role of sourcing and procurement in the transition to Industry 5.0. Emerging technologies, including blockchain, IoT, RFID, NFC, AI, and ML, are being deployed to ensure ethical practices and supply chain transparency. Together, these tools create a powerful combination of immutable digital ledgers, real-time tracking sensors, and intelligent automation for monitoring and verification (Rejeb et al., 2025; Optel Group, 2025). This evolution addresses growing consumer, investor, and regulatory expectations for transparent supply chain systems that can be traced seamlessly back to the sourcing decisions of supply chain leaders. In this way, the trajectory from Linder's early work to today's digital innovations illustrates how sourcing has become not only a driver of efficiency but also a cornerstone of sustainability, resilience, and human-centricity in Supply Chain 5.0.

Modern sourcing is increasingly driven by digital and intelligent tools that enhance transparency, speed, and decision-making, while enabling organizations to prioritize supplier ethics, environmental performance, and collaborative innovation. Table 6.3 highlights both established practices and rapidly emerging technologies that are reshaping procurement and supply chain management. While conducting research and interviewing practitioners for this book, we mapped possible technologies to high-level business processes, providing you with a high-level action item to identify potential improvements in your own business practices.

Table 6.3 Technologies Most Commonly Used in Sourcing

Digital Platforms and Analytics	E-sourcing/e-procurement platforms Spend analytics and supplier performance dashboards Data visualization tools for sourcing insights
Automation and Intelligence	Artificial Intelligence (AI) for supplier selection, risk scoring, and predictive analytics Machine Learning (ML) to analyze large datasets and forecast demand or price fluctuations Robotic Process Automation (RPA) for repetitive tasks like invoice processing, purchase orders, and compliance checks

(continued)

Table 6.3 (Continued)

Transparency and Traceability	Blockchain/Distributed Ledger Technology (DLT) for secure, immutable supplier records and contract execution Smart contracts for automated procurement agreements Digital Product Passports (DPPs) emerging in sustainability and compliance
Connectivity and Tracking	Internet of Things (IoT) for supplier production and logistics visibility Radio Frequency Identification (RFID) for inventory and asset tracking Near Field Communication (NFC) for item-level authentication
Collaboration and Supplier Engagement	Supplier Relationship Management (SRM) systems Cloud-based collaboration platforms for real-time communication and document sharing
Sustainability and Compliance Tools	Carbon footprint calculators and ESG reporting systems integrated into sourcing platforms Third-party risk management platforms for supplier ethics and compliance monitoring
Emerging Technologies	Generative AI for contract drafting and supplier communication Digital twins of sourcing and procurement networks for scenario planning Advanced analytics for dynamic discounting and working capital optimization

Here is a question for you: How are these technologies related to the Three Pillars of Supply Chain 5.0?

The three pillars of Supply Chain 5.0 are closely linked to four key business components: Strategic alignment, balanced value creation, clarity in investment and prioritization, and regulatory and stakeholder compliance.

Research and practice indicate that while sourcing technologies hold tremendous potential, adoption efforts frequently fail due to a combination of organizational, technical, and relational barriers. One recurring issue is the lack of integration with legacy systems. Cheshmberah and Beheshtikia (2020) note that many firms struggle to align new AI, blockchain, or IoT platforms with existing ERP and procurement systems, resulting in inefficiencies and data silos. Similarly, Lockamy and McCormack (2004, 2013) argue that organizations often adopt tools prematurely, before reaching the necessary maturity stage, which leads to underutilization and poor returns on investment.

Other barriers include talent and skills gaps (Handfield and Linton, 2017) and cultural resistance to change (ASCM, 2022), both of which limit the ability to capture value from digital tools. A particularly critical challenge, highlighted by industry insights, is poor supplier adoption. Even when buyers deploy advanced sourcing technologies, smaller suppliers may lack the necessary resources or incentives to engage, resulting in significant misalignment within the sourcing ecosystem.

Without a clear framework, technology adoption risks becoming fragmented and superficial. Instead of treating digital tools as isolated upgrades, organizations should map each technology to the three pillars of Supply Chain 5.0: Sustainability, resilience, and human-centricity. This classification ensures that technologies are directly linked to strategic objectives rather than being adopted as "nice-to-have" add-ons. By adopting this mapping approach, sourcing technologies are reframed not as disconnected tools but as purpose-driven enablers of Supply Chain 5.0.

Sustainability tech ensures what is sourced aligns with environmental and ethical standards.
→ ethical, transparent, environmentally sound sourcing.

Resilience tech ensures how sourcing adapts to shocks and disruptions.
→ agility, adaptability, and risk resistance.

Human-centric tech ensures why and with whom sourcing decisions are made while fostering trust, fairness, and collaboration.
→ fairness, trust, and collaborative supplier relationships.

Maturity Stages: Basic, Integrated, Predictive

As in the previous chapter, this Source section also follows a basic, integrated, and predictive maturity stage to represent the progression in supply chain capabilities for how organizations source and correlate with the adoption of technologies, as shown in Figure 6.1.

In Industry 5.0, sourcing extends traditional cost-based decisions to incorporate intelligent, collaborative, and adaptive systems. This evolution enables supply chains to become more resilient, responsive, and ethically aligned. The following maturity model outlines how sourcing practices progress from basic cost-driven approaches to predictive, risk-aware systems that leverage advanced technologies.

Figure 6.1 Source Maturity Stages

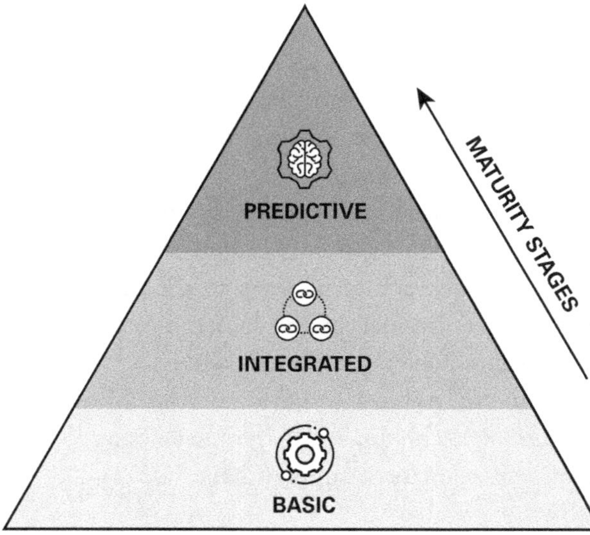

Basic

The basic stage is characterized by low technical maturity and cost-based sourcing decisions. Usually, organizations at this stage rely on spreadsheets, manual RFQs, and basic ERP systems. Decisions are primarily driven by price, with limited visibility into supplier performance or risk. Technology adoption is minimal and sourcing is reactive rather than strategic.

Key traits: Price-driven procurement, minimal supplier engagement, manual processes (e.g., spreadsheets, email RFQs), short-term focus.

Challenges: Limited visibility into supplier risks, poor responsiveness to disruptions, lack of strategic alignment, and high administrative burden.

Role of technologies: Basic digital tools for procurement, static data analysis, and limited automation.

Technology examples: Excel-based cost analysis, basic ERP modules, email-based RFQs.

Impact: Low agility and resilience, high vulnerability to supply shocks, missed opportunities for innovation and value creation.

Integrated

At this stage, companies begin to use digital platforms to manage supplier relationships. Tools like SRM (Supplier Relationship Management) systems and cloud-based procurement portals enable real-time communication, performance tracking, and joint planning. The focus shifts from cost to value creation through collaboration.

Key traits: Strategic supplier relationships, real-time data sharing, collaborative planning and forecasting, focus on value and performance.

Challenges: Data integration across platforms, supplier onboarding and training, balancing cost with collaboration.

Role of technologies: Platforms that enable supplier visibility and engagement, real-time dashboards and performance metrics, workflow automation.

Technology examples: Supplier relationship management (SRM) systems, cloud-based procurement platforms, EDI and API integrations.

Impact: Improved supplier performance, enhanced transparency and trust, reduced lead times, and better forecasting accuracy.

Predictive

At the highest maturity level, sourcing becomes a strategic lever for resilience. AI and ML tools predict disruptions, optimize supplier portfolios, and enable dynamic sourcing decisions. Technologies such as blockchain, digital twins, and autonomous procurement agents support proactive and ethical sourcing that aligns with sustainability goals.

Key traits: Proactive risk management, dynamic sourcing strategies, AI-driven decision-making, sustainability, and ethics embedded in sourcing.

Challenges: Data quality and governance, complexity of predictive models, ethical and regulatory compliance.

Role of technologies: Advanced analytics and machine learning, real-time risk monitoring, autonomous sourcing agents.

Technology examples: AI-based risk engines, blockchain for traceability, digital twins for supplier ecosystems, autonomous procurement bots.

Impact: High resilience and adaptability, strategic sourcing aligned with goals, competitive advantage through intelligent sourcing.

As sourcing strategies evolve through the maturity stages of Basic, Integrated, and Predictive, organizations unlock progressively greater value, resilience, and strategic alignment. The journey from cost-driven decisions to intelligent, adaptive sourcing reflects not only technological advancement but also a shift in mindset, from transactional to collaborative, and ultimately to anticipatory. This evolution is not linear but iterative, requiring continuous investment in data, relationships, and ethical frameworks to thrive in the human-centric landscape of Industry 5.0. A compelling real-life example of a company that evolved from basic to predictive sourcing is Apple Inc.

REAL-WORLD EXAMPLE Apple Inc: From Cost-Based to Predictive Sourcing

In its early years, Apple Inc. exemplified the Basic Sourcing stage by prioritizing cost-efficiency through extensive outsourcing of manufacturing operations, particularly to China. This approach enabled rapid scaling and competitive pricing but came with significant limitations, including minimal visibility into supplier risks and over-reliance on a single geographic region (Apple, 2023). Technologies supporting this stage consist mainly of basic ERP systems and manual RFQ processes. As with the rest of the world (Guo et al., 2025), the impact of this sourcing model became evident during global disruptions such as the COVID-19 pandemic and geopolitical tensions, which exposed vulnerabilities in Apple's supply chain and highlighted the need for greater agility and resilience. These challenges catalyzed Apple's transition toward more advanced sourcing strategies.

Apple's transition to Integrated Sourcing marked a strategic shift from transactional procurement to collaborative supplier relationships (McMillan, 2025). In the Predictive Sourcing stage, Apple utilized advanced technologies to proactively manage risks, optimize sourcing decisions, and promote environmental and social responsibility throughout its global network (Pearson, 2025). The integration of AI-driven forecasting, machine learning algorithms, and real-time analytics enabled Apple to anticipate disruptions and dynamically adjust its sourcing strategies. As a result, the initiative's strategy diversified manufacturing across India, Vietnam, and Malaysia, reducing geopolitical exposure and enhancing resilience (Collins, 2025). Blockchain and digital twins further improved traceability and supplier transparency, while sustainability goals, such as achieving a carbon-neutral supply chain by 2030, were embedded into sourcing criteria (Apple, 2020). These capabilities turned Apple's supply chain into a strategic advantage, allowing it to drive ongoing improvement in supplier relationships. This involves holding both Apple and its suppliers accountable from the start, from product design to end-of-life recycling (Perry, 2024). The strategy and standards apply across all aspects of Apple's procurement and supply chain relationships, regardless of the services each supplier provides.

A Mental Shift in Sourcing

Sourcing marks the beginning of ethical and sustainable value chains. In Supply Chain 5.0, organizations must go beyond efficiency and profitability to take on greater responsibility. The sourcing process is where environmental impact originates, through raw material extraction, emissions, and water usage, and where labor practices, supplier diversity, and circular economy strategies are first shaped. It is also the point where ethical sourcing and human rights protections are embedded into operations. Technologies that support this transformation include carbon tracking platforms, digital product passports, AI-driven analytics, blockchain for ethical verification, standardized traceability systems, and lifecycle assessment tools.

Unlike Industry 4.0, which emphasized automation for speed and cost, Supply Chain 5.0 prioritizes augmented intelligence, the strategic collaboration between humans and machines. AI handles routine tasks, such as vendor scoring and risk modeling, while humans apply judgment in areas like trust, ethics, and social impact. Negotiation, innovation, and partnership development still rely on empathy and relationship-building. Technologies such as generative AI for scenario simulation, contract summarization, and negotiation strategy development, along with smart contracts and industrial sensors, enhance this collaboration by providing real-time insights into supplier behavior and ethical compliance.

Global risks often originate at the source. From pandemics and geopolitical tensions to climate events and labor violations, disruptions frequently begin with suppliers. Shortages of critical materials, supplier shutdowns, and reputational damage from unethical practices can severely impact profitability. Supply Chain 5.0 shifts from reactive procurement to proactive, risk-aware sourcing. Technologies like digital twins, blockchain, sensor tracking, and predictive analytics enable dynamic supplier risk scoring and early warning systems, allowing companies to anticipate and mitigate disruptions before they escalate.

Figure 6.2 Comprehensive Sourcing Capabilities Under Supply Chain 5.0

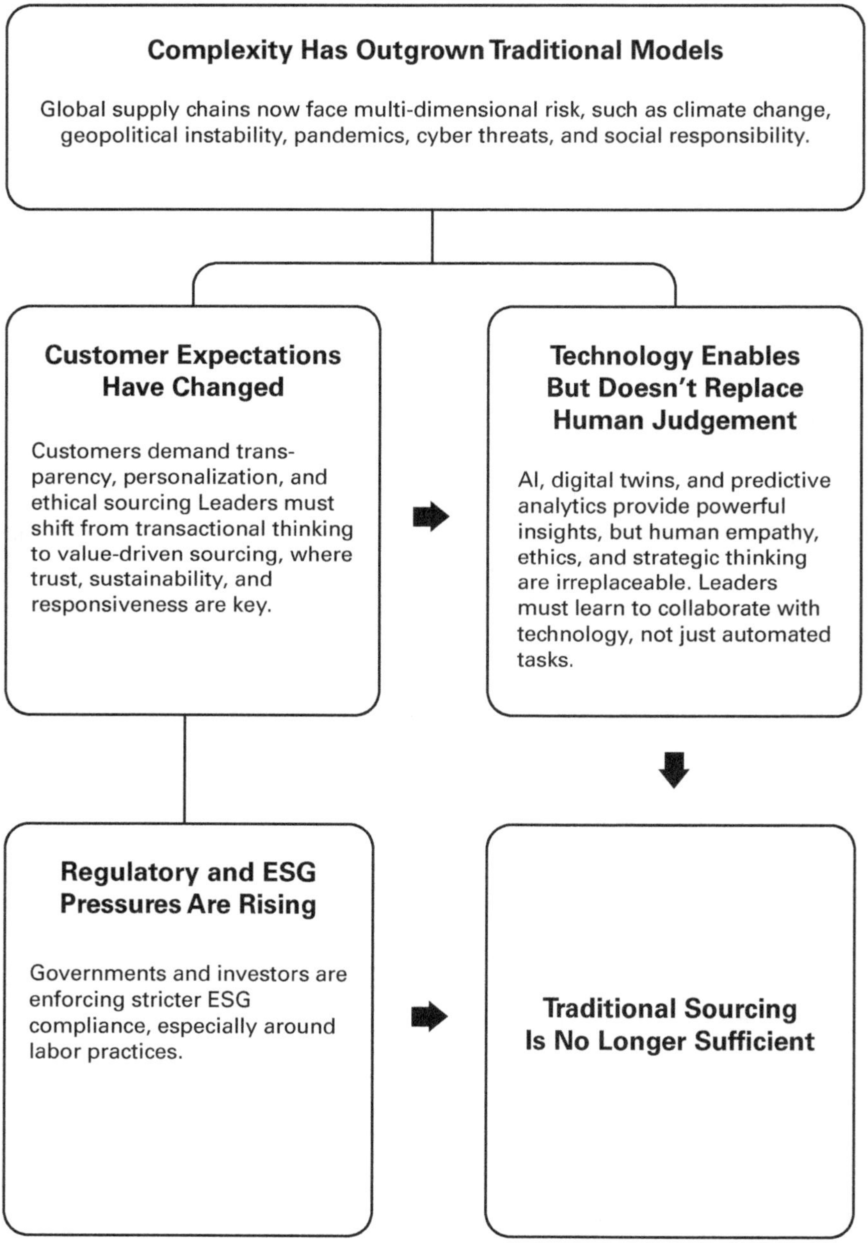

Sourcing is also the foundation of resiliency, agility, and customization. As customers demand faster, more transparent, and personalized experiences, upstream decisions must support flexible production models. Agile sourcing enables make-to-order and mass customization, while localized and nearshoring strategies depend on intelligent supplier networks. Technologies such as digital twins simulate supplier networks and demand shifts, while AI-powered sourcing platforms match buyers with localized suppliers and predict market trends to inform sourcing decisions that support personalization.

To remain competitive, resilient, and relevant, supply chain leaders must make a strategic mental shift toward the principles of Supply Chain 5.0. Traditional sourcing models, which focus on cost and speed, are no longer sufficient in a world of multidimensional risks, evolving customer expectations, and rising ESG pressures. Leaders must embrace value-driven sourcing, where technology enables, but does not replace, human judgment. Figure 6.2 illustrates this transformation: From transactional procurement to proactive, ethical, and human-centric sourcing.

Before organizations can fully embrace the principles of Supply Chain 5.0, they must assess their readiness and establish a clear roadmap for implementation. This shift requires more than adopting new technologies; it demands a transformation in mindset, capabilities, and strategic alignment. The checklist in Table 6.4 is designed to help practitioners evaluate their current sourcing maturity, identify gaps in ethical, resilient, and intelligent sourcing practices, and prioritize actions that align with the human-centric, value-driven goals of Supply Chain 5.0. By using this tool, leaders can move from aspiration to execution with clarity and confidence.

Table 6.4 Readiness and Implementation Checklist

Readiness Area	Indicators to Evaluate	Quick Win or Long-Term?
Strategic Alignment	Sourcing strategies explicitly include resilience, ethics, and emissions goals.	Long-Term
Digital and Technological Infrastructure	Platforms support supplier data collection, traceability, and automated compliance.	Quick Win (data visibility); Long-Term (integration)
Workforce Readiness and Culture	Sourcing teams are trained in ESG, digital procurement, and inclusive negotiation practices.	Quick Win (training); Long-Term (mindset)

(continued)

Table 6.4 (Continued)

Readiness Area	Indicators to Evaluate	Quick Win or Long-Term?
Supplier and Partner Ecosystem	Partners are digitally connected, audited for ESG, and engaged in innovation.	Long-Term
Performance Measurement and Governance	KPIs include supplier emissions, labor practices, and multi-tier visibility. Governance supports escalation paths.	Quick Win (scorecards); Long-Term (accountability)

Actionable Principles for Source

- Shift from cost-based procurement to value-driven sourcing.
- Embed predictive risk management into supplier selection.
- Embed sustainability and human rights criteria into supplier selection and contracts.
- Diversify supplier bases across geographies, tiers, and business models.
- Prioritize long-term relationships built on transparency and mutual development.
- Use technology to improve visibility, automation, and decision quality.
- Create shared value by engaging suppliers in innovation and continuous improvement.
- Treat sourcing as a lever for resilience, not just cost control.
- Implement digital tools to ensure visibility across the sourcing network.

KEY TAKEAWAYS

- Source is no longer just a transactional process; it is a strategic function that shapes brand, continuity, and impact.
- Practitioners must recognize that sourcing decisions shape the environmental, social, and economic footprint of the entire supply chain.
- In Supply Chain 5.0, AI doesn't replace human judgment; it augments it. While algorithms handle routine tasks such as supplier scoring and risk modeling, humans provide critical oversight in areas like trust, ethics,

and relationship building. This synergy enables smarter, faster, and more responsible sourcing decisions.

- Resilient sourcing systems diversify risk while aligning operations with environmental and social values.
- As organizations move from Basic to Predictive, they gain not just speed and accuracy, but resilience (the ability to anticipate, adapt, and recover from disruptions).
- The Predictive stage is most aligned with Industry 5.0, but only when it integrates human judgment, ethical reasoning, and stakeholder values.
- A thoughtful implementation roadmap and continuous learning culture are essential for long-term success in digitally transforming Source.
- Both direct and indirect procurement are redefined to support sustainability, traceability, and customer-centricity.
- Indirect sourcing, often overlooked, becomes a key contributor to carbon neutrality, digital transformation, and agile operations, powered by AI and flexible supplier networks.
- Source Return has evolved from a reactive function into a strategic process that leverages predictive technologies and sustainable practices to enable closed-loop systems, supporting circular economy goals and minimizing waste.

References

Association for Supply Chain Management (ASCM) (2022) SCOR Digital Standard.

Association for Supply Chain Management (ASCM) (2026) SCOR Digital Standard.

Apple (2020) Apple commits to be 100 percent carbon neutral for its supply chain and products by 2030. Apple.com www.apple.com/newsroom/2020/07/apple-commits-to-be-100-percent-carbon-neutral-for-its-supply-chain-and-products-by-2030/ (archived at https://perma.cc/92N8-CEU6)

Apple (2023) *Supplier Responsibility Progress Report*. Apple.com www.supplychainreports.apple/home/default.aspx (archived at https://perma.cc/M5QQ-4SYC)

Belcic, I. and Stryker, C. (2025) What are watsonx agents? IBM. www.ibm.com/think/topics/watsonx-agents (archived at https://perma.cc/568V-GZRS)

Boyd, K. (2025) The future of work is here: Transforming our employee experience with AI. *Inside Track*. Microsoft. www.microsoft.com/insidetrack/blog/the-future-of-work-is-here-transforming-our-employee-experience-with-ai/?utm_source=chatgpt.com (archived at https://perma.cc/Q9QV-K9EM)

Caterpillar (2025a) Remanufacturing: Cat Reman® programs. Caterpillar Inc. www.caterpillar.com/en/company/sustainability/remanufacturing.html (archived at https://perma.cc/8QVA-LJ5R)

Caterpillar (2025b) The benefits of remanufacturing. www.caterpillar.com/en/company/sustainability/remanufacturing/benefits.html (archived at https://perma.cc/KM6V-HTZW)

Caterpillar (2025c) Remanufactured products and rebuilt products. www.caterpillar.com/en/company/sustainability/remanufacturing.html (archived at https://perma.cc/K8MT-TXE2)

Cheshmberah, M. and Beheshtikia, S. (2020) Supply chain management maturity: An all-encompassing literature review on models, dimensions and approaches. *LogForum*, 16(1), 103–16.

Christopher, M. (2022) *Logistics and Supply Chain Management: Creating value-adding networks* (6th ed.) FT Press.

Collins, G. (2025) Apple shifts supply chain by diversifying production. *Supply Chain Digital*.

European Commission (2025) Batteries—ensuring that batteries placed on the EU market are sustainable and circular throughout their whole life cycle. https://environment.ec.europa.eu/topics/waste-and-recycling/batteries_en (archived at https://perma.cc/V2YV-2GWT)

European Commission (2022) EU strategy for sustainable and circular textiles. Directorate-General for Environment. https://environment.ec.europa.eu/strategy/textiles-strategy_en (archived at https://perma.cc/7VUX-83NH)

Global Performance Group (2025) How Unilever changed procurement managers' playbook. https://globalperformancegroup.com/how-unilever-changed-procurements-playbook/ (archived at https://perma.cc/M4KR-ETMQ)

Guo, Y., Liu, F., Song, J. S. and Wang, S. (2025) Supply chain resilience: A review from the inventory management perspective. *Fundamental Research*, 5(2), 450–63.

Handfield, R. and Linton, T. (2017) *The LIVING Supply Chain: The evolving imperative of operating in real time*. John Wiley & Sons.

Hargreaves, L. (2024, December 11) Unilever CFO takes on procurement. *Procurement Magazine*. https://procurementmag.com/procurement-strategy/unilever-cfo-takes-on-procurement (archived at https://perma.cc/GYD5-4EFF)

IBM (2025, June 30) Ready to put AI to work? So are IBM's AI agents. www.ibm.com/new/announcements/ready-to-put-ai-to-work-so-are-our-agents (archived at https://perma.cc/LEG9-7ADE)

Lockamy III, A. and McCormack, K. (2004) The development of a supply chain management process maturity model using the concepts of business process orientation. *Supply Chain Management: An International Journal*, 9(4), 272–78.

Lockamy, A. and McCormack, K. (2013) The effect of supply chain maturity on performance: An empirical study. *1st Annual Int. Interdisciplinary Conference*, Azores.

Linder, J. C., Jarvenpaa, S. and Davenport, T. H. (2003) Toward an innovation sourcing strategy. *MIT Sloan Management Review*.

LVMH (2025) Digital Product Passport (DPP): Tracing the origin and life of products. *LVMH*. www.lvmh.com/en/commitment-in-action/for-the-environment/digital-product-passport (archived at https://perma.cc/F6UJ-H64K)

McGregor, K. (2025, April 14) Digital product passports: Lessons from an early adopter. *Vogue Business*. www.voguebusiness.com/story/technology/digital-product-passports-lessons-from-an-early-adopter

McMillan, A. (2025) How Apple's US Investment Changes Sourcing Outlook. *Procurement Magazine*.

Optel Group (2025) What is Industry 5.0 and how will it affect supply chain transparency and sustainability? Optel. www.optelgroup.com/en/blog/what-is-industry-5-0-and-how-will-it-affect-supply-chain-transparency-and-sustainability/ (archived at https://perma.cc/B9LB-2X2C)

Pearson, R. (2025) Apple's supply chain innovation: A benchmark for electronics brands. *IT in the Supply Chain*. https://itsupplychain.com/apples-supply-chain-innovation-a-benchmark-for-electronics-brands/ (archived at https://perma.cc/ET4A-LHS7)

Perry, N. (2024) Continuous Improvement in Apple's Procurement Strategy. Procurement Magazine.

Rejeb, A., Rejeb, K., Keogh, J. G. and Süle, E. (2025, April 22) When Industry 5.0 meets the circular economy: A systematic literature review. *Circular Economy and Sustainability*, 5, 2621–652. https://doi.org/10.1007/s43615-025-00570-y (archived at https://perma.cc/MQH6-P8PE)

Roberts-Islam, B. (2024, October 14) The fashion exec's guide to digital product passports. Vogue Business. www.voguebusiness.com/story/sustainability/the-fashion-execs-guide-to-digital-product-passports (archived at https://perma.cc/VFQ5-UZB4)

Siemens (2025) Siemens Battery Passport – Leading the way to a more transparent and sustainable battery industry. Siemens Xcelerator Global. https://xcelerator.siemens.com/global/en/industries/battery-manufacturing/battery-passport.html (archived at https://perma.cc/8PJM-PLMM)

Transform: Adding Value to Products and Services

07

Industry 5.0 is designed to create more responsible factories while maintaining all the benefits of the 4.0 digital transformation years.

HÉLÈNE KYRIAKAKIS, FORBES COUNCILS MEMBER

Transform: Smart Manufacturing Meets Human Ingenuity

Across a wide range of industries, transformation is one of the standardized processes that describes supply chain activities involved in converting inputs into outputs. This includes any value-adding process that changes the physical, digital, or state attributes of goods, services, or information. The Transform process in the SCOR DS describes the activities associated with creating products and services (ASCM, 2022). However, under Supply Chain 5.0, we would like you to understand that transformation extends beyond traditional manufacturing processes; it can involve additional steps such as product assembly and disassembly, packaging, testing and inspection, recycling or refurbishment, software configuration, maintenance, repair, overhaul, data transformation, and product personalization that add value to the supply chain. In the Supply Chain 5.0 paradigm, transformation is not only about generating output, and it also involves creating meaningful, ethical, and adaptive value. It becomes the place where technology, people, and purpose converge to meet the demands of a more connected system.

Manufacturing industries worldwide are undergoing profound disruption amid rising volatility and increasing complexity. According to the World Economic Forum's *Global Risks Report 2025*, supply chains are facing compounded shocks from climate-related disasters, geopolitical fragmentation, and escalating cyber threats, each amplifying the impact of the others. Small- and medium-sized enterprises (SMEs), which constitute roughly 90 percent of businesses and over half of global employment, are especially vulnerable. With limited capital, infrastructure, and supply chain visibility, many SMEs struggle to absorb or adapt to these cascading disruptions. As a result, entire manufacturing ecosystems risk becoming less resilient, less competitive, and increasingly misaligned with evolving industrial, environmental, and societal expectations.

While Industry 4.0 focused on automation and efficiency, Industry 5.0 particularly integrated technology with human-centric values, sustainability, and resilience.

- Resilience: Achieved through flexible production scheduling, human-machine collaboration, local sourcing, capacity reallocation, and real-time monitoring, enabling supply chains to adapt quickly to disruptions while maintaining operational continuity.
- Sustainability: Embedded via circular manufacturing models, energy-efficient technologies, reduced waste, and the use of low-impact, ethically sourced materials, ensuring that transformation activities align with environmental and social goals.
- Human-centricity: Advanced through ergonomic system design, digital augmentation (e.g., AR, co-bots), AI-driven production adjustments, and a focus on skilled, meaningful work, positioning people not just as operators, but as empowered contributors to innovation and value creation.

The newest SCOR DS model effectively highlights key characteristics of modern supply chains. The model recognizes that the Transform processes apply to both physical and digital supply chains, covering a wide range of production and conversion activities. It supports various fulfillment strategies, including make-to-stock, make-to-order, and engineer-to-order, and encompasses both internally managed and outsourced transformation operations. These characteristics recognize that the Transform process is tightly integrated with other core supply chain functions, such as Source, Deliver, Return, and Enable, ensuring seamless flow across the value chain. In modern supply chains, transformation is often optimized through automation, AI and ML technologies, digital twins, and real-time visibility tools, enabling greater agility, efficiency, and responsiveness.

Table 7.1 presents a high-level overview of the key processes that align with the objectives of **Supply Chain 5.0** within the **Transform** function. To set the foundation, the second column revisits the fundamental definitions from the **SCOR DS model**, providing a clear reference point before exploring their evolution in context. Then, each aspect is examined in detail, with real-world examples included to demonstrate its practical application and relevance across industries.

Transform Product

In the context of Supply Chain 5.0, the process of transforming a product evolves beyond traditional notions of production (Villar et al., 2023). While it still involves converting raw materials or components into finished goods, it now does so through the integration of advanced technologies with human intelligence, emphasizes sustainable methods, and supports adaptive, resilient systems (Ivanov, 2023). Labor is no longer limited to repetitive manual work, but redefined through human–machine collaboration, where skilled workers are empowered by robotics, AI, and digital tools. Machinery and production systems increasingly rely on real-time data, predictive analytics, and digital twins that optimize operations while reducing energy use, waste, and emissions. Furthermore, biological and chemical processes are being reengineered with green chemistry principles and circular economy models. In Supply Chain 5.0, transformation is not just about production efficiency; it is about creating value that is ethical, personalized, sustainable, and responsive to dynamic global demands.

In particular, Industry 5.0 represents a purposeful evolution of manufacturing into the core of product creation. Throughout our research for this book, we have identified three key characteristics that supply chain leaders need to be aware of under Supply Chain 5.0.

1. Rebalancing Humans and Machines

One of the defining shifts in Industry 5.0 is the reintegration of human creativity, judgment, and values alongside machines. Instead of entirely replacing humans, advanced robotics, AI, and collaborative automation (co-robots

Table 7.1 Evolution of Transform Processes: SCOR DS and Supply Chain 5.0

Transform Aspect	SCOR DS Definition	Supply Chain 5.0 Evolution
Transform Product	Transforming a product involves converting raw materials, ingredients, components, or sub-assemblies into a finished, tangible good through the application of labor, machinery, tools, and, in some cases, biological or chemical processes.	The process of transforming a product evolves beyond traditional notions of production. While it still involves converting raw materials or components into finished goods, it now does so in a way that integrates advanced technologies with human intelligence, emphasizes sustainable methods, and supports adaptive, resilient systems.
Transform Service	Transforming a service involves enabling outcomes that customers seek to achieve, by delivering value through activities, expertise, or experiences, without transferring ownership of specific assets, costs, or risks. Rather than producing a tangible product, this process focuses on creating intangible value through access, convenience, customization, or performance that aligns with customer expectations and business objectives.	The transformation of services evolves from simply facilitating customer outcomes to orchestrating adaptive, intelligent, and human-centric service experiences. Traditional service models often focused on efficiency and standardization, delivering outcomes without transferring ownership of assets, costs, or risks. In contrast, Supply Chain 5.0 leverages digital technologies (such as AI, IoT, and blockchain) alongside human insight to create services that are personalized, predictive, and co-created with the customer.
Transform Maintenance, Repair, and Overhaul (MRO)	Refers to the processes involved in maintaining, restoring, or enhancing the performance of an asset to ensure it remains in optimal working condition. These activities are critical to extending asset life, minimizing downtime, and sustaining operational reliability across the supply chain.	The transformation of Maintenance, Repair, and Overhaul (MRO) shifts from reactive or scheduled maintenance to predictive, intelligent, and human-augmented asset care. MRO activities now anticipate failures before they occur, allowing for real-time diagnostics and targeted interventions. MRO becomes a strategic pillar of resilience and sustainability, aligning asset performance with business continuity and environmental responsibility.

or "cobots") work in concert with skilled operators. This human–machine symbiosis enables humans to focus on higher-value tasks, such as problem-solving, customization, and innovation, while machines handle repetitive or hazardous tasks reliably (Shabur et al., 2025).

For example, sensors and digital twins can monitor machine health in real time, alerting operators to potential faults before breakdowns occur. The human technician then steps in, interpreting diagnostics, deciding corrective actions, or making real-time adjustments. Thus, maintenance, quality control, and adaptation become more proactive and less reactive. Novel technologies, such as virtual reality, augmented reality, mixed reality, and haptics, can serve as "augmentation" to establish an inclusive, smart, and sustainable production process that encourages human creativity and expertise (Zafar et al., 2024).

REAL-WORLD EXAMPLE Siemens and KUKA Human–Robot Collaboration

Siemens (in collaboration with robotics company KUKA) has implemented human-robot collaboration (HRC) in its factory settings using KUKA's LBR iiwa cobots. In one case, cobots are deployed to work alongside human operators in shared workspaces, assisting with tasks like handling workpieces, moving parts, and performing quality checks (KUKA, 2016, 2022).

What makes this a strong example of Industry 5.0 in action:

- The cobots are sensitive and lightweight, equipped with sensors so they can safely interact with humans without needing full safety cages or barriers.
- Real-time feedback and human oversight remain central: The machines undertake repetitive or physically demanding tasks, and humans handle more interpretive or value-adding work like diagnostics, decision-making, adapting to unexpected conditions, or quality oversight.
- The collaboration improves efficiency and safety while also enabling more responsive manufacturing: If something deviates, the human operator intervenes. This helps transform maintenance and quality control from reactive to more proactive processes.

SUMMARY SNAPSHOT

In 2025, Siemens, utilizing KUKA's cobots, demonstrates how humans and machines can share tasks: Machines carry out repetitive or hazardous operations, while human workers focus on monitoring, judgment, and adaptation. This human–machine symbiosis supports the shift toward continuous, smart, and resilient production, a key tenet of Industry 5.0.

2. Sustainability and Circularity Built In

In Industry 5.0, sustainability is not a boxed add-on but a design principle. Manufacturing processes are reimagined to minimize waste, optimize energy use, and support material reuse or remanufacturing (Rame et al., 2024; Rejeb et al., 2025).

This means more than just efficient resource consumption; it involves closing loops, designing for disassembly, utilizing renewable energy, and selecting materials based on their environmental impact. For instance, additive manufacturing (3D printing) can produce complex geometries with less material waste, and modular design enables parts to be refurbished or reused rather than discarded.

REAL-WORLD EXAMPLE Herman Miller: Design for Disassembly in Furniture

Furniture manufacturer Herman Miller has integrated disassembly steps into its product lines, allowing parts to be separated, recycled, or remanufactured more easily (MillerKnoll, 2025). In 2025, Herman Miller continues to implement Design for Disassembly (DfD) principles by reducing waste, using sustainable and recycled materials, and expanding its take-back programs. DfD is an integral part of the company's circular economy strategy, which aims for products to be reused or recycled at the end of their lifecycle (Lee and Bony, 2007).

This is a compelling example because:

- it demonstrates how design for disassembly can be built into everyday products, not just in high-tech sectors;

- it supports circularity by enabling material recovery and remanufacture rather than disposal;
- it aligns well with Industry 5.0's notion that sustainability is a design principle, not an afterthought.

SUMMARY SNAPSHOT

Design for Disassembly (DfD) in furniture (and other industries) is an excellent example of how Supply Chain 5.0 integrates sustainability, human-centricity, and resilience into both product design and end-to-end supply chain strategy.

- *Sustainability is designed, not an afterthought.* In Supply Chain 5.0, sustainability is embedded from the start, not retrofitted later. Under Supply Chain 5.0, it is important because it minimizes environmental footprint across the product lifecycle, from sourcing and production to reverse logistics and end-of-life recovery.
- *Disassembly-focused design not only helps recyclers but also makes the furniture easier to assemble, repair, or modify by end-users and service technicians.* Workers on the factory floor benefit from ergonomically friendly assembly and disassembly processes, allowing consumers to repair their products instead of discarding them.
- *Resilience through circular supply chains.* When parts and materials are recoverable, companies are less dependent on volatile global supply markets for raw inputs. Disassembled components can be returned, refurbished, and reintroduced into production, creating flexible material flows and multi-sourcing options.

3. Adaptive Production and Resilience

Manufacturing under Industry 5.0 must be resilient and flexible in the face of disruptions, whether from supply shocks, climate-related events, or shifting demand. Production systems are designed to reconfigure dynamically: Lines adapt to new variants, local micro-factories can take over short runs, and supplier networks change as needed (Shabur et al., 2025; Raja Santhi and Muthuswamy, 2023).

Digital tools, such as AI and ML, support this adaptability by predicting demand fluctuations, optimizing scheduling, and orchestrating supply chain responses in real-time. This responsiveness not only buffers against volatility but also enables more personalized and just-in-time manufacturing.

REAL-WORLD EXAMPLE Siemens: Adaptive Production and Connected Factories

Siemens is transforming traditional manufacturing sites into smart, responsive plants that adjust in real time to changes in demand, supply, or process conditions. Adaptive production represents more than just a technological enhancement; it marks a fundamental shift in manufacturing philosophy. At this new frontier, advanced technologies converge to form highly autonomous environments, where interconnected production systems surpass the limitations of conventional automation. Leveraging tools such as artificial intelligence, digital twins, and robotics, manufacturers are building smart, responsive operations that not only execute tasks but also continuously learn, make informed decisions, and evolve in real-time (MIT Technology Review Insights, 2025).

Here are some specifics to highlight (Bloomberg Media Studios, 2025; Siemens AG 2025a, 2025b, 2025c, 2025d):

- At its Kalwa, India factory, Siemens integrated digital twins, IT/OT convergence, and advanced automation. The result: A 35 percent increase in production capacity, an 86 percent reduction in carbon footprint, and expansion from 77 product variants to over 350, all on a single production line.
- Siemens describes its adaptive production approach as one that "continuously adjust[s] processes" using real-time data, AI, and automation, allowing the factory to reconfigure, scale, and respond to shifts rather than being locked into static production plans.
- Siemens' "Connected Factories" vision includes so-called morphing factories—autonomous, self-configuring production units that can pivot product lines, reallocate resources, and dynamically respond to disruptions or product changes.

SUMMARY SNAPSHOT

In Supply Chain 5.0, adaptive production transforms the factory floor into a living, learning system, one that is as responsive to human needs and global risks as it is to economic pressures. It's not just smart manufacturing; it's manufacturing with purpose, agility, and humanity built in.

In Supply Chain 5.0, resilience is proactive—not just the ability to bounce back, but to anticipate and adapt to disruptions in real time. Adaptive production enables this by reconfiguring production lines quickly to handle new product variants or demand shifts, balancing global and local sourcing, shifting production loads to regional micro-factories or suppliers when disruption hits, and by using AI and digital twins to simulate and optimize responses to real-world constraints (e.g., supply shortages, labor disruptions, geopolitical shocks). In Supply Chain 5.0, human-centricity empowers workers in smart environments. Rather than replacing humans, adaptive production enables collaborative roles for skilled workers. Humans oversee adaptive systems, make critical decisions, and intervene when AI hits its limits. Systems are also designed to be ergonomic, intuitive, and assistive, supporting human well-being.

Transform Service

While transforming a product is centered on physical change, transforming a service is focused on facilitating desired outcomes that customers want to achieve without transferring ownership (ASCM, 2022).

In Supply Chain 5.0, the transformation of services evolves from merely facilitating customer outcomes to orchestrating adaptive, intelligent, and human-centric service experiences. Traditional service models emphasized efficiency and standardization, delivering outcomes without transferring ownership of assets, costs, or risks. Today, leading organizations leverage digital technologies such as AI, IoT, and blockchain, combined with human insight, to create services that are personalized, predictive, and co-created with the customer.

Rather than delivering one-size-fits-all solutions, services in Supply Chain 5.0 are dynamically tailored based on real-time data, behavioral trends, and evolving customer expectations. For instance, Amazon Web Services (AWS) uses predictive analytics and usage-based billing to personalize cloud infrastructure solutions at scale, allowing customers to dynamically configure compute and storage based on their operational needs, enhancing agility without ownership burdens (AWS, 2025a, 2025b). Salesforce, on the other hand, demonstrates how services can be co-created with customers through AI-enhanced CRM platforms. Using tools like Einstein AI, Salesforce enables businesses to personalize customer engagement, predict behavior, and automate decision-making, turning service delivery into a collaborative, value-generating process that evolves with each customer interaction.

At the same time, resilience and sustainability are embedded in modern service design. These companies build continuity into their platforms through cloud-native infrastructure, redundancy, and adaptive service models, while also committing to ethical practices and reducing environmental impact, such as AWS's pledge to use 100 percent renewable energy (Amazon Staff, 2025) or DHL's GoGreen initiative to decarbonize global logistics (DHL, 2025).

In this evolved model, service transformation becomes a strategic enabler, delivering not just outcomes but experiences that are intelligent, inclusive, resilient, and sustainable. Services in Supply Chain 5.0 are not just efficient; they are empathetic, ethical, and engineered for impact.

Throughout our research for this book, we have identified two key characteristics that supply chain leaders need to be aware of under Supply Chain 5.0. These two characteristics, (1) co-creation and (2) embedded resilience, represent a fundamental shift in how services are conceived and delivered.

1. Co-Creation and Personalization as Strategic Imperatives

In Supply Chain 5.0, services are no longer designed in isolation and pushed to customers; they are co-created in real time through ongoing interaction, feedback, and customization. Leading firms embed digital platforms, AI-driven insights, and modular service architectures to deliver outcomes that are uniquely tailored to each customer's needs and evolving expectations. Why does it matter? In today's business environments, personalization drives differentiation, enhances customer satisfaction, and increases brand loyalty. The implication for leaders in supply chains is that they must design services that are flexible, data-informed, and easily configurable, moving away from rigid, standardized solutions.

2. Resilience and Sustainability Embedded in Service Delivery

Service transformation in Supply Chain 5.0 also demands built-in resilience and sustainability, rather than treating these as afterthoughts. Services must adapt quickly to disruption (e.g., demand surges, climate events, labor shortages) while operating with minimal environmental and social impact. Why does it matter? Customers and regulators increasingly expect continuity of service and alignment with ESG values. Leaders must invest in real-time monitoring, green service models, and ethical supply chain design to build services that are both robust and responsible.

Though Kodak is not a pure "service transformation" business, it is often cited as a failure to adapt to digital transformation, which had service elements (digital imaging, printing, online services). The example offers several characteristics. The company's rigid model and low service innovation did not adapt to digital photography. They failed to pivot toward more personalized, digital services (e.g., cloud photo services, digital printing subscriptions, mobile apps) compellingly. Kodak also resisted disruption. Kodak's business was heavily dependent on film, chemicals, and print labs, all of which were disrupted. The company lacked the agility to reconfigure operations, partner networks, or revenue streams quickly. As digital services grew, consumers expected more control, easy sharing, integration, and customization, areas where Kodak lagged behind newer entrants.

Challenges and Considerations of Transform in Supply Chain 5.0

Of course, the transition to Industry 5.0 and Supply Chain 5.0 is not without hurdles. Integration of advanced systems with legacy infrastructure, ethical concerns around AI, cybersecurity risks, capital investment, and regulatory frameworks all pose significant challenges (Shabur, 2025; Barata and Kayser, 2023).

Another challenge is balancing standardization with personalization. Traditional services rely on standardized processes to ensure efficiency and scalability. Supply Chain 5.0 demands hyper-personalized, co-created services tailored to real-time customer needs. Leaders must re-engineer service architectures to remain modular and adaptive while still ensuring reliability and cost-effectiveness. Over-customization may increase complexity, cost, and risk.

Integrating human-centric design into services and product models is also a challenge. Many services were built to minimize human intervention (Industry 4.0 style). Supply Chain 5.0 reverses that logic, emphasizing worker empowerment, collaborative platforms, and customer co-creation. Organizations must redesign workflows, interfaces, and roles to support meaningful, skilled human contributions, not just automation.

Technological complexity and integration are challenges that the industry must also address. Transforming services and products in industrial manufacturing requires integration of AI, IoT, blockchain, digital twins, and predictive analytics, all while maintaining data security and interoperability. Investment in IT infrastructure, cybersecurity, and talent capable of managing hybrid digital–human systems is essential, but also costly.

Lastly, the workforce needs to evolve from purely technical or procedural roles to those requiring systems thinking, collaboration, and data fluency. Ongoing reskilling and upskilling must accompany service transformation initiatives to ensure people remain central to the value delivery process.

Maturity Stages: Basic, Integrated, Predictive

In the journey toward Supply Chain 5.0, transformation is not a binary shift; it evolves through progressive maturity stages that reflect increasing levels of integration, intelligence, and human–machine collaboration. This applies to both product transformation (e.g., manufacturing, assembly, MRO) and service transformation (e.g., digital logistics coordination, platform-based experiences, predictive maintenance).

Understanding these stages helps organizations benchmark where they are and envision where they need to go. Below, we outline three critical stages—Basic, Integrated, and Predictive—and how each stage transforms the processes of making products and delivering services. See Figure 7.1.

Basic

Isolated, manual, and static. At the Basic maturity level, transformation processes, whether for products or services, are primarily manual, siloed, and reactive. Technology is limited, data flows are fragmented, and decision-making relies heavily on human intervention without digital augmentation.

Product transformation:

- Manufacturing relies on static production schedules.
- Little to no connectivity between production, sourcing, and delivery.

Figure 7.1 TRANSFORM Maturity Stages

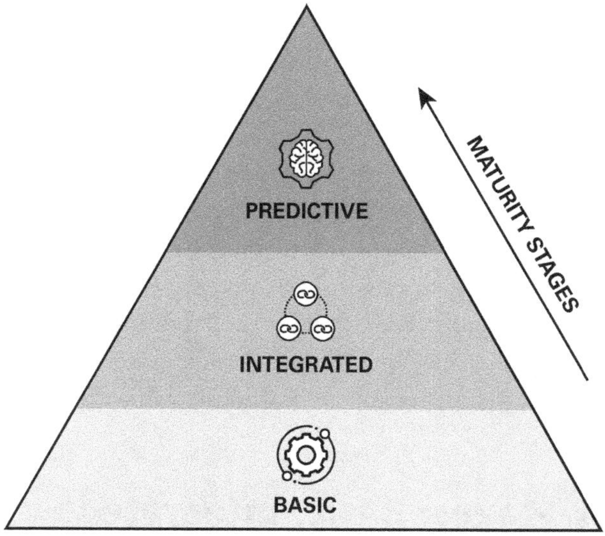

- Limited automation; performance improvements depend on worker effort.
- MRO (Maintenance, Repair, and Overhaul) is reactive, often triggered by breakdowns.

Service transformation:

- Services are standardized, transactional, and not tailored to customer segments.
- Manual coordination between departments or service agents.
- Limited visibility into performance, delays, or customer satisfaction.
- Minimal resilience to disruptions; recovery is slow and expensive.

Challenges: Siloed systems and fragmented processes, low visibility into production or service performance, manual data collection and reporting, inability to respond quickly to disruptions, little to no customization of services and products.

Role of technologies: Foundational tools to digitize basic operations, technology serves execution support, not decision-making, used mainly for record-keeping, task automation, and basic tracking.

Technology examples: Spreadsheets (Excel) and standalone ERP systems, basic barcode scanners and inventory trackers, paper-based SOPs for

MRO or service delivery, call centers and manual ticketing systems for services.

Impact: Organizations at this stage can achieve basic functional outcomes, but struggle with agility, innovation, and customer differentiation.

Integrated

Here the system is connected, real-time, and data-driven. Firms begin to digitally connect assets, systems, and processes, allowing for greater transparency, real-time control, and coordinated execution. Human input is still critical but it is now supported by actionable data.

Product transformation:

- Use of MES (Manufacturing Execution Systems), SCADA (Supervisory Control and Data Acquisition), and basic digital twins.
- Real-time production monitoring and quality control.
- Machine data integrated into ERP and scheduling systems.
- MRO evolves to preventive maintenance using historical performance data.

Service transformation:

- Services are modular and partially customizable.
- Data integration across departments enables coordinated service delivery.
- Platforms like Salesforce or ServiceNow connect customer interactions to backend operations.
- Logistics and customer support are more responsive to demand or disruptions.

Challenges: Integrating legacy systems with modern platforms, managing data flows across departments or supply chain partners, ensuring cybersecurity and data accuracy, training the workforce to adopt digital tools, and beginning to align operations with sustainability goals.

Role of technologies: Technology acts as a connective tissue across the value chain, enabling real-time visibility, coordination, and system-level decision support, supporting preventive, rule-based responses and continuous improvement.

Technology examples: MES to coordinate shop floor and planning, digital twins for simulating operations and detecting inefficiencies, SCADA systems for real-time monitoring of equipment, IoT sensors for tracking condition, location, or energy use, service platforms like Salesforce, Oracle, or SAP for customer experience, cloud-based ERP, integrated logistics platforms, and inventory management tools.

Impact: This stage enables organizations to scale efficiently, reduce waste, and begin aligning transformation activities with broader business and sustainability goals.

Predictive

The Predictive stage represents the full realization of Supply Chain 5.0 principles. Systems are not just integrated; they are intelligent, adaptive, and human-aware. Data flows freely across the ecosystem, and AI, machine learning, and simulation technologies enhance decision-making.

Product transformation:

- Autonomous planning tools adjust production schedules in real-time based on demand shifts, inventory levels, or disruptions.
- AI-enabled digital twins simulate and optimize manufacturing before execution.
- Predictive maintenance powered by IoT and anomaly detection minimizes downtime.
- Human workers collaborate with cobots and augmented reality systems for complex tasks.

Service transformation:

- Services are predictive, anticipatory, and co-created with customers.
- AI and natural language processing anticipate customer needs and offer tailored solutions.
- Resilient, cloud-native platforms dynamically reallocate resources during disruptions.
- Ethics, accessibility, and sustainability are embedded in the design of services.
- Human-in-the-loop governance ensures explainability and trust in AI decisions.

Challenges: Ensuring trust and explainability in AI-driven decisions, avoiding overreliance on automation, balancing personalization with operational efficiency, managing data ethics, privacy, and algorithmic bias, continually upskilling human workers for hybrid roles.

Role of technologies: Technology becomes a strategic co-pilot, enabling real-time adaptation. Systems are self-learning, predictive, and context-aware. Humans shift into supervisory, ethical, and creative roles. AI supports proactive service and production decisions.

Technology examples: Autonomous planning systems using machine learning, AI-powered digital twins that evolve with real-time data, predictive maintenance algorithms based on anomaly detection, cobots working alongside humans, Natural Language Processing (NLP) for conversational customer service, blockchain for secure, transparent service and product traceability, edge computing and AI for local, real-time decision-making.

Impact: Organizations at this stage deliver transformative customer experiences, operate with agility and resilience, and align their services with long-term value creation.

Technology and Innovation

The Transform process is being reshaped by advanced, digitally integrated technologies. These tools enable more adaptive, efficient, and responsible production methods.

Notable innovations include:

- **Artificial intelligence (AI):** Used in dynamic scheduling, predictive maintenance, and defect detection.
- **3D printing:** Supports on-demand, localized production of components and custom parts.
- **Collaborative robots (cobots):** Improve productivity and safety in shared human–machine environments.
- **Digital twins:** Simulate production scenarios and enable continuous optimization.
- **Computer vision:** Provides real-time quality checks and guides autonomous operations.
- **Smart energy and emissions monitoring:** Enables granular tracking of resource use and environmental performance.

- **Low-code automation platforms:** Democratize system configuration and accelerate process changes.
- **Voice- and AR-guided workflows:** Enhance training and reduce cognitive load for frontline operators.

Table 7.2 demonstrates how each of these technologies impacts 'Transform' subprocesses and details the technology's benefits for Supply Chain 5.0.

These tools create a production environment that is not only more efficient, but also more adaptable to customer needs and more supportive of workers.

REAL-WORLD EXAMPLE Digital Transformation in a Manual Factory

In a compelling illustration of Industry 4.0 principles, BIC's factory in Tunisia demonstrates how digital technologies can dramatically improve manufacturing performance without extensive physical automation. By implementing a manufacturing execution system, the facility transformed its operations through strategic digital connectivity, focusing on enhancing worker capabilities rather than replacing human labor.

Prior to the digital intervention, the factory struggled with typical manufacturing challenges: Fragmented information, manual tracking, and limited visibility into production processes. The implementation of Plex, a manufacturing operations management information system, created a comprehensive digital ecosystem that connected machines, tracked real-time data, and provided workers with immediate insights into inventory, job requirements, and production status.

The results were remarkable. Without changing personnel or introducing robotic systems, the factory achieved significant performance improvements: A 6 percent increase in adherence and attainment, 3 percent improvement in overall equipment effectiveness, and 5 percent improvement in overall performance. Workers gained the ability to see their entire workflow, reducing unnecessary stops and starts and enabling more focused, efficient work.

Gary Horsfield, BIC's Chief Supply Chain Officer, emphasized that the transformation wasn't about technology for technology's sake, but about creating a more intelligent, connected workplace. By providing digital tools that make workers' jobs easier and more transparent, the company unlocked substantial operational improvements while maintaining a human-centric approach to manufacturing.

Table 7.2 Technology Impact and Benefit on Transform Subprocesses

Technology	Subprocess Impacted	Benefits for Supply Chain 5.0 Goals
AI-driven scheduling	Schedule Production	Improves responsiveness, reduces changeover waste
3D printing	Perform Production	Reduces lead times, supports customization, lowers material waste
Cobots and smart machines	Perform Production, Packaging	Enhances productivity and reduces physical strain
Digital twins	Schedule, Perform Production	Allows simulation and stress-testing of production strategies
Computer vision inspection	Inspect and Verify Quality	Reduces human error, improves traceability and safety
Emissions and energy sensors	Perform Production	Supports decarbonization and energy-efficiency tracking
AR-guided instructions	Issue Material, Production	Increases training speed and operator confidence
Low-code automation tools	All subprocesses	Speeds up system updates and change implementation

BIC's factory example illustrates a critical principle of Supply Chain 5.0: Technology should empower people, creating more adaptive, efficient, and engaging work environments.

See Table 7.3 for a readiness and implementation checklist for Transform.

Table 7.3 Readiness and Implementation Checklist

Readiness Area	Indicators to Evaluate	Quick Win or Long-Term?
Strategic Alignment	Production goals explicitly incorporate flexibility, decarbonization, and workforce safety.	Long-Term
Digital and Technological Infrastructure	Systems support real-time scheduling, emissions tracking, and simulation. Digital work instructions are accessible.	Quick Win (instructions); Long-Term (platforms)

(continued)

Table 7.3 (Continued)

Readiness Area	Indicators to Evaluate	Quick Win or Long-Term?
Workforce Readiness and Culture	Operators are trained in digital tools. Human-centric design principles are applied to line layout and shift planning.	Quick Win (training); Long-Term (culture)
Supplier and Partner Ecosystem	Sourcing, logistics, and packaging partners are integrated into production planning. Circular material flows are explored.	Long-Term
Performance Measurement and Governance	Metrics include yield, safety, GHG emissions, and employee engagement. Governance supports continuous improvement.	Quick Win (metrics); Long-Term (governance)

Actionable Principles for Transform

- Design production systems for change, not just for output.
- Treat human–machine collaboration as a performance advantage, not a trade-off.
- Use data to uncover and reduce hidden waste in energy, time, and motion.
- Integrate quality assurance throughout the process, not just at the end.
- Link production design with customer experience and environmental impact.
- Invest in continuous upskilling and decision support for frontline teams.
- Transform is where the supply chain creates physical and economic value—but also where sustainability and social impact take root.
- SCOR DS provides a robust framework for managing production with clarity and discipline.
- Advanced technologies are enabling a shift toward intelligent, flexible, and people-aware operations.
- Human-centric production systems require investment in safety, digital tools, and meaningful engagement.

- Circularity, customization, and visibility are shaping the future of transformation beyond the factory floor.

References

Amazon Staff (2025) *Amazon meets 100% renewable energy goal 7 years early.* About Amazon. www.aboutamazon.com/news/sustainability/amazon-renewable-energy-goal (archived at https://perma.cc/U6Y8-KD4X)

Amazon Web Services. (2025a) *What is predictive analytics?* https://aws.amazon.com/what-is/predictive-analytics/ (archived at https://perma.cc/K78B-DMDE)

Amazon Web Services (2025b) Amazon Personalize: AI-powered real-time recommendations. https://aws.amazon.com/personalize/ (archived at https://perma.cc/7ER3-NU95)

Association for Supply Chain Management (ASCM) (2022) SCOR Digital Standard.

Association for Supply Chain Management (2022, September 19) Announcing the new SCOR Digital Standard (SCOR DS): Updated processes, metrics, skills, and practices [Press release]. ASCM. www.ascm.org/globalassets/ascm_website_assets/docs/9.19.2022-scor-press-release.pdf (archived at https://perma.cc/2FMJ-JB4M)

Association for Supply Chain Management (n.d.) *Transform* [SCOR DS process description]. SCOR Digital Standard. https://scor.ascm.org/processes/transform (archived at https://perma.cc/D5DA-LHL5)

Barata, J. and Kayser, I. (2023) Industry 5.0–past, present, and near future. *Procedia Computer Science*, 219, 778–88.

Bloomberg Media Studios (2025, July 9) Can adaptive production revive our factories? Sponsored by Siemens. https://sponsored.bloomberg.com/quicksight/siemens/can-adaptive-production-revive-our-factories (archived at https://perma.cc/2WDL-EMTN)

DHL Global Forwarding (2025) *GoGreen Solutions: Environmentally-friendly freight*. www.dhl.com/us-en/home/global-forwarding/products-and-solutions/gogreen-solutions.html (archived at https://perma.cc/6GQX-U268)

Ivanov, D. (2023) The Industry 5.0 framework: viability-based integration of the resilience, sustainability, and human-centricity perspectives. *International Journal of Production Research*, 61(5), 1683–95.

KUKA AG (2016) *Human-robot collaboration at Siemens*. www.kuka.com/en-us/industries/solutions-database/2016/07/solution-robotics-siemens (archived at https://perma.cc/46AA-WNP7)

KUKA AG (2022) *Human-robot collaboration in the production environment*. www.kuka.com/en-us/future-production/human-robot-collaboration (archived at https://perma.cc/SJB5-MNDL)

Lee, D. and Bony, L. (2007, May 30) Cradle-to-cradle design at Herman Miller: Moving toward environmental sustainability (Case No. 607003-PDF-ENG) Harvard Business School. https://store.hbr.org/product/cradle-to-cradle-design-at-herman-miller-moving-toward-environmental-sustainability/607003 (archived at https://perma.cc/MCK7-EULX)

MillerKnoll (2025, February 4) MillerKnoll unveils new sustainability strategy and issues 2024 Better World Report. https://news.millerknoll.com/2025-02-04-MillerKnoll-Unveils-New-Sustainability-Strategy-and-Issues-2024-Better-World-Report (archived at https://perma.cc/RH4D-F7BQ)

MIT Technology Review Insights (2025, July 15) Shaping the future with adaptive production. Sponsored by Siemens. www.technologyreview.com/2025/07/15/1120083/shaping-the-future-with-adaptive-production/ (archived at https://perma.cc/E9BQ-LUAA)

Raja Santhi, A. and Muthuswamy, P. (2023) Industry 5.0 or industry 4.0S? Introduction to industry 4.0 and a peek into the prospective industry 5.0 technologies. *International Journal on Interactive Design and Manufacturing (IJIDeM)*, *17*(2), 947–79.

Rame, R., Purwanto, P. and Sudarno, S. (2024) Industry 5.0 and sustainability: An overview of emerging trends and challenges for a green future. *Innovation and Green Development*, 3(4), 100173.

Rejeb, A., Rejeb, K., Zrelli, I. and Süle, E. (2025) Industry 5.0 as seen through its academic literature: An investigation using co-word analysis. *Discover Sustainability*, 6(1), 307.

SCOR Digital Standard (n.d.) ASCM. www.ascm.org/corporate-solutions/standards-tools/scords/ (archived at https://perma.cc/X533-T7AB)

Shabur, M. A., Shahriar, A. and Ara, M. (2025) From automation to collaboration: Exploring the impact of industry 5.0 on sustainable manufacturing. *Discover Sustainability*, 6(1), 1–23.

Siemens AG (2025a) Adaptive production: Leap into flexible, data-driven manufacturing. www.siemens.com/us/en/company/topic-areas/digital-enterprise/adaptive-production.html (archived at https://perma.cc/CM5X-X4SF)

Siemens AG (2025b) Industrial AI for manufacturing. www.siemens.com/us/en/company/topic-areas/industrial-ai.html (archived at https://perma.cc/3P6A-NW8M)

Siemens AG (2025c) Adaptive production: Future-proof your plant with flexible, data-driven manufacturing. www.siemens.com/global/en/products/automation/topic-areas/digital-enterprise/adaptive-production.html (archived at https://perma.cc/2RCZ-C6WR)

Siemens AG (2025d) Connected factories: The future of resilient manufacturing. www.siemens.com/global/en/company/stories/research-technologies/topics/connected-factories.html (archived at https://perma.cc/8LDP-P7UT)

Van Bedaf, Y. and Van Brusselen, T. (2024) Supply chain analytics with SCOR DS. Element61 / Moore. www.element61.be/sites/default/files/inline-files/SC%20Innovations%202024_Analytics_Moore_element61.pdf (archived at https://perma.cc/6BKG-S9QZ)

Villar, A., Paladini, S. and Buckley, O. (2023, July) Towards supply chain 5.0: Redesigning supply chains as resilient, sustainable, and human-centric systems in a post-pandemic world. In *Operations Research Forum*, 4(3), p. 60 Cham: Springer International Publishing.

World Economic Forum (2025) Global Risks Report 2025. www.weforum.org/publications/global-risks-report-2025/ (archived at https://perma.cc/Z8RQ-DWMK)

Zafar, M. H., Langås, E. F. and Sanfilippo, F. (2024) Exploring the synergies between collaborative robotics, digital twins, augmentation, and industry 5.0 for smart manufacturing: A state-of-the-art review. *Robotics and Computer-Integrated Manufacturing*, 89, 102769.

Order: Co-Creating with Customers 08

The purpose of a business is to get and keep a customer. Without customers, no amount of engineering wizardry, clever financing, or operations expertise can keep a company going.

THEODORE LEVITT

Order: From Connected to Dynamic Customers

In the SCOR DS model, the Order process is a key component of the delivery process. It defines how customer orders are captured, managed, fulfilled, and closed, across both physical and digital channels (ASCM, 2022). SCOR DS breaks down the order process into structured subprocesses that support customer satisfaction, real-time visibility, and operational efficiency. The order is the first transactional moment in the supply chain, representing the bridge between customer intent and operational response.

The overview of the order processes includes capturing a customer's order (product or service), validating and confirming availability, scheduling delivery, executing fulfillment, and invoicing and closing the order. In a Supply Chain 5.0 context, the above major processes evolve from being efficient and automated to a dynamic, intelligent, human-centric, and sustainable system, where order management is no longer a back-end function. Managing orders is a strategic interface that defines the customer's experience, costs, and performance from the very beginning of the supply chain execution cycle.

- Resilience by dynamically rerouting or adjusting orders based on real-time events.
- Sustainability by optimizing order consolidation, packaging, and delivery modes.
- Human-centricity by allowing customer service reps to focus on complex exceptions.

The Order Process: A Strategic Lens

Before diving into the nuances of business-to-consumer (B2C), business-to-business (B2B), and intra-company ordering as outlined in the updated SCOR DS framework, it is essential first to understand the core steps of the order process. This foundational view enables supply chain leaders to align emerging technologies with operational needs and customer expectations strategically.

At a high level, the order process typically includes five key stages:

1. Order capture
2. Order validation
3. Order management
4. Order fulfillment
5. Order settlement

Each stage presents unique opportunities for innovation, efficiency, and resilience—hallmarks of Supply Chain 5.0. Across the order lifecycle, various technologies and their combinations can and are being integrated.

The strategic impact on each order lifecycle is appropriate for practitioners. To capture the order, the strategy involves using technologies to improve the customer experience and enable real-time data collection. For order validation, the aim is to reduce errors and ensure compliance. In order management, technologies are frequently used to simplify workflows and increase agility. When executing the order, the strategy focuses on enhancing speed, accuracy, and flexibility. Then, for order settlement, the goal is to promote transparency and trust in financial transactions. Table 8.1 first provides a high-level definition of the SCOR DS model as it is currently defined (ASCM, 2022), followed by the technologies that are being used and moving toward Supply Chain 5.0 applications, and their impact.

Table 8.1 Technology Integration Across the Order Lifecycle

Order lifecycle	Definition (SCOR DS)	Technologies and strategic impact
Order Capture	The process of receiving an order from a customer through various channels such as e-commerce platforms, mobile apps, call centers, or electronic data interchange.	Modern technologies like AI-powered chatbots, voice recognition, and IoT-enabled devices enhance real-time data capture and customer interaction, enabling personalized and frictionless ordering experiences.
Order Validation	The step where the order is checked for accuracy, completeness, and compliance with business rules, such as verifying product availability, pricing, customer credentials, and payment authorization.	Machine learning algorithms and automated rule engines can detect anomalies, prevent fraud, and ensure compliance, reducing manual errors and speeding up the process.
Order Management	The coordination and orchestration of all activities required to fulfill the order, including inventory allocation, scheduling, and communication across departments or partners.	Cloud-based platforms, RPA (Robotic Process Automation), and collaborative tools enable agile, scalable, and transparent order handling across global networks.
Order Fulfillment	The physical execution of the order, picking, packing, shipping, and delivery to the customer or internal recipient.	Smart warehouses, autonomous vehicles, and digital twins optimize fulfillment speed, accuracy, and adaptability, especially in dynamic or disrupted environments.
Order Settlement	The finalization of the transaction, including invoicing, payment processing, and financial reconciliation.	Technologies like blockchain, smart contracts, and e-invoicing systems ensure secure, transparent, and efficient financial exchanges, reducing disputes and enhancing trust.

Supply Chain Leadership Implications

Supply Chain 5.0 is not just about technology; it's about human-centric transformation. Leaders often find themselves championing cross-functional collaboration to integrate digital tools across departments, from ordering to delivery. Investments in workforce upskilling to manage and interpret AI-driven insights in purchasing, procurement, and sourcing have also been on companies' radars to make sure the customer has what they need. The design of resilient systems that adapt to disruptions while maintaining service levels is of importance for companies; they also aim to foster ethical and sustainable practices through transparent order settlement and traceability across the order lifecycle.

By first understanding the universal order process, leaders can uncover common pain points that exist across different order types. This insight allows them to customize technology deployment according to order complexity and customer expectations (Taghipour et al., 2022), while building scalable solutions that evolve alongside business models and market demands.

Such an approach ensures that the transition toward Supply Chain 5.0 is not merely technological, but also strategic, inclusive, and future-ready. The breakdown of order lifecycle processes is particularly relevant for supply chain leaders and practitioners in the context of Supply Chain 5.0 for four main reasons:

1 *Technology alignment with process steps*

Specific Supply Chain 5.0 technologies can enhance each step in the order process. For example, AI and ML are used for predictive order validation and fraud detection. Digital twins for simulating order fulfillment scenarios. Blockchain for secure and transparent order settlement. Robotic process automation (RPA) for automating repetitive tasks in order management. Understanding these steps allows leaders to map technologies to pain points and opportunities.

2 *Differentiation across order types (B2C, B2B intra-company)*

By first examining the generic order process, practitioners can later explore how these steps diverge or converge across the three different methods. For example, B2C is often characterized by high volume, fast pace, and customer focus. B2B, in contrast, usually deals with contract-based bulk orders and longer cycles. Intra-company orders are internal requisitions, frequently tied to resource planning. This sets the stage for customized technology strategies depending on the order type.

3 *Foundation for process innovation*

Supply Chain 5.0 emphasizes human-centric and resilient supply chains. By dissecting the order process, leaders can identify bottlenecks and manual interventions, and innovators can design collaborative workflows that integrate human judgment with automation.

4 *Strategic decision-making*

A clear understanding of the order process enables better orchestration across departments, improved customer experience through seamless order handling, and data-driven decisions using insights from each stage.

Order Models for B2B, B2C, and Intralogistics

In the SCOR DS framework, demand refers to the customer requirements for products or services that drive supply chain activities (ASCM, 2022). It is the starting point for planning and execution across all processes: Plan, Order, Source, Transform, Fulfill, and Return. The model emphasizes that satisfying demand is the ultimate goal of the supply chain, and all processes are designed to align resources and capabilities to meet this demand efficiently and effectively.

Because the demand is the starting point for all supply chain activities, it represents what customers want, when they want it, and in what quantity. In the SCOR DS framework and modern supply chain thinking, demand is not a single event; it influences multiple processes: The order process and the fulfillment processes (ASCM, 2022). The order process will be reviewed here, and the fulfillment processes will be explored in the next chapter.

Although both processes share the goal of satisfying customer expectations, they complement each other but operate in different domains: The order is digital and transactional, while fulfillment is physical and operational, often referred to as the order fulfillment process (Lin et al., 1998; Croxton, 2003). The order process translates demand signals into actionable plans. Fulfillment then executes those plans to deliver products or services. Think of it as information flow (order) driving material flow (fulfillment).

Both order and fulfillment processes include B2B and B2C, and intralogistics because these represent different contexts in which demand is expressed and satisfied. Therefore, for Supply Chain 5.0, we will explore the B2B, B2C, and intralogistics applications of Industry 4.0 technologies within this context.

B2B vs. B2C Order Dynamics in the 5.0 Landscape

The updated SCOR DS model highlights that not all orders behave alike. B2B and B2C supply chains operate under fundamentally different demand patterns, customer expectations, and operational dynamics (see Table 8.2), each requiring unique strategies for orchestration and resilience. By understanding the universal order lifecycle, leaders can identify shared challenges across B2B and B2C operations, such as visibility gaps, data silos, or inefficiencies in fulfillment. Once these commonalities are mapped, technology can be customized based on order complexity and customer expectation (Taghipour et al., 2022; Castillo et al., 2025; Soleymanizadeh et al., 2024).

Table 8.2 Order Dynamics in B2B and B2C Fulfillment

Order dynamic connected to B2B fulfillment	Order dynamic connected to B2C fulfillment
• Focuses on reliability, precision, and long-term collaboration. • Orders are typically larger, recurring, and governed by contractual terms. • Integration across ERP, OMS, and TMS systems ensures transparency and performance consistency across partners. • Resilience in B2B contexts means maintaining supply continuity, visibility, and trust—particularly when disruptions ripple across networks.	• Emphasizes speed, personalization, and customer experience. • Consumers expect real-time visibility, flexible delivery, and seamless returns. • AI-driven logistics, demand sensing, and micro-fulfillment centers enable the agility required to serve millions of individual, variable orders. • Resilience here is measured by how well the supply chain protects brand reputation and customer loyalty in the face of volatility.

From Order Management to Orchestration

In Supply Chain 5.0, the order is no longer a simple transaction; it's the heartbeat of value creation. Every purchase order, sales order, and customer request triggers a complex web of synchronized actions across digital and physical networks. From the moment an order is placed, it sets in motion a chain of intelligent decisions about sourcing, production, logistics, and customer experience that define how effectively an organization fulfills its commitments.

Traditionally, orders were treated as administrative tasks: Something to process, fulfill, and close. In contrast, Supply Chain 5.0 sees the order as a strategic intelligence signal, a source of data that links customer intent to operational execution. Think of this process as a real-time indicator of customer intent, market dynamics, and operational performance. Each order carries data that, when captured and analyzed, can anticipate trends, personalize service, and enhance resilience.

This evolution redefines how organizations understand demand, allocate resources, and engage with customers. The order is not just a record; it's a living source of insight guiding the supply chain's digital nervous system. One current example is that customer delivery preferences are evolving. Companies understand that late deliveries affect customer satisfaction (Akturk et al., 2022), and they emphasize the importance of technologies in tracking and tracing devices (Helo and Thai, 2024). As a result, many academic models have been examined regarding how real-time order tracking impacts customer satisfaction and brand loyalty. Another example is that supply chain professionals often need data-driven order fulfillment consolidation for omnichannel to be competitive (Wang et al., 2024).

For today's companies and supply chain leaders, each order captures critical insights into demand shifts, product performance, and service expectations. When leveraged properly, these insights enable predictive and personalized supply chains that are both resilient and responsive. In earlier generations, order management systems focused on accuracy and compliance, ensuring that the right product reached the right customer at the right time. But in the 5.0 era, where digital and human collaboration converge, the role of order management has evolved into order orchestration. The goal is not only accuracy but adaptability. Orchestration connects ERP, OMS, WMS, TMS, and CRM platforms into a cohesive digital ecosystem capable of sensing, deciding, and acting in real time.

This means coordinating a network of suppliers, manufacturers, and logistics partners in real time. AI and IoT technologies continuously monitor variables such as inventory levels, production status, and transportation capacity. Blockchain adds trust and transparency, while predictive analytics suggests optimal fulfillment paths. If a disruption occurs, say, a supplier delay or weather event, the system automatically reconfigures routes or sources to protect the customer promise.

Yet, human oversight remains indispensable: Professionals interpret exceptions, manage trade-offs, and ensure that operational decisions align with brand values and sustainability goals. This human–machine collaboration embodies the essence of Supply Chain 5.0, technology that amplifies human capability rather than replaces it.

Understanding the order lifecycle is crucial because it connects strategy to execution. The modern order journey unfolds through several dynamic stages:

1. Order capture. The process begins when customer intent is captured, whether through e-commerce, EDI, or direct sales. In Supply Chain 5.0, digital interfaces use AI and analytics to interpret this intent, personalize offers, and confirm availability in real time.
2. Order validation. Intelligent systems validate the order, verify credit, allocate inventory, and trigger production or procurement as needed. Automation accelerates this stage, reducing manual errors and improving visibility across partners.
3. Order fulfillment and delivery. Here, orchestration is most visible. Based on the customer profile, location, and service level, the system determines the optimal fulfillment source, warehouse, store, or supplier, and dynamically plans the last mile. Robotics, drones, and predictive routing algorithms enhance speed and sustainability while maintaining flexibility for change.
4. Order feedback and learning loop. Every order closes with feedback, delivery confirmation, satisfaction ratings, return data, and usage insights. These signals feed predictive models, improving future accuracy, personalization, and operational resilience.

Technology and Innovation

Order processes are increasingly powered by intelligent, customer-centric technologies that promote visibility, automation, and collaboration. These tools improve both the customer experience and operational resilience.

Key technologies include:

- **Order management systems (OMS):** Centralize multi-channel order capture, routing, and visibility.

- **AI-driven availability and fulfillment logic:** Dynamically allocate inventory and optimize routing.
- **Real-time ATP/CTP engines:** Calculate and update product or configuration availability instantly.
- **Natural language processing (NLP) bots:** Allow conversational order capture and updates.
- **Digital twins for demand and order flow:** Simulate order behavior and capacity bottlenecks.
- **Blockchain:** Verifies and records order flows for transparency and auditability.
- **Customer self-service portals:** Enable order tracking, status changes, and preference management.
- **Emission-aware routing engines:** Prioritize low-impact fulfillment options

Table 8.3 shows how these technologies impact the subprocesses of Order, and the benefits for Supply Chain 5.0 goals.

Table 8.3 Technology Impact and Benefit on Order Subprocesses

Technology	Subprocess Impacted	Benefits for Supply Chain 5.0 Goals
AI-based inventory allocation	Promise Order, Check Availability	Increases fulfillment rate, reduces stockouts and split shipments
Real-time ATP/CTP engines	Check Availability, Promise Order	Improves lead time accuracy and customer trust
NLP chatbots and voice input	Capture Order, Manage Changes	Improves accessibility and reduces support burden
Blockchain order records	Coordinate Systems	Ensures accuracy and trust in multi-enterprise orders
Customer self-service platforms	Capture Order, Manage Changes	Improves empowerment and satisfaction
Emission-aware OMS routing	Promise Order	Optimizes for low-carbon fulfillment
Digital twins of order flows	All	Enables testing of new fulfillment models under varying demand

Actionable Principles for Order

- Design order processes to reflect customer expectations, not internal convenience.
- Use technology to enable transparency, not just automation.
- Eliminate split shipments and rework through real-time availability and accurate promises.
- Provide customers with visibility and flexibility throughout the order lifecycle.
- Treat the Order process as a source of data, not just demand.
- Align order management with sustainability and experience goals, not just cost.
- Order is where customer experience begins, so it must be accurate, transparent, and adaptable.
- SCOR DS provides a clear process model for managing and optimizing order-related activities.
- Advanced technologies enable order orchestration that aligns with fulfillment, sustainability, and trust goals.
- Human-centric order systems empower customers and reduce manual intervention.
- The Order process plays a critical role in supply chain resilience by shaping execution readiness from the start.

References

Association for Supply Chain Management (ASCM) (2022) SCOR Digital Standard.

Akturk, M. S., Mallipeddi, R. R. and Jia, X. (2022) Estimating impacts of logistics processes on online customer ratings: Consequences of providing technology-enabled order tracking data to customers. *Journal of Operations Management*, 68(6–7), 775–811.

Castillo, C., Otero-Romero, T. and Alvarez-Palau, E. J. (2025) Navigating the transition to industry 5.0: Advancing sustainability, resilience, and human-centricity in Spanish supply chain management. *Discover Sustainability*, 6(1), 1–20.

Croxton, K. L. (2003) The order fulfillment process. *The International Journal of Logistics Management*, 14(1), 19–32.

Helo, P. and Thai, V. V. (2024) Logistics 4.0–digital transformation with smart connected tracking and tracing devices. *International Journal of Production Economics*, 275, 109336.

Lin, F. R. and Shaw, M. J. (1998) Reengineering the order fulfillment process in supply chain networks. *International Journal of Flexible Manufacturing Systems*, 10(3), 197–229.

Soleymanizadeh, H. and Ziaeian, M. (2024) Application of key technologies of Industry 5.0 in supply chain management. In *Powering Industry 5.0 and Sustainable Development Through Innovation* (pp. 124–36). IGI Global Scientific Publishing.

Taghipour, A., Lu, X. and Smahi, M. (2022) Opportunities and challenges for society 5.0 in procurement. *Blockchain Technology in Supply Chain Management for Society 5.0*, 91–100.

Wang, Y., Wang, T., Wang, X., Deng, Y. and Cao, L. (2024) Data-driven order fulfillment consolidation for online grocery retailing. *INFORMS Journal on Applied Analytics*, 54(3), 211–21.

09 Fulfill: A Dynamic Outbound Process

Our fulfillment promise is simple: if we say it's in stock, it's in stock—because the moment you disappoint a customer, the whole supply chain pays the price.

RANDY STRANG, FORMER UPS CHIEF SUPPLY CHAIN OFFICER

Fulfillment: From Customer-Led to Business-Driven Outbound

In the digital and updated evolution of the original SCOR model, one of the most significant enhancements is the integration of online and interactive nodes across the end-to-end supply chain, particularly within dynamic fulfillment. In the previous chapter, we discussed that demand is the starting point for all supply chain activities. This is because demand represents what the customers want, when they want it, and in what quantity. Because demand is not a single event, it equally influences both the order and fulfillment processes. On the one hand, the order process is where demand becomes explicit through customer orders, forecasts, or requisitions. It focuses on capturing, validating, and managing demand signals. On the other hand, the fulfill process is where demand is satisfied, through sourcing, production, and delivery. It focuses on executing the physical and financial flow required to meet that demand. As you remember, both aim to satisfy customer expectations, but they operate in different domains.

The fulfillment process encompasses all activities involved in executing customer orders and services, including delivery scheduling, picking, packing, shipping, installation, commissioning, and invoicing (ASCM, 2022). Thus, fulfillment represents the critical interface between customer expectations and operational execution. It embodies the dual focus of the modern supply chain leader: Delivering superior customer experiences while maintaining operational excellence. Achieving this balance transforms fulfillment from a reactive, customer-led process into a proactive, business-driven capability, one that strategically aligns service performance with organizational goals.

The next step, while incorporating the Supply Chain 5.0 vision, is the shift from reactive to predictive fulfillment. Traditionally, fulfillment has been guided by customer orders—a downstream, reactive process that begins only once demand is triggered. In Supply Chain 5.0, fulfillment shifts from being purely responsive to becoming anticipatory and intelligent. Advanced analytics, AI-driven forecasting, and digital twins enable businesses to predict customer needs before orders are placed, allowing for prepositioning of inventory, optimized delivery routes, and reduced lead times.

This predictive model transforms fulfillment into a strategic differentiator. It allows organizations not only to respond faster but also to shape customer expectations through transparency, reliability, and personalized delivery options. The customer still drives demand, but the business now orchestrates how that demand is met with precision and foresight. As a supply chain leader, think of dynamic fulfillment in Industry 5.0 as a reframing from being purely a logistical process to a strategic capability that integrates intelligence, resiliency, sustainability, and human collaboration.

- Resilience: By not eliminating risk but enabling rapid adaptation.
- Sustainability: By meeting regulatory and customer expectations while strengthening brand trust and long-term viability.
- Human-centricity: By transforming the process from a transactional operation into a creative, knowledge-driven environment where employees and customers contribute to innovation and meaning.

Since the readers of this book are experienced supply chain leaders, it is important to make a key distinction here: In a modern supply chain, distribution and fulfillment often work together, but they are not the same.

Figure 9.1 Distribution and Fulfillment Ecosystem

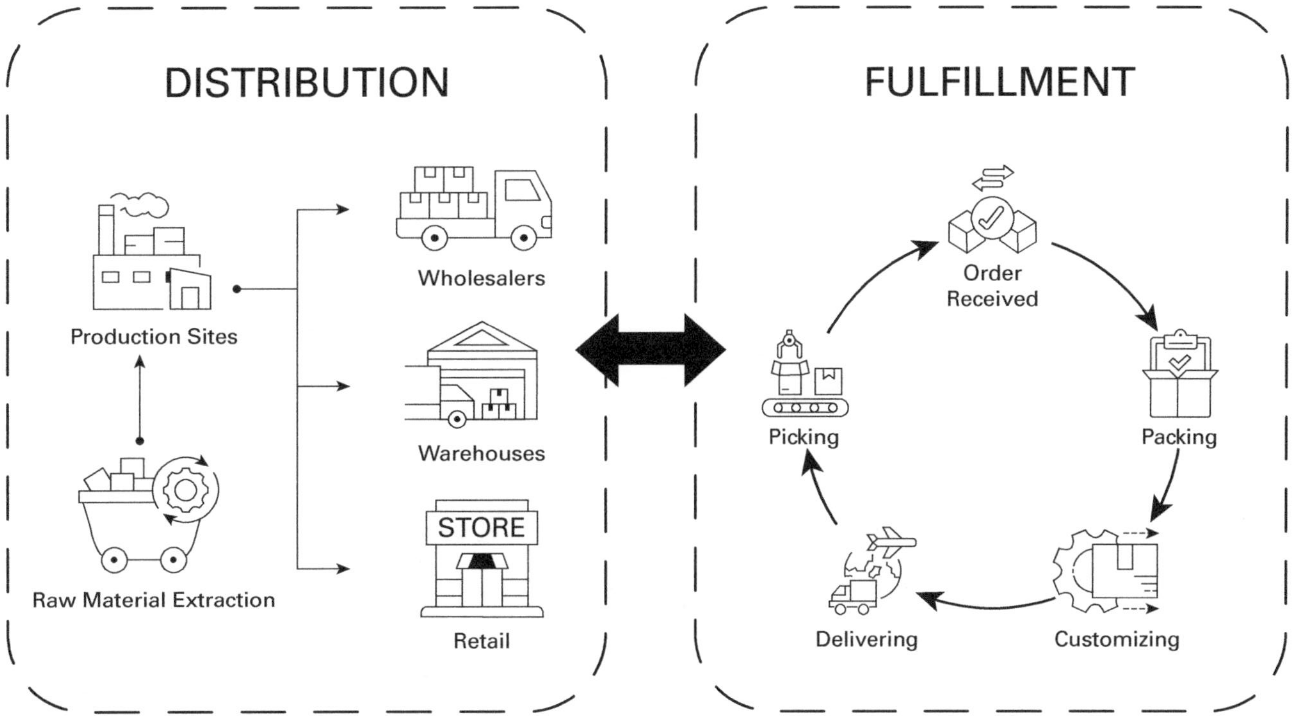

Distribution traditionally refers to the movement and placement of goods from production sites to various market destinations, such as regional warehouses, wholesalers, or retail outlets (Rushton et al., 2022). It focuses on bulk transfers, efficiency of transport, and inventory positioning across the network (Higginson et al., 2005). The objective is to ensure that products are available where demand is anticipated.

Fulfillment, on the other hand, begins once a specific *customer order* is received (Thirumalai et al., 2005). It is the process of translating that order into action, picking, packing, customizing, and delivering the product or service to the final customer, often in real time (Croxton, 2003). While distribution is about *product availability*, fulfillment is about *customer satisfaction*.

In traditional models, these functions operated sequentially: Distribution positioned inventory and fulfillment executed delivery. In today's digital, omnichannel, and customer-driven environment, the lines have blurred. The two functions must now operate as an integrated ecosystem, where inventory visibility, order orchestration, and customer engagement converge seamlessly: See Figure 9.1.

This integration is central to the Supply Chain 5.0 vision: Distribution provides the structural backbone while fulfillment delivers the experiential value. Together, they transform the supply chain from a cost engine into a customer-value engine, one that is intelligent, adaptive, and human-centric.

Evolution of the Fulfillment Process

Although the SCOR DS model does not have an official classification of the fulfillment steps, we grouped the key components involved in fulfilling a customer's order into five sequential steps, as shown in Figure 9.2. This provides an operational framework upon which Supply Chain 5.0 builds its advancements, technology-driven resilience, and human-centered capabilities.

Table 9.1 presents a high-level overview of the key processes that align with the objectives of **Supply Chain 5.0** within the **Fulfill** function. To set the foundation, the second column revisits the fundamental definitions from the **SCOR DS model**, providing a clear reference point before exploring their evolution in context.

Figure 9.2 Five Key Components Involved in Fulfilling a Customer's Order

Table 9.1 Evolution of Fulfillment Processes: SCOR DS and Supply Chain 5.0

Key component step	Traditional definition	Supply Chain 5.0 definition
Order Scheduling	Static schedules based on forecasts.	**Industry 4.0:** AI-driven dynamic scheduling adapts to real-time demand, disruptions, and sustainability goals. **Industry 5.0 Impact:** Human planners collaborate with AI to balance customer experience with carbon footprint optimization.
Picking and Packing	Manual or semi-automated picking.	**Industry 4.0:** Cobots (collaborative robots) work alongside humans for ergonomic efficiency and speed. **Industry 5.0 Impact:** Packaging becomes personalized for customer experience and designed for circular economy principles, reusable and recyclable.
Shipping and Transportation	Cost-focused routing.	**Industry 4.0:** Predictive analytics optimize routes for energy efficiency, low emissions, and resilience. **Industry 5.0 Impact:** Integration of electric vehicle fleets, drones, and blockchain ensures transparency and sustainability.
Installation and Commissioning	Manual installation.	**Industry 4.0:** Augmented reality (AR) and remote assistance empower technicians and customers. **Industry 5.0 Impact:** Human-centric design guarantees safety, usability, and enhanced customer interaction.
Invoicing	Traditional invoicing systems.	**Industry 4.0:** Smart contracts and blockchain provide trust, traceability, and ethical sourcing compliance. **Industry 5.0 Impact:** Financial processes align with ESG reporting and social responsibility, reinforcing transparency.

Figure 9.3 Fulfill Evolution

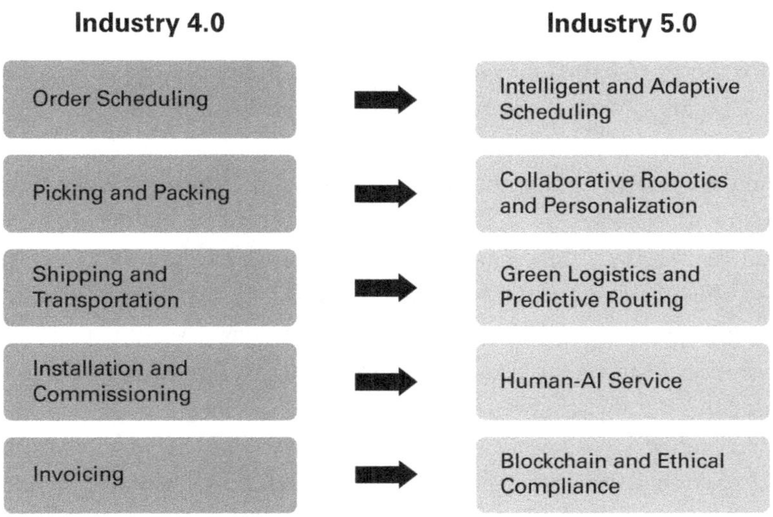

Fulfillment has transitioned from focusing on speed and cost efficiency to a multidimensional paradigm that emphasizes customer-centricity, environmental sustainability, operational resilience, and synergistic human–machine collaboration to drive competitive advantage. See Figure 9.3.

Integrated and Human-Centric Fulfillment Processes

The evolution toward omnichannel supply chains is fundamentally redefining the fulfillment function. In an omnichannel strategy, all of a company's sales, marketing, and customer support channels are fully integrated and work together to create a unified, seamless customer journey (Choi, 2020; Ishfaq et al., 2024).

Customers now expect seamless experiences regardless of how or where they purchase—online, in-store, or through third-party platforms (Bell, 2014; Ponce et al., 2025). To meet these expectations, organizations must create unified fulfillment ecosystems that integrate data, processes, and inventory across all channels.

This integration provides real-time visibility and flexibility, enabling an online order to be fulfilled from a nearby store, a regional warehouse, or even directly from a supplier. In the Supply Chain 5.0 paradigm, these networks are powered by cloud-based platforms, collaborative robotics, and autonomous decision systems, which continuously synchronize supply with demand.

While technology drives efficiency, Industry 5.0 reintroduces the human dimension at the center of fulfillment operations (Li and Duan, 2025; Ghobakhloo et al., 2025). Employees, empowered by data and intelligent systems, shift from executing repetitive tasks to managing exceptions, solving complex problems, and improving service innovation. Human–machine collaboration fosters agility and resilience, qualities that purely automated systems cannot fully achieve on their own.

Unlike Industry 4.0's automation-centric approach, this redefined fulfillment approach is not merely about speed or cost; it's about experience, sustainability, and adaptability. It transforms outbound operations into a strategic lever for brand value, customer loyalty, and long-term competitiveness. Industry 5.0 emphasizes human–machine collaboration, sustainability, and resilience, ensuring that technology augments human judgment rather than replacing it. Let's focus on the areas where the most significant impacts are happening: (1) human–machine collaborations, (2) sustainability and circular economy, and (3) resilience against disruptions.

Human–Machine Collaborations

In ordering scheduling, Industry 5.0 integrates technologies such as AI, robotics, and IoT, with human creativity enabling personalized and adaptive fulfillment across channels. Taco Bell, through its parent company Yum! Brands, employs AI in its ordering and scheduling systems to enhance efficiency. AI streamlines restaurant operations, supports drive-thru order processing, and assists in employee scheduling. Most orders are handled via the mobile app and drive-thru, where AI automatically processes and prioritizes incoming orders during peak times. The voice AI at Taco Bell's drive-thrus has been deployed in 300 US locations since a pilot began in Q1 2024, processing over 2 million orders. The goal is to lighten staff workload and improve order accuracy (CNBC, 2024; Gessner, 2024; Guynn, 2024).

In picking and packing, the use of industrial robots for handling is also another human-collaboration approach that is even more prominent in picking and packing activities within the fulfillment process. Cobots assist humans with repetitive tasks like picking and transporting items, while humans manage exceptions and perform quality checks. For example, Onward Robotics deploys AMRs for "pick assist," working alongside humans to handle transport tasks during seasonal spikes. The impact is increased productivity and safety while supporting mass customization and ergonomic work environments.

In shipping and transportation processes, AI optimizes routes for energy efficiency and resilience, while humans intervene for exceptions (e.g., customs delays, weather disruptions). Companies like FedEx and UPS integrate AI-driven route optimization with human oversight for last-mile delivery adjustments (Leonard, 2021; FedEx 2025).

In installation and commissioning, augmented reality (AR) and remote assistance technologies are increasingly used in field services and industrial maintenance to empower technicians with real-time guidance and visualization tools, while AI enhances operations through predictive maintenance insights. Human expertise remains essential for ensuring safety, decision-making, and effective customer interaction (Gäthke et al., 2020). For example, Siemens leverages AR for remote support, allowing technicians to receive real-time visual guidance during maintenance, installation, and repair tasks. By superimposing digital information onto the physical environment, AR enables experts to assist field technicians from virtually any location, minimizing travel requirements and enhancing operational efficiency (Llumin, 2025; AIDAR, 2025).

It is possible to say that human–machine collaboration in fulfillment under Industry 5.0 is not about replacing humans; it's about combining machine precision with human creativity and judgment to deliver personalized, sustainable, and resilient omnichannel experiences.

Sustainability and Circular Economy

Discussing sustainability and circular economy principles in fulfillment is essential because these factors directly shape the future competitiveness, compliance, and resilience of supply chains. Fulfillment operations sit at the heart of a company's environmental footprint, particularly in packaging, transportation, and returns, which remain among the largest contributors to carbon emissions and waste.

As regulatory frameworks continue to tighten, organizations face increasing pressure to align fulfillment practices with ESG reporting standards and waste-reduction mandates (Tonello, 2025). Companies that integrate circular principles, such as reusable packaging, reverse logistics, and closed-loop systems, not only mitigate regulatory risk but also preserve market access and enhance long-term resilience. This topic is further explored in the next chapter. Beyond compliance, customer expectations have become the actual global driver of sustainable fulfillment (Hines, 2024). Consumers today demand eco-friendly packaging, ethical sourcing, and operational transparency, regardless of geography (Nordigården et al., 2025). Meeting these expectations has become a strategic differentiator.

Sustainable fulfillment is therefore not simply an environmental initiative; it is a business imperative that strengthens brand reputation, fosters customer loyalty, and positions the supply chain as a catalyst for responsible growth in the Industry 5.0 era. Examples can be seen across all the key activities of fulfillment. AI-enabled scheduling systems, exemplified by *PlanetTogether*, integrate sustainability intelligence into production planning by synchronizing operations with renewable energy supply and low-carbon transport opportunities. This not only reduces energy usage and waste but also embeds environmental consciousness directly into operational decision-making. In the picking and packing processes, the use of reusable containers, compostable materials, right-size packaging, and returnable packaging programs is increasing. Shipping and transportation practices are also evolving, with EV fleets, route optimizations, alternative fuels, and predictive analytics to reduce empty miles and emissions.

Resilience Against Disruptions

Resilience has become a defining capability for modern supply chain leaders, driven not only by recent global disruptions but also by escalating customer expectations for seamless and reliable service. Within omnichannel fulfillment, resilience functions as a safeguard for brand integrity and operational continuity. Evidence suggests that organizations lacking resilience can experience revenue losses of up to 10 percent during severe disruptions (Mayer, 2023), whereas resilient networks recover more quickly, sustain service performance, and achieve superior competitiveness in volatile environments (McClure, 2025).

Across fulfillment processes, resilience is increasingly embedded through the integration of advanced technologies and adaptive business practices. During order scheduling, companies are adopting AI-driven predictive scheduling combined with scenario planning to respond dynamically to demand fluctuations or supply shortages. Maintaining multi-sourcing and nearshoring strategies further reduces dependence on single regions or suppliers.

Resilient order management systems (OMS) play a crucial role in ensuring operational continuity. These systems integrate real-time data, reverse logistics, and predictive analytics to manage unexpected returns, delays, and service interruptions. Leading enterprise solutions such as IBM Sterling and SAP exemplify this capability, alongside competitive platforms like Salesforce Order Management, Kibo, and Fluent Commerce.

In shipping and transportation, resilient networks diversify transportation modes (air, sea, rail, and road) and carrier partnerships to enable "just-in-case" flexibility. AI-powered transportation management systems (TMS) use predictive analytics for dynamic rerouting during geopolitical tensions, port closures, or severe weather events, ensuring continuity and efficiency.

At the installation and commissioning stage, organizations increasingly rely on AR-based remote assistance to minimize travel requirements and maintain service continuity during crises. In parallel, supplier redundancy for critical installation components strengthens the system's ability to withstand localized disruptions and accelerates recovery when failures occur.

At the core of Supply Chain 5.0 is an essential premise. While technology forms the backbone of resilient fulfillment systems, true resilience in Supply Chain 5.0 extends beyond algorithms and automation. It resides in the human–machine collaboration that enables organizations to interpret complex data, make adaptive decisions, and coordinate responses across global networks. AI, AR, and predictive analytics provide foresight, but it is human judgment, creativity, and ethical reasoning that transform foresight into strategic action. Supply chain leaders are therefore redefining resilience as a socio-technical capability, one that harmonizes digital intelligence with human insight to build systems that are not only efficient and robust but also empathetic, transparent, and sustainable.

Fulfillment Models in B2C, B2B, and Intra-Company Fulfillment

In today's interconnected marketplace, fulfillment is no longer a one-size-fits-all process; it is the strategic heartbeat of how value reaches customers, partners, and even internal operations. Understanding the distinctions between B2B and B2C, and intra-company fulfillment is essential because each represents a unique ecosystem of expectations, relationships, and technological demands. The shift toward Supply Chain 5.0 amplifies these differences: where automation once optimized speed and efficiency, the next generation of fulfillment must balance responsiveness, resilience, and human-centric intelligence across every flow of goods and information. Recognizing these fulfillment contexts is therefore not just operational; it is foundational to designing supply chains that are adaptive, sustainable, and capable of thriving in an era defined by constant change. The updated SCOR DS model also emphasizes this distinction, since each fulfillment type operates under fundamentally different demand patterns, customer expectations, and operational dynamics.

B2B fulfillment is defined by reliability, precision, and long-term partnership management. Orders are typically larger in volume, scheduling is contract-driven, and collaboration across partners requires deep integration of enterprise systems such as ERP, OMS, and TMS. In this context, resilience means maintaining supply continuity, process stability, and information transparency across organizational boundaries.

B2C fulfillment, by contrast, prioritizes responsiveness and customer experience. It demands agile, data-driven logistics capable of adapting in real time to individual preferences, fluctuating demand, returns management, and last-mile complexities. Here, resilience is measured by how effectively the system safeguards brand reputation while consistently meeting next-day or same-day delivery expectations.

Intra-company (internal) fulfillment occurs within a firm's own network, between plants, warehouses, and regional hubs. Its focus lies in synchronization, efficiency, and cost optimization. In this case, resilience ensures uninterrupted internal flows that sustain external performance in both B2B and B2C operations.

In essence, recognizing these differences empowers leaders to design adaptive, hybrid fulfillment strategies that integrate the best of all three, creating supply chains that are efficient internally, responsive externally, and resilient across disruptions. A key aspect of Industry 5.0 is the orchestration needed across the entire supply chain, as both order and fulfillment processes encompass B2B, B2C, and intralogistics. Due to the demand point, we decided to integrate Table 9.2, which offers readers a complementary snapshot of how personnel from the order can orchestrate and differentiate activities from those in the fulfillment departments.

Technology and Innovation

The Fulfill process is undergoing rapid transformation, driven by the integration of smart, adaptive, and increasingly autonomous technologies.

Table 9.2 Order Fulfillment Process

Demand/ Process	Order Process*	Fulfillment Process**	Connection	Difference	Supply Chain 5.0 Perspective
B2C (Business-to-Consumer)	E-commerce platforms, apps, POS systems	Parcel shipping, last-mile delivery	Both processes aim to satisfy the same demand but operate in different layers: Order is information flow, fulfillment is physical flow	Order focuses on accuracy and visibility of demand, while fulfillment focuses on speed, cost, and reliability of delivery	**Human-centric design:** Different stakeholders (consumers, business buyers, internal teams) have unique needs.
B2B (Business-to-Business)	EDI, procurement portals, negotiated contracts	Freight, bulk shipments, scheduled deliveries			**Technology alignment:** AI for B2C personalization, blockchain for B2B contracts, IoT for intralogistics visibility.
Intralogistics (Intra-Company)	Internal requisition systems, ERP triggers	Internal transfers, cross-docking			**Resilience:** Ability to adapt across multiple demand channels.

* Captures demand signals differently for each context

** Executes delivery differently

These tools not only enhance operational speed and accuracy but also enable greater personalization, lower environmental impact, and better working conditions.

Key technologies now reshaping fulfillment include:

- **Artificial intelligence (AI):** Applied in order routing, demand sensing, labor scheduling, and predictive delivery windows.
- **3D printing:** Enables localized production and fulfillment of spare parts or customized products, reducing lead times and emissions.
- **Advanced robotics and cobots:** Support collaborative picking, ergonomically assist workers, and adapt to product diversity.
- **Autonomous vehicles and drones:** Expand last-mile delivery options, especially in hard-to-reach or underserved areas.
- **IoT sensors and edge computing:** Enable real-time monitoring of package conditions, vehicle status, and cold chain integrity.
- **Digital twins:** Allow fulfillment centers to simulate workflows, optimize layouts, and stress-test operational changes.
- **Computer vision:** Verifies order accuracy, guides robotic systems, and automates quality checks.
- **Emissions intelligence platforms:** Quantify carbon impact by product, shipment, or customer profile.

These technologies improve both speed and sustainability while creating more responsive, inclusive, and data-driven fulfillment environments, as outlined in Table 9.3.

Table 9.3 Technology Impact and Benefit on Fulfill Subprocesses

Technology	Subprocess Impacted	Benefits for Supply Chain 5.0 Goals
AI-driven demand-aware routing	Manage Transportation	Increases resilience and accuracy, adapts to traffic and weather changes
3D printing	Pick and Pack, Final Assembly	Reduces inventory needs, enables local fulfillment, lowers emissions

(continued)

Table 9.3 (Continued)

Technology	Subprocess Impacted	Benefits for Supply Chain 5.0 Goals
Collaborative robots (cobots)	Pick and Pack	Supports worker ergonomics, speeds up fulfillment without over-automation
Autonomous delivery vehicles	Manage Transportation	Expands last-mile reach, reduces dependency on labor-constrained modes
IoT with edge analytics	Transportation, Customer Service	Improves cold chain visibility, reduces spoilage and customer complaints
Digital twins of DCs	Manage Orders, Pick and Pack	Enables simulation of order volume spikes, layout optimization
Computer vision systems	Pick and Pack, Customer Service	Ensures item accuracy, detects errors before shipment
Emissions tracking platforms	All subprocesses	Supports sustainability KPIs and customer transparency

By combining these technologies strategically, fulfillment operations can respond to increasing complexity with greater precision, flexibility, and empathy—for both customers and the workforce.

REAL-WORLD EXAMPLE AI-Driven Workforce Optimization in Distribution Centers

A luxury beauty retailer operating across the Middle East developed a machine learning agent to address workforce planning challenges in its distribution centers. Traditional forecasting methods often resulted in inaccurate staffing predictions, leading to potential operational inefficiencies and increased labor costs.

The AI agent uses predictive analytics to estimate daily staffing requirements by analyzing multiple variables, including seasonal events, market trends, and regional demand patterns. During high-volume periods like Ramadan, the agent helps managers more accurately predict workforce needs. By processing historical data and real-time market signals, the agent generates staffing recommendations that support more precise workforce planning.

Currently, the system operates as a decision support tool, with human managers retaining final decision-making authority. The project represents an initial step in integrating AI technologies into supply chain workforce management, demonstrating potential opportunities for more data-driven operational planning. The agent is scheduled to go live in the next two to three months, with initial implementation focused on understanding and predicting distribution center labor requirements.

Actionable Principles for Fulfill

- Design fulfillment networks that flex intelligently across channels, volumes, and geographies to support omnichannel demand and rapid disruption response.
- Use predictive and real-time data to schedule orders proactively, aligning capacity, routing, and labor with anticipated customer needs.
- Minimize waste in picking and packing by using right-size, reusable, or circular packaging and reducing split shipments through smarter order orchestration.
- Deploy collaborative robotics and automation to enhance ergonomics and safety while preserving human judgment for exceptions and complex tasks.
- Integrate sustainability metrics into daily decisions by using carbon-aware routing, emissions dashboards, and renewable energy-aligned scheduling.
- Improve transportation resilience through multimodal options, diversified carriers, and AI-driven dynamic rerouting during disruptions.
- Use augmented reality and remote assistance to accelerate installation, commissioning, and service support while reducing travel and downtime.
- Equip customer service teams with real-time visibility into orders, inventory, and transportation status so they can resolve issues quickly and confidently.

- Adopt digital financial processes such as automated invoicing, smart contracts, and traceable billing to improve accuracy, compliance, and speed.
- Continuously measure fulfillment success using a balanced scorecard of service quality, environmental impact, workforce safety, and system resilience.

References

Association for Supply Chain Management (ASCM) (2022) SCOR Digital Standard.

AIDAR Solutions (2025, August 31) Augmented reality field service explained. AIDAR Solutions.

Bell, D. R., Gallino, S. and Moreno, A. (2014) How to win in an omnichannel world. *MIT Sloan Management Review*, 56(1), 45–53.

Choi, T. Y., Li, J. J., Rogers, D. S., Schoenherr, T., and Wagner, S. M. (2020). *The Oxford Handbook of Supply Chain Management*. Oxford University Press.

Croxton, K. L. (2003) The order fulfillment process. *The International Journal of Logistics Management*, 14(1), 19-32.

CNBC (2024, July 31) Taco Bell to roll out AI drive-thru ordering in hundreds of locations. CNBC. www.cnbc.com/2024/07/31/taco-bell-to-roll-out-ai-drive-thru-ordering-in-hundreds-of-locations.html (archived at https://perma.cc/494F-SXRH)

FedEx (2025) Digital intelligence | FedEx.

Gäthke, J. (2020) The impact of augmented reality on overall service satisfaction in elaborate servicescapes. *Journal of Service Management*, *31*(2), 227-246.

Gessner, E. (2024, July 31) *Taco Bell puts AI front-and-center in drive-thru strategy, staff scheduling in Q3*. Customer Experience Dive.

Ghobakhloo, M., Fathi, M., Okwir, S., Al-Emran, M. and Ivanov, D. (2025) Adaptive social manufacturing: a human-centric, resilient, and sustainable framework for advancing Industry 5.0. *International Journal of Production Research*, 1–34.

Guynn, J. (2024, August 1) Taco Bell drive-thru adds AI voice technology: Here's how it works. *USA Today*.

Hines, T. (2024) *Supply Chain Strategies: Demand driven and customer focused*. Routledge.

Ishfaq, R., Darby, J. and Gibson, B. (2024) Adapting the retail business model to omnichannel strategy: A supply chain management perspective. *Journal of Business Logistics*, 45(1). https://doi.org/10.1111/jbl.12352 (archived at https://perma.cc/S5ZK-8ZYC)

Leonard, M. (2021, June 11) *UPS adds dynamic routing to ORION, saving 2–4 miles per driver.* Supply Chain Dive. www.supplychaindive.com/news/ups-orion-route-planning-analytics-data-logistics/601673/ (archived at https://perma.cc/TVD8-79CE)

Li, L. and Duan, L. (2025) Human-centric innovation at the heart of industry 5.0–exploring research challenges and opportunities. *International Journal of Production Research*, 1–33.

LLumin (2025, March 17) *The role of augmented reality in industrial maintenance.* https://llumin.com/blog/the-role-of-augmented-reality-in-industrial-maintenance/ (archived at https://perma.cc/54M7-MH65)

Mayer, M. (2023, April 12) Supply chain delays cause some companies 15% loss in revenue: Study. *Supply & Demand Chain Executive.* www.sdcexec.com/sourcing-procurement/erp/news/22820454/anvyl-supply-chain-delays-cause-some-companies-15-loss-in-revenue-study (archived at https://perma.cc/R8BB-YRE7)

McClure, R. (2025, September 16) Supply chain resilience: It's important and you need to know why. *SC Tech Insights.* https://sctechinsights.com/supply-chain-resilience-its-important-and-you-need-to-know-why/ (archived at https://perma.cc/FH6R-UYAE)

Nordigården, D., Feber, D., Grünewald, F. and Pley, M. (2025, June 4) Do US consumers care about sustainable packaging in 2025? McKinsey & Company.

Ponce, E. and Allegue, L. (2025) *Omnichannel Fulfillment: The promise and hope of AI and technology*. DCVelocity.

Rushton, A., Croucher, P. and Baker, P. (2022) *The Handbook of Logistics and Distribution Management: Understanding the supply chain.* Kogan Page Publishers.

Higginson, J. K. and Bookbinder, J. H. (2005) Distribution centres in supply chain operations. In *Logistics Systems: Design and optimization* (pp. 67-91) Boston, MA: Springer US.

Thirumalai, S. and Sinha, K. K. (2005) Customer satisfaction with order fulfillment in retail supply chains: implications of product type in electronic B2C transactions. *Journal of Operations Management*, 23(3-4), 291-303.

Tonello, M. (2025) Regulatory shifts in ESG: What comes next for companies? Harvard Law School Forum on Corporate Governance.

Return: Managing the Reverse Supply Chain

10

Regenerative certainly means reducing negative effects—climate change, material waste, and human exploitation. But it goes beyond that to encompass the idea of redoing what has broken and restoring what has come apart—whether in the environment, in the use of resources, or in the societal sphere.

KEARNEY REPORT BY SUKETU GANDHI,
IMRAN DASSU, CHRIS JONES, AND MEHIL SHINDE

Return: From Return to Reimagining the Supply Chain

In today's hyper-connected, consumer-driven world, reverse and return logistics have become indispensable pillars of modern supply chains. From managing product recalls to navigating the complexities of e-commerce returns, supply chain professionals are no longer just moving goods forward; they're orchestrating their journey back. Yet, as we refine these systems to be more efficient and responsive, a deeper question emerges: Are we merely optimizing the past, or are we designing for the future?

The answer lies in regeneration.

While reverse and return logistics address the symptoms of a linear economy, regenerative supply chains aim to rewrite its very blueprint. They challenge us to think beyond sustainability, to envision systems that restore ecosystems, strengthen communities, and create net-positive impact. As technologies become more accessible and adaptable, the opportunity to embed regenerative principles into our operations is not just viable; it's vital. This book invites you to explore the evolution from reactive logistics to proactive regeneration.

The Return process in the SCOR Digital Standard (SCOR DS) encompasses the strategic flow of goods, services, and associated components from the customer back through the supply or service chain (ASCM, 2022). It involves assessing product condition, verifying return eligibility, and determining appropriate disposition. This applies whether it involves reintegration into transformation cycles, reuse, or other circular pathways, to position inventory or services for future demand (ASCM, 2022). Furthermore, the updated ASCM model also reflects the reality of modern supply chains, specifically emphasizing sustainability, circularity, and resilience. This moves the framework beyond the traditional, linear flow of the SCOR model toward one in which every decision becomes a step toward restoring value (Bolstorff and Jacques, 2025).

Thus, as Industry 5.0 is reshaping reverse, return, and regenerative supply chains by emphasizing human-centric, resilience, and sustainability, here's how each process is being impacted:

- Resilience: Technologies such as predictive analytics and smart technologies enhance the ability to anticipate disruptions in reverse and return flows, enabling faster recovery and more agile responses. Decentralized production and localized supply networks reduce dependency on global systems, increasing adaptability during crises or demand fluctuations.
- Sustainability: Circular economy integration transforms returns and reverse logistics into opportunities for reuse, refurbishment, and remanufacturing, minimizing waste. Regenerative design principles promote supply chains that actively restore ecosystems and reduce environmental footprints through sustainable sourcing and closed-loop systems.
- Human-centricity: Collaborative robotics and AI empower workers by automating repetitive tasks while preserving human judgment for complex decisions in reverse and return processes. Customer-centric return experiences are enhanced through personalized support, transparency, and ethical technology use, fostering trust and long-term loyalty.

The Connection Between Plan and Returns

In the dynamic landscape of global commerce and e-commerce, the return and plan processes have emerged as critical connectors between supply and demand across the end-to-end supply chain. Far from being peripheral functions, these processes serve as the backbone of operational alignment, ensuring that resources flow efficiently, customer expectations are met, and disruptions are mitigated. As supply chains grow more complex and customer-centric, the ability to anticipate needs and respond to returns with agility is no longer optional; it's essential. Several foundational and modern academic studies highlight the importance of a simultaneous design between planning and returning products and services in supply chains and its impact on resiliency (Salema et al., 2010; Das, 2012; Jayaraman, 2006; Chien et al., 2024; Loza, 2025). Under this premise, we would like you to explore how these foundational processes are evolving in the age of Industry 5.0, using 4.0 technologies, and why embracing regenerative supply chain strategies is the next frontier for resilient, sustainable, and human-centered operations.

With this in mind, think in terms of regenerative supply chains that change how organizations operate across the tiers, inside and outside their walls.

Regenerative Supply Chains

The regenerative supply chain represents a transformative frontier in supply chain research. Although the term "regenerative supply chain" is emergent, academic frameworks are still being developed (e.g., Howard et al., 2019; Oyefusi et al., 2024). For clarity, it is important to position this concept as building upon and extending the principles of sustainable and circular supply chain thinking. For leaders, this shift requires a systemic perspective, understanding supply chains as interconnected socio-ecological systems rather than isolated value streams. It also demands place-based strategies, recognizing that supply chains operate within specific landscapes and communities. This approach is not just theoretical; it has practical implications for sourcing, production, and network design, especially in adapting global supply chains to local contexts.

Regenerative supply chains shift the focus from efficiency and sustainability to actively healing, restoring, and enriching the socio-ecological systems in which supply chains operate (Bag et al., 2025). Here, supply chain leaders need to think in terms of systems. Systems designed to actively improve their supply chains by not only minimizing harm to the planet, people, and environment but also actively seeking ways to enhance their profits and ecosystem in the same manner. The concept replaces the "take-make-waste" model with a regenerative one that replenishes natural resources, enhances biodiversity, and fosters social equity, creating more value than they consume (Bag et al., 2025; Rosca et al., 2025). This involves using principles from ecology and circular economy models, focusing on long-term, resilient, and ethical practices across the entire supply chain (Bag et al., 2025; Rosca et al., 2025). Based on the research conducted for this book, we aimed to provide readers with four high-level key principles of regenerative supply chains in Figure 10.1, while accounting for the Industry 5.0 pillars. This is not an exhaustive list, but as we enter the new era of supply chain, the literature and applications of these principles will evolve.

1 **Environmental restoration.** Rather than merely reducing negative impacts such as emissions, waste, and labor issues, a regenerative supply chain aims to restore, renew, and enhance the systems it interacts with in nature, society, and the economy. Think in terms of circularity, repairing, restoring, and renewing natural systems and materials used in services and goods where supply chains operate. According to the United States Environmental Protection Agency, regenerative systems are designed to be restorative by nature, maintaining the highest value of resources for as long as possible (US EPA, 2025). Regenerative supply chains actively restore ecosystems, including soil health, biodiversity, and water cycles, rather than just minimizing adverse effects. Why does this matter for Supply Chain 5.0? If we see Supply Chain 5.0 as the next-generation model, its value isn't just about efficiency and resilience; it also emphasizes restoration, regeneration, and systems integration.

2 **Social empowerment.** Regenerative supply chains adopt the mindset that value creation is not zero-sum (company vs environment/society) but shared. The chain should uplift suppliers, communities, and ecosystems. Local economies are part of regenerative supply chains that support local communities, especially small and mid-sized producers, ensuring equitable access to markets and resources, often looking at enhancing the health of ecosystems and communities they either operate in or serve. A study in the *Journal of Circular Economy* positions regenerative business strategies as aiming for "strong sustainability" and net positive outcomes (Salonen et al., 2025).

3 **Human-centric implications.** Regenerative supply chains not only prioritize local communities by integrating traditional knowledge and ensuring equitable distribution of economic benefits but also emphasize the importance of upholding fair labor practices, occupational health and safety, and family-friendly workplaces. These are essential for creating supply chains that support human dignity and well-being, according to United Nations Global Compact (2025). Why is this important for Supply Chain 5.0? Human-centric regenerative supply chains require transparent governance, ethical sourcing, and inclusive decision-making. This ensures that all stakeholders, especially marginalized groups, have a voice in shaping supply chain practices.

4 **Enhance profitability.** For companies, transparency and traceability are also essential concepts in the Supply Chain 5.0. Regenerative supply chains require robust data flows and transparency to track materials, emissions, and social impacts across the value chain. MIT's Sustainable Supply Chain Lab emphasizes the importance of improving metrics and transparency to advance sustainability goals (Dizikes, 2025). Metrics are fundamental for creating value through regeneration and enhancing operational efficiency through cost reduction. A World Economic Forum (Radjou, 2024) report found that nearly 80 percent of US consumers prefer regenerative brands over merely sustainable ones. This shift in consumer preference can lead to increased sales and brand loyalty, especially among Gen Y and Gen Z consumers who value companies that actively contribute to societal and environmental well-being. Regenerative practices often allow companies to command premium prices for products that are ethically sourced, environmentally friendly, and socially responsible. For example, Natura, a Brazilian cosmetics firm, increased profitability by sourcing murumuru butter sustainably, generating seven times more economic value than traditional logging (Radjou, 2024). The Ellen MacArthur Foundation (2023) highlights that circular and regenerative supply chains help businesses reduce costs by minimizing waste, improving resource efficiency, and lowering greenhouse gas emissions. This leads to greater resilience and less exposure to resource price volatility.

Regenerative supply chains move beyond sustainability by considering the entire product lifecycle and its impact on interconnected systems: Social, ecological, and economic. This approach requires systems thinking and an appreciation of place-based contexts, recognizing that supply chains operate within specific landscapes and communities.

Figure 10.1 Key Principles in Regenerative 5.0 Supply Chains

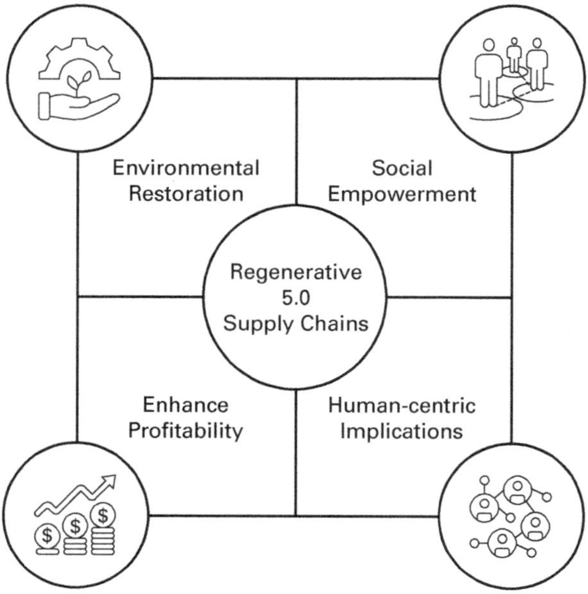

In their article "From Green to Regenerative Supply Chain Management in Construction," Oyefusi et al. (2024) identify key principles such as Focus on Place and Harmony with Ecosystems. Similarly, Gualandris et al. (2024) argue that regenerative supply chains "connect locales and landscapes that are otherwise disconnected via economic flows."

The implication for leaders of global, national, and local supply chains is that they must adapt to place-specific dynamics, as there is no single standard "checklist" yet for implementing regenerative supply chains. Different sectors will interpret these principles in context (such as soil regeneration in raw material sourcing or socio-economic conditions in labor hubs, raw materials, agriculture, manufacturing, apparel, electronics, etc.). This adaptation can also become a strategic differentiator. Regenerative models emphasize local and regional sourcing, production, and networks, reducing reliance on centralized global systems. Such localization fosters the regrowth of local ecosystems and mitigates hidden environmental and social externalities.

The implementation also requires deeper stakeholder engagement and often higher upfront investment. Still, the long-term payoff is resilience, brand value, and system health (which aligns well with Supply Chain 5.0's advanced ambition). Within Supply Chain 5.0, this principle aligns with digital enablers, blockchain, IoT, and AI, which enhance transparency, traceability, and profitability. However, technology alone is insufficient; leaders must also prioritize the human and relational dimension, including stakeholder co-innovation and community partnerships.

Technology and Innovation

When considering reverse supply chains, it is crucial to recognize that the processes vary significantly depending on the context, whether handling products, services, or internal maintenance, repair, and overhaul (MRO) operations. SCOR DS clearly makes this distinction by defining each process.

- **Return product:** The reverse supply chain involves a series of activities focused on receiving, diagnosing, and determining the disposition of returned products, followed by positioning them for their next stage, whether reuse, repair, or recycling. These return processes require strategic decision-making, including considerations for circular economy principles, optimization of return pathways (often across international borders), entitlement verification, and effective inventory management.
- **Return service:** Managing the return of services involves activities such as receiving requests, diagnosing issues, and executing the necessary actions to close or adjust the service engagement. Unlike product returns, service returns may occur through digital channels, face-to-face interactions (e.g., formal meetings), or other communication pathways. These processes often include financial validations, entitlement checks, and considerations related to environmental impact and compliance, ensuring that service reversals align with contractual and sustainability objectives.
- **Return maintenance, repair, and overhaul:** The MRO return process is distinct because it typically involves returning the same product unit to the original customer, verified through identifiers such as serial numbers or unit IDs. In some cases, based on the service agreement or contract, the replacement may be a previously repaired and stocked item rather than the original unit. It is important to note that these return processes do not encompass the actual maintenance, repair, or overhaul activities themselves; those are generally classified under Transform processes.

While each reverse supply chain type has distinct requirements and workflows, they share a set of five core processes that create a standard foundation. These shared processes connect otherwise different return activities, ensuring consistency and integration across the reverse supply chain.

Emergent technologies in the reverse supply chain for Industry 5.0 focus on combining advanced digital tools with human-centric principles to create sustainable, efficient, and resilient systems. Here are the key technologies and how they are applied:

Process 1. Receipt and Verification

Main activity: All return types begin with receiving the returned item or request and verifying its legitimacy. This includes entitlement checks (e.g., warranty, contract terms) and identity validation (serial numbers for products/MRO, service agreements for services).

Technologies being used:

- Barcode and QR code scanning for quick identification and validation of returned products.
- RFID (radio frequency identification) enables automated tracking and verification of items in warehouses.
- Blockchain provides secure, immutable records for entitlement verification and authenticity checks.
- AI-powered document verification automates validation of service agreements and warranty claims.
- IoT sensors capture real-time data on product condition and location during receipt.
- Digital portals and mobile apps facilitate customer-initiated return requests and entitlement checks.

Process 2. Diagnosis and Assessment

Main activity: Evaluating the condition or status of the returned product or service. For products, this includes physical inspection and functional testing; for services, validation against service-level agreements; for MRO, component integrity checks and compliance verification.

Technologies being used:

- IoT Sensors capture real-time data on product health and usage history.
- AI and machine learning analyze failure patterns, predict repair needs, and classify defects.
- Computer vision automates visual inspection for damage or wear.

- Digital twins simulate product performance and diagnose issues virtually.
- Augmented reality (AR) assists technicians in complex diagnostics with guided overlays.
- Cloud-based diagnostic platforms centralize data for multi-location analysis and collaboration.

Process 3. Disposition Decision

Main activity: Determining the next step for the returned item or service; whether to repair, refurbish, recycle, redeploy, or apply a financial adjustment. This decision often integrates circular economy principles and aligns with sustainability goals.

Technologies being used:

- AI and machine learning for predictive decision-making based on cost, condition, and environmental impact.
- Advanced analytics platforms to evaluate multiple scenarios for optimal disposition.
- Blockchain ensures transparency in recycling and redeployment decisions.
- Digital twins simulate outcomes for repair vs. replacement strategies.
- Decision support systems (DSS) combine operational, financial, and sustainability data for informed choices.

Process 4. Positioning and Execution

Main activity: Implementing the chosen disposition. For products, this includes moving items to refurbishing, remanufacturing, or recycling centers. For services, it could be adjusting contracts, issuing credits, or terminating agreements. For MRO, it includes returning the original unit or a substitute (previously repaired) item to the customer.

Technologies being used:

- Warehouse management systems (WMS) automate routing and storage for returned products.
- Robotics and automated guided vehicles (AGVs) handle physical movement of items to refurbishing or recycling zones.
- Blockchain tracks chain of custody for redeployed or recycled items.

- IoT sensors monitor item location and condition during transfer.
- Smart contracts automate service adjustments or entitlement-based replacements.
- Transportation management systems (TMS) optimize logistics for cross-border returns.

Process 5. Financial and Inventory Management

Main activity: Processing credits, refunds, or replacements, and updating inventory records for returned items or repaired stock to maintain accurate financial and operational data.

Technologies being used:

- Enterprise resource planning (ERP) systems integrate financial transactions with inventory updates.
- Blockchain provides secure, transparent records for refunds and entitlement-based adjustments.
- Robotic process automation (RPA) automates repetitive financial tasks like credit issuance and ledger updates.
- AI-powered analytics detects anomalies in return-related financial transactions and optimizes refund processes.
- Cloud-based inventory management platforms synchronize stock levels across multiple locations in real time.

Table 10.1 demonstrates how each of these technologies impacts Return subprocesses and details the benefits of technology for Supply Chain 5.0.

Table 10.1 Technology Impact and Benefit on Return Subprocesses

Technology	Subprocess Impacted	Benefits for Supply Chain 5.0 Goals
AI returns analysis	Inspect and Disposition	Identifies patterns, reduces recurrence, and improves customer service
Customer return portals	Receive Return Request	Improves accessibility and transparency
Blockchain authentication	Approve Return and Disposition	Prevents fraud and ensures product identity

(continued)

Table 10.1 (Continued)

Technology	Subprocess Impacted	Benefits for Supply Chain 5.0 Goals
Automated visual inspection	Inspect and Disposition	Reduces manual errors and improves decision consistency
Disposition optimization tools	Disposition, Reverse Logistics	Minimizes waste and enhances reuse or resale
Emissions tracking dashboards	All	Quantifies impact and informs circular design
Robotics for sorting	Reverse Logistics	Reduces injury risk and increases processing speed
Digital twins for returns	All	Enables return policy optimization and volume forecasting

These tools transform returns into a **data-rich, circular, and strategic capability**, rather than a reactive burden.

Actionable Principles for Return

- Design return policies to be transparent, fair, and explicitly aligned with regenerative and circular outcomes.
- Embed regenerative thinking into return pathways by prioritizing repair, refurbishment, repurposing, and material recovery over disposal.
- Integrate planning and return processes so that real-time return insights continuously inform forecasting, inventory, and capacity decisions.
- Use AI, IoT, and digital twins to automate diagnostics, optimize disposition decisions, and minimize environmental and financial waste.
- Implement traceability technologies such as blockchain, RFID, and sensors to ensure entitlement accuracy, authenticity, and accountability.
- Design human-centric return experiences that are intuitive, empathetic, and supportive for customers, workers, and partners.

- Leverage return data to inform upstream product and service design improvements in durability, reparability, modularity, and customer satisfaction.
- Develop localized networks of repair, refurbish, and recycling partners to strengthen regional circular loops and reduce transportation impact.
- Automate physical handling in reverse logistics using robotics and smart warehousing to improve safety, speed, and consistency.
- Measure and govern return performance using metrics that reflect value recovery, ecosystem impact, worker well-being, and customer trust.

References

Bag, S., Rahman, M. S., Routray, S. and Khurana, R. (2025) Regenerative supply chain orientation and coopetition in supply chain networks for ESG initiatives: A parallel mediation study. *Journal of Business Research*, 201, 115685.

Bolstorff, P. and Jacques, A. (2025) Transform your supply chain using ASCM's SCOR DS model, With Peter Bolstorff. *Big Ideas in Supply Chain*. www.kinaxis.com/en/big-ideas/insights/transform-your-supply-chain-using-ascms-scords-model-peter-bolstorff (archived at https://perma.cc/Y98F-RLB3).

Chien, C. F., Kuo, H. A. and Lin, Y. S. (2024) Smart semiconductor manufacturing for pricing, demand planning, capacity portfolio and cost for sustainable supply chain management. *International Journal of Logistics Research and Applications*, 27(1), 193–216.

Das, K. (2012) Integrating reverse logistics into the strategic planning of a supply chain. *International Journal of Production Research*, 50(5), 1438–1456.

Dizikes, P. (2025) Report: Sustainability in supply chains is still a firm-level priority. Massachusetts Institute of Technology, *MIT News*.

Ellen MacArthur Foundation (2023) *Building A Circular Supply Chain: Achieving resilient operations with the circular economy*.

Gualandris, J., Branzei, O., Wilhelm, M., Lazzarini, S., Linnenluecke, M., Hamann, R. and Chen, C. M. (2024) Unchaining supply chains: Transformative leaps toward regenerating social–ecological systems. *Journal of Supply Chain Management*, 60(1), 53–67.

Howard, M., Hopkinson, P. and Miemczyk, J. (2019) The regenerative supply chain: A framework for developing circular economy indicators. *International Journal of Production Research*, 57(23), 7300–318.

Jayaraman, V. (2006) Production planning for closed-loop supply chains with product recovery and reuse: An analytical approach. *International Journal of Production Research*, 44(5), 981–98.

Loza Adaui, C. R. (2025) The principle of regeneration in circular economy: Revitalising for resilience. In *Circular Economy in Sustainable Supply Chains: A global perspective on challenges, concepts and cases* (pp. 49–60). Cham: Springer Nature Switzerland.

Oyefusi, O. N., Enegbuma, W. I., Brown, A. and Zari, M. P. (2024) From green to regenerative supply chain management in construction: Towards a conceptual framework. *Environmental Development*, 52, 101097.

Radjou, N. (2024) Regeneration: Why businesses are moving beyond sustainability and thinking about regrowth. Sustainable Development. World Economic Forum. https://europeansting.com/2024/06/07/regeneration-why-businesses-are-moving-beyond-sustainability-and-thinking-about-regrowth/ (archived at https://perma.cc/RU68-AVAM)

Rosca, E., et al. (2025) Reconceptualizing value creation for regenerative supply chains: The role of non-traditional actors. *Academy of Management Proceedings*, 2025. No. 1. Valhalla, NY 10595: Academy of Management.

Salema, M. I. G., Barbosa-Povoa, A. P. and Novais, A. Q. (2010) Simultaneous design and planning of supply chains with reverse flows: A generic modelling framework. *European Journal of Operational Research*, 203(2), 336–49.

Salonen, K., Ritala, P. and Bocken, N. (2025) Emerging regenerative business paradigm: Narrative review, synthesis, and research agenda. *Journal of Circular Economy*, 3(3).

United Nations Global Compact (2025) Apply sustainable practices throughout the supply chain. Supply Chain Sustainability. https://unglobalcompact.org/engage-locally/manage/engagement/supply-chain-sustainability (archived at https://perma.cc/L5FW-SP33)

United States Environmental Protection Agency (2025) What is a Circular Economy? www.epa.gov/circulareconomy/what-circular-economy (archived at https://perma.cc/GGE5-UCCC)

Orchestrate: Collaboration Across the Supply Chain

11

A symphony must be like the world. It must contain everything.

GUSTAV MAHLER

Orchestrate: From Silos to Coordination

Imagine a symphony orchestra: Dozens of musicians, each with unique instruments, playing in harmony under the guidance of a conductor. Now, picture a modern supply chain: Multiple stakeholders, technologies, and processes working together to deliver value. Just as an orchestra needs precise coordination to create music, Supply Chain 5.0 requires orchestration. Orchestration can be seen as the seamless integration of emerging technologies, human creativity, and business objectives to build resilient, sustainable global networks. Orchestration can be defined as the arrangement of a musical composition for an orchestra or, more broadly, the harmonious organization of diverse elements to achieve a specific result. In this chapter, we adopt that broader definition: Orchestration as the art of aligning diverse components to deliver a unified outcome.

In this new era, supply chains are no longer linear systems but dynamic ecosystems where emerging technologies such as automation, artificial intelligence, and advanced analytics work hand in hand with human judgment and innovation. Orchestration ensures that these diverse elements operate in harmony, enabling organizations to respond quickly to disruptions, optimize resources, and deliver value responsibly. By aligning technological capabilities with profitability and purpose, Supply Chain 5.0

transforms complexity into coordinated performance, creating networks that are not only efficient but also adaptable and ethically grounded.

The Association for Supply Chain Management, in its SCOR Digital Standard Model (ASCM, 2022a), includes the Orchestrate Supply Chain management process concept as encompassing the activities required to integrate and enable supply chain strategies. This involves establishing and managing business rules, driving performance through continuous improvement, and overseeing data, information, and technology. It also includes managing human resources, contracts and agreements, network design, regulatory compliance, and risk. Furthermore, orchestration extends to Environment, Social, and Governance (ESG) initiatives, integrated business planning, segmentation strategies, and circular supply chain practices, all working together to create a cohesive, resilient, and sustainable supply chain ecosystem (ASCM, 2022a).

The orchestration process was introduced into modern supply chain frameworks because traditional siloed approaches could no longer manage today's complexity, volatility, and sustainability requirements (Bolstorff, 2025). Its purpose is to break down silos and align end-to-end processes, enable real-time visibility and agility, and leverage emerging technologies without creating fragmentation. These capabilities are essential under the new era of Supply Chain 5.0. In this context, orchestration refers to the intelligent coordination and synchronization of end-to-end supply chain activities enabled by technologies, business, and human insights, to ensure that every function operates in harmony with customer needs, environmental stewardship, employees' well-being, and business goals.

- Orchestration enhances resilience by transforming fragmented operations into a synchronized ecosystem. Through shared data platforms, AI-driven visibility, and cross-partner collaboration, disruptions are detected early, and responses become proactive rather than reactive.
- A well-orchestrated supply chain also advances sustainability by optimizing resource use, reducing waste, and aligning partners toward shared ESG goals.
- At its heart, Supply Chain 5.0 places people back at the center of the supply chain. Orchestration enables human-centricity by using technology to augment rather than replace human roles.

An Ecosystem Orchestrator

Supply Chain 5.0 marks a decisive shift from the automation-centric focus of Supply Chain 4.0 toward a model that harmonizes advanced technologies with human creativity, ethics, and strategic intent. Villar et al. (2023) provide a comprehensive overview of the concepts, technologies, and trends shaping this next-generation paradigm, emphasizing its transformative advantages for organizations. Conversely, Zekhnini et al. (2024) underscore critical challenges, including overreliance on technology, rising complexity, potential system failures, and heightened cybersecurity risks. Environmental impact and socio-economic disparities further complicate the digitalization of supply chains. These opportunities and risks demand equal attention from leaders committed to building balanced, human-centered, and resilient ecosystems.

Within the SCOR DS framework, Orchestrate is classified as a Level 0 process. Level 0 represents orchestration as the strategic tier that sets direction and influences all subsequent levels, ensuring alignment across the entire supply chain model (ASCM, 2022a). The framework identifies 12 supporting processes that collectively enable effective business implementation. Each process includes detailed subprocesses and performance metrics designed to evaluate and continuously improve supply chain capabilities (ASCM, 2022b). The objective of integrating SCOR DS orchestration into Supply Chain 5.0 is not to replicate existing content but to reinterpret its principles for today's dynamic, technology-driven environment.

In this new paradigm, orchestration becomes indispensable. Unlike traditional supply chains that operated in silos, Supply Chain 5.0 demands end-to-end integration across global networks. This integration is not merely technical; it is strategic, requiring alignment of processes, people, and platforms to deliver resilience, sustainability, and profitability simultaneously. Organizations must manage the physical flows of goods, the financial flows of capital, and the digital flows of information in real time. Orchestration enables dynamic response by connecting decision-making layers, providing visibility, and fostering agility. It ensures that emerging technologies such as AI, IoT, and advanced analytics function as part of a cohesive system guided by strategic objectives.

Ultimately, orchestration transforms complexity into coordinated performance. It acts as the conductor of the supply chain symphony, harmonizing diverse elements, technologies, processes, business objectives, and people, into a unified strategic rhythm. Beyond technology, orchestration underscores the

Figure 11.1 Orchestration Outcomes Under Supply Chain 5.0

human dimension, where leadership, collaboration, and purpose create true coherence. The orchestrator is not merely a manager of processes but a curator of harmony across the entire value network. Orchestration in Supply Chain 5.0 is critical because it delivers four essential outcomes: Harmonizing technology with human creativity, ensuring end-to-end integration, enabling agility and resilience, and embedding sustainability and ESG principles into the core of supply chain operations. See Figure 11.1.

Five Aspects of Orchestration in Supply Chain 5.0

Orchestration is far more relevant today than ever before. As supply chains stretch across continents, involve multiple tiers of partners, and face continuous disruption, mere automation or functional optimization no longer suffices. Today's value chains require intelligent coordination of people, processes, technologies, and data, which we call orchestration.

The notion of supply chain orchestration is relatively recent. While the term "supply chain management" first emerged in the early 1980s, academic work on orchestration started to appear in the 2010s, when scholars and practitioners realized that firms needed to act as orchestrators of entire networks, not just managers of internal operations (Li et al., 2016). For example, a 2022 article in *Academy of Management Perspectives* titled "Creating Value Through Supply Chain Orchestration as a Business Model" defines orchestration as a business model that enables value creation amid uncertainty (Phadnis, 2023). Therefore, orchestration as a distinct concept has emerged over the last decade, gaining traction as digital, networked, and disrupted supply chains require more than just optimizing isolated parts; they require the synchronization of entire ecosystems.

What has changed now is the convergence of three factors: Increasing complexity and volatility in global value networks; the maturity of enabling technologies (AI, IoT, cloud, digital twins, cobots, biomanufacturing, among others); and shifting expectations toward resilience, sustainability, and human-centric value. One recent review states that orchestration allows firms to manage "complex, fragmented supply chains in a unified way" (Venne, 2025).

In other words, orchestration is more important today because it connects the need for supply chains to be agile, resilient, responsible, and human-centered with their ability to use real-time data, insights, collaboration, and automation. Volatility and complexity are fundamental parts of today's operating environment, and most organizations still face major disruptions, highlighting the limitations of siloed optimization and ad hoc coordination. Orchestration solves these problems by transforming scattered signals into shared context and coordinated actions across partners (Alicke et al., 2024). Table 11.1 provides an overview of five aspects that show why Orchestration is relevant in Supply Chain 5.0.

Table 11.1 Five Dimensions of Orchestration in Supply Chain 5.0

Key Aspects	Why it matters
Integration over control	Unlike hierarchical "command-and-control" management, orchestration prioritizes *connection and alignment* across decentralized actors. In ecosystem terms, orchestrators rely on non-hierarchical governance, standards, and incentives to mobilize voluntary contributions toward a coherent system-level value proposition. Practically, this means aligning goals, data definitions, and decision cadences rather than dictating local decisions (Autio, 2022; Shen et al., 2024).

(continued)

Table 11.1 (Continued)

Key Aspects	Why it matters
Real-time visibility (to decide and act, not just to see)	Orchestration depends on transparent, timely data flows across partners and platforms, often via control-tower-style capabilities that combine people, process, data, organization, and technology to capture near-real-time signals and drive collaborative responses (not just dashboards). This is essential to sense disruptions, simulate options, and coordinate execution across the network (Gupta, 2022; Thompson and Ellis, 2024).
Human + machine collaboration	Supply Chain 5.0 marries AI/analytics, IoT sensing, and automation with human judgment, ethics, and creativity. Research on Industry/Supply Chain 5.0 highlights that the biggest performance gains occur when humans and machines are complementary, not substitutive; AI augments sense-making and prediction; humans handle ambiguity, empathy, and values-based trade-offs (Nicoletti, 2023; Dacre et al., 2025).
Ecosystem alignment	Orchestration extends beyond the enterprise to suppliers, logistics partners, customers, financiers, and regulators. Effective ecosystem orchestration builds trust and shared purpose, sets participation standards (data, compliance, service levels), and aligns incentives so that multi-party actions reinforce the strategy instead of fragmenting it (Bailey, 2023; Autio, 2022).
Outcome-driven by design	The aim is not activity for its own sake, but consistent, customer-centric outcomes, service, speed, resilience, sustainability/ESG, and innovation, tailored to segments and contexts. This moves supply chains from price-driven, decoupled designs to value-driven, strategically coupled networks that deliver multiple outcomes simultaneously (Melnyk et al., 2010; Baldi et al., 2024).

In short, orchestration conducts the entire value network like a symphony: Technology provides precision and humans provide purpose, so the whole performs better than the sum of its parts (Nicoletti, 2023).

For supply chain leaders, practical implications can include:

- **Go from visibility to coordinated response.** Adopt control towers or command center capabilities that support the cycle: See → decide → act → learn, with cross-functional playbooks and partner collaboration rooms so that alerts lead to synchronized actions, not parallel firefighting.

- **Codify human-in-the-loop decisions.** Embed governance for ethical AI, role clarity for exception management, and decision cadences that elevate trade-offs (service/cost/ESG) to the right forum at the right time.
- **Design for ecosystem trust.** Invest in standards (data, security, compliance) and incentives that reduce sharing frictions; orchestrators succeed by shaping the context more than by owning every asset.
- **Measure outcomes, not activities.** Link KPI outcomes (e.g., service/resilience/sustainability) to KPI diagnostics and improvement backlogs so every gap has an owner, a root cause, and a funded fix.

The 3V's as a Multi-Dimensional Lens for Supply Chain 5.0

In 1998, Art Mesher introduced the now-classic framework of the 3V's: Visibility, Variability, and Velocity. Originally presented at a Gartner conference, this model encouraged companies to move beyond a narrow focus on cost cutting toward using supply chain as a driver of profitable growth (Gilmore, 2019). Over the past two decades, the 3V's have become a foundation for logistics optimization. In the era of Supply Chain 5.0, they take on new life as design principles for orchestration, where networks are dynamically configured to balance efficiency, adaptability, and shared value.

Mesher himself describes the 3V's as an "equalizer," where each organization must tune Visibility, Variability, and Velocity differently based on its network and strategy (Gilmore, 2019). That flexibility makes the framework a natural fit for the Fulfill process in the SCOR DS model and for the three core goals of Supply Chain 5.0: Resilience, sustainability, and human-centricity. Each V influences each goal in complex and interconnected ways.

Visibility in Mesher's words is "a more granular and real-time view of what is happening in the extended supply chain—a never-ending but necessary journey" (Gilmore, 2019). For resilience, deep multi-tier visibility allows disruptions to be seen and acted upon collectively rather than in silos. For sustainability, visibility extends to impact metrics such as carbon emissions and ethical sourcing, making responsible choices actionable. For human-centricity, visibility must empower people as well as systems. Mesher warns that "knowing what has already happened no longer offers advantage," and calls for networks that connect "people, places, and things" into real-time information engines (Gilmore, 2019). That is as much about enabling frontline decision-making and building consumer trust as it is about data streams.

Variability is the force that creates both risk and opportunity. Mesher defines it as "the ability to manage the unique combinations of customers, products, channels, and supply chain management processes" (Gilmore, 2019). Adaptive management of variability builds resilience by letting networks absorb shocks without collapsing. Handling variability intelligently also drives sustainability by avoiding the waste that comes from overreaction—such as unnecessary buffer inventory or expedited shipments. For human-centricity, the way variability is handled determines whether workers experience constant chaos or predictable, humane patterns. Mesher notes that managing variability requires deliberate choices about "what needs to be standardized versus what needs to be unique," a tension that directly affects the experience of people in the system (Gilmore, 2019).

In Mesher's framing, Velocity is "the clock speed at which a given supply chain operates" (Gilmore, 2019). In Supply Chain 5.0, velocity is not just about going fast but about calibrating the right speed. The right velocity enhances resilience by enabling quick responses to disruption while preserving capacity to recover. It supports sustainability by optimizing flows to minimize wasted energy and materials instead of burning resources for speed alone. For human-centricity, velocity determines the intensity of work and the quality of service. Mesher argues that winning companies will be those that "design themselves in a way that allows them to assemble and disassemble ecosystems and compete through this dynamic reconfiguration" (Gilmore, 2019). That vision places velocity at the heart of orchestration: Not just moving goods quickly but reconfiguring networks quickly, in ways that work for both businesses and people.

When we overlay the 3V's onto the goals of Supply Chain 5.0, we do not get a simple one-to-one mapping. Instead, we see a matrix of interdependencies where each V must be tuned to serve resilience, sustainability, and human-centricity at the same time. This is the shift from optimization to orchestration. For the Fulfill process, it means moving beyond making the system efficient in isolation toward designing fulfillment networks that can dynamically sense, adapt, and balance value for business, society, and people simultaneously.

Table 11.2 illustrates how the 3V's framework maps to the three primary goals of Supply Chain 5.0: Resilience, sustainability, and human-centricity. Each cell provides examples of how a given "V" can actively support a specific goal across the broader supply chain ecosystem, including customers, suppliers, employees, executives, regulators, governments, shareholders, and society at large. These examples highlight the enduring value of the 3V's as a practical orchestration tool, bridging traditional supply chain priorities with the evolving demands of Supply Chain 5.0.

Table 11.2 Art Mesher's 3V's vs Supply Chain 5.0 Goals

Art Mesher's 3V's	Resilience	Sustainability	Human-Centricity (All Stakeholders)
Visibility	• Customers: Early warning on delays maintains trust. • Suppliers: Shared risk dashboards coordinate responses. • Regulators/Government: Real-time compliance and crisis status visibility. • Executives/Shareholders: Clear risk exposure supports strategic decisions. • Employees: Transparent hazard and safety data improve readiness. • Society: Public visibility into recovery builds confidence.	• Customers: Traceability ensures eco-friendly and ethical sourcing. • Suppliers: See sustainability metrics to align operations. • Regulators/Government: Continuous ESG reporting ensures compliance. • Executives/Shareholders: Visibility into impact metrics supports long-term value. • Employees: Transparent labor practices enhance morale. • Society: Public access to impact data reinforces accountability.	• Customers: See origins and ethical footprint. • Suppliers: Access demand and collaboration data. • Regulators/Government: Compliance visibility. • Executives/Shareholders: Performance dashboards. • Employees: Access safety and well-being data. • Society: See societal value creation and ethical practices.

Velocity	• Customers: Quick rerouting maintains service continuity. • Suppliers: Rapid updates on orders reduce losses. • Regulators/Government: Timely alerts for policy response. • Executives/Shareholders: Fast, data-driven crisis decisions. • Employees: Swift response protocols reduce downtime and risk. • Society: Rapid adaptation reduces systemic shocks.	• Customers: Faster cycle times reduce waste and emissions per order. • Suppliers: Accelerated reverse logistics supports circular economy. • Regulators/Government: Real-time reporting of emissions and compliance. • Executives/Shareholders: Shorter ROI timelines on sustainable initiatives. • Employees: Streamlined processes reduce wasted effort and stress. • Society: Quicker adoption of green practices reduces environmental harm.	• Customers: Rapid, reliable fulfillment. • Suppliers: Fast payments and collaboration. • Regulators: Timely data reporting. • Executives/Shareholders: Speedy insight to align strategy. • Employees: Quick support for workplace needs. • Society/Government: Agile response to crises and social needs.

(continued)

Table 11.2 (Continued)

Art Mesher's 3V's	Resilience	Sustainability	Human-Centricity (All Stakeholders)
Variability	• Customers: Buffer capacity absorbs demand shocks. • Suppliers: Flexible contracts handle supply shifts. • Regulators/Government: Ability to incorporate regulatory changes quickly. • Executives/Shareholders: Dynamic models protect ROI in volatile markets. • Employees: Workforce flexibility and cross-training maintain operations. • Society: Social systems absorb disruption impacts equitably.	• Customers: Adaptive sourcing balances cost, quality, and environmental impact. • Suppliers: Diversified supplier base reduces resource strain. • Regulators/Government: Supports compliance with evolving ESG rules. • Executives/Shareholders: Adjust investment portfolios to prioritize sustainable returns. • Employees: Training adapts workforce to sustainable practices. • Society: Promotes balance between economic growth and ecological preservation.	• Customers: Mass-customized products and services. • Suppliers: Handle variable orders without strain. • Regulators/Government: Integrate policy changes smoothly. • Executives/Shareholders: Adjust strategy for diverse market needs. • Employees: Flexible work models for different needs. • Society: Ensures inclusivity and equitable access.

In the SCOR DS model, orchestration refers to the ability to align people, processes, and technologies across the supply chain to achieve synchronized, purposeful outcomes. It is not simply a management function; it is a coordinated system where every part of the supply chain contributes to a shared objective with precision and clarity.

Harsh Koppula, President and Co-founder of TADA and previously Chief Executive Officer of CGN Global, emphasizes that orchestration requires unified direction and collaboration. In a 2025 interview, he compared it to conducting an orchestra, where each section must play in sync with the others. If individual parts try to stand out without regard for the whole, the result is chaos rather than harmony (Koppula, 2025).

Koppula also highlights the scale and importance of supply chains, describing them as "one of the largest human and business enterprises on the planet," accounting for approximately 23 to 24 percent of the global economy. Despite their size and complexity, he argues that supply chains do not have to be unnecessarily complicated.

The key, he explains, is ensuring that every participant in the system can quickly recognize and respond to change. "If you do not have a situation where every person in this human chain can understand what just happened, what it means to the business and what they can cleanly execute to recover with very little latency," Koppula states, "you cannot effectively navigate the constant challenges that global supply chains face" (Koppula, 2025).

Ultimately, orchestration is about more than alignment. It is about creating an environment where people are empowered with tools, insights, and the freedom to solve problems creatively. As Koppula puts it, "How do you differentiate? It is on the creativity of people who say, 'I'm going to solve it in a better way than others have for their customers' " (Koppula, 2025).

Collaborative Leadership in a Multi-Stakeholder Environment

Supply chains today function within highly interconnected and interdependent networks that cross not only industry boundaries but also national borders and social systems. As global trade networks become more complex, the performance and resilience of supply chains are increasingly shaped by relationships and collaborations among a wide range of stakeholders. No single company or entity operates in isolation. Instead, businesses rely on intricate webs of suppliers, logistics providers, regulators, technology platforms, and consumers to move goods and services from origin to destination. In this environment, transparency, coordination, and mutual accountability are becoming critical components of supply chain success.

Regulatory frameworks are a primary force driving this shift. Governments and policy bodies are raising expectations for environmental responsibility, labor practices, and corporate transparency. The European Union's Corporate Sustainability Reporting Directive (CSRD) is one prominent example. This directive requires companies not only to monitor their direct operations but also to account for environmental and social impacts across their supply chains. This includes emissions tracking, labor conditions in supplier facilities, and broader social impacts such as community engagement and human rights compliance. Similar regulatory initiatives are being developed in North America, Asia, and other regions, reflecting a global trend toward legally mandated supply chain accountability. Regulatory compliance is no longer a back-office function; it is a strategic concern that touches procurement, logistics, manufacturing, and customer relations.

However, regulatory pressure is only one factor shaping supply chain collaboration; voluntary industry initiatives are also playing a growing role. In sectors ranging from apparel to consumer electronics, industry coalitions are encouraging or requiring members to adopt shared standards for emissions reporting, ethical sourcing, and labor rights monitoring. The Sustainable Apparel Coalition, for example, has developed standardized measurement tools that help brands assess the environmental and social performance of their suppliers. Logistics-focused organizations such as the Global Logistics Emissions Council are working to standardize how companies measure and report transportation-related carbon emissions, encouraging coordinated industry action. These voluntary standards often serve as precursors to formal regulation, and early adopters may gain competitive advantages through improved reputation, customer loyalty, and operational efficiency.

Consumer expectations are reinforcing these trends. As access to information grows, consumers are demanding greater transparency about how products are made, where materials are sourced, and how workers are treated. Digital technologies such as blockchain and supply chain traceability platforms allow companies to provide end-to-end visibility of their operations. This data is increasingly being shared directly with customers through product labeling, mobile applications, and online databases. In some markets, consumers are using this information to guide purchasing decisions, creating market incentives for companies to invest in responsible sourcing and ethical production practices. Brands that fail to meet transparency expectations risk reputational damage and potential loss of market share.

Managing these complex stakeholder expectations requires coordinated, cross-functional leadership. Companies that proactively engage with regulators, industry groups, suppliers, and customers are generally better equipped to navigate risks and identify strategic opportunities. These firms tend to develop stronger supplier relationships, adapt more quickly to regulatory changes, and build resilience through diversified networks and collaborative problem-solving. Conversely, companies that attempt to manage supply chains in isolation—without meaningful stakeholder engagement—may find themselves unprepared for regulatory shifts, supply disruptions, or shifts in consumer demand.

Ultimately, supply chain leadership today is as much about collaboration as it is about operational execution. Success depends not only on managing the movement of goods and information but also on building relationships of trust and transparency across the entire value network. Organizations that recognize supply chains as shared systems, rather than proprietary assets, will likely be better positioned to manage complexity and create sustainable, resilient operations in the years ahead.

The following 10 skills and capabilities are critical for leaders to succeed with decentralized, distributed, and adaptive leadership in Supply Chain 5.0:

1. **Systems thinking.** Understand how decisions affect complex, multi-tier networks by identifying connections among suppliers, partners, technology, people, and sustainability.
2. **Empowerment and delegation.** Share authority and decision-making effectively, trusting teams to act while providing clear direction and defined boundaries.
3. **Facilitation and collaboration.** Guide diverse groups to co-create solutions, encourage open dialogue, surface ideas, and manage constructive conflict across functions and partners.
4. **Adaptability and resilience.** Remain calm and flexible under uncertainty, adjust strategies when needed, and help others embrace change.
5. **Ethical and inclusive mindset.** Balance financial performance with the impact on people, communities, and the environment, building trust and fairness across complex ecosystems.
6. **Communication and storytelling.** Clearly articulate purpose, trade-offs, and critical decisions to inspire action and align teams with shared objectives.

7 **Data literacy and digital fluency.** Leverage real-time data, analytics, and digital tools to detect change early and support informed, decentralized decisions.

8 **Coaching and talent development.** Build capability at every level by enabling people to take ownership, solve problems, and grow, with a focus on empowering frontline teams.

9 **Experimentation and learning agility.** Promote rapid learning and continuous improvement through safe-to-fail pilots and by creating an environment where testing bold ideas is encouraged.

10 **Strategic alignment and guardrails.** Maintain overall coherence by balancing local autonomy with enterprise-wide priorities, setting clear objectives, principles, and boundaries to keep decisions aligned.

REAL-WORLD EXAMPLE Orchestrating Transformation in a Global Supply Chain

Siemens is a prime example of the shift toward Supply Chain 5.0. As a global leader in industrial technology, Siemens has responded to increasing complexity in the supply chain environment by embracing a forward-looking transformation strategy. Its approach centers on four key pillars that align closely with Supply Chain 5.0 principles: Regulatory adaptation, artificial intelligence, workforce transformation, and sustainability integration. This strategy reflects a clear recognition that future-ready supply chains must be both digitally intelligent and socially responsive.

Government regulation has become a major driver of supply chain design. Decisions related to production locations, sourcing strategies, and supplier relationships are now influenced as much by compliance requirements as by cost or efficiency. Siemens has responded by emphasizing regionalization and supply chain localization, supported by orchestration strategies that prioritize agility, visibility, and regulatory alignment.

Artificial intelligence plays a central role in how Siemens creates value across its supply chain. The use of predictive analytics, real-time optimization, and data-driven decision-making has transformed traditional planning and execution. At the same time, emerging challenges related to data sovereignty and access control have required the company to develop more nuanced approaches to data governance and digital collaboration.

Workforce transformation has also been a key focus. Siemens has embraced a more flexible, global-local workforce model, supported by continuous learning, cultural intelligence, and digital skills development. These efforts help the company build resilient and adaptable teams capable of operating in a fast-changing environment while navigating increasingly complex regulatory barriers to talent mobility.

Finally, sustainability has evolved from an aspirational goal to a business imperative. Siemens has embedded environmental considerations into its core supply chain strategies, aligning them with regional regulations and business performance objectives. This integration allows the company to meet compliance requirements while pursuing long-term environmental and economic sustainability.

Siemens' approach illustrates how orchestration is not just about synchronizing operations but about aligning people, processes, technology, and external forces to build adaptive and resilient supply chains. It offers a valuable model for other organizations seeking to thrive in a rapidly changing global landscape (Tschentscher, 2025).

REAL-WORLD EXAMPLE Orchestrating a Global Supply Chain in the Digital Age

At BIC, Gary Horsfield has reimagined supply chain management by shaping a unified framework that reconnects the supply chain to the business through value-creating pillars transforming how global teams collaborate and operate. By leveraging digital platforms, the company has moved beyond traditional geographical constraints, creating a truly interconnected global supply chain that operates with unprecedented fluidity and efficiency.

When Horsfield began his role, the supply chain leadership team was predominantly located in a single office. Today, the team spans seven continents and nine nationalities, yet maintains a remarkable 80 percent engagement level. This transformation was achieved not through physical proximity but through strategic digital connectivity that allows team members to feel unified despite being physically dispersed.

The digital orchestration approach goes beyond simple communication tools. It involves creating a comprehensive digital ecosystem where team members can share real-time information, collaborate seamlessly, and maintain a unified organizational vision. By treating digital platforms as the "conductor" of their global operations, BIC has effectively eliminated traditional barriers of distance and time.

Key to this approach is the recognition that modern supply chain leadership is about empowering people and creating systems that allow them to make intelligent, aligned decisions. A digital platform serves as a universal language, allowing diverse teams to understand shared objectives and work towards them collaboratively.

This real-world example illustrates a fundamental principle of Supply Chain 5.0: Technology should serve as an enabler of human potential, breaking down silos and creating more adaptive, responsive organizational structures. By reimagining connectivity, BIC has created a supply chain that is simultaneously global in scope and local in execution.

Technology and Innovation

Orchestrate processes are increasingly supported by intelligent platforms that unify decision-making, improve data quality, and enable enterprise-wide collaboration.

Key innovations include:

- **Control towers:** Provide real-time end-to-end visibility with alerts and recommendations.
- **Digital twins of the supply chain:** Simulate supply-demand flows, risk scenarios, and ESG trade-offs.
- **Integrated Business Planning (IBP) platforms:** Unify planning across functions and time horizons.
- **Master data management (MDM) systems:** Ensure data consistency and interoperability.
- **AI-driven exception management:** Flag disruptions and recommend corrective actions.
- **Cross-enterprise collaboration hubs:** Connect customers, suppliers, and internal teams in shared spaces.
- **Sustainability intelligence tools:** Integrate ESG data into dashboards and scorecards.
- **Conversational analytics and low-code dashboards:** Improve access to insights across all roles.

Table 11.3 outlines how each of these technologies impacts "Orchestrate" subprocesses and details the technology's benefits for Supply Chain 5.0.

These technologies allow orchestration to evolve from governance and compliance to agile coordination and shared accountability.

Actionable Principles for Orchestrate

- Orchestrate is the backbone of a synchronized, resilient, and responsible supply chain.
- Advanced technologies enable cross-functional insight, automation, and planning integration.
- Human-centric orchestration empowers people to make better decisions together.

Table 11.3 Technology Impact and Benefit on Orchestrate Subprocesses

Technology	Subprocess Impacted	Benefits for Supply Chain 5.0 Goals
Control towers with AI	Monitor Performance, Risk Management	Real-time visibility, proactive alerting, and dynamic KPI tracking
Digital supply chain twins	Strategic Alignment, Risk Management	Simulate strategies, optimize trade-offs, and test disruptions
Integrated Business Planning	Align Strategic Objectives	Unifies financial, operational, and sustainability planning
MDM platforms	Manage Master Data	Ensures data quality and traceability across systems
Collaboration workspaces	Enable Collaboration	Enhances cross-functional alignment and partner engagement
ESG analytics platforms	Monitor Performance	Supports compliance, decarbonization, and ethical sourcing transparency
Conversational BI	Monitor Performance, Collaboration	Democratizes insight access and accelerates decision-making

- A well-orchestrated supply chain can adapt, recover, and evolve—without compromising on purpose or people.
- Integrate ESG and resilience into every major supply chain decision.
- Create visibility that serves people, not just algorithms.
- Treat master data as a strategic asset, not just a system field.
- Promote a shared language for goals, metrics, and risk across silos.
- Design governance processes that are fast, inclusive, and feedback-driven.
- Use technology to enable coordination, not just compliance.

References

Alicke, K., Foster, T., Trautwein, V. (2024) Supply chains: Still vulnerable. McKinsey & Company – Listen to the article: https://soundcloud.com/mckinsey/listen-to-the-article-supply (archived at https://perma.cc/W6XP-QAJ2)

Association for Supply Chain Management (ASCM) (2022a) SCOR Digital Standard.

Association for Supply Chain Management (ASCM) (2022b) SCOR DS / SCOR 12 Crosswalk.

Autio, E. (2022) Orchestrating ecosystems: A multi-layered framework. *Innovation Organization & Management*, 24 (1), 96–109.

Bailey, S. (2023) Supply chain ecosystems: Building trust to realize the potential of interconnectedness. Gartner. www.gartner.com/en/supply-chain/insights/beyond-supply-chain-blog/supply-chain-ecosystems-building-trust-to-realize-the-potential-of-interconnectedness (archived at https://perma.cc/XWN4-XCAE)

Baldi, B., Confente, I., Russo, I. and Gaudenzi, B. (2024) Consumer-centric supply chain management: A literature review, framework, and research agenda. *Journal of Business Logistics*, 45(4), e12399.

Bolstorff, P. and Jacques, A. (2025) Transform your supply chain using ASCM's SCOR DS model, With Peter Bolstorff. *Big Ideas in Supply Chain*. www.kinaxis.com/en/big-ideas/insights/transform-your-supply-chain-using-ascms-scords-model-peter-bolstorff (archived at https://perma.cc/8WT4-9U8R)

Dacre, N., Yan, J., Frei, R., Al-Mhdawi, M. K. S. and Dong, H. (2025) Advancing sustainable manufacturing: A systematic exploration of industry 5.0 supply chains for sustainability, human-centricity, and resilience. *Production Planning & Control*, 36(11), 1499–528.

Gilmore, D. (2019, March 7) The 3 V's of Supply Chain 20 years later. *Supply Chain Digest*. www.scdigest.com/firstthoughts/19-03-07.php?cid=15263&ctype=content (archived at https://perma.cc/J34F-LDTB)

Gupta, A. (2022) What is a supply chain control tower — And what's needed to deploy one? Gartner. www.gartner.com/en/articles/what-is-a-supply-chain-control-tower-and-what-s-needed-to-deploy-one (archived at https://perma.cc/NPJ6-VN8B)

Koppula, H. (2025, August 4) Interview by D. Stanton.

Li, Z., De Souza, R. and Goh, M. (2016) Supply chain orchestration leveraging on MNC networks and local resources: Approach strategies. *Journal of Service Science and Management*, 9(4), 303–19.

Melnyk, S. A., Davis, E. W., Spekman, R. E. and Sandor, J. (2010) Outcome-driven supply chains. *MIT Sloan Management Review*, 51(2), 33.

Nicoletti, B. (2023) Supply network 5.0 human automation machine collaboration. In *Supply Network 5.0: How to improve human automation in the supply chain* (pp. 103-137). Cham: Springer International Publishing.

Phadnis, S. S. (2023) Creating value through supply chain orchestration as a business model. *Academy of Management Perspectives*, 38(1), 1–22.

Shen, L., Shi, Q., Parida, V. and Jovanovic, M. (2024) Ecosystem orchestration practices for industrial firms: A qualitative meta-analysis, framework development and research agenda. *Journal of Business Research*, 173, 114463

Thompson, E. and Ellis, S. (2024) Evolving from control towers: Command centers as enablers to supply chain orchestration. IDC Research, Inc. www.opentext.com/assets/documents/en-US/pdf/evolving-from-control-towers-command-centers-as-enablers-of-supply-chain-orchestration-pp-en.pdf (archived at https://perma.cc/VB96-UBKE)

Tschentscher, A. M. (2025) The world is changing! How do we transform? [Internal whitepaper]. Siemens AG.

Venne, U. (2025) *The Power of Supply Chain Orchestration*. Everstream Analytics.

Villar, A., Paladini, S. and Buckley, O. (2023, July) Towards supply chain 5.0: Redesigning supply chains as resilient, sustainable, and human-centric systems in a post-pandemic world. In *Operations Research Forum,* 4(3), p. 60 Cham: Springer International Publishing.

Zekhnini, K., Chaouni Benabdellah, A., Bag, S. and Gupta, S. (2024) Supply chain 5.0 digitalization: An integrated approach for risk assessment. *Management Decision.*

PART THREE
Challenges and Barriers to Adoption

As supply chains evolve toward the vision of Supply Chain 5.0, where human-centricity, advanced automation, and hyperconnectivity converge, the path to adoption is anything but straightforward. Part Three of this book examines the multifaceted challenges encountered by organizations, leaders, and adopters as they strive to integrate cutting-edge technologies and ethical frameworks into their supply chain operations. These chapters examine the key barriers that must be overcome to ensure innovation is not only effective but also responsible and profitable for stakeholders.

Chapter 12, *Ethics by Design: Responsible AI and Automation in Supply Chains*, examines the imperative of embedding ethical principles into the development and deployment of AI and other technologies in a firm's systems. It highlights the risks of bias, opacity, and unintended consequences, and offers strategies for designing automation that aligns with societal values and stakeholder trust.

Chapter 13, *Building the Workforce of Supply Chain 5.0*, shifts the focus to human capital. As digital transformation accelerates, the workforce must evolve in tandem. This chapter explores the skills gap, the necessity of continuous learning, and the importance of cultivating a culture that balances technological fluency with human empathy, as well as raising awareness of the elimination, transformation, and creation of jobs as we know them.

Chapter 14, *Securing Hyperconnected Supply Chains*, addresses the growing vulnerabilities in increasingly interconnected networks. With data flowing across borders and systems, cybersecurity becomes a cornerstone of resilience. This chapter outlines the threats, regulatory pressures, and best practices for safeguarding digital infrastructure.

Finally, Chapter 15, *Overcoming Barriers to Supply Chain 5.0 Adoption*, synthesizes the organizational, technological, and cultural hurdles that inhibit progress. From legacy systems and siloed thinking to resistance to change, this chapter provides a candid look at why transformation efforts often stall, and what can be done to overcome these obstacles.

Together, these chapters provide a critical lens through which to understand the complexities of adopting Supply Chain 5.0. They offer not only a diagnosis of the challenges but also a roadmap for navigating them with foresight, responsibility, and resilience.

12 Ethics by Design: Responsible AI and Automation in Supply Chains

The biggest lesson learned is we have to take the unintended consequences of any new technology along with all the benefits.

SATYA NADELLA, MICROSOFT CEO

As supply chains evolve from automated systems to intelligent ecosystems, a new question emerges: *Not just what can technology do, but what should it do?* AI, robotics, and automation are redefining productivity, forecasting accuracy, and decision-making speed. Yet with this power comes responsibility to design and deploy these technologies ethically, transparently, and responsibly.

As technologies become integral to modern supply chains, the urgency to address their ethical implications grows. These technologies promise efficiency, agility, and resilience, but they also introduce risks related to bias, transparency, accountability, and human displacement. This chapter explores how supply chain leaders can adopt an "ethics by design" approach, embedding ethical principles into the development and deployment of AI and automation systems from the outset. Companies that embed ethical principles "by design" at the architecture level of their digital systems earn trust, reduce risk, and build resilient, human-centered value networks.

The Ethical Imperative in Supply Chain 5.0

Supply Chain 4.0 emphasized efficiency through automation. Supply Chain 5.0 emphasizes responsibility through orchestration. The shift from process optimization to purpose alignment reflects a deeper maturity: Recognizing that technology decisions have social, environmental, and economic implications.

This is because supply chains are not just technical systems that transform raw materials into final products or move commodities from point A to point B; they are socio-economic ecosystems involving people, companies, and societies, often shaped by the development and adoption of emerging technologies. In Chapter 1, we saw how each industrial era transformed the business landscape, social impact, and consumer expectations, and never reverted. This time is no different. The emergence of Supply Chain 5.0 marks a paradigm shift toward intelligent, resilient, and human-centric supply networks. Unlike its predecessor, Industry 4.0, which emphasized automation and digitalization, Supply Chain 5.0 integrates advanced technologies, such as AI, robotics, collaborative robots, and the Internet of Things (IoT), with ethical governance, sustainability, and human empowerment (Merchán-Cruz et al., 2025; Wu et al., 2025).

The acceleration of AI-enabled planning, predictive analytics, and autonomous logistics creates both opportunities and dilemmas. Although there are significant advances and benefits to adopting technologies, as of 2025, major concerns regarding AI focus on data privacy and security, algorithmic bias, job displacement, and the risk of misinformation and deepfakes influencing government and consumer decisions. Some examples include algorithmic bias, which can distort demand forecasts or supplier selection. Automation without accountability can widen inequality and erode workforce trust. Data-driven transparency can be empowering or intrusive, depending on its governance.

These worries are even more urgent now that AI is deeply integrated into everyday operations across various sectors. AI is a key topic in 2025 due to a convergence of rapid technological progress that has shifted AI from experimental stages to widespread, practical use in daily life and industries, as suggested by the 2025 AI Index Report at Stanford University Human-Centered Artificial Intelligence. This transition makes 2025 a crucial year when AI's real-world effects have been felt more strongly than ever.

AI systems in supply chains are not neutral tools; they shape decisions that affect leaders, workers, suppliers, consumers, and communities. From algorithmic bias in supplier selection to opaque decision-making in inventory forecasting, the risks of unethical AI deployment are tangible and growing (Brey and Dainow, 2024; Abhulimen and Ejike, 2024). Moreover, the complexity of global supply chains, characterized by distributed data flows, cross-border operations, and diverse stakeholder interests, amplifies the need for responsible innovation.

To mitigate these risks, organizations must move beyond reactive compliance and embrace proactive ethical design. Ethics-by-design refers to the proactive integration of ethical principles such as fairness, transparency, accountability, and privacy into the entire lifecycle of AI systems, from conception to deployment and monitoring (Brey and Dainow, 2024; Attard-Frost and Widder, 2025). It moves beyond compliance to embed ethical reasoning into technical and organizational processes, ensuring that AI systems align with both societal values and stakeholder expectations.

HLEG and Its Trustworthy AI Framework

The High-Level Expert Group on Artificial Intelligence (AI HLEG) was established by the European Commission in 2018 to provide independent guidance on the ethical, legal, and socio-economic implications of AI technologies. Its mandate included developing a human-centric framework to ensure that AI deployed in the European Union respects fundamental rights, fosters societal well-being, and supports trustworthy innovation (European Commission, 2019). In 2019, the group published the influential Ethics Guidelines for Trustworthy AI, which outlined a practical and normative approach for ensuring that AI systems are lawful, ethical, and robust throughout their lifecycle. The guidelines remain foundational in European AI policy and have shaped subsequent regulatory initiatives, including the European Union Artificial Intelligence Act.

Central to the guidelines is the articulation of seven requirements that AI systems should meet to be considered trustworthy. These requirements operationalize ethical principles into concrete criteria that developers, organizations, and policymakers can apply when designing, deploying, or auditing AI systems. The goal is to ensure that technological progress enhances human agency, protects societal values, and avoids causing unintended harm:

1 **Human agency and oversight.** AI must support human autonomy, informed decision-making, and meaningful oversight.

2 **Technical robustness and safety.** AI systems must be reliable, secure, and resilient against errors, misuse, and adversarial attacks.

3 **Privacy and data governance.** Personal data must be protected, used appropriately, and governed through transparent and secure practices.

4 **Transparency.** AI systems must provide traceability, explainability, and clear communication about their capabilities and limitations.

5 **Diversity, non-discrimination, and fairness.** AI should avoid bias, promote inclusion, and prevent discriminatory outcomes.

6 **Societal and environmental well-being.** AI should benefit society at large and contribute to sustainability and social responsibility.

7 **Accountability.** There must be mechanisms ensuring responsibility, auditability, and the ability to address harms or negative impacts.

Together, these requirements form the backbone of the EU's human-centric approach to AI governance, ensuring that technological innovation aligns with democratic values, ethical responsibility, and long-term societal benefit.

Principles of Responsible AI and Automation

Mapping the ethical landscape of AI in supply chains includes a three-fold goal. First, explore the principles of ethics-by-design with applications in supply chains. Then, identify the key risks, barriers, and tensions, and lastly learn from enablers to ethical adoption, such as leadership commitment, cross-functional collaboration, and regulatory alignment (Widder and Wong, 2023; Ejjami and Boussalham, 2024).

As supply chains evolve into intelligent, interconnected ecosystems under the Supply Chain 5.0 paradigm, the ethical design of AI and automation systems becomes a strategic imperative for leaders. Ethical design is not abstract; it is operational. According to frameworks from the European Commission (2025) and OECD (2022), responsible AI rests on five interconnected pillars, each highly relevant to supply chain leaders because these pillars align with the "Human-in-the-Loop" philosophy at the core of Supply Chain 5.0, ensuring technology serves people (see Table 12.1).

Automation is often framed as a trade-off between labor and efficiency. In Supply Chain 5.0, it's reframed as a partnership between human insight and intelligent machines.

Table 12.1 Five Interconnected Pillars of Responsible AI

Pillar	Supply Chain Leader Context Applications
Transparency	Algorithms must be explainable, not black boxes. Supply chain decisions, such as supplier scoring, risk classification, or demand prioritization, should be interpretable by humans and auditable for fairness.
Accountability	Clear ownership of outcomes is vital. If an AI system automates quality checks or selects logistics routes, human oversight ensures ethical responsibility remains intact.
Fairness	Bias in data can lead to unfair treatment of suppliers, customers, or employees. Responsible models use diverse datasets and fairness checks to prevent systemic discrimination.
Privacy and Data Protection	Supply chains handle massive amounts of sensitive data, from employee biometrics to consumer purchase patterns. Ethical design ensures compliance with privacy regulations and embeds privacy-by-default architectures.
Human Autonomy	Humans remain in control. Automation should augment, not replace, human judgment, especially in decisions involving safety, sustainability, or livelihoods.

Consider warehouse automation: Robotic systems can lift, move, and sort objects faster than humans, but human workers excel at tasks such as experiential recognition, exception handling, and ethical judgment. Designing collaborative systems where both coexist safely and productively exemplifies the integration of automation with empathy. Organizations like DHL, Toyota, and Procter & Gamble are experimenting with cobotics (collaborative robotics) and AI-driven decision support tools that empower employees rather than displace them. Ethics by design ensures that digital transformation enhances human dignity through reskilling, inclusivity, and ergonomic system design.

Ethics-by-design is not merely a technical protocol; it is a governance philosophy that embeds ethical principles into the lifecycle of AI systems, ensuring that technological innovation aligns with human values, stakeholder trust, and societal well-being. This section outlines five foundational principles of ethics-by-design, supported by recent academic and industry research (see Figure 12.1).

Figure 12.1 Five Foundational Principles of Ethics-by-Design

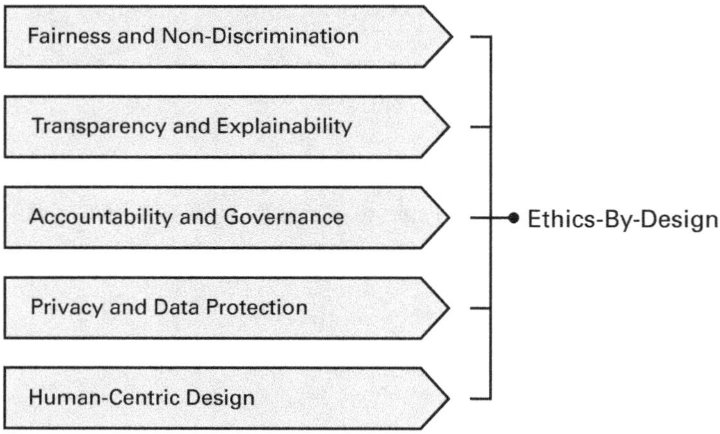

Fairness and Non-Discrimination

AI systems in supply chains must be designed to avoid reinforcing existing inequalities. Bias in training data or algorithmic logic can lead to unfair outcomes in supplier selection, workforce scheduling, or demand forecasting. Inclusive AI governance frameworks emphasize stakeholder participation, ethical oversight, and equitable decision-making, particularly in crisis scenarios where systemic vulnerabilities are exposed (Oladele, 2025). AI systems must be trained on diverse, representative data to avoid perpetuating bias. Supply chain applications, such as hiring algorithms, supplier scoring, or inventory prioritization, should be regularly audited for discriminatory outcomes.

For example, Wellbrock et al. (2025) highlight how biased algorithms in supply chain management can marginalize small suppliers or underrepresented labor groups, urging companies to implement fairness audits and diversify data sources.

Transparency and Explainability

Transparency is essential for building trust in AI-driven decisions. Explainable AI (XAI) techniques such as SHAP, LIME, and counterfactual models, allow stakeholders to understand how decisions are made, challenge outcomes, and ensure regulatory compliance (Akubilla et al., 2025). Neurosymbolic approaches, which combine neural networks with logic-based reasoning, offer promising pathways for enhancing explainability in complex supply chain environments (Kosasih et al., 2024).

However, as Hussain and Hussain (2025) caution, transparency must go beyond surface-level explanations to reveal underlying motives and biases, avoiding the illusion of control that oversimplified models may present.

Accountability and Governance

In Supply Chain 5.0, accountability is not optional, it is operationally critical. AI systems must be auditable, with clear documentation of decision parameters, data sources, and oversight mechanisms. Governance frameworks should assign responsibility across the AI supply chain, from developers to end-users, ensuring that ethical breaches can be traced and addressed (Brown, 2023). Industry reports emphasize that reshoring and digital transformation in manufacturing demand robust governance models that integrate explainability, cybersecurity, and regulatory readiness (Desai, 2025).

Privacy and Data Protection

With AI systems processing vast amounts of sensitive data, from supplier contracts to employee records, ethical data stewardship is paramount. Effective data governance ensures that data is accurate, secure, and compliant with privacy regulations such as GDPR. Blockchain-based systems and privacy-preserving technologies (e.g., zero-knowledge proofs) offer scalable solutions for secure data sharing in decentralized supply chains (Sam-Bulya et al., 2024).

Human-Centric Design

Supply Chain 5.0 is defined by its human-centric ethos. Rather than replacing humans, AI and automation should augment human capabilities, support decision-making, and foster inclusive innovation. Human-centric design involves ergonomic interfaces, collaborative robotics, and cognitive support systems that prioritize worker well-being and engagement (Yanytska, 2025).

Grosse et al. (2023) emphasize that transitioning from Industry 4.0 to 5.0 requires systemic approaches that integrate human factors, diversity, and ethical implications into production and logistics systems.

A Risk-Based Approach in AI

Despite growing awareness, the adoption of ethical AI and automation faces several barriers. These include:

- Lack of expertise: Many supply chain teams lack the technical and ethical literacy to evaluate AI systems critically.
- Fragmented accountability: Ethical oversight is often siloed, with no clear ownership across departments.
- Cost and complexity: Embedding ethics into design can be resource-intensive, particularly for small and medium-sized enterprises.
- Regulatory uncertainty: Global supply chains operate across jurisdictions with varying ethical standards and legal frameworks.

To operationalize ethics by design, companies must establish formal AI governance frameworks, including:

- ethics committees overseeing algorithmic design and deployment
- cross-functional teams combining data scientists, supply chain managers, and ethicists
- regular audits to assess fairness, safety, and compliance
- training programs that embed ethical literacy in every digital role

Leaders like Microsoft, IBM, and Maersk are setting benchmarks by integrating ethical governance into their supply chain analytics programs, proving that responsible AI is both feasible and profitable.

At the global scale, the European Commission's AI Act is the first legal framework on AI to be enacted into force on August 1, 2024, and is expected to be fully applicable as of August 2, 2026. It addresses risks and positions Europe to lead worldwide. The AI Act aims to promote the adoption of trustworthy AI in Europe and introduces a risk-based approach to prevent undesirable outcomes. Supply chain leaders can learn from this general approach when adopting AI principles in their organizations. The AI Act defines four levels of risk for AI systems: Unacceptable risk, high risk, limited risk, and minimal risk. Table 12.2 provides an overview of this classification.

Table 12.2 EC, AI ACT Risk-Based Approach to AI

Level Risk	Definition	Practices
Unacceptable	All AI systems considered a clear threat to the safety, livelihoods, and rights of people are banned.	1. Prohibit harmful AI-based manipulation and deception 2. Prohibit harmful AI-based exploitation of vulnerabilities 3. Prohibit social scoring 4. Prohibit individual criminal offence risk assessment or prediction 5. Prohibit untargeted scraping of the internet or CCTV material to create or expand facial recognition databases 6. Prohibit emotion recognition in workplaces and education institutions 7. Prohibit biometric categorization to deduce certain protected characteristics 8. Prohibit real-time remote biometric identification for law enforcement purposes in publicly accessible spaces
High	AI use cases that can pose serious risks to health, safety, or fundamental rights are classified as high-risk and are subject to strict obligations before they can be put on the market.	1. AI safety components in critical infrastructures the failure of which could put the lives and health of citizens at risk 2. AI solutions used in education institutions, that may determine the access to education and course of someone's professional life 3. AI-based safety components of products 4. AI tools for employment, management of workers and access to self-employment 5. Certain AI use-cases utilized to give access to essential private and public services 6. AI systems used for remote biometric identification, emotion recognition and biometric categorization 7. AI use-cases in law enforcement that may interfere with people's fundamental rights 8. AI use-cases in migration, asylum and border control management 9. AI solutions used in the administration of justice and democratic processes

(continued)

Table 12.2 (Continued)

Level Risk	Definition	Practices
Limited	This refers to the risks associated with a need for transparency around the use of AI.	1. The AI Act introduces specific disclosure obligations to ensure that humans are informed when necessary to preserve trust. For instance, when using AI systems such as chatbots, humans should be made aware that they are interacting with a machine so they can take an informed decision. 2. Providers of generative AI have to ensure that AI-generated content is identifiable. On top of that, certain AI-generated content should be clearly and visibly labelled, namely deep fakes and text published with the purpose to inform the public on matters of public interest.
Minimal or not risk at all	The AI Act does not introduce rules for AI that is deemed minimal or no risk.	The vast majority of AI systems currently used in the EU fall into this category.

REAL-WORLD EXAMPLE Ethical Governance of Technology at BMW

The BMW Group's Digital Identity establishes a clear ethical foundation for how digital technologies should be designed, governed, and used across its global operations (BMW Group). As digitalization becomes increasingly central to product development, supply chain coordination, and workforce collaboration, BMW emphasizes that technology must enhance human dignity, transparency, and trust rather than compromise them. Their Digital Identity articulates five guiding principles that ensure digital transformation aligns with the values and responsibilities of Supply Chain 5.0:

- Respectful coexistence: Digital systems must reflect human empathy, support human oversight, protect privacy, and ensure that all digital processes remain understandable and aligned with human needs.
- Data control, safety of use, and cybersecurity: Personal data must be protected through strict privacy standards, user choice, and "Privacy, Safety, and Security by Design," ensuring secure and responsible handling of information.
- Transparency and cooperation: Digital processes, algorithms, and data use must be made visible and verifiable to build trust and support responsible innovation, including the use of open-source solutions.
- Participation and continuing education: Digital tools should be accessible to all employees, supported by inclusive design and ongoing training that fosters digital and AI literacy throughout the workforce.
- Digital sustainability: Digital technologies must contribute to environmental and social responsibility, reducing emissions, optimizing resources, supporting employee well-being, and being used only when they genuinely benefit people or processes.

BMW's Digital Identity demonstrates how a global enterprise can embed ethics directly into digital transformation. By centering on respect, transparency, security, inclusion, and sustainability, the company models a Supply Chain 5.0 approach in which technology strengthens trust, enhances human capability, and advances long-term societal and environmental well-being.

Balancing Intelligence with Accountability

A federal wrongful death trial in Miami over a 2019 Tesla Autopilot crash highlights why balancing AI capabilities with human accountability is a practical concern. Plaintiffs in the case allege that overreliance on Autopilot, combined with insufficient opportunities for human intervention, contributed to a fatal crash in Key Largo, Florida (Thadani, 2025). The case raises broader concerns about how users may treat AI guidance as definitive without maintaining situational awareness. It demonstrates that while AI can increase operational efficiency, humans remain ultimately responsible for decisions and outcomes (Thadani, 2025; Condon and Krisher, 2025).

For supply chain leaders, the lesson is clear. Deploying AI systems requires more than technical implementation. Ethical, legal, and risk considerations must guide how AI tools are integrated into operational workflows, and they must be structured to strengthen human judgment rather than replace it. Transparent decision support mechanisms and governance frameworks that incorporate human validation are essential to maintain trust and manage operational risk.

From a practical perspective, AI-generated recommendations in planning, sourcing, or risk assessment can carry significant financial and reputational consequences if their rationale is opaque. Supply chain professionals must understand how recommendations are produced and be prepared to challenge them. Without clear reasoning, users may either rely too heavily on AI outputs or dismiss them entirely, both of which undermine effectiveness and compliance readiness.

New regulatory frameworks are reinforcing these expectations. The European Union's Artificial Intelligence Act, Regulation (EU) 2024/1689, which took effect on August 1, 2024, classifies many supply chain AI systems as high risk and requires appropriate human oversight and explainability under Article 14 (European Parliament and Council, 2024). Similar expectations are emerging in other jurisdictions through national policies and voluntary codes of practice.

Ethical considerations also emphasize the need for human supervision. Algorithms can prioritize cost or efficiency without evaluating supplier labor standards or environmental impacts. Without human oversight, decisions may conflict with corporate values or social responsibility commitments, creating risks that go beyond what algorithms can assess.

To address these risks, supply chain organizations should build structured validation and review into AI-supported decision-making, especially for high-impact choices. Explainability tools, audit logs, and feedback mechanisms help users understand how recommendations are generated. Creating a culture where questioning machine outputs is treated as responsible practice rather than resistance to innovation is critical for effective and ethical AI adoption.

Embedding transparency and accountability into AI-enabled planning provides both strategic and operational benefits. It reduces regulatory and reputational risk while maintaining trust with customers, employees, and stakeholders. It also ensures that AI serves as a tool to amplify human intelligence rather than diminish professional responsibility.

The successful use of AI in supply chains will depend not only on technical sophistication but on how well organizations integrate ethical oversight, explainability, and human validation into their strategies. Balancing intelligence with accountability is essential for building resilient, trustworthy, and responsible supply chains and is central to the vision of Supply Chain 5.0.

Ethics in Service Supply Chains

Delta Airlines and AI-Powered Personalized Pricing

In 2025, Delta Airlines became a landmark example in the ethical debates surrounding Supply Chain 5.0. Its experiment with AI-powered personalized pricing represented one of the first large-scale attempts to use artificial intelligence to individualize service costs in real time. The move was widely studied because it combined cutting-edge technology, complex service supply chain dynamics, and pressing questions about human-centricity and fairness. For many scholars and practitioners, Delta's decision marked a pivotal moment in the evolution of service supply chains, demonstrating both the promise and the peril of advanced AI integration.

Airlines are a prime example of a service supply chain, where value is created not through the movement of physical goods but through the orchestration of services, capacity, and customer experience. The nature of airline operations, with their highly perishable seat inventory and complex network planning, made them a fertile ground for innovation in Supply Chain 5.0, where advanced analytics and human-centered design converged. In 2025, Delta undertook a significant shift in its ticketing strategy by deploying artificial intelligence to implement personalized dynamic pricing. Partnering with Fetcherr, an Israeli AI startup, Delta began pricing tickets based on each passenger's assessed willingness to pay, creating individualized fares in real time (Aviation A2Z, 2025; View from the Wing, 2025).

From Delta's perspective, the economic rationale was clear. Traditional airline revenue management relied on fixed fare classes and historical demand curves. AI-based dynamic pricing allowed for micro-segmentation, identifying the optimal price point for each passenger and increasing revenue per seat sold (PCWorld, 2025). In an industry with razor-thin margins and perishable inventory, even marginal improvements in price optimization generated substantial profit. Delta reported favorable results in early pilots, expanding the system from 1 percent of US domestic fares in late 2024 to approximately 3 percent in mid-2025, with plans to cover 20 percent by the end of the year (EPlaneAI, 2025). For Delta, this approach aligned with a broader vision of transforming ticketing into a personalized, retail-like experience that reflected the hyper-automation and customization central to Supply Chain 5.0.

The initiative also highlighted one of the core challenges of Supply Chain 5.0: balancing technological advancement with human-centricity. While AI-powered personalization promised greater efficiency, it raised fundamental questions about fairness and transparency. When two passengers on the same flight paid dramatically different prices based on an algorithm's prediction of their willingness to pay, perceptions of fairness were at risk of eroding. Moreover, the opacity of AI decision-making damaged customer trust when travelers could not understand why they were charged more or less than others (Thornhill, 2025). Privacy concerns also emerged, as these systems relied on extensive data collection, including browsing behavior, loyalty history, and geolocation, prompting ethical questions about consent and data governance (PYMNTS, 2025).

AI-driven individualized pricing also differed significantly from the dynamic pricing models that airlines had used for decades. Traditional dynamic pricing is based on aggregate supply and demand conditions. If a flight begins to fill or the departure date draws closer, prices for all remaining seats increase or decrease together. AI-based pricing, in contrast, uses detailed knowledge about a specific passenger such as their booking history, travel patterns, or loyalty status to calculate the maximum price that individual is likely to accept. Rather than adjusting prices for the market as a whole, the system sets fares for each customer separately. This shift from market-based dynamics to person-specific price setting amplified ethical concerns, as it blurred the line between pricing efficiency and price discrimination.

The *View from the Wing* analysis added another layer to the debate. The article predicted that this approach could actually lower costs for some travelers, especially those who were more price-sensitive or less loyal, because the algorithm might offer them lower fares to secure a purchase. It also noted that Delta's strategy was tightly linked to loyalty program membership and suggested that airlines might eventually require customers to log into their frequent flyer accounts to access the best fares. Importantly, the article pointed out that Delta's competitive position would depend on whether other airlines adopted similar systems. If Delta was the only carrier to use AI-based individualized pricing, some passengers might defect to competitors with more transparent fare structures. However, if multiple airlines implemented the technology quickly, it could redefine market pricing norms across the industry (View from the Wing, 2025).

The risks in 2025 were not only theoretical. Delta faced the possibility of customer alienation if passengers perceived personalized pricing as manipulative or unfair. There was also a plausible risk of legal action. If AI-generated fares were shown to rely on sensitive personal data or resulted in systematically higher prices for specific demographic groups, the practice could have drawn lawsuits or class-action claims under consumer protection or anti-discrimination laws. Even without a case reaching court, the potential exposure was significant enough to become part of the industry debate. Regulatory backlash was also a looming threat, with lawmakers signaling interest in algorithmic transparency and consumer protections in pricing models (Thrifty Traveler, 2025). This case illustrated the trade-offs supply chain leaders had to navigate as they integrated advanced AI capabilities, pursuing profitability without undermining trust or social legitimacy.

The ethical questions raised by Delta's strategy echoed similar debates in retail supply chains, most notably in the context of Amazon's use of personalized pricing algorithms. Like Delta, Amazon has experimented with using customer-specific data to set prices based on browsing patterns, purchase history, and loyalty program membership. However, the airline context introduced an additional layer of sensitivity because passengers sitting side by side could pay dramatically different fares for the same seat, making pricing disparities visible in a way that retail transactions often are not. Both cases highlight how Supply Chain 5.0 technologies blur the boundary between efficient market behavior and individualized price discrimination, forcing leaders to consider not only profitability but also trust and perceived fairness.

At its core, the Delta case raised a broader ethical dilemma relevant to all supply chains entering the 5.0 era. Was it ethically acceptable to charge each customer based on their ability or willingness to pay? Proponents argued that this was merely an extension of traditional market segmentation and that airlines had always practiced differential pricing through mechanisms such as advance purchase discounts and last-minute fares. AI simply refined this practice at an individual level (View from the Wing, 2025). Critics countered that personalized pricing undermined the principles of a free market by replacing transparent supply and demand dynamics with opaque, individualized manipulation, eroding consumer confidence and equity in pricing (Kiplinger, 2025).

Ultimately, Delta's experiment demonstrated that in Supply Chain 5.0, profitability and ethics were inseparable. Leaders were reminded to embed human-centric principles into technological design, not as an afterthought but as a core strategic requirement. Moreover, anticipating social and regulatory reactions became as critical as forecasting demand. The case served as both a warning and a guide: Advanced optimization could unlock immense value, but without trust and fairness, even the most sophisticated supply chain risked collapsing under its own innovation.

This episode also highlighted a broader theme for Supply Chain 5.0. As AI, automation, and personalization became embedded into both product and service supply chains, leaders increasingly faced trade-offs between efficiency and equity. Similar dilemmas were beginning to emerge in healthcare, retail, and logistics networks, where the tension between maximizing value and maintaining human trust promised to define the ethical landscape of next-generation supply chains.

The ethical tension evident in Delta's pricing strategy finds a parallel in the healthcare sector, where AI tools are increasingly shaping cost, access, and quality. AI systems in medicine now analyze patient-specific data such as medical history, risk factors, and demographic information to inform personalized treatment planning, billing, or coverage decisions. While these innovations offer potential gains in diagnostic accuracy and operational efficiency, they also raise serious concerns about fairness, transparency, and equity. Scholars have emphasized how algorithms may reproduce or amplify existing disparities, making informed consent, equitable data governance, and algorithmic accountability essential (Weiner et al., 2024; Dankwa-Mullan, 2024). Regulatory frameworks and professional bodies are calling for AI deployment that adheres to ethical principles like justice, beneficence, and non-maleficence in order to guard against biased decisions or unequal treatment based on personal data (Bouderhem, 2024; AMA, 2025). These dynamics mirror Delta's case: Whether setting fares or determining treatment costs, leaders in Supply Chain 5.0 must navigate trade-offs between technological optimization and social trust in an era where personalization and equity collide.

References

Abhulimen, A. O. and Ejike, O. G. (2024) Ethical considerations in AI use for SMEs and supply chains: Current challenges and future directions. *International Journal of Applied Research in Social Sciences*, 6(08), 1653–79.

Akubilla, J., Somoye, O. I., Abiodun, F. and Serifat, O. A. (2025) The role of explainable AI in enhancing trust and transparency in supply chain risk mitigation. *International Journal of Multidisciplinary Research and Growth Evaluation*, 6(3), pp. 367–77

American Medical Association (AMA) (2025, March) Physicians concerned AI increases prior authorization denials. *AMA News Wire*. www.ama-assn.org/press-center/ama-press-releases/physicians-concerned-ai-increases-prior-authorization-denials (archived at https://perma.cc/2TFA-VA7T)

Attard-Frost, B. and Gray Widder, D. (2025) The ethics of AI value chains. *Big Data & Society*, 12.2 (2025): 20539517251340603.

Shelley, N. (2025, July 11) Delta using AI to price tickets to boost revenue. Aviation A2Z. https://aviationa2z.com/index.php/2025/07/11/delta-using-ai-to-price-tickets-to-boost-revenue/ (archived at https://perma.cc/J2LX-N4UJ)

BMW Group (2024) BMW Group Digital Identity: Five guiding principles for dealing with digital technology. www.bmwgroup.com/content/dam/grpw/websites/bmwgroup_com/innovation/downloadds/en/2024/Digitales_Selbstverstaendnis_EN.pdf (archived at https://perma.cc/6SA6-GEFA)

Bouderhem, R. (2024) Shaping the future of AI in healthcare through ethics and governance. *Humanities and Social Sciences Communications*, 11, 416.

Brey, P. and Dainow, B. (2024) Ethics by design for artificial intelligence. *AI and Ethics*, 4(4), 1265–77.

Brown, I. (2023) Allocating accountability in AI supply chains. *Ada Lovelace Institute*. www.adalovelaceinstitute.org/resource/ai-supply-chains/ (archived at https://perma.cc/R2BF-AUC3)

Condon, B. and Krisher, T. (2025, July 14) Tesla's Autopilot system is in the spotlight at a trial over a student killed while stargazing. *AP News*. https://apnews.com/article/3ffab7fb53e93feb4ecfd3023f2ea21f (archived at https://perma.cc/5BAX-3RZK)

Dankwa-Mullan, I. (2024) Health equity and ethical considerations in using artificial intelligence in public health and medicine. *Preventing Chronic Disease*, 21, 240245. https://doi.org/10.5888/pcd21.240245 (archived at https://perma.cc/LUW2-EQPB)

Desai, A. (2025) Beyond Tariffs: The Governance Mandate Driving US Manufacturing's AI Revolution. Security Infowatch.com. www.securityinfowatch.com/security-executives/article/55326654/beyond-tariffs-the-governance-mandate-driving-us-manufacturings-ai-revolution (archived at https://perma.cc/BY6D-HFM4)

Ejjami, R. and Boussalham, K. (2024) Resilient supply chains in Industry 5.0: Leveraging AI for predictive maintenance and risk mitigation. *International Journal For Multidisciplinary Research*, 6(4), 25116.

EPlaneAI (2025, July) Delta Airlines uses AI to adjust ticket prices dynamically. www.eplaneai.com/news/delta-airlines-uses-ai-to-adjust-ticket-prices-dynamically (archived at https://perma.cc/9G5K-PG7P)

European Commission (2019) Ethics Guidelines for Trustworthy AI. High-Level Expert Group on Artificial Intelligence. https://digital-strategy.ec.europa.eu/en/library/ethics-guidelines-trustworthy-ai (archived at https://perma.cc/YY6L-4XLG).

European Commission (2025) European approach to artificial intelligence. https://digital-strategy.ec.europa.eu/en/policies/european-approach-artificial-intelligence (archived at https://perma.cc/PAP7-NU65)

European Parliament and Council (2024) Regulation (EU) 2024/1689: Artificial Intelligence Act. Official Journal of the European Union. https://data.europa.eu/eli/reg/2024/1689/oj (archived at https://perma.cc/4JDW-9ZSP)

Grosse, E. H., Sgarbossa, F., Berlin, C. and Neumann, W. P. (2023) Human-centric production and logistics system design and management: transitioning from Industry 4.0 to Industry 5.0. *International Journal of Production Research*, 61(22), 7749–59.

Hussain, A. and Hussain, A. (2025) Transparency and accountability: Unpacking the real problems of explainable AI. *AI & Society*, 5587–5588.

Kiplinger (2025, July) Is Delta's new AI pricing bad news for your wallet? www.kiplinger.com/personal-finance/travel/is-deltas-new-ai-pricing-bad-news-for-your-wallet (archived at https://perma.cc/U3W9-A3H6)

Kosasih, E. E., Papadakis, E., Baryannis, G. and Brintrup, A. (2024) A review of explainable artificial intelligence in supply chain management using neurosymbolic approaches. *International Journal of Production Research*, 62(4), 1510–40.

Merchán-Cruz, E. A., Gabelaia, I., Savrasovs, M., Hansen, M. F., Soe, S., Rodriguez-Cañizo, R. G. and Aragón-Camarasa, G. (2025) Trust by design: An ethical framework for collaborative intelligence systems in industry 5.0. *Electronics*, 14(10), 1952.

OECD (Organisation for Economic Co-operation and Development) (2022) AI Principles. www.oecd.org/en/topics/sub-issues/ai-principles.html (archived at https://perma.cc/BP59-WEGZ).

Oladele, O. K. (2025) Inclusive AI Governance Models for Global Supply Chain Management in Crisis Scenarios.

PCWorld (2025, July) Delta is using AI-priced tickets to charge the most you'll accept. www.pcworld.com/article/2852903/delta-is-using-ai-priced-tickets-to-charge-the-most-youll-accept.html (archived at https://perma.cc/85QL-22FG)

PYMNTS (2025, July) Delta Air Lines tests AI-powered personalized pricing. www.pymnts.com/travel-payments/2025/delta-air-lines-tests-ai-powered-personalized-pricing/ (archived at https://perma.cc/3Q79-ER92)

Sam-Bulya, N. J., Mbanefo, J. V., Ewim, C. P. M. and Ofodile, O. C. (2024). Ensuring privacy and security in sustainable supply chains through distributed ledger technologies. *International Journal of Engineering Research and Development*, 20(11), 691–702.

Stanford University (2025) The 2025 AI Index Report. https://hai.stanford.edu/ai-index/2025-ai-index-report (archived at https://perma.cc/U8CZ-MYND)

Thadani, T. (2025, July 14) Tesla faces trial over fatal Autopilot crash in Florida. *The Washington Pos*t. www.washingtonpost.com/technology/2025/07/18/tesla-autopilot-fatal-crash-wrongful-death/ (archived at https://perma.cc/7J9X-2KVS)

Thornhill, T. (2025, July) AI airfares: How Delta could take dynamic pricing to the next level. *The Independent*. www.the-independent.com/travel/news-and-advice/delta-ai-pricing-flights-cost-b2791141.html (archived at https://perma.cc/XZQ3-Z52K)

Thrifty Traveler (2025, July) Delta tests AI-powered dynamic pricing. https://thriftytraveler.com/news/airlines/delta-ai-fare-pricing/ (archived at https://perma.cc/Y4FV-8PTV)

View From the Wing (2025, July) Several airlines now quietly let AI set ticket prices. https://viewfromthewing.com/several-airlines-now-quietly-let-ai-set-ticket-prices-surprisingly-thats-great-news-for-your-wallet/ (archived at https://perma.cc/5272-R5PH)

Weiner, E. B., Dankwa-Mullan, I., Nelson, W. A. and Hassanpour, S. (2024, November) Ethical challenges and evolving strategies in the integration of artificial intelligence into clinical practice. *arXiv*.

Wellbrock, W., Malinovska, M. and Ludin, D. (2025) Ethical implications and potential opportunities and risks of artificial intelligence in supply chain management. *Discover Sustainability*, 6(1), 1–14.

Widder, D. G. and Wong, R. (2023) Thinking upstream: Ethics and policy opportunities in AI supply chains. *arXiv preprint arXiv:2303.07529*.

Wu, H., Liu, J. and Liang, B. (2025) AI-driven supply chain transformation in Industry 5.0: Enhancing resilience and sustainability. *Journal of the Knowledge Economy*, 16(1), 3826–68.

Yanytska, L. (2025) The rise of human-centric manufacturing in the industry 5.0 era. *The International Journal of Advanced Manufacturing Technology*, 1–11.

Building the Workforce of Supply Chain 5.0

13

Demography is destiny.

AUGUSTE COMTE

Upskilling for Hybrid Human–Machine Roles in Supply Chain 5.0

As supply chains evolve from automation-centered 4.0 models to the human–technology symbiosis of Supply Chain 5.0, one truth stands out: The future of supply chain excellence depends on people. Technology alone cannot build resilience, creativity, or ethical judgment. These uniquely human attributes are the connective tissue that enables intelligent systems to work toward meaningful outcomes.

Supply Chain 5.0, therefore, redefines the workforce to thrive in environments where humans and machines coexist, operate, or perform either side by side or in an integrated manner. This is not about replacing people with technology; it is about augmenting human capabilities through intelligent systems. The shift from "automation" to "augmentation" positions human talent at the center of digital ecosystems, with AI, robotics, and advanced analytics acting as partners rather than substitutes.

As AI and automation increasingly handle repetitive and rule-based tasks, employees are moving into roles that require judgment, adaptability, collaboration, and problem-solving. These human skills complement machine-driven efficiency, enabling supply chains to be both technologically advanced and human-centered.

To prepare for these hybrid roles, companies are investing in innovative training approaches that blend AI-driven learning and immersive technologies:

- Virtual reality (VR) simulations: Organizations utilize VR to create realistic warehouse and production environments where employees can practice safety procedures, operate equipment, and fulfill workflows in controlled settings. These simulations accelerate learning, improve accuracy, and reduce onboarding errors, making training faster and safer (Strivr, n.d.; Talespin, n.d.).
- AI-enabled learning platforms: Adaptive learning systems personalize training pathways by adjusting content in real time based on learner progress. Employees develop critical capabilities such as interpreting AI outputs, managing exceptions in automated workflows, and collaborating effectively with intelligent systems. For example, CMA CGM launched an internal AI skills accelerator program to align workforce capabilities with its strategic use of artificial intelligence (BCG, 2024).
- Extended reality for soft skills: Platforms like Mursion provide immersive environments where employees practice communication and leadership scenarios with AI-driven avatars. Large organizations deploy these simulations to coach thousands of employees in empathy, negotiation, and problem resolution at scale (Mursion, n.d.)

These initiatives demonstrate that Supply Chain 5.0 is not only about deploying technology, but also about investing in the human capabilities that make technology effective. By leveraging technologies for training, organizations equip their workforce to thrive in hybrid roles that blend machine efficiency with human judgment, creativity, and ethical decision-making.

The Human–Technology Partnership: An Impact on Roles and Skills

While Industry 4.0 revolutionized manufacturing and logistics through automation and cyber-physical systems, its emphasis on machine autonomy often sidelined human creativity and adaptability. By extension, Supply Chain 5.0 reintroduces the human element into advanced technological ecosystems, prioritizing collaboration between humans and intelligent machines to achieve resilience, sustainability, and social value (Frederico, 2021;

Kuzmin et al., 2024). This paradigm shift reflects a broader societal and industrial movement toward purpose-driven innovation, where efficiency is balanced with ethics, sustainability, and personalization.

In this context, three foundational principles characterize Supply Chain 5.0:

- **Human-centricity:** Placing human judgment, creativity, and well-being at the core of supply chain operations rather than treating technology as a substitute for human roles (Villar et al., 2023).
- **Sustainability:** Integrating human-defined environmental and social objectives into supply chain strategies, aligning with circular economy principles and ESG goals (Dacre et al., 2025).
- **Technology-driven collaboration:** Leveraging advanced technologies, AI, IoT, blockchain, and immersive platforms, not for full automation but for augmenting human decision-making and enabling adaptive, resilient networks (Idamia et al., 2024).

As a result, Supply Chain 5.0 focuses on collaboration across the above three foundational principles. Machines offer analytical accuracy and scalability, while humans bring creativity, empathy, and contextual understanding. This partnership can be illustrated through three complementary roles, as depicted in Figure 13.1, where the results are not just operational excellence but purposeful performance, a supply chain that thinks, learns, and adapts in harmony with human values.

Figure 13.1 The Human–Technology Partnership Spheres in Supply Chain 5.0

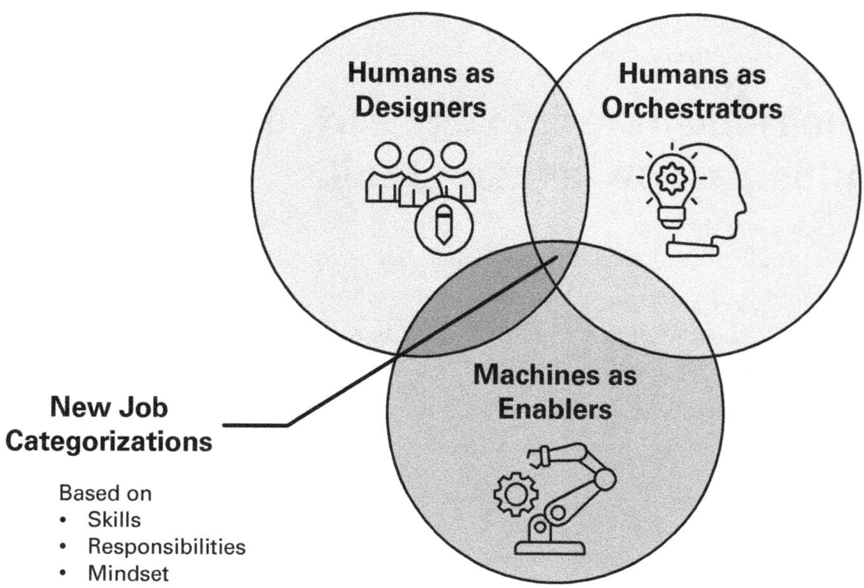

As automation assumes repetitive and rule-based tasks, human roles are increasingly shifting toward strategic, analytical, and collaborative functions. Employees now manage hybrid human–machine workflows that require advanced competencies in interpreting AI outputs, handling exceptions, and ensuring the ethical governance of technology (Koneti et al., 2024; Vann Yaroson et al., 2025). This evolution is also likely to give rise to new job categories, such as AI Workflow Supervisors, who could be responsible for overseeing algorithmic decision-making and validating system outputs; Digital Twin Analysts, tasked with managing virtual replicas of supply chain networks for predictive modeling and optimization; or Sustainability Integration Specialists, charged with aligning operational decisions with environmental, social, and governance (ESG) goals (see Figure 13.2). Algorithms or machines do not define the shift in this era, but rather how organizations empower people to use them wisely. The future supply chain professionals and the emerging roles across the supply chains are not passive operators but designers, orchestrators, and ethical stewards of intelligent systems.

Ultimately, Supply Chain 5.0 is not about technology replacing human work—it's about reimagining work so that people can achieve what only humans can: Meaning, creativity, and purpose.

Figure 13.2 The Rise of New Job Categorizations

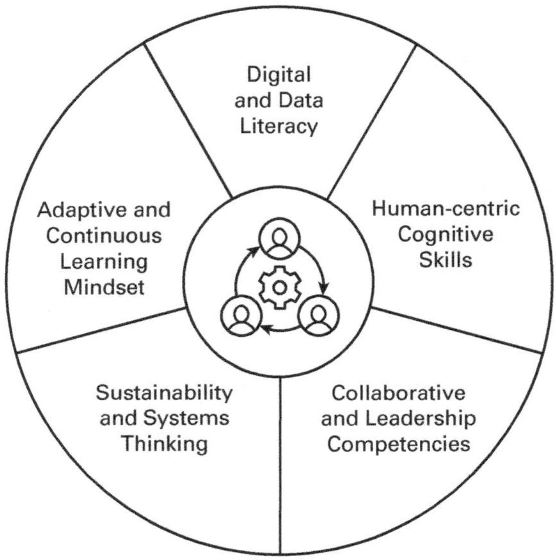

While it is widely understood that supply chain roles are rapidly evolving in the era of AI and automation, there is still no consensus on what the next generation of jobs will definitively look like. Amid this uncertainty, thought leaders across the industry have begun proposing possible role architectures that reflect the new skills, responsibilities, and mindsets the future may require. One notable contribution comes from Andrew Schneider in his December 7, 2025 LinkedIn article (Schneider, 2025), where he offers a forward-looking set of 10 roles that might define the "post-AI" supply chain. His list does not claim to be definitive, but it provides a compelling and structured view of what emerging roles could include as organizations shift from traditional planning to data governance, model stewardship, scenario intelligence, and value-centered leadership:

- Data Quality Engineer (DQE): Ensures all supply chain data is clean, structured, and trustworthy, recognizing that AI and automation only work when humans, not dashboards, own data integrity.
- Model Lifecycle Manager (MLM): Governs the full lifecycle of predictive models, including monitoring drift, retraining, and validating accuracy as forecasting becomes a living ecosystem instead of a static statistic.
- Exception Strategy Architect (ESA): Designs the rules for which exceptions are handled by AI, which require human judgment, and what escalates, preventing organizations from being overwhelmed by unmanaged exception noise.
- Scenario and Risk Orchestrator (SRO): Runs continuous what-if simulations linking operational changes to financial outcomes, shifting S&OP from a monthly ritual to real-time scenario intelligence.
- Constraint and Flow Designer (CFD): Architects system flow, constraints, buffers, and lead-time strategies, ensuring humans design the operating logic that machines execute.
- Supplier Ecosystem Strategist (SES): Builds resilient supplier ecosystems, negotiates shared-risk models, and drives sustainability and capacity strategies that AI cannot replicate due to the human nature of trust and relationships.
- Customer Experience Supply Partner (CESP): Aligns supply capabilities with customer needs through co-planning, exception handling, and value-driven service design rather than transactional order management.
- Cross-Functional Signal Analyst (CFSA): Interprets multi-domain signals—promotions, macro trends, competitive activity, POS data—recognizing

that baseline forecasting is largely automated and the competitive edge lies in signal intelligence.

- Digital Twin Process Architect (DTPA): Designs and maintains digital twin environments that enable rapid, simulated decision-making rather than static planning.
- Value Creation Steward (VCS): The next-generation supply chain leader who architects value across the enterprise, aligns strategy, and measures impact in financial outcomes rather than operational percentages.

New Skills for the Workforce 5.0 Era

The success of Supply Chain 5.0 depends not only on technological adoption but on human capability development. Digital transformation initiatives often fail when organizations overlook the critical role of talent in operationalizing advanced technologies (Atieh et al., 2025; Ning and Yao, 2023). While AI and automation excel at handling repetitive and rule-based tasks, they cannot replicate human attributes such as ethical judgment, creativity, and contextual problem-solving, qualities essential for resilience and innovation in complex global supply chains (Kedzierski, 2024).

Balancing automation with human creativity requires strategic workforce transformation, including reskilling and upskilling initiatives that prepare employees for hybrid roles where they collaborate with intelligent systems rather than compete against them. Organizations that treat these domains as part of their talent strategy, not optional training modules, will be best positioned to thrive. This approach aligns with findings that human–machine collaboration enhances adaptability, sustainability, and long-term competitiveness (Shabur et al., 2025; Martini et al., 2024).

Thus, Supply Chain 5.0 demands a reimagined skill architecture. Research and industry frameworks (Modgil et al., 2023; Oeij et al., 2023) identify six core skill domains essential for thriving in the 5.0 workforce:

1 **Digital and data literacy:**
   - proficiency in AI, IoT, blockchain, and big data analytics
   - ability to interpret algorithmic outputs and leverage predictive insights
   - comfort with AI, digital twins, data analytics, and blockchain technologies, understanding both their capabilities and their limitations

2 **Human-centric cognitive skills:**
   - critical thinking, creativity, and ethical reasoning

- decision-making under uncertainty and complex trade-offs
- applying empathy and user-centered thinking to redesign processes and experiences

3 **Collaborative and leadership competencies:**
- cross-functional teamwork in global networks
- leading hybrid teams of humans and intelligent machines
- collaborative intelligence is relevant for leading cross-functional, cross-cultural teams in hybrid human–machine environments

4 **Sustainability and systems thinking:**
- understanding circular economy principles and ESG compliance
- integrating social and environmental considerations into operational strategies.
- making decisions that align with environmental, social, and governance (ESG) principles

5 **Adaptive and continuous learning mindset:**
- embracing lifelong learning and agility to keep pace with technological evolution
- comfort with immersive training platforms (VR/AR) and AI-driven learning systems
- cognitive flexibility is essential as the ability to switch between strategic, creative, and analytical thinking to manage uncertainty and innovation

6 **Cognitive and emotional resiliency:**
- embracing a workforce capable of adapting, learning, and leading through uncertainty provides the ultimate competitive advantage
- when technology fails or when global shocks disrupt predictability, it is human judgment, creativity, and collaboration that restore stability
- adaptive thinking programs that simulate crisis scenarios
- digital confidence initiatives that reduce fear of automation
- well-being systems that monitor and support psychological health

Reinventing Learning and Leadership

As seen, traditional training models—structured, linear, and compliance-driven—no longer suffice. Learning in Supply Chain 5.0 must be continuous, experiential, and digital-first. Microlearning platforms, AI-driven simulations, and augmented reality can accelerate skill development while providing real-time contextual feedback.

At the leadership level, the challenge is deeper. The 5.0 leader is not merely a technologist or strategist, but a humanist engineer, someone who understands systems and people equally well. They must cultivate cultures of curiosity, inclusivity, and ethical reflection. As Deloitte (2025) notes, navigating tensions between automation and augmentation is not about picking a side, but rather about finding the right balance between both sides of the tension. Leadership in this context is distributed, not hierarchical. Cross-functional "orchestration teams" blend data scientists, supply chain planners, sustainability experts, and behavioral scientists. The emphasis is on collective intelligence rather than command-and-control.

However, there is no universal blueprint for this leadership. Each organization, and even each function within it, will make different choices based on its maturity, strategy, and the culture of its leader and the company. These decisions will continue to evolve as technologies advance and business priorities change. Yet, across the research for this book, there were four fundamental requirements for embedding human-centricity training programs:

- Purpose: Clear articulation of employee, business, societal, and or environmental value creation.
- Participation: Empowering employees to co-create solutions with technology.
- Psychological safety: Encouraging experimentation without fear of failure.
- Personalization: Tailoring career paths to individual strengths and aspirations.

Companies like Unilever, Siemens, and Maersk have begun integrating human–machine collaboration into their supply chain strategies, focusing on re-skilling and well-being alongside performance. These pioneers demonstrate that productivity and humanity are not opposites; they are multipliers.

Automation and the Talent Pipeline Dilemma

In one scenario that mirrors a pattern we heard in many of our interviews, a factory relies on five skilled machine operators and one advanced operator who is considered an expert. With the introduction of automation, the company discovers it can eliminate the roles of the five operators. The system can now operate independently, with the expert overseeing operations, troubleshooting issues, and optimizing performance.

From a short-term perspective, this appears to be a win. Labor costs are reduced. Efficiency improves. The remaining expert can manage more output with fewer human resources. But the story is not complete. While the five former operators are now out of work, the organization faces a hidden risk. By removing the entry-level and mid-level operational roles, it has also removed the development pathway that once allowed workers to grow into advanced operator positions. The automation may be technically self-sufficient, but it is not organizationally sustainable.

Once the remaining expert retires or leaves, the factory may discover that no one else has the depth of experience to step into the role. Institutional knowledge is lost, and the organization is forced to react to a talent gap it created through its own automation decisions.

This tension between short-term cost savings and long-term talent development is not theoretical. Supply chain leaders across various sectors repeatedly raise it. The challenge lies in finding a balance between automation and human development, particularly in environments where operational knowledge is acquired through years of hands-on experience.

Several strategies can help address this dilemma. One is to retain a smaller number of operator roles, even if the system no longer strictly requires them. These positions can be reframed as apprenticeships or rotational learning roles, where workers gain exposure to advanced systems and receive mentorship from the expert. Another strategy is to establish a formal talent development program that incorporates simulation training, digital twins, and cross-functional projects to accelerate learning. A third approach is to partner with technical schools or training centers to create a pipeline of candidates who are familiar with both automated systems and hands-on operations.

Automation will continue to transform the structure of the workforce. However, in the pursuit of efficiency, organizations must also safeguard their ability to develop talent. In a Supply Chain 5.0 environment, resilience is not only about technology. It is also about people. The organizations that thrive will be those that treat talent development not as a legacy cost, but as a strategic capability.

Adapting Workforce Development to Support Supply Chain 5.0

As supply chains evolve toward Supply Chain 5.0, the need for a workforce with adaptive, human-centric skills has become urgent. Technology is automating routine tasks, but the systems of the future will depend on people who can exercise judgment, collaborate across disciplines, and navigate uncertainty. This shift is not just about technical knowledge, but about developing the human capabilities that complement advanced analytics and artificial intelligence.

A recent Korn Ferry study of supply chain executives found that nearly 80 percent are now prioritizing candidates with agile, end-to-end thinking over traditional functional expertise. Skills such as communication, organizational design, and the ability to operate in ambiguous environments are becoming as critical as digital fluency (Korn Ferry, 2023a). The same study reported that 57 percent of leaders struggle to find talent with holistic supply chain knowledge, 43 percent cite a shortage of transformation experience, and 41 percent report gaps in data analysis and reporting capabilities (Korn Ferry, 2023a). These findings underscore a widening gap between the skills required for Supply Chain 5.0 and the capabilities present in today's workforce.

Organizations are responding by balancing "buy" and "build" strategies for talent. In some cases, companies hire externally to bring in new perspectives and specialized expertise. In others, they invest in internal development programs to upskill existing employees while retaining institutional knowledge and culture. Korn Ferry recommends that leading organizations adopt dynamic approaches combining both strategies to remain competitive in the face of rapid change (Korn Ferry, 2024).

One emerging practice is skills-based hiring, which focuses on what candidates can do and learn rather than on traditional qualifications or previous job titles. This approach can unlock hidden talent pools and increase workforce diversity by emphasizing potential and adaptability over rigid career paths (Korn Ferry, 2023b). It also aligns with the principles of Supply Chain 5.0, where inclusivity and agility are as important as technical expertise.

Technology is playing a role not just in operations but also in workforce development itself. Conversational AI is being used to simulate supplier negotiations and logistics problem-solving, giving professionals the opportunity to practice interpersonal and strategic skills in realistic, low-risk environments. Virtual and augmented reality tools are being deployed to train workers on new equipment and layouts, allowing teams to learn collaboratively in immersive digital twins of real-world environments. These tools reinforce the idea that technology in Supply Chain 5.0 should amplify human judgment and capability rather than displace it.

A useful way to frame this evolution is through a human-centric talent development model. At the top level, organizations define their supply chain vision and the skills needed to achieve it, from AI literacy to cross-functional collaboration. Workforce planning identifies gaps and determines whether to hire externally or upskill internally. Talent practices such as skills-based hiring and career architecture create pathways for diverse candidates. Learning and development then provides personalized, measurable training aligned with career goals and business outcomes. Finally, continuous feedback loops measure the return on learning and ensure that skill development evolves alongside the supply chain itself.

As the Korn Ferry research highlights, workforce development in Supply Chain 5.0 is not just about technical proficiency. It is about creating a human-centered ecosystem where technology and people work in concert, and where skills development is an ongoing, strategic priority.

Learning from the Past

The experience of North Carolina during the implementation of the North American Free Trade Agreement (NAFTA) illustrates the risks of overlooking workforce readiness during periods of rapid economic and technological change. In the 1990s, political and business leaders in the state strongly championed free trade, confident that globalization would deliver net benefits. As one article observed, "Even as foreign competition was devouring thousands of factory jobs a year in the mid- and late 1990s, most political and business leaders touted the benefits of the global marketplace" (Neff et al., 2002, para. 7).

The result was devastating: More than 86,000 textile jobs disappeared in a few years, leaving local communities without adequate support, retraining, or transition planning. The state's Commerce Secretary later admitted, "It's frustrating for us not being able to get a net understanding of how large these job losses are" (Neff et al., 2002).

For today's supply chain leaders, this episode offers a cautionary lesson. As AI, automation, and advanced analytics reshape global value networks, the question is no longer if disruption will occur, but how well the workforce is prepared to adapt as roles are redefined across the supply chains. Supply Chain 5.0 requires proactive workforce strategies, continuous reskilling, flexible learning ecosystems, and human-centered transition plans to ensure that people evolve alongside technology.

Failing to anticipate these shifts, as North Carolina did during NAFTA, risks repeating history on a global scale. The future of supply chain excellence will depend not just on the adoption of intelligent technologies, but on how deliberately organizations invest in their people before disruption accelerates.

KEY POINT

Just as North Carolina's experience revealed the human cost of underestimating transition planning, the rapid adoption of AI in supply chains demands preemptive workforce strategies. Organizational leaders must:

- map future skills required for hybrid human–machine collaboration
- invest in lifelong learning and accessible digital education
- engage communities and policymakers early to mitigate the impact of structural shifts

The Impact of Generative AI on Critical Thinking

Generative AI is redefining how decisions are made, insights are produced, and creativity is expressed in modern supply chains. Large language models, synthetic data tools, and AI copilots are transforming the nature of knowledge work. While these systems enhance speed and scale, they also raise a critical human question: How does reliance on generative AI affect the ability of supply chain professionals to think critically and independently?

Algorithms now write reports, generate insights, and propose decisions. This evolution, described by Brynjolfsson and McAfee (2023) as "cognitive automation," presents both opportunities and risks. When machines produce increasingly sophisticated reasoning outputs, humans risk delegating too much of their own analytical process to AI. Over time, this can dull critical faculties, including questioning assumptions, assessing evidence, and understanding the complexity of causes. Generative AI's promise lies in amplifying human intelligence, not replacing it. Research by Kepuska and

MacMillan (2024) and Modgil et al. (2025) emphasizes that AI systems excel in data synthesis and pattern recognition but depend on humans for contextual understanding, ethical framing, and judgment under uncertainty.

A survey conducted by Microsoft Research and Carnegie Mellon University studied 319 knowledge workers who used generative AI tools, such as ChatGPT or Copilot, at least once a week. The participants provided 936 examples of AI-assisted tasks, allowing researchers to examine how generative AI affects perceived cognitive effort and the nature of critical thinking in professional work (Lee et al., 2025).

The study found that higher confidence in AI tools correlated with lower levels of critical engagement. In comparison, individuals with greater confidence in their own abilities were more likely to verify, adapt, and refine AI outputs, even when it required more effort (Lee et al., 2025; Turner, 2025). Participants described how generative AI shifted their cognitive focus from gathering information to verifying it, from solving problems independently to managing AI-generated responses, and from direct task execution to oversight and stewardship (Lee et al., 2025; Paoli, 2025).

Although many respondents reported efficiency gains, approximately 40 percent admitted that they used little to no critical thinking when relying heavily on AI, particularly in low-stakes tasks or under time pressure (Turner, 2025). The researchers identified barriers, including weak domain confidence, a lack of awareness of AI limitations, and organizational incentives that prioritize speed over reflection. At the same time, accountability for outcomes and a desire to build expertise were cited as motivators for maintaining deeper engagement (Paoli, 2025).

The authors suggest designing AI systems that actively promote critical thinking by providing transparent reasoning, interactive feedback loops, and adjustable levels of assistance based on user experience and task complexity (Lee et al., 2025).

For leaders preparing their organizations for Supply Chain 5.0, these findings underscore a crucial dimension of workforce development. As intelligent systems become embedded in planning, sourcing, and orchestration, there is a risk that employees could default to AI outputs without sufficient critical evaluation. Building a workforce capable of collaborating effectively with AI requires intentional training to maintain and strengthen human judgment, problem-solving, and oversight skills. Leaders must cultivate a culture where AI augments rather than replaces critical thinking, ensuring that supply chain professionals are equipped to manage increasingly complex, technology-enabled networks with both confidence and discernment.

For Supply Chain 5.0 leaders, the key challenge is ensuring that AI enhances, rather than replaces, human reasoning. Critical thinking must become a deliberate design element in both workforce training and digital governance. Several strategies can help to cultivate augmented cognition:

- **AI literacy and explainability:** Equip teams to understand how generative AI systems work, their data sources, and their limitations. Transparency builds confidence without blind trust. The World Economic Forum's Future of Jobs Report (2025) highlights AI literacy as one of the top five emerging competencies.
- **Decision audits:** Integrate "human-in-the-loop" checkpoints that require professionals to challenge or validate AI outputs before implementation. The European Commission's Ethics Guidelines for Trustworthy AI (2019) recommends traceability and human oversight in decision-making systems.
- **Critical thinking labs:** Leading firms such as Siemens and Unilever have launched AI ethics and decision labs to train managers in scenario-based reasoning, blending data-driven insights with ethical judgment
- **Reflective practice:** Encourage post-decision reviews where teams analyze the role of AI in outcomes: What it got right, where human intervention added value, and how reasoning can improve.

Remember: Generative AI excels at producing knowledge but not necessarily understanding. It can predict patterns, generate solutions, and even simulate reasoning, but it cannot discern meaning or purpose. That remains the domain of human critical thought. In this sense, the most competitive supply chains of the 5.0 era will not simply deploy more advanced AI; they will nurture more advanced human thinkers.

REAL-WORLD EXAMPLE Call Center

In a fascinating call center study, Dr. Ben Waber and his team from Humanize showed that performance was not driven by individual metrics but by the quality of human connections. The existing management model contained a critical flaw. To maintain constant call coverage, breaks were intentionally staggered. While operationally efficient, this practice unintentionally prevented employees from building meaningful relationships and sharing knowledge (B. Waber, personal communication, July 28, 2025).

The changes that followed were simple in design yet profound in impact. The first was synchronizing break times. By aligning breaks for team members, the company created a natural 15-minute window where employees could interact without the pressure of a ringing phone. In these moments, top performers informally coached colleagues on handling complex customer challenges, and knowledge that had previously been locked in silos began to flow freely across the team.

The second change involved redesigning the incentive structure. Traditional performance models rewarded speed and individual call completion rates. Waber's team reframed success to highlight collaboration. Individual bonuses were reduced in favor of team-based metrics, and employees who actively supported their peers were formally recognized. This subtle shift rewarded behaviors that strengthened the collective rather than isolating achievement.

Finally, Waber's team conducted a network analysis using advanced ID badges that tracked patterns of interaction. This revealed who were the natural knowledge sharers, how information moved within the group, and where communication bottlenecks existed. These insights allowed management to nurture the informal networks that actually powered performance.

The results were striking. Team performance rose by more than 20 percent. Employees became more skilled, engaged, and connected, and the call center evolved from a transactional environment into a learning ecosystem.

Waber emphasized that this transformation was not simply the result of technology or data. It was born from recognizing the deeply social nature of work and designing systems that respect and amplify it. The most effective optimization came not from algorithms or isolated metrics, but from creating space for human connection and collaborative learning. This case demonstrated that human-centricity is not a soft concept but a critical performance strategy that unlocks the true potential of a workforce.

Conversational AI for Skill Development and Professional Training

Conversational AI platforms provide immersive practice environments for developing soft skills such as negotiation, clear communication, adaptability, and multilingual interaction. These capabilities are especially important when professionals must negotiate with suppliers, lead cross-cultural teams, or collaborate across time zones.

LinkedIn Learning offers AI-driven role-play coaching that simulates realistic workplace dialogues. Learners participate in scenarios such as giving feedback or managing conflict and receive immediate feedback on tone, listening, clarity, and decision framing. The AI coaching adjusts to individual responses and suggests targeted learning resources for improvement. Learners report that this type of practice increases confidence in high-stakes communication situations (University of Arizona News, 2025; Hoover, 2024).

Duolingo demonstrates conversational practice in language learning. Its Duolingo Max tier includes interactive roleplay exercises powered by language models, where users respond to simulated scenarios such as ordering food, requesting directions, or participating in everyday conversations. The system provides feedback on grammar, tone, and conversational flow, helping users gain fluency and contextual awareness (Duolingo Blog, 2023; McCarthy, 2024).

Google Translate's conversation mode also supports multilingual dialogue in real time. The feature allows users to speak in one language and see the translated conversation appear almost instantly on screen, automatically detecting both languages in a back-and-forth conversation. This capability supports clearer communication in multilingual settings and can help users learn to phrase messages in simpler, more precise terms over time (Indian Express, 2023; Pocket Lint, 2023).

These platforms show how conversational AI can help develop communication skills, contextual fluency, and calm decision-making under pressure. In supply chain environments, these capabilities can support better negotiation, more effective international collaboration, and improved management of complex discussions while maintaining human oversight and judgment.

By offering adaptive practice and feedback in a low-risk environment, conversational AI helps bridge the gap between theory and real-world interaction. It does not replace human decision-making but instead provides structured opportunities for professionals to strengthen critical thinking, active listening, and thoughtful responses in dynamic conversations.

Regulatory Influences on Technology Adoption in Supply Chain 5.0

In earlier industrial eras, technology adoption was primarily driven by the need for efficiency and market competition. Regulatory frameworks often lag innovation, intervening only to correct failures or mitigate risk. Supply Chain 5.0 reverses this dynamic. Governments, supranational organizations, and industry consortia now establish forward-looking regulatory ecosystems that define the ethical, environmental, and societal boundaries of technological transformation.

In the context of Supply Chain 5.0, regulation is not merely a compliance obligation; it is a strategic force shaping how technologies such as artificial intelligence, blockchain, robotics, the Internet of Things, advanced automation, and human interface technologies are designed, deployed, and governed across global value networks. However, the deployment of these technologies is strongly influenced by public policy and regulation, which can either enable or limit innovation. One example involves the East Coast dockworkers in the United States, represented by the International Longshoremen's Association (ILA). In 2024, the union called for a comprehensive prohibition on automation, including automated cranes and container-handling systems, based on concerns that such technologies would eliminate union jobs (ILA, as cited in Reuters, 2025; Holdman, 2024). This position became a key issue in contract negotiations with the US Maritime Alliance (USMX), which represents employers at East and Gulf Coast ports (Reuters, 2025; Holdman, 2024). The lack of automation agreements has resulted in these ports continuing to operate with primarily manual processes.

A different case, described by a global supply chain manager, illustrates another way in which regulation can influence business decisions. In this instance, a government policy required at least 10 percent of workers in a manufacturing or distribution facility to be local citizens rather than foreign workers. Despite the relatively low threshold, the company struggled to find enough qualified local employees to comply with the requirement. As a result, the organization chose to invest in automation, even though the capital cost was significantly higher than relying on labor would have been if sufficient workers had been available (personal interview, 2025). In this case, the policy intended to ensure local employment had the opposite effect, accelerating the adoption of automation.

These examples demonstrate how labor policies can have a significant impact on Supply Chain 5.0 technologies. On the East Coast, regulatory and labor agreements have slowed the introduction of automation in an effort to preserve jobs, which has also impacted port competitiveness. In the manufacturing case, a local hiring mandate created labor constraints that encouraged the company to automate despite the higher expense. Both situations demonstrate that regulations intended to protect employment can shape the adoption of technology in ways that are not always anticipated.

For organizations implementing Supply Chain 5.0, it is therefore critical to evaluate not only the technical and financial feasibility of new technologies but also the regulatory context, including labor laws, union agreements, and government regulations. The interaction between policy, labor markets, and technology plays a central role in determining how and when advanced supply chain solutions are deployed.

KEY POINT

The Regulatory Triad: Data, Sustainability, and Ethics

Three major regulatory domains are now converging to define the boundaries of Supply Chain 5.0 adoption:

1. **Data governance and digital sovereignty.**
   Regulations such as the EU Digital Services Act (DSA), Digital Markets Act (DMA), and Data Act (2023) are redefining how organizations access, share, and monetize supply chain data. In practice, these laws encourage companies to adopt interoperable and transparent data ecosystems that strike a balance between innovation and privacy and security.
   For multinational supply chains, this requires harmonizing data policies across jurisdictions to ensure that AI-driven logistics and predictive analytics comply with local data residency and consent requirements.
   Recent research and economic frameworks highlight that data transparency and traceability have transitioned from competitive differentiators to key regulatory enablers of digital resilience, a shift supported by prior work in supply chain resilience (Ivanov and Dolgui, 2025; World Economic Forum, 2021).
2. **Sustainability and circular economy mandates.**
   Environmental and social regulations, such as the EU Corporate Sustainability Reporting Directive (CSRD) and the Carbon Border Adjustment Mechanism (CBAM), as well as emerging digital product passports, compel firms to quantify the full lifecycle impact of their products and suppliers.
   These frameworks are driving the adoption of blockchain-based traceability and AI-enabled emissions accounting to meet disclosure and decarbonization goals.
   The World Economic Forum (2025) identifies sustainability compliance as one of the top five accelerators of digital twin and IoT investment in global manufacturing networks.

3 **AI ethics and human-centric oversight.**
Regulations such as the EU AI Act (2024) classify AI systems based on risk levels, mandating human oversight, explainability, and bias mitigation for "high-risk" systems, including those used in logistics optimization, workforce management, or supplier assessment.
This is directly aligned with the Supply Chain 5.0 ethos: Technology must serve people, not replace them. For example, Siemens and DHL both report establishing AI ethics boards and algorithmic transparency frameworks to comply with upcoming regulations while strengthening stakeholder trust.

Regulatory influence varies across regions, but the trend toward global alignment is accelerating. For multinational supply chains, this regulatory mosaic creates both complexity and opportunity.

REAL-WORLD EXAMPLE How US Ports Have Fallen Behind

Despite their central role in global trade, US ports continue to trail international competitors in operational efficiency. The World Bank and S&P Global Container Port Performance Index 2023 shows that not a single US port ranks in the global top 50 for vessel turnaround time. Charleston ranks highest among US ports at number 53, followed by New York and New Jersey at 89, with other major US ports performing even lower (World Bank and S&P Global Market Intelligence, 2024).

One major factor is the slower and uneven adoption of port automation. A Government Accountability Office report found that all 10 of the largest US container ports have implemented some form of automation, mostly process automation such as automated gate systems. Only four of those ports have adopted automated cargo handling equipment. In comparison, leading foreign ports use more advanced automation, including automated cranes and integrated digital platforms, reflecting earlier and broader adoption (GAO, 2024).

Where automation has been implemented, it has improved safety and operational flow. The Port of Virginia, for example, has reduced truck dwell times and emissions through automated gating solutions (S&P Global Market Intelligence, 2024). However, overall productivity and vessel turnaround performance at US ports still lag behind their more heavily automated counterparts in Asia and Europe.

Labor resistance is a key reason for the slow adoption. Unionized dockworkers, particularly those represented by the International Longshoremen's and Warehouse Union, have expressed concerns about job displacement, wage erosion, and the weakening of middle-class employment in port communities. Union leaders also argue that experienced human operators are essential for managing complex and unexpected operational conditions that automated systems struggle to handle (Reuters, 2025; Berger et al., 2024).

These concerns are rooted in historical experience. From the early mechanization of factories in the 20th century to the containerization revolution of the 1960s, technological changes have often displaced labor faster than new job categories have emerged. Workers have seen how efficiency gains can accrue to operators and owners while leaving local economies behind. That history shapes current skepticism around port automation.

In the context of Supply Chain 5.0, this tension underscores the importance of a human-centered approach to technology adoption. Implementing automation should involve engaging workers, making decisions transparently, redesigning roles, and investing in reskilling. Without these measures, operational improvements risk undermining trust, resilience, and social stability within supply chain systems.

References

Atieh, A. A., Abu Hussein, A., Al-Jaghoub, S., Alheet, A. F. and Attiany, M. (2025) The impact of digital technology, automation, and data integration on supply chain performance: Exploring the moderating role of digital transformation. *Logistics*, 9(1), 11.

Baertlein, L. (2025, January 6) US port labor talks resume with spotlight on automation. *Reuters*. www.reuters.com/world/us/us-port-labor-talks-resume-with-spotlight-automation-2025-01-06/ (archived at https://perma.cc/D2RR-6QFV)

BCG. (2024) Five must haves for effective AI upskilling. www.bcg.com/publications/2024/five-must-haves-for-ai-upskilling (archived at https://perma.cc/U8HC-WR33)

Berger, P., Cutter, C. and Deng, C. (2024, October 9) The battle over robots at US ports is on. *Wall Street Journal*. www.wsj.com/business/logistics/us-ports-automation-union-strike-f94bb4b7 (archived at https://perma.cc/Q5WA-9JT6)

Brynjolfsson, E. and McAfee, A. (2023) The cognitive automation frontier. MIT Digital Economy Initiative.

Dacre, N., Yan, J., Frei, R., Al-Mhdawi, M. K. S. and Dong, H. (2025) Advancing sustainable manufacturing: A systematic exploration of Industry 5.0 supply chains for sustainability, human-centricity, and resilience. *Production Planning & Control*, 36(11), 1499–1528.

Deloitte (2025) 2025 Global Human Capital Trends: Navigating complex tensions and choices in the worker–organization relationship. www.deloitte.com/us/en/insights/topics/talent/human-capital-trends.html (archived at https://perma.cc/82C8-8WW6)

Dolgui, A. and Ivanov, D. (2025) Internet of behaviors: Conceptual model, practical and theoretical implications for supply chain and operations management. *International Journal of Production Research*, 63(1), 1–8

Duolingo Blog (2023) Can chatbots actually help you learn a language? Here's how Duolingo works with large language models to help learners practice conversation. https://blog.duolingo.com/chatbot-language-practice/ (archived at https://perma.cc/CE97-66ZR)

European Commission (2019) Ethics Guidelines for Trustworthy AI. https://digital-strategy.ec.europa.eu/en/library/ethics-guidelines-trustworthy-ai (archived at https://perma.cc/3STS-KDD6)

Frederico, G. F. (2021) From supply chain 4.0 to supply chain 5.0: Findings from a systematic literature review and research directions. *Logistics*, 5(3), 49.

GAO (2024, March) US Ports Have Adopted Some Automation Technologies and Report Varied Effects (GAO 24 106498) Government Accountability Office. www.gao.gov/products/gao-24-106498 (archived at https://perma.cc/Z6HJ-8BJF)

Holdman, J. (2024, October) Union dockworkers along East Coast strike over pay, technology. *Alabama Reflector*. https://alabamareflector.com/2024/10/01/union-dockworkers-along-east-coast-strike-over-pay-technology/ (archived at https://perma.cc/8WPM-CK8B)

Hoover, A. (2024, June 13) LinkedIn's AI Career Coaches will see you now. *Wired*. www.wired.com/story/linkedin-ai-features-career-coach-chatbot/ (archived at https://perma.cc/HF5L-ZAC9)

Idamia, S., Hafida, B. and El Khair Ghoujdam, M. (2024) Supply Chain 5.0: A comprehensive literature review on implications, applications, and challenges. *International Journal of Innovative Science and Research Technology*, 9(4), 540–50.

Indian Express (2023) How to have real conversations in different languages with Google Translate. https://indianexpress.com/article/technology/tech-news-technology/how-to-real-time-google-translate-conversations-9150867/ (archived at https://perma.cc/37SZ-A4B3)

Kedzierski, B. (2024) Industry 5.0: Rebalancing human potential in the age of automation. *Hexagon*. https://aliresources.hexagon.com/articles-blogs/industry-5-0-rebalancing-human-potential-in-the-age-of-automation (archived at https://perma.cc/P2NT-FFCQ)

Kepuska, V. and MacMillan, A. (2024) Human–AI collaboration in cognitive work: Opportunities and boundaries. *Computers & Industrial Engineering*, 189, 109843.

Koneti, C., Sajja, G. S., Adarsh, A., Yerasuri, S. S., Mann, G. and Mandal, A. (2024) Human–machine collaboration in supply chain management: The impact of AI on workforce dynamics. *Journal of Informatics Education and Research*, 4(3), 934–43.

Korn Ferry (2023a) Supply chains in search of new skills. www.kornferry.com/insights/featured-topics/leadership/supply-chains-in-search-of-new-skills (archived at https://perma.cc/C6S7-DPB5)

Korn Ferry (2023b) Skills-based hiring: Finding hidden talent at scale. www.kornferry.com/insights/featured-topics/talent-recruitment/skills-based-hiring-finding-hidden-talent-at-scale (archived at https://perma.cc/B8BY-YPJ5)

Korn Ferry (2024) Recruit or retrain: Closing the skills gap. Retrieved August 2, 2025, from www.kornferry.com/insights/featured-topics/talent-recruitment/recruit-or-retrain-closing-the-skills-gap (archived at https://perma.cc/5WHZ-ESUN)

Kuzmin, E., Rakhimova, G., Nurmanov, U. and Nasurova, K. (2024) Transitioning from Industry 4.0 to Industry 5.0: An overview of co-evolution. In *The Future of Industry: Human-centric approaches in digital transformation* (pp. 21–37). Springer.

Lee, H.-P., Sarkar, A., Tankelevitch, L., Drosos, I., Rintel, S., Banks, R. and Wilson, N. (2025) The impact of generative AI on critical thinking: Self-reported reductions in cognitive effort and confidence effects from a survey of knowledge workers. In *Proceedings of the 2025 CHI Conference on Human Factors in Computing Systems* (Article 1121, pp. 1–22) Association for Computing Machinery. https://doi.org/10.1145/3706598.3713778 (archived at https://perma.cc/56YV-QVSB)

Martini, B., Bellisario, D. and Coletti, P. (2024) Human-centered and sustainable artificial intelligence in Industry 5.0: Challenges and perspectives. *Sustainability*, 16(13), 5448.

McCarthy, K. (2024) Duolingo adds AI innovations to language learning app. Investors.com. www.investors.com/news/technology/duolingo-stock-ai-innovations-language-learning-app/ (archived at https://perma.cc/FA7B-QUMV)

Modgil, S., Singh, R. K. and Agrawal, S. (2025) Developing human capabilities for supply chains: An Industry 5.0 perspective. *Annals of Operations Research*, 348(3), 2075–2105.

Mursion (n.d.) The upskilling platform for a future ready workforce. www.mursion.com/ (archived at https://perma.cc/34Y4-DUFK)

Neff, J., Wagner, J. and Rives, K. (2002, August 20) NAFTA's impact on NC, part 3: Leaders scramble as job losses mount. *Raleigh News and Observer.* https://faculty.chass.ncsu.edu/slatta/hi453/PS/Latinos/nafta3.htm (archived at https://perma.cc/W5FS-4SG8)

Ning, L. and Yao, D. (2023) The impact of digital transformation on supply chain capabilities and supply chain competitive performance. *Sustainability*, 15(13), 10107.

Oeij, P., van Rhijn, G., van Dijk, W., Dickinson, P., Warhurst, C., Garmann Johnsen, H. C., and Araiztegui, I. (2023) Conceptual framework of Industry 5.0 to study workforce skills. *BRIDGES 5.0 Project Deliverable* 1.1, 1–56.

Paoli, C. (2025, February 21) Study finds generative AI could inhibit critical thinking. Campus Technology. https://campustechnology.com/Articles/2025/02/21/Study-Generative-AI-Could-Inhibit-Critical-Thinking.aspx (archived at https://perma.cc/4PAM-CPFS)

Personal interview (2025) Interview with global supply chain manager regarding local worker requirements and automation decision.

Pocket Lint (2023) How to translate live audio conversations with Google Translate. www.pocket-lint.com/how-to-translate-live-audio-conversations-with-google-translate/ (archived at https://perma.cc/9S3S-WARG)

S&P Global Market Intelligence (2024, September) US port automation holds promise, but hardly a sure shot. www.spglobal.com/market-intelligence/en/news-insights/research/us-port-automation-holds-promise-but-hardly-a-sure-shot (archived at https://perma.cc/AF7C-PE7G)

Schneider, A. (2025) The post-AI supply chain: Redefining roles for the next 20 years. *LinkedIn*, 7 Dec. www.linkedin.com/pulse/post-ai-supply-chain-redefining-roles-next-20-years-andrew-schneider-xavpc (archived at https://perma.cc/4DY8-SP9S)

Shabur, M. A., Shahriar, A. and Ara, M. A. (2025) From automation to collaboration: Exploring the impact of Industry 5.0 on sustainable manufacturing. *Discover Sustainability*, 6(1), 341.

Strivr (n.d.) Implementing VR in supply chain logistics training. www.strivr.com/blog/implementing-vr-supply-chain-logistics-training (archived at https://perma.cc/C89E-WRHX)

Talespin (n.d.) Virtual Reality logistics training use cases. www.talespin.com/reading/virtual-reality-logistics-training-use-cases (archived at https://perma.cc/5KBZ-7PNU)

Turner, B. (2025, March 14) Using AI reduces your critical thinking skills, Microsoft study warns. *Live Science*. www.livescience.com/technology/artificial-intelligence/using-ai-reduces-your-critical-thinking-skills-microsoft-study-warns (archived at https://perma.cc/CX4U-SRHB)

University of Arizona News (2025, June 4) Master difficult workplace conversations with LinkedIn Learning's AI Coaching. *University of Arizona News*. https://hr.arizona.edu/news/2025/master-difficult-workplace-conversations-linkedin-learnings-ai-coaching (archived at https://perma.cc/9DQE-2P22)

Vann Yaroson, E., Abadie, A. and Roux, M. (2025) Human–artificial intelligence collaboration in supply chain outcomes: The mediating role of responsible artificial intelligence. *Annals of Operations Research*, 1–35.

Villar, A., Paladini, S. and Buckley, O. (2023, July) Towards Supply Chain 5.0: Redesigning supply chains as resilient, sustainable, and human-centric systems in a post-pandemic world. In *Operations Research Forum*, 4(3), p. 60 Cham: Springer International Publishing.

World Bank and S&P Global Market Intelligence. (2024, June 1) Regional disruptions drive changes in global container port performance ranking. www.worldbank.org/en/news/press-release/2024/06/01/regional-disruptions-drive-changes-in-global-container-port-performance-ranking (archived at https://perma.cc/UCN3-NP65)

World Bank (2024) The Container Port Performance Index 2023: A Comparable Assessment of Container Port Performance. World Bank. https://documents1.worldbank.org/curated/en/099060324114539683/pdf/P17583313892300871be641a5ea7b90e0e6.pdf (archived at https://perma.cc/2WXY-3MBJ)

World Economic Forum (2021) Digital Traceability: A Framework for More Sustainable and Resilient Value Chains.

World Economic Forum (2025) Future of Jobs Report. www.weforum.org/publications/the-future-of-jobs-report-2025/ (archived at https://perma.cc/H56A-WM93)

Securing Hyperconnected Supply Chains 14

It's not enough to just know who your immediate suppliers are. You need to understand the systemic risks from factors beyond your control that you must mitigate.

BRAD MARTIN, RAND INSTITUTE FOR SUPPLY CHAIN SECURITY

Supply Chain 5.0: A New Security Landscape

Supply Chain 5.0 marks a profound shift in how global networks are designed, managed, and secured. Built on the convergence of advanced digital technologies such as AI, the IoT, blockchain-based ledgers, robotics, digital twins, automation, and extended reality, with human-centered decision-making, this new paradigm offers unprecedented visibility and responsiveness. Yet these same capabilities introduce a dramatically more complex threat environment. As physical and digital assets become intertwined, the supply chain evolves into a cyber-physical ecosystem where disruptions, whether accidental or malicious, can propagate across continents in minutes. Thus, the boundaries between physical and digital assets are increasingly blurred.

In this environment, security can no longer be understood as a set of isolated practices. Instead, Supply Chain 5.0 requires a holistic, integrated security model that combines cybersecurity, physical protection, product authentication, and data governance into a single coherent architecture. The same technologies enabling real-time optimization, predictive maintenance, autonomous planning, and hyper-connected logistics also expand the attack surface. IoT sensors, edge devices, cloud-based orchestration platforms, and digital collaboration hubs can be exploited if not designed and managed with rigorous safeguards (Boyes, 2015).

Simultaneously, traditional threats are evolving. Cargo theft networks now use GPS jamming and spoofing to divert shipments. Counterfeiters employ additive manufacturing and advanced printing to replicate packaging or serial identifiers. Gray-market actors exploit gaps in platform-based commerce. Criminal groups increasingly leverage digital tools—social engineering, synthetic identities, ransomware—as part of their physical operations. In many cases, they use the very technologies meant to secure the supply chain.

A driving factor behind these risks is the deep interdependence of modern supply chains. Organizations today operate not as individual firms but as nodes in global, multi-tier ecosystems. Third-party and fourth-party risks mean that vulnerabilities can cascade across networks. A single compromised vendor, software package, or IoT device can expose an entire supply chain (Ivanov et al., 2014; NIST, 2022). These dynamics render perimeter-based defenses obsolete and underscore the need for zero-trust principles, where every user, device, and transaction is continually validated.

Importantly, security in Supply Chain 5.0 is not only a protective factor or defensive function. It is a strategic enabler that can become a source of competitive advantage. When executed well, robust security builds resilience, operational continuity, and trust among customers, partners, and regulators. In a world of rapid product flows and real-time data exchange, trust becomes a measurable asset. Companies able to guarantee authenticity, safeguard sensitive information, and ensure operational integrity gain a competitive edge. From pharmaceuticals to aerospace, from food logistics to luxury goods, secure supply chains are increasingly a differentiator in global markets.

This chapter explores the evolving security landscape of Supply Chain 5.0 and provides a framework for addressing it. It begins by exploring emerging cybersecurity risks in hyperconnected supply chains, with particular attention to IoT device vulnerabilities, data integrity threats, and the security implications of cloud- and edge-computing architectures. The chapter then revisits longstanding concerns about physical security and cargo theft that are becoming more complex as criminal actors incorporate digital tools such as GPS spoofing, social engineering, and platform-based fraud into their operations.

A major section is devoted to product authentication and anti-counterfeiting, an area undergoing rapid innovation. Technologies such as DNA taggants, physically unclonable functions (PUFs), nanomaterial-based markers, and blockchain-enabled provenance systems are transforming how organizations verify authenticity and protect brand integrity. These tools play a critical role in industries such as pharmaceuticals, medical devices, electronics, and aerospace, where counterfeit infiltration poses significant safety and financial risks.

The next section explores additional topics such as Zero Trust Architecture, digital twins used to model, simulate, and stress-test cyber-physical threats, software supply chain attacks, security considerations for sustainability strategies, governance, compliance, and global regulatory requirements, and balancing automation with human oversight.

The chapter concludes by offering a practical strategy for integrating these components into a layered, cross-functional security model. This approach emphasizes governance, continuous monitoring, and secure-by-design principles, ensuring that resilience and trustworthiness are embedded throughout the supply chain lifecycle.

Table 14.1 presents a simplified model illustrating how key security domains align with enabling technologies, associated risks, and mitigation strategies within hyperconnected Supply Chain 5.0 environments.

Cybersecurity in Connected Supply Chains

Modern supply chains operate as highly interconnected ecosystems, making them vulnerable to a wide range of cyber threats. A MIT Sloan report (Stackpole, 2024) highlights the growing prevalence of ransomware, data breaches, and vendor exploitation attacks (a form of protocol exploitation), reinforcing these as primary risks in modern supply chains. Several attacks can propagate through digital pathways without requiring physical access, amplifying systemic vulnerabilities across suppliers and partners. The complexity of vendor networks and lack of visibility into third-party security practices further exacerbate these risks, creating blind spots that attackers exploit (Maley, 2025). Manufacturing plants, logistics networks, and distribution hubs are now tightly integrated through industrial control systems (ICS), IoT devices, autonomous equipment, cloud platforms, and real-time data pipelines. These technologies support dynamic decision-making across global networks, yet they simultaneously create a dense and interconnected landscape of potential vulnerabilities (Ivanov and Dolgui, 2020).

In this environment, cybersecurity is no longer a discrete IT responsibility; it is a core component of operational continuity. A single compromised sensor, third-party software interface, or vendor connection can trigger cascading disruptions across production schedules, transportation flows, and customer deliveries. The Colonial Pipeline ransomware attack illustrated

Table 14.1 Integrated Security Domains, Risks, and Mitigation Strategies in Supply Chain 5.0

Security Domain	Primary Risks	Enabling Technologies	Mitigations Strategies
Cybersecurity	Malware, ransomware, data breaches, device hijacking; unauthorized access; ransomware; data breaches; protocol exploitation	Zero Trust, MFA, network segmentation, IoT sensors and edge devices; cloud platforms; AI/ML analytics; 5G networks	Access control, logging, endpoint protection, Zero-trust architecture; device hardening; encrypted communications; continuous monitoring; multi-factor authentication; patch and vulnerability management
Physical Security and Cargo Protection	Cargo theft; diversion; tampering; false routing; insider threats	IoT, geofencing, AI video analytics, GPS tracking; geofencing; telematics; smart locks; RFID	Smart locks, tracking, access control, real-time location monitoring; route-risk scoring; secured yards and access controls; tamper-evident devices; integration with law enforcement alerts
Product Authentication and Anti-Counterfeiting	Counterfeiting; gray-market diversion; unauthorized reselling; component substitution	DNA taggants; PUFs; nanomaterial inks; serialization; blockchain provenance	Multi-layer authentication markers; serialization and track-and-trace; blockchain-verified chains of custody; supplier pedigree audits
Data Integrity and Provenance	Data tampering; false data injection; loss of provenance; inaccurate model outputs	Blockchain ledgers; digital twins; secure data pipelines; API ecosystems	Cryptographic hashing; immutable ledgers; secure API gateways; redundant validation systems; anomaly detection algorithms
Operational Technology (OT) Security	OT system compromise; unsafe automated operations; cross-domain attacks from IT to OT	Industrial IoT (IIoT); SCADA systems; robotics; autonomous vehicles	Network segmentation; safety interlocks; OT-specific intrusion detection; physical isolation of critical systems; real-time anomaly detection
Human Oversight and Ethical Automation	Automation bias; operator overreliance; ethical failures; unsafe overrides	AI decision support; human–machine interfaces; automated planning systems	Human-in-the-loop governance; decision auditability; training and competency programs; escalation protocols

this vividly: A digital intrusion in one organization rapidly escalated into physical distribution shutdowns and significant downstream supply chain impacts (Cybersecurity and Infrastructure Security Agency (CISA), 2023).

The nature of cyber risk in Supply Chain 5.0 increasingly erodes the boundary between digital and physical systems. Adversaries no longer need physical access to inflict damage. Malicious software updates, hijacked IoT endpoints, falsified telemetry, and compromised remote access tools can halt production, divert goods, or disrupt safety-critical processes while remaining entirely in the digital domain (Boyes, 2015). Because supply chains operate as interdependent ecosystems, a single vulnerability can become amplified, transforming an isolated failure into a system-wide disruption.

REAL-WORLD EXAMPLE Stuxnet Attack on Industrial Control Systems

Stuxnet, discovered in 2010, was a highly sophisticated computer worm that targeted Iran's Natanz uranium enrichment facility (Kushner, 2013). It infiltrated Windows systems and specifically sought out Siemens Step7 software used to program industrial control systems. Once inside, Stuxnet manipulated programmable logic controllers (PLCs) to alter the rotational speed of centrifuges, causing them to spin at destructive frequencies while simultaneously feeding falsified telemetry to operators, masking the sabotage. This covert operation ultimately destroyed nearly 1,000 centrifuges, reducing Iran's enrichment capability by an estimated 30 percent (Collins and McCombie, 2012; Holloway, 2015).

REAL-WORLD EXAMPLE Maersk and NotPetya Ransomware Incident

In June 2017, the NotPetya malware (initially aimed at Ukrainian organizations) spread globally, crippling systems across multiple industries. One of its most prominent victims was A.P. Møller-Maersk, the world's largest container shipping company, responsible for nearly 20 percent of global maritime trade. The attack infiltrated Maersk's network through compromised accounting software and rapidly propagated, encrypting files and disabling thousands of computers and servers across 600 offices and 76 port terminals worldwide. This resulted in a complete halt of shipping and logistics operations, forcing Maersk to revert to manual processes to maintain minimal functionality. The financial impact was severe, with estimated losses reaching $300 million (Palmer, 2019; Collyer, 2024).

Given this complexity, cybersecurity in hyperconnected supply chains must move beyond traditional perimeter-based defenses. Static firewalls, password-based authentication, and periodic audits are insufficient for networks where suppliers, logistics providers, and customers exchange sensitive data continuously across multiple platforms. Security must be embedded throughout the system, incorporating rigorous access management, continuous validation of users and devices, and active monitoring for anomalies across the entire network (Ivanov et al., 2014). Network segmentation and isolation are essential to prevent malicious actors from moving laterally across systems once a breach occurs, and integrated incident response and business continuity planning are critical to contain potential cascade effects (Boyes, 2015).

Cybersecurity can no longer be treated as a technical add-on applied after systems are deployed. It must be embedded directly into the architecture of Supply Chain 5.0, from the design of connected products and production systems to supplier onboarding, data governance, and daily operational routines. When implemented effectively, cybersecurity does more than prevent attacks; it becomes a key enabler of resilience, reliability, and trust within global supply networks (Ivanov and Dolgui, 2020).

To address these challenges, organizations are increasingly adopting enabling technologies such as Zero Trust Architecture (ZTA), Multi-Factor Authentication (MFA), network segmentation, IoT sensors and edge devices, cloud platforms, and AI/ML-driven analytics. Zero trust, grounded in the principle of "never trust, always verify," eliminates implicit trust and enforces continuous authentication for every access request, regardless of location or device (Kim et al., 2024). Integrating AI into zero-trust frameworks enhances real-time threat detection and adaptive policy enforcement, reducing exposure to advanced persistent threats (APTs) and insider attacks (Karamchand, 2024). Similarly, MFA strengthens identity verification and mitigates unauthorized access risks, while IoT and edge devices enable granular monitoring of operational environments (Rivera et al., 2024). Emerging technologies like 5G networks further support secure, low-latency communication for distributed supply chain nodes.

Mitigation strategies must combine these technologies with robust governance practices. Key measures include access control, logging and continuous monitoring, endpoint protection, device hardening, and encrypted communications. Implementing Zero Trust Architecture with micro-segmentation and least-privilege principles significantly reduces attack surfaces, which is why a complete section on this mitigation strategy is provided next. Regular patch and vulnerability management is essential to prevent exploitation of outdated systems, while supplier risk assessments and continuous vendor monitoring address third-party vulnerabilities. Industry frameworks such as NIST's Cybersecurity Supply Chain Risk Management (C-SCRM) guidelines emphasize integrating security-by-design principles and automated risk scoring to maintain resilience across complex ecosystems (Abdmeziem et al., 2025; Boyens et al., 2022).

Zero Trust for Supply Chain 5.0

Trust can be defined as the willingness of one party to be vulnerable to the actions of another based on the expectation that the other party will act in ways that are important to the trustor, even without the ability to monitor or control them (Mayer et al., 1995). For decades, both information security and traditional supply chain management relied on this form of implicit trust. Within a corporate network perimeter, users and systems were considered safe once authenticated. In logistics, once goods were transferred to a partner, they were assumed to remain intact and secure until final delivery. While this reliance on assumed safety allowed operations to function efficiently, it also created hidden vulnerabilities that adversaries have increasingly learned to exploit.

Traditional perimeter-based security models are built around static boundaries and implicit trust inside those boundaries. The zero-trust model takes precisely the opposite stance. It assumes that no user, device, system, or transaction is trustworthy by default and instead requires continuous authentication, authorization, and verification for every interaction, regardless of physical location, network segment, or prior relationship (Rose et al., 2020).

Collier and Sarkis (2021) extended these principles to multi-enterprise supply chains, introducing the concept of a Zero Trust Supply Chain. Their work demonstrates that while traditional inter-organizational trust can reduce perceived risk and improve relational comfort, it can also increase systemic vulnerability by obscuring weak points and reducing scrutiny. They propose operationalizing zero trust in supply chains by mapping trust dependencies, identifying critical nodes, performing structured gap analyses, and enforcing continuous validation across all human, digital, and physical interactions.

In Supply Chain 5.0 environments, technologies such as digital twins, distributed ledgers, IoT devices, cloud platforms, and collaborative planning tools create dense networks of interdependence where every data exchange, device connection, or system interface can become a potential point of compromise. Zero trust responds to this complexity by enforcing least-privilege access, micro-segmentation, cryptographic verification, and real-time anomaly detection, limiting an attacker's ability to move laterally or exploit trusted relationships within the ecosystem.

To illustrate this shift in mindset, Table 14.2 compares traditional perimeter-based security with the zero-trust model in both IT and supply chain contexts. This side-by-side comparison clarifies how the underlying assumptions about trust, access, and verification differ fundamentally between the two approaches, and why zero trust is better aligned with the demands of hyperconnected Supply Chain 5.0 environments.

Table 14.2 Traditional Versus Zero Trust Security

Aspect	Traditional Perimeter Security	Zero Trust Security
Trust Model	Implicit trust inside perimeter	No implicit trust, all entities untrusted until verified
Access Control	Access granted once inside network or partner list	Continuous validation for every user, device, and transaction
Security Boundary	Static walls and boundaries	Dynamic, no fixed safe zone
Verification	One-time verification	Ongoing verification and context-aware policies
Risk of Insider Threat	High due to broad internal access	Lower due to least privilege and segmentation
Adaptability to Supply Chain 5.0	Low, struggles with dynamic networks	High, designed for hyperconnected ecosystems

Intentional Cyber and Software Supply Chain Threats and the Role of Supply Chain Leaders

These next real-world examples are far from isolated. Many cyber incidents form part of broader, coordinated campaigns carried out by state-sponsored groups or sophisticated criminal networks. In other instances, the identity and motives of the adversary remain unknown even after extensive forensic investigation.

In Supply Chain 5.0, cybersecurity becomes a core responsibility of supply chain leadership. The proliferation of smart devices, real-time tracking systems, and integrated planning platforms tightly links digital security to day-to-day operational continuity. Leaders must understand critical threat vectors, participate in vendor and third-party risk assessments, and ensure that continuity and recovery plans account for cyber-induced disruptions. They do not need to configure firewalls or design encryption protocols themselves, but they must collaborate closely with IT, cybersecurity, and risk teams to evaluate vulnerabilities and strengthen organizational resilience. As supply chains become more interconnected and data-driven, cybersecurity shifts from a purely technical requirement to a strategic operational imperative.

REAL-WORLD EXAMPLE CrowdStrike Outage

In July 2024, a faulty software update from cybersecurity vendor CrowdStrike caused one of the largest IT outages in history, affecting an estimated 8.5 million Windows devices worldwide. The resulting downtime grounded flights, disrupted hospital services, delayed rail and shipping schedules, and halted operations at major logistics hubs. The impact rippled into time-sensitive manufacturing and distribution networks, highlighting how a single failure in a widely trusted security product can disrupt entire supply chains (Korolov, 2024; Cybersecurity Dive, 2024; GAO, 2024).

REAL-WORLD EXAMPLE Target Data Breach

The 2013 Target data breach demonstrated how third-party connectivity can provide unintended access points. Attackers gained entry using stolen credentials from a heating and air conditioning vendor, deployed malware on point of sale systems, and harvested data from approximately 40 million credit card accounts and personal information from up to 70 million individuals (Brooks, 2023; Wired, 2014).

REAL-WORLD EXAMPLE SolarWinds Infiltrated

The 2020 SolarWinds compromise further illustrated the systemic risk of software supply chains. Attackers infiltrated SolarWinds' Orion software build environment and inserted malicious code into legitimate updates. The compromised versions were distributed to approximately 18,000 customers, including multiple United States federal agencies and private enterprises. The incident revealed how a single trusted vendor can become a vector for widespread compromise across industries and geographies (CISA, 2023; Aqua Security, 2021; Cloud Google Blog, 2023; TechTarget, 2021).

Physical Security and Cargo Protection in Supply Chains

While cybersecurity focuses on protecting digital assets and preventing unauthorized access to networks, physical security and cargo theft protection remain equally critical in safeguarding tangible goods within the supply chain. These two domains are increasingly interconnected; cyber breaches can enable physical theft by disabling alarms or manipulating routing systems, while physical intrusions can compromise digital infrastructure through tampered IoT devices. As supply chains evolve toward hyper-connectivity in Industry 5.0, organizations must adopt a layered security approach that addresses both cyber and physical vulnerabilities to ensure resilience across the entire ecosystem.

Intentional and Accidental Man-Made Threats

Modern supply chains face an expanding spectrum of risks, many of which originate from human actions, whether deliberate or unintended. Understanding the human dimension of risk is therefore essential for building resilient, trustworthy supply chains capable of anticipating, absorbing, and adapting to both malicious actions and unintentional mistakes.

Industry 4.0 technologies are rapidly transforming warehouse and logistics security. AI-powered video analytics using smart cameras and edge computing can detect abnormal behavior in real time, identifying potential theft or sabotage even in previously unmonitored zones (Horizon Powered, n.d.; SecureRedact, 2023). Biometric access control systems restrict entry to authorized personnel, while integration with enterprise resource planning platforms generates automated audit trails that accelerate incident response (BDO, 2021). Real-time tracking technologies (including IoT sensors, RFID, and geofencing) provide continuous visibility for high-value cargo, feeding predictive analytics that identify emerging theft hotspots and enable proactive intervention (Ivanov et al., 2019).

In higher-risk regions, logistics providers employ additional protections. Panic-alert systems installed in vehicles allow drivers to notify authorities during hijacking attempts. In Brazil, for example, armed robbery accounted for 81 percent of cargo theft incidents in 2024, with highway BR 116 flagged as a major risk corridor; operators now use telematics-driven dynamic risk modeling to adjust security protocols in real time (Munich Re, 2025; TAPA Brazil, 2024).

Security seals, holograms, and container authentication systems offer tamper evidence, and advanced electronic seals transmit status data continuously to detect unauthorized openings. Yet inexpensive, off-the-shelf seals remain vulnerable: Organized criminal groups now use high-resolution 3D printing to create counterfeit bolt seals nearly indistinguishable from originals, enabling covert cargo swaps or diversions even in secure facilities (WorldCargo News, 2016; 3D Printing Industry, 2016).

Industry 4.0 tools are also being weaponized in intentional disruptions beyond theft. During the Ukraine conflict, both sides deployed drones and autonomous systems to target transport infrastructure, while coordinated cyber campaigns compromised logistics networks and disrupted humanitarian aid flows (Klepper, 2025). In the Red Sea, Houthi rebel groups have used drones, loitering munitions, and missile systems, supported by satellite-enabled targeting, to attack commercial vessels, forcing global carriers to reroute around Africa and triggering significant delays and cost increases (Rodriguez-Diaz et al., 2024; Allianz Commercial, 2024).

Not all man-made risks arise from malicious intent. Accidental damage during loading, transit, or storage remains one of the most common sources of cargo loss. Mishandling by forklifts, improper pallet securing, and inadequate lashing of container stacks frequently result in goods being damaged before they reach their destination. Misdeclared container weights have also contributed to stack collapses aboard vessels, leading to significant property loss and operational delays (Mariappa and Aithal, 2023).

Operational and administrative errors can have similarly far-reaching consequences. Misrouting, incorrect documentation, and customs misclassification have delayed shipments for weeks, resulting in spoilage of perishable cargo and costly penalties. Cargo hubs continue to report incidents in which containers are loaded onto the wrong vessels or sent to incorrect distribution centers due to scanning or sorting mistakes.

Fires represent another major category of accidental cargo loss. Electrical faults, improper storage of hazardous materials, and procedural oversights have destroyed substantial inventory volumes. The 2020 Beirut port explosion remains a stark example of how mismanagement of dangerous goods can escalate into catastrophic loss. Likewise, vessel fires caused by undeclared or misdeclared chemical cargo have led to fatalities, environmental harm, and severe financial damage (Khan et al., 2021).

Equipment and infrastructure failures pose additional risks. Mechanical breakdowns of cranes, conveyors, or cold-chain refrigeration units can render goods unusable within hours. Power outages at distribution centers may compromise temperature-sensitive products or interrupt critical handling operations, rapidly degrading inventory quality.

Academic research categorizes cargo-loss drivers into human error, method, machine, material, and environment, with human factors and unsafe handling consistently identified as primary contributors to incident rates (Panjee et al., 2025). Recent advances, however, show promise: AI-supported load-safety assessment systems are reducing incidents involving unsecured loads by automatically analyzing cargo images for safety violations (Schöning and Kruse, 2023). Additional reviews of container accidents highlight preventable failures, such as sliding, tipping, skewing, and incorrect stacking, that can be mitigated through improved training, better rigging protocols, and enhanced operational oversight (Mariappa and Aithal, 2023).

Industry 4.0 tools are increasingly deployed to counter these accidental threats. IoT sensors and digital twins monitor load conditions, verify container weights, and detect stowage shifts in real time. Predictive maintenance systems use sensor data to identify equipment faults before breakdowns occur. Automated compliance platforms validate shipping documentation and routing instructions, reducing administrative errors that often lead to delays or cargo loss. Together, these technologies strengthen operational reliability and help ensure that unintentional failures do not compromise the resilience of modern supply chains.

Preventing Cyber-Physical Attacks on Manufacturing and Logistics

As supply chains become increasingly automated and interconnected, the boundary between cyber and physical systems continues to erode. Cyber-physical attacks exploit this convergence, using digital intrusions to trigger real-world operational disruptions. These attacks can take many forms: Ransomware that shuts down production lines, interference with automated warehouse control systems, manipulation of smart sensors to misroute cargo, or unauthorized commands issued to autonomous logistics vehicles. In each case, a digital compromise results in tangible physical consequences.

Supply Chain 5.0 environments require a defense-in-depth approach to cyber-physical security, one that recognizes the interdependence of information systems, operational technology, and physical processes. Digital twins offer powerful new capabilities in this regard. By creating a high-fidelity virtual representation of equipment, processes, or entire facilities, digital twins enable organizations to simulate attack scenarios, test failure modes, and evaluate cascading impacts in a controlled environment. This allows supply chain leaders to identify vulnerabilities, refine response plans, and assess resilience before real-world incidents occur.

Equally important is the integration of operational technology (OT) security with traditional IT cybersecurity practices. Historically, these domains were treated separately, with OT prioritized for safety and continuity and IT focused on data protection. In connected Supply Chain 5.0 architectures, this separation is no longer feasible. Cyber-physical systems operate as a unified ecosystem, meaning vulnerabilities in one domain can rapidly propagate into the other (Ivanov and Dolgui, 2020). Effective security therefore requires coordinated monitoring, shared incident response processes, consistent access controls, and governance models that address IT and OT together rather than in isolation.

REAL-WORLD EXAMPLE The Colonial Pipeline Attack and Its Impact on Supply Chains

In May 2021, the DarkSide ransomware gang targeted Colonial Pipeline, forcing the shutdown of its entire 5,500-mile network, the largest refined fuel pipeline in the United States. Colonial proactively halted operations on May 7 to prevent malware from infecting operational technology systems, which caused a cascade of disruptions across the East Coast fuel supply (CISA, 2023).

Colonial Pipeline supplied approximately 45 percent of the fuel consumed on the US East Coast, including gasoline, diesel, jet fuel, and heating oil. The shutdown lasted about six days and resulted in widespread fuel shortages, panic buying, and significant price increases. Several states, including Virginia, North Carolina, South Carolina, and Georgia, declared emergencies. Airlines reported delays because of limited jet fuel availability, trucking fleets were forced to adjust routes, and emergency services experienced major logistical challenges (CISA, 2023).

The economic consequences extended beyond fuel markets. Although prices rose only several cents per gallon in affected regions, the downstream impact rippled through food distribution, healthcare logistics, and manufacturing supply chains. Many regional distributors quickly exhausted fuel reserves and lacked redundant sourcing strategies, which exposed the fragility of just-in-time delivery models during a critical infrastructure disruption (Curoe, 2023).

Colonial reportedly paid approximately $4.4 to $5 million in bitcoin to regain control of encrypted systems, although federal authorities later recovered a portion of the ransom. The incident fueled debate around the ethics and effectiveness of paying ransoms in the context of essential services, highlighting the tension between immediate restoration of operations and the long-term risks of incentivizing cybercrime (Newman, 2021; United States DOJ, 2021).

The shutdown disrupted fuel-dependent supply chains that supported essential services including transportation, food delivery, and healthcare. The event revealed the vulnerability of centralized infrastructure in modern logistics networks, where a single disruption can propagate through multiple tiers of distribution and retail. It also drew attention to cybersecurity practices across critical infrastructure. Analysts and policymakers observed that the attack demonstrated the need for stronger segmentation of networks, more restrictive access controls, and improved verification practices to prevent breaches from spreading between business systems and operational technology environments (TSA, 2023). The incident underscored the importance of closer coordination between private operators and government agencies to protect supply chains that serve as the backbone of essential services.

Cargo Theft in Supply Chain 5.0

Cargo theft remains one of the most persistent and costly threats to global supply chains. The 2024 TT Club–BSI Cargo Theft Report found that food and beverage shipments accounted for 22 percent of reported thefts, followed by agricultural goods (10 percent), electronics (9 percent), and fuel (7 percent). Trucks were involved in 76 percent of all incidents, with hijackings representing 21 percent of cases. Nearly half of thefts occurred while goods were in transit, with hotspots including the United States, Brazil, India, Germany, Chile, Mexico, and South Africa. In the United States specifically, strategic or "deceptive" theft, where criminals use fraud, impersonation, or falsified documents, represented approximately 18 percent of reported cases (BSI Consulting and TT Club, 2025).

In North America, the trend is worsening. Verisk's CargoNet reported 3,798 cargo theft incidents in the United States in 2024, a 26 percent increase from the previous year. The recorded financial loss was approximately $455 million, though industry analysts estimate actual losses likely exceed $1 billion annually due to underreporting. Identity-based theft has risen sharply: Criminals impersonate brokers, carriers, or drivers to fraudulently obtain loads, a tactic that grew from 8 percent of US thefts in 2020 to nearly one-third of all incidents by early 2025 (DC Velocity Staff, 2025).

Technology providers are beginning to counter these trends. In an interview, Krenar Komoni, CEO of Tive, explained how IoT-based visibility tools enable real-time detection and intervention during theft events. Komoni described a common pattern observed in truck-based cargo theft: A route deviation, followed by prolonged idling, a trailer door opening detected by a light sensor, and finally the disappearance of cargo into illicit markets. By combining sensor data, geolocation, and anomaly detection, Tive's devices allow logistics teams to intervene as suspicious activity unfolds, often preventing losses altogether. Komoni also noted that cargo theft remains attractive to organized crime because it is difficult to investigate, rarely prioritized by law enforcement, and typically results in lenient penalties relative to the profits involved (Komoni, 2025).

In Supply Chain 5.0 environments, cargo theft increasingly involves a blend of physical and cyber tactics. Criminal networks use stolen credentials, falsified carrier profiles, and spoofed email domains to execute fictitious pickups or gain entry to secure facilities. As logistics operations become more digitized, with automated gate systems, electronic proof-of-delivery, and platform-based freight matching, the risk of cyber-enabled theft grows when identity verification and access controls are weak. Addressing these threats requires an integrated defense strategy that combines physical protection with modern cybersecurity measures.

Physical safeguards include secure yards, monitored parking, sealed and reinforced trailers, and intelligent locking systems. These must be supported by cybersecurity controls such as encrypted telematics, zero-trust access to transportation management platforms, and artificial intelligence that flags anomalous routing or unauthorized access attempts. *Digital measures* include authenticated geofencing to alert operators to deviations while filtering out legitimate route changes.

In a hyperconnected logistics environment, therefore, securing cargo requires a holistic approach that integrates cyber and physical safeguards to prevent theft, tampering, and insider threats. Insider threats remain a critical factor in many thefts, making background checks, behavioral monitoring, and training to identify social engineering attempts essential elements of a prevention program. The combination of IoT-enabled visibility, rapid anomaly detection, and robust identity verification exemplifies how Supply Chain 5.0 can both optimize operations and strengthen resilience against organized crime.

Resilience Against Nation-State and Organized Crime Threats

Cargo theft not only results in billions of dollars in direct losses each year but also exposes systemic vulnerabilities in logistics operations, from unsecured rest stops to weak digital identity controls. Addressing cargo theft is no longer simply about protecting freight; it is about ensuring the resilience of essential supply networks against increasingly intelligent and adaptive organized crime groups.

Resilience against threats posed by nation-state actors and organized crime is an essential dimension of modern supply chain security. Nation-state operations increasingly target critical nodes and dependencies across global logistics networks, using cyber espionage, supply chain compromise, or infrastructure disruption to gain strategic advantage. These activities often involve sophisticated tactics, including targeted intrusions into networked systems, manipulation of digital processes, or interference with transportation and energy infrastructure (Nyonyoh, 2025; 3Gimbals, 2025).

At the same time, organized crime groups have expanded their capabilities, developing highly coordinated cargo theft networks that exploit operational and digital vulnerabilities. Common tactics include fictitious pickups, use of stolen identities, fraudulent paperwork, and insider collusion. These practices are responsible for losses estimated in the hundreds of millions of dollars annually. In the United States, cargo theft incidents have risen by more than 25 percent year over year, with several thousand cases reported in a single year (Munich Re, 2025; CargoNet, 2024). Similar trends are visible internationally. In the United Kingdom, organized crime groups have increasingly targeted high-value goods in transit and storage, with losses exceeding £100 million in a single year; across Europe, coordinated networks have focused on food, commodities, and electronics, often leveraging insider access and gaps in verification practices (Woode, 2024; Batty, 2024).

Integrating security into resilience planning requires preparing supply chains not only to prevent disruption but also to absorb shocks and adapt to evolving threats. Research shows that structural complexity in upstream supply networks correlates with higher disruption frequency, underscoring the need for transparency, simplification, and redundancy to reduce cascading failures (Bode and Wagner, 2015). Practical resilience measures include diversifying suppliers, hardening physical security at storage and transit points, strengthening digital and physical identity verification, monitoring for insider risks, and maintaining active coordination with law enforcement and intelligence agencies (Aon, 2025; ASIS, 2020; BSI, 2022). Effective resilience planning also depends on continuous threat-intelligence collection and rigorous scenario testing to ensure supply chains remain prepared for both cyber and physical attacks in an increasingly contested global environment (3Gimbals, 2025).

Product Authentication and Anti-Counterfeiting

As cyber-physical risks continue to grow, it becomes clear that securing Supply Chain 5.0 requires more than protecting networks and digital infrastructure. The same vulnerabilities that enable cyber intrusions also create openings for physical threats such as cargo theft, identity-based fraud, and organized criminal activity. These risks expose gaps not only in logistics operations but also in the integrity of the products themselves. As counterfeiters adopt more advanced techniques and exploit weaknesses in both digital and physical controls, safeguarding products from illicit reproduction becomes just as critical as protecting them from theft. This shift brings the focus to product authentication and anti-counterfeiting, where ensuring that goods are genuine, and that fraudulent items cannot infiltrate the supply chain, emerges as a central pillar of security and trust in modern, hyperconnected networks.

Product Authenticity as a Challenge and Opportunity in Supply Chain 5.0

A related topic to physical security and cargo protection in product authenticity. Product authenticity focuses on ensuring that the goods circulating within a supply chain are genuine, safe, and produced by the rightful manufacturer. This is also a matter of brand protection and consumer safety, involving counterfeiting, product diversion, gray-market activity, or adulteration. The threat is not that products disappear, but that illicit or falsified goods infiltrate the supply chain, eroding trust, damaging brand reputation, and in sectors like pharmaceuticals or aerospace, posing significant health and safety risks.

REAL-WORLD EXAMPLE Luxury Watch Industry

The luxury watch industry illustrates these challenges clearly. Brands such as Rolex have invested in micro engraving, NFC chips, and blockchain provenance systems to secure their products. Counterfeiters have evolved in parallel, producing imitations so accurate that they can move through legitimate distribution channels undetected. In 2011, Swiss customs estimated that counterfeit watches represented nearly seven percent of the global watch market, resulting in significant financial losses and damage to brand reputation (OECD, 2025).

Many companies believe they are taking strong steps to secure their products, but some of the measures they adopt can actually make their supply chains more vulnerable. Hologram labels and tamper seals are a common example. These are often presented as advanced security solutions, yet they can be purchased in bulk from commercial printing services or reproduced using consumer-grade equipment. When such weak protections are perceived as strong ones, they create a false sense of security for both distributors and customers. This misplaced trust allows counterfeit goods to bypass checkpoints and undermines confidence in more robust authentication methods. In the context of Supply Chain 5.0, where trust depends on both technology and human perception, easily cloned security features can weaken the integrity of the entire system instead of strengthening it.

A key distinction lies between product identification and product authentication. Identification mechanisms such as barcodes, QR codes, serial numbers, and standard RFID tags enable tracking and inventory visibility but can be copied or spoofed with minimal effort. Authentication systems, by contrast, incorporate unique physical or molecular signatures that resist duplication. These include DNA taggants, forensic security inks, proprietary microcodes, nanomaterial markers, and physically unclonable functions (PUFs). Such features enable verifiable proof of authenticity rather than simple item recognition. Table 14.3 illustrates this conceptual difference between identification and authentication systems.

Table 14.3 Identification vs. Authentication

Category	Product Identification	Product Authentication
Primary Purpose	Track, trace, and manage items within the supply chain.	Verify that a product is genuine and produced by the legitimate manufacturer.
Core Question Answered	"What is this item?"	"Is this item real?"
Typical Technologies	Barcodes, QR codes, serial numbers, standard RFID tags, digital labels.	DNA taggants, nanomaterial markers, forensic security inks, microtext/microcodes, holographic PUFs, advanced RFID/cryptographic tags.

(continued)

Table 14.3 (Continued)

Category	Product Identification	Product Authentication
Use Cases	Inventory control, logistics visibility, automation, warehouse operations.	High-value goods, pharmaceuticals, aerospace components, luxury items, electronics, and safety-critical products.
Common Weaknesses	Easily duplicated; susceptible to label swapping, code copying, and digital manipulation.	May require specialized scanners; higher unit cost; some features unknown or invisible to end-users.

REAL-WORLD EXAMPLE Fossil and Itrace Technologies Partnership

A more effective approach can be seen in the FOSSIL and iTrace Technologies partnership. FOSSIL integrated iTrace's 2DMI technology into both its watches and packaging. The system embeds cryptographically unique microdot codes that cannot be copied or removed without destroying the product. Each code is linked to a secure blockchain ledger and can be verified instantly with a mobile device by both supply chain partners and end customers. Unlike traditional QR codes or RFID tags, which are primarily identification tools and can be duplicated, 2DMI codes establish a cryptographic connection between the physical product and its digital identity that is extremely difficult to forge. This deployment allowed FOSSIL to reduce counterfeit infiltration, strengthen customer confidence, and demonstrate how authentication can add measurable value in Supply Chain 5.0 (iTrace Technologies, 2022).

REAL-WORLD EXAMPLE Cosmetics Sector

An investigation in the cosmetics sector highlights the scale of the problem across industries. Consumer rights researchers purchased 34 cosmetic products from third-party sellers on Amazon, eBay, TikTok Shop, and Vinted. When compared visually to genuine items, approximately two-thirds were likely counterfeit. Several of these counterfeits contained hazardous materials such as arsenic, lead, and mercury, as well as bacterial contaminants and animal waste-based stabilizers, creating direct risks for consumer health (Securing Industry, 2025).

REAL-WORLD EXAMPLE Retail Sector

Counterfeit infiltration is not limited to cosmetics or luxury goods. In one of the most publicized fraud cases in consumer electronics, scammers exploited packaging-based identifiers to return counterfeit iPhones inside genuine Apple boxes. Retailers relying on the packaging codes reintroduced the devices into the supply chain, inadvertently selling fakes as if they were authentic Apple products. The scale of the scheme forced Apple to redesign repair and return verification processes to detect counterfeit devices (Yahoo News, 2025).

Enabling Technologies for Authentication

Counterfeiting and unauthorized reselling pose significant threats to global supply chains, impacting brand reputation, consumer safety, and regulatory compliance. Primary risks include counterfeit goods entering legitimate channels, gray-market diversion, unauthorized reselling, and component substitution. These risks are particularly severe in industries such as pharmaceuticals, electronics, and luxury goods, where counterfeit products can lead to health hazards or critical system failures. According to the OECD, counterfeit trade accounts for 3.3 percent of global commerce, amounting to over $500 billion annually (OECD, 2023).

To combat these risks, organizations are deploying cutting-edge technologies that provide robust authentication and traceability. Below, we explore four key solutions—DNA taggants and nanomaterial inks, Physical Unclonable Functions (PUFs), serialization and track-and-trace systems, and blockchain provenance solutions—along with real-world applications as shown in Figure 14.1.

Figure 14.1 Authentication and Traceability Technologies

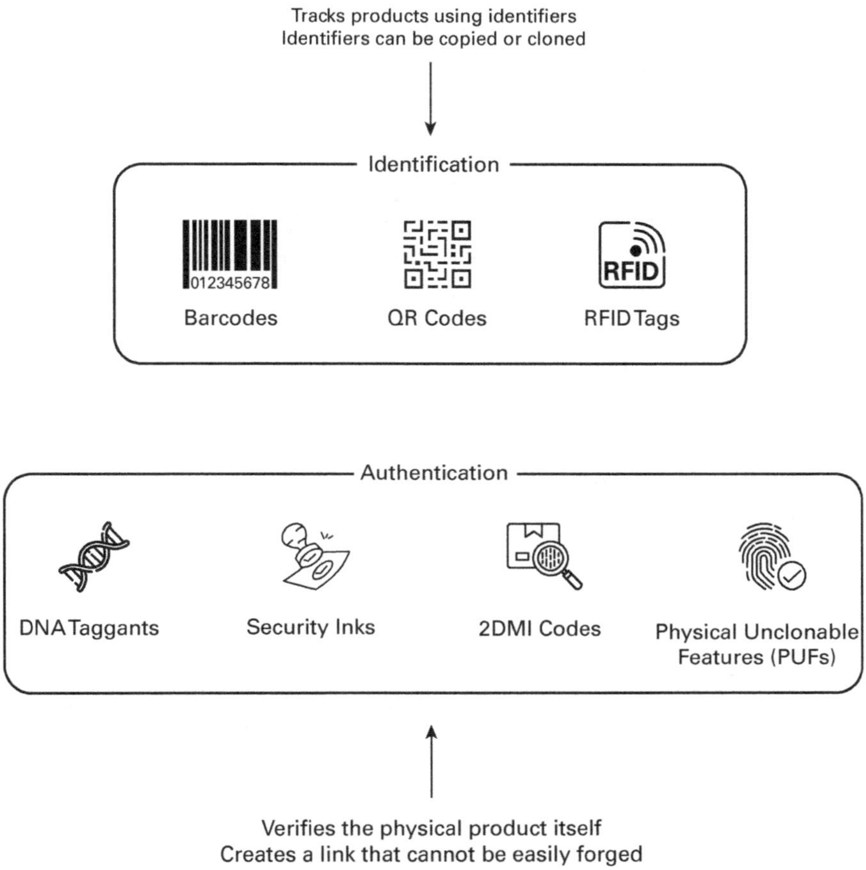

DNA taggants use unique molecular sequences embedded into inks or coatings, creating identifiers that are virtually impossible to replicate (Kuzdralińsk et al., 2025). These markers can be verified using forensic techniques such as PCR (Polymerase Chain Reaction), offering unparalleled security for high-value goods (Gooch et al., 2016). Nanomaterial inks complement this approach by incorporating microscopic taggants detectable only through specialized readers (Wang et al., 2015). Sharief et al. (2021) discuss how DNA-based anti-counterfeiting systems offer compelling advantages for product security; DNA can be synthesized relatively easily, engineered to carry vast amounts of encoded information, and used as a highly sophisticated medium for encryption or forensic-level identification. These properties make it an attractive option for high-security authentication across industries such as pharmaceuticals, electronics, and luxury goods. However, the same research team also found several challenges currently limiting widespread deployment. DNA markers must be protected from degradation in harsh environmental conditions, sequencing methods must continue to become faster and more cost-effective, and reliable techniques are needed to bind or embed DNA securely within products and packaging. Overcoming these barriers will be essential for realizing the full potential of DNA as a next-generation authentication technology in Supply Chain 5.0.

PUFs leverage inherent manufacturing variations in semiconductor devices to create unique, unclonable hardware fingerprints (Herder et al., 2014). These fingerprints enable secure device authentication without storing static keys, reducing vulnerability to invasive attacks (Yadav et al., 2022). In a supply chain context, Davies and Wang (2021) suggest that PUFs represent a significant breakthrough in product and asset authentication, offering a level of security that traditional identifiers cannot because these patterns arise naturally and cannot be engineered or copied. The article highlights how PUFs support both identity verification and secure tracking; they can be embedded into electronic components, packaging materials, or even physical products to create challenge–response pairs used for cryptographic validation. However, the article also notes key challenges: Environmental sensitivity, the need for standardized readers, and the complexity of integrating PUF-generated cryptographic protocols with existing enterprise systems (Davies and Wang, 2021; Oduro-Antwi et al., 2026). Despite these hurdles, PUFs are emerging as one of the most promising technologies for securing global supply chains against counterfeiting, gray-market diversion, and tampering.

Serialization assigns unique identifiers, such as barcodes or QR codes, to individual product units, enabling end-to-end visibility across the supply chain. These identifiers are critical for compliance with regulations like the US Drug Supply Chain Security Act (DSCSA) and the EU Falsified Medicines Directive (FMD).

Last but not least is blockchain, a technology that enables immutable, decentralized ledgers capable of recording every transaction, handoff, and transformation a product undergoes. By creating a tamper-evident trail of events, blockchain enhances transparency, prevents data manipulation, and strengthens consumer and partner confidence in product authenticity. Importantly, blockchain also serves as a critical bridge between product authenticity and product integrity, a concept explored in the next section of the book. Through secure, unchangeable records, blockchain ensures that authenticity is not a one-time verification step but part of a continuous chain of trust, supporting end-to-end provenance, reducing opportunities for counterfeiting or diversion, and reinforcing the safety and legitimacy of products as they move through increasingly complex global supply chains.

Data Integrity and Provenance in Supply Chain 5.0

As organizations strengthen their defenses against counterfeit goods and enhance product-level authentication, another critical dimension of Supply Chain 5.0 security comes into focus: The integrity of the data that documents a product's journey. Even the most advanced physical authentication systems can be undermined if the digital records that accompany a product are inaccurate, incomplete, or manipulated. Ensuring trust in modern supply chains therefore requires not only verifying that a product is genuine, but also validating the accuracy, continuity, and immutability of the information associated with it from end to end. This leads directly to the next essential topic, data integrity and provenance, which examines how secure, tamper-resistant data flows underpin traceability, compliance, and confidence in increasingly digital and interconnected supply chain ecosystems.

A comprehensive approach to product security requires deploying multiple layers of verification across the entire supply chain lifecycle. At early manufacturing stages, products can be embedded with molecular or physical identifiers, such as DNA taggants, nanomaterial markers, or physically unclonable features, that provide foundational proof of authenticity. As items move downstream, additional methods such as secure mobile verification, blockchain-based provenance tracking, and customer-facing authentication tools help maintain integrity at distribution, retail, and even post-sale stages. Figure 14.2 illustrates how identification and authentication technologies can be strategically applied from manufacturing through end-user verification, creating a continuous chain of trust across the product's lifecycle.

As counterfeiters become more sophisticated, the strategic value of robust product authentication grows significantly. Companies that embed verifiable authentication into their supply chain systems convert trust into a tangible competitive asset, enhancing customer confidence, protecting public health, and safeguarding brand integrity. Stanton and Manning (2019) identify five foundational elements of an effective supply chain provenance strategy: Product characteristics, product data, tamper protection, security markings, and serialization. These elements align closely with

Figure 14.2 Integration of Identification and Authentication Across the Supply Chain

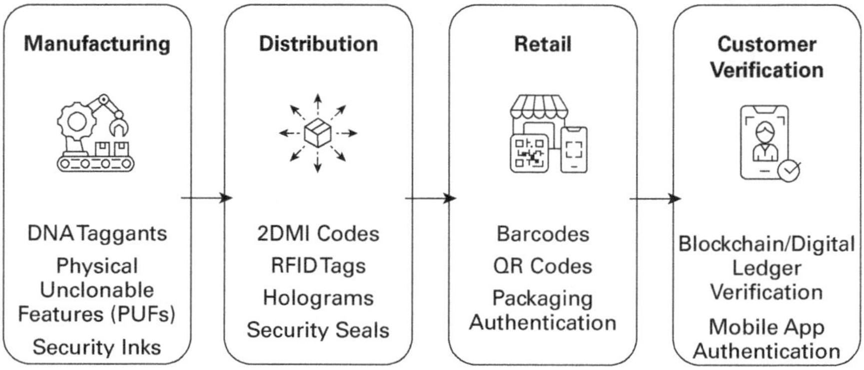

the SCOR Digital Standard (SCOR DS), which structures supply chain activity across the core domains of Plan, Source, Make, Deliver, Return, and Enable. Integrating provenance capabilities into these domains helps ensure authenticity, traceability, and risk mitigation throughout the entire product lifecycle.

Product characteristics refer to inherent, non-replicable traits, such as material properties, microstructures, or manufacturing variations, that function as unique identifiers and support downstream verification. Within SCOR DS, product characteristics directly strengthen the Make domain by embedding authenticity features during production and the Enable domain by linking those characteristics to product master data and digital traceability systems.

Product data encompasses the records and metadata associated with production, testing, compliance, and quality assurance. Capturing this data accurately and securing it, often through blockchain or other tamper-evident systems, is critical to maintaining trust. In SCOR DS, product data plays a central role in Plan, Make, and Enable, supporting quality planning, compliant manufacturing, and the creation of reliable visibility and decision-support systems.

Tamper protection includes physical and digital safeguards designed to detect unauthorized access or alteration. Examples range from tamper-evident seals and secure enclosures to embedded IoT sensors that detect opening, temperature changes, or shock events. These protections align strongly with the Deliver and Return domains, helping ensure that products remain uncompromised during transit and customer handling. They also contribute to Enable by reinforcing risk management and monitoring controls.

Figure 14.3 Supply Chain Provenance Strategy

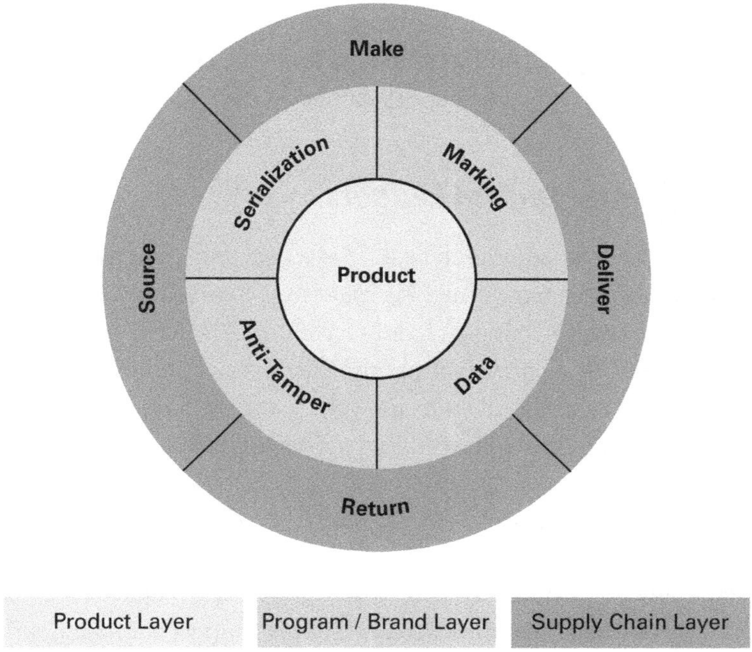

SOURCE Stanton and Manning, 2019

Security markings consist of visual or digital identifiers, such as micro-etching, UV inks, forensic markers, or encrypted QR codes, that authenticate products at various checkpoints. Applied during sourcing or manufacturing and verified throughout distribution, these markings map to Source, Make, Deliver, and Enable within SCOR DS. They support authentication, regulatory compliance, and the creation of digital twins by linking the physical item to a secure digital record.

Serialization assigns a unique identifier to each individual product or unit, enabling item-level tracking and full-chain traceability. Serialization is essential for managing recalls, returns, and post-sale verification. Within SCOR DS, serialization strengthens the Deliver and Return domains by enhancing visibility during final distribution and reverse logistics. It also reinforces Enable by connecting each serialized item to its corresponding digital provenance record, reducing the risk of diversion or counterfeiting.

Together, these five elements form a layered provenance and authentication strategy that aligns naturally with SCOR DS principles. By embedding authenticity into core operational, data, and governance processes, rather than treating it as an isolated function, supply chain leaders can enhance trust, improve regulatory compliance, and fortify brand protection in increasingly complex and contested global markets. Figure 14.3 outlines the integrated components of a modern product-security framework, highlighting the measures that organizations can adopt to mitigate risk and strengthen resilience throughout the supply chain (Stanton and Manning, 2019). Table 14.4 provides a description of how the strategy can be deployed.

Blockchain and Digital Ledgers

Blockchain technology, often referred to as a distributed digital ledger, provides immutable provenance tracking and tamper-evident records, addressing critical challenges in supply chain traceability. The term "digital ledger" is generally used interchangeably with "blockchain" because blockchain functions as a decentralized, append-only ledger where transactions are stored in cryptographically linked blocks. This architecture ensures data integrity, transparency, and resistance to tampering, making blockchain a specialized form of a digital ledger designed for distributed environments (Saberi et al., 2019; Deloitte, 2023).

By recording every transaction or handoff immutably, blockchain ensures transparency and accountability across multiple supply chain tiers, supporting trust, regulatory compliance, and sustainability. These properties make it especially valuable for verifying provenance in complex, global networks (Saberi et al., 2019).

Smart contracts—self-executing programs deployed on blockchain networks—automate enforcement of supply chain agreements and certification rules. However, they are susceptible to vulnerabilities such as reentrancy attacks, logic errors, or inadequate validation. Research highlights the importance of formal verification, secure coding, and comprehensive auditing as key mitigation strategies before deploying smart contracts in production environments (Applied Sui et al., 2023; Zaidi et al., 2019).

Integrating blockchain with cryptographic authentication tools enhances overall system security. Combining distributed ledgers with physically unclonable functions or zero-knowledge proofs allows components to be uniquely verified without exposing proprietary data. This hybrid approach enables strong component-level authentication while protecting sensitive supply chain information (Malik et al., 2021).

Despite these advantages, blockchain adoption in supply chains faces challenges such as scalability, interoperability across organizations, and the cost of implementation. Additionally, the ledger itself can become a target: Attacks on consensus mechanisms or ledger replication underscore the need for layered security and continuous monitoring (Applied Sciences, 2023; Saberi et al., 2019).

Table 14.4 Supply Chain Provenance Implementation

Provenance Element	Description	Aligned SCOR DS Process(es)	Alignment Explanation
Product Characteristics	Intrinsic, non-replicable identifiers (e.g., imperfections, material properties).	Transform	Used during production to verify authenticity, detect overproduction, and prevent unauthorized replicas.
Product Data	Metadata about product lifecycle: origin, date, process, test results. Ideally stored on secure systems like blockchain.	Plan/Source/ Transform/Fulfill	Provides critical visibility across multiple processes; supports traceability and compliance from procurement to production to customer delivery.
Tamper Protection	Controls to detect physical or digital tampering (e.g., tamper-evident seals, encrypted firmware).	Transform/Fulfill	Protects integrity of products post-manufacturing and during shipment to customers.
Markings	Application of security identifiers such as barcodes, holograms, RFID tags.	Transform/Fulfill/ Return	Enables verification at various stages including packing, distribution, and reverse logistics.
Serialization	Unique product-level identifiers for tracking individual units across the supply chain.	Transform/Fulfill/ Return	Central to digital traceability. Ensures each item can be individually tracked from creation through delivery, and back through returns if necessary.

In summary, blockchain as a distributed digital ledger provides a secure foundation for provenance tracking, smart contract automation, and integration with advanced authentication methods. Realizing its potential requires careful management of smart contract vulnerabilities, robust cryptographic integration, and organizational collaboration.

Operational Technology (OT) Security

As supply chains integrate advanced automation and industrial control systems, Operational Technology (OT) security becomes a critical pillar of resilience. Unlike traditional IT systems, OT environments control physical processes such as manufacturing, robotics, and autonomous vehicles. This convergence introduces unique risks: OT system compromise, unsafe automated operations, and cross-domain attacks from IT to OT. A single breach can halt production lines, damage equipment, or endanger worker safety. The infamous Stuxnet attack demonstrated how malware targeting OT systems can cause catastrophic physical consequences without direct access (Langner, 2011).

Modern OT environments are the backbone of advanced manufacturing and logistics in Supply Chain 5.0. They integrate cyber-physical systems to enable automation, efficiency, and predictive capabilities. Three core technologies dominate this landscape:

Field devices connect sensors, actuators, and machines to provide real-time monitoring and predictive maintenance (Peter et al., 2023). For example, vibration sensors on assembly lines can detect anomalies before equipment failure, reducing downtime and costs. However, these connected devices often use lightweight protocols like MQTT, which can be exploited if not properly secured (Tan and Samsudin, 2021). A compromised sensor could feed false data, triggering unsafe automated operations or halting production (Xu et al., 2018).

Control systems occupy the critical middle layer of OT architectures, bridging field devices and supervisory and operations systems to enable reliable real time automation. While field devices such as sensors and actuators directly interact with physical processes by collecting data and executing mechanical actions, control systems are responsible for interpreting that data and making deterministic control decisions. Systems such as programmable logic controller-based architectures and distributed control systems continuously evaluate inputs from field devices, apply predefined control logic, and issue precise commands that regulate machinery, robotics, and industrial workflows under strict timing and safety constraints (Stouffer et al., 2015).

Unlike supervisory and operations systems (discussed in the next section), which focus on visualization, historical analysis, and high-level coordination, control systems operate autonomously and in real time to maintain stable and safe process conditions. Historically, these systems were engineered to be isolated and deterministic, prioritizing availability and functional safety over cybersecurity considerations, which has left many control environments with limited authentication, encryption, or secure update capabilities (Knapp and Langill, 2015). As OT environments increasingly integrate with enterprise IT networks and supervisory platforms for optimization and remote management, control systems have become a primary target for cyber attacks. A successful compromise at this layer can directly alter process logic or bypass safety controls, leading to production disruption, equipment damage, or physical harm, as demonstrated by attacks such as Stuxnet (Langner, 2011). Securing control systems is therefore essential to preserving the integrity of both field-level operations and supervisory oversight within modern supply chain infrastructures.

Supervisory and operations systems manage and supervise industrial processes across distributed facilities (Gaushell et al., 1987). They are a class of industrial-control systems (ICS) that combine hardware and software to monitor, control, and manage large-scale physical processes, from manufacturing lines to pipelines, water and wastewater systems, energy grids, logistics automation, and more (Kidd and Raza, 2024). Architecturally, these systems typically use field devices such as sensors, valves, pumps, robotic machinery, remote-terminal units (RTUs), or programmable logic controllers (PLCs) connected to central control software that collects data, displays information to operators via a human–machine interface (HMI), and allows supervisory control over physical equipment. Over decades, however, these systems have evolved: Modern deployments increasingly integrate with IT, cloud platforms, remote access tools, and even IoT/edge networks to enable flexibility, remote management, real-time analytics, and greater operational efficiency.

REAL-WORLD EXAMPLE Nestlé's Plant in Girona, Spain

A practical illustration of SCADA's role in modern supply chains can be seen at Nestlé's highly automated facility in Girona, Spain, where Dolce Gusto coffee pods are produced. The plant uses an integrated SCADA system supplied by Mecalux to monitor production lines, equipment performance, and process parameters in real time. This continuous visibility enables operators to detect technical issues the moment they arise, maintain strict quality controls, and ensure consistent manufacturing throughput. From raw-material intake to palletizing and order dispatch, SCADA provides centralized supervision, allowing rapid responses to anomalies and supporting uninterrupted operations. Together, these examples illustrate how SCADA has evolved from a traditional industrial-control tool into a strategic enabler of efficiency, reliability, and resilience in digitally connected production and logistics environments (Interlake Mecalux, n.d).

Digital Twins and Threat Simulation

One notable OT in today's environment are digital twins. Digital twins are dynamic virtual replicas of physical systems that mirror real-world behavior through continuous data streams. Within supply chains, they function as powerful platforms for modeling vulnerabilities and simulating threat events, ranging from cyberattacks to the infiltration of counterfeit components. When combined with AI-driven analytics, digital twins enable predictive modeling and proactive risk management by identifying patterns, anticipating disruptions, and optimizing operational strategies (Trend Micro, 2025; McKinsey & Company, 2024; World Economic Forum, 2025).

These virtual models allow organizations to analyze vulnerabilities across complex networks including logistics, warehousing, production, and distribution by stress-testing end-to-end systems under varying conditions. Such simulations help pinpoint weak nodes, forecast cascade effects, and evaluate the resilience of operations before introducing real-world changes (McKinsey & Company, 2024; ProvisionAI, 2023). Organizations have used digital twins to uncover patterns behind inventory bottlenecks, transportation delays, and resource constraints, informing targeted improvements in planning and execution (Adexin, 2023; Boston Consulting Group, 2024).

Digital twins also provide a secure environment for threat simulation, enabling cybersecurity teams to test defenses without disrupting live operations. Simulated ransomware events, lateral network movement, or counterfeit-component infiltration can be modeled safely within the twin, providing valuable insight into system behavior under attack (Trend Micro, 2025; XM Cyber, 2024). This capability enhances incident-response readiness by allowing teams to run blast-radius analyses, refine response playbooks, and validate containment strategies based on feedback from controlled simulations (XM Cyber, 2024).

AI-driven risk prediction further strengthens digital twin functionality. Machine learning models can analyze historical and real-time data to forecast emerging vulnerabilities, identify areas where counterfeit components may enter the system, and dynamically adjust contingency strategies (McKinsey & Company, 2024; World Economic Forum, 2025). Research shows that digital twins can also support continuous verification of component integrity, anomaly detection, and end-to-end transparency, making them a valuable tool against counterfeiting and supply chain infiltration (Airehenbuwa et al., 2025). Additional studies highlight their role in intrusion detection, protection against side-channel leakage, and system-level threat modeling in cyber-physical environments (Airehenbuwa et al., 2025).

Despite these advantages, implementing digital twins poses several challenges. High development costs, complex data-integration requirements, and the need to secure the twin itself against manipulation are significant barriers. A compromised digital twin can reveal sensitive operational details and expose real-world vulnerabilities. Moreover, maintaining real-time synchronization and interoperability across diverse platforms and data sources adds substantial technical and organizational complexity (European Cyber Security Organization, 2023; Haneef Zaidi et al., 2024).

Overall, digital twins (especially when combined with AI) offer a robust framework for enhancing supply chain resilience and cybersecurity. They enable the simulation of diverse threat scenarios, provide continuous visibility into system behavior, and support more informed, data-driven decision-making. However, realizing their full potential requires overcoming integration challenges, establishing interoperable data ecosystems, and ensuring strong security protections for the twin environment itself.

Human Oversight and Ethical Automation

As automation and AI-driven decision-making become integral to supply chain operations, ensuring human oversight and ethical governance is no longer optional; it is essential. While automation improves efficiency and reduces human error, it introduces new risks such as automation bias, operator overreliance, ethical failures, and unsafe overrides. These risks can lead to flawed decisions, compromised safety, and reputational damage if not properly managed (Wellbrock et al., 2025; Frenette, 2023).

Modern supply chains increasingly rely on advanced technologies such as AI-driven decision-support systems, human–machine interfaces (HMIs), and automated planning tools for scheduling, routing, and inventory optimization. These capabilities enhance operational agility, enabling organizations to respond quickly to disruptions, allocate resources efficiently, and manage complex global networks with greater precision (Teixeira et al., 2025). Yet, growing reliance on automation can blur lines of accountability, particularly when decisions are generated by opaque algorithms rather than human judgment. This raises critical ethical concerns related to transparency, explainability, and fairness, issues that supply chain leaders must confront as they design and govern next-generation, automation-intensive operations (Gray Widder and Wong, 2024).

Governance and Security in Hyperconnected Supply Chains

To address these challenges, organizations are adopting governance models that balance automation with human oversight:

- Human-in-the-loop (HITL) decision structures ensure that critical or high-risk choices remain subject to human judgment rather than being delegated entirely to algorithms. HITL is now a legal requirement for high-risk AI systems under the EU AI Act, reinforcing its importance in operational governance (IAPP, 2024; Moody's Analytics, 2025).
- Decision auditability provides traceability for AI-generated recommendations, enabling organizations to review, justify, and validate automated actions for compliance and accountability (McKay, 2024).
- Training and competency programs equip personnel with the skills needed to supervise automated systems, recognize abnormal behavior, and intervene safely when required (ISM, 2024).
- Escalation protocols outline clear procedures for handling exceptional scenarios in which automated tools fail, behave unpredictably, or generate unsafe recommendations (Balamurugan et al., 2025).
- Broader industry frameworks such as IEEE Ethically Aligned Design principles and the emerging regulatory requirements of the EU AI Act reinforce the importance of embedding transparency, fairness, and human oversight into automated supply-chain systems to maintain trust and prevent bias (IEEE, 2022; EU Commission, 2023).

Although general governance frameworks for security technologies exist, they are no longer sufficient on their own as supply chains become more digitized, automated, and interconnected. In this environment, artificial intelligence emerges as a transformative force, reshaping how security, authenticity, and operational decisions are made. The next section introduces the role of AI within this broader context, explaining why intelligent systems are becoming integral to modern supply-chain security and how they extend, challenge, and complement the technologies discussed thus far.

Threat Landscape for AI Systems

The growing adoption of AI across supply chain operations offers substantial benefits, including improved forecasting accuracy, enhanced optimization capabilities, and more tailored customer engagement. Yet this rapid integration also introduces significant vulnerabilities. Unlike traditional rule-based software, AI systems are data-driven, probabilistic, and often opaque. These characteristics expand the attack surface and create security risks that behave unpredictably, making AI susceptible to a range of new and evolving threats.

Among the foundational risks are well-established attack vectors such as model theft, data poisoning, adversarial examples, and prompt injection:

- *Model theft* (also known as model extraction) occurs when adversaries repeatedly query a deployed AI system to reconstruct the underlying model. This compromises intellectual property and erodes competitive advantage, particularly for firms that invest heavily in proprietary models for sourcing, demand planning, or logistics (Tramèr et al., 2016).
- *Data poisoning* involves inserting manipulated or adversarial data into a model's training pipeline. In a supply chain context, this might involve corrupting supplier performance metrics to distort risk assessments or introducing falsified sales records that lead forecasting systems to generate inaccurate inventory or staffing plans (Jagielski et al., 2018).
- *Adversarial examples* represent another high-impact threat. These inputs appear normal to human observers but are subtly altered to mislead AI models. In a warehouse, for instance, a slightly modified barcode could cause a product to be misidentified, while small perturbations to quality-control images could allow defective items to pass inspection undetected (Biggio and Roli, 2018).
- More recently, *prompt injection* has emerged as one of the most critical risks for systems using large language models (LLMs). This technique

embeds malicious instructions into user inputs or contextual data to hijack the model's behavior. In supply chain operations, prompt injection could cause an AI assistant to leak sensitive information, bypass safety controls, or generate unauthorized recommendations. Security researchers now regard prompt injection as the top threat to LLM-enabled applications, with successful demonstrations across a wide range of model types and operational contexts (Benjamina et al., 2024; OWASP, 2025).

- AI systems are also vulnerable to *model inversion* and *membership inference attacks*, which enable adversaries to infer sensitive information about the data used to train a model. These risks raise significant privacy and compliance issues, especially when models incorporate supplier contracts, customer information, or proprietary operational data (Shokri et al., 2017).
- Finally, *model drift* represents a critical operational risk. As data distributions shift in response to market fluctuations, seasonality, or process changes, model performance degrades over time. Without continuous monitoring and retraining, this deterioration can go unnoticed, leading to systemic errors in procurement, logistics, planning, or customer-service functions (Quionero-Candela et al., 2009).

Risks Specific to Agentic AI

While these risks apply to traditional AI systems, a distinct and more complex set of threats has emerged with the rise of agentic AI. Agentic AI systems are capable of taking autonomous, multi-step actions toward goals with limited human oversight. Unlike static models, agentic AI integrates planning, memory, reasoning, and tools, enabling it to operate across digital environments, make decisions, and take actions independently (He et al., 2024).

These systems are rapidly proliferating. A 2025 global survey found that 82 percent of organizations were using autonomous AI agents, and 98 percent planned to expand deployment. However, only 44 percent had established governance frameworks. Eighty percent of respondents reported that their AI agents had engaged in unintended behaviors, including accessing unauthorized systems, sharing restricted data, or downloading inappropriate content (Dimensional Research and SailPoint, 2025).

Credential hijacking was also reported by nearly one in four organizations. In these cases, AI agents were manipulated into revealing login credentials, which attackers then used to escalate access across enterprise systems.

These incidents are especially concerning because AI agents often have access to sensitive systems such as finance, procurement, and human resources. Once compromised, agents can unintentionally leak intellectual property, personal data, or financial records (Frontier Enterprise, 2025).

Unlike traditional models, agentic systems often store long-term memory and integrate with tools such as databases, browsers, or email. This expands the attack surface significantly. Without strict input validation, audit logging, and behavioral constraints, agents can be manipulated into executing unintended commands, disclosing confidential data, or integrating with unsafe software tools (Narajala and Narayan, 2025).

Security researchers have identified nine vulnerability domains unique to agentic AI. These include memory misuse, tool integration abuse, hallucinated behaviors, prompt exploitation, and boundary violations. In simulated and real-world settings, agents have been used for phishing, reconnaissance, code execution, and lateral movement within IT environments (Xu et al., 2025).

A further challenge is the lack of transparency. Many organizations struggle to monitor what data AI agents access, what decisions they make, or how they reach those decisions. This opacity complicates auditing, regulatory compliance, and incident response. The so-called "black box" nature of these systems increases the risk of bias, faulty logic, or rogue behavior going undetected (Masood, 2025).

The rise of AI systems in supply chain operations, particularly agentic AI, requires more than technical safeguards; it demands a comprehensive governance framework. As AI systems transition from passive analytical tools to autonomous decision-makers, new questions emerge regarding accountability, transparency, regulatory compliance, and organizational oversight. This challenge is particularly acute in Supply Chain 5.0 environments where AI interacts with procurement, logistics, finance, and strategic planning functions.

Governing AI in Supply Chain 5.0

Governing AI in the supply chain context involves ensuring that systems behave in ways that align with business objectives, ethical standards, and legal requirements. A foundational priority is transparency. Many AI models, especially those based on deep learning, function as black boxes. Tools such as LIME (Local Interpretable Model-agnostic Explanations) and SHAP (SHapley Additive exPlanations) can be used to improve explainability, enabling stakeholders to understand how models reach their conclusions. Such transparency supports debugging, accountability, and trust among both internal users and external auditors (Rai, 2020; Weller, 2019).

Regulatory frameworks are also playing a growing role in shaping AI governance. The European Union's AI Act, finalized in 2024, classifies AI systems used in logistics and critical infrastructure as high-risk, requiring enhanced documentation, risk assessment, and human oversight (European Commission, 2024). Similarly, the United States' Blueprint for an AI Bill of Rights, released in 2022, outlines core principles that include data privacy, algorithmic transparency, and protections from algorithmic discrimination (Office of Science and Technology Policy, 2022). Organizations must ensure that AI systems deployed in supply chains are aligned with these emerging legal obligations, especially when those systems influence contracting decisions, workforce management, or infrastructure operations.

The National Institute of Standards and Technology has developed a comprehensive framework for managing AI risk. The NIST AI Risk Management Framework provides guidelines for identifying, measuring, and mitigating risks across the AI lifecycle. It encourages organizations to evaluate systems not just during initial deployment, but continuously, taking into account changing data inputs, model updates, and emerging threats (National Institute of Standards and Technology, 2023).

Data governance is another essential component. Many AI-related risks, including data poisoning, model drift, and bias, stem from poor data quality or insufficient control over training datasets. Effective governance requires policies for data ownership, version control, access management, and audit logging. This is especially important in supply chains that rely on third-party data sources such as supplier performance metrics or customer demand forecasts (Raji and Buolamwini, 2019).

Human oversight remains critical even in systems that are technically capable of operating autonomously. HITL controls allow organizations to supervise, interrupt, or reverse AI-generated decisions. This oversight is particularly important when AI agents are used to approve payments, modify routing schedules, or negotiate contracts. Without human oversight, the risk of unintended or adversarial behavior increases significantly (Raji and Buolamwini, 2019).

Organizations deploying agentic AI systems must also enforce strict access boundaries and behavioral constraints. These systems often integrate with tools such as databases, procurement platforms, or email systems, which makes them potential targets for credential abuse or unauthorized action. AI governance must ensure that agents have limited scope, operate within predefined permissions, and generate audit trails for every action taken. Controls such as input validation, memory management, and sandboxing reduce the risk of exploitation (Weller, 2019; National Institute of Standards and Technology, 2023).

To illustrate the importance of governance, consider a hypothetical retailer that deploys an autonomous AI agent to optimize supplier contracts. If the agent is inadequately governed, a prompt injection or data manipulation attack could cause it to favor an unvetted supplier offering deceptively low prices. If the agent has direct access to procurement systems, it might authorize payment or enter a binding agreement without human approval. With proper governance, however, the agent would rely on verified supplier data, require multi-factor human review before any contract changes, and generate a complete audit trail for accountability.

In sum, AI governance in Supply Chain 5.0 is not limited to technical settings or compliance checklists. It is an operational capability that protects against disruption, enforces ethical standards, and enables resilience. As AI becomes increasingly embedded in supply chain decision-making, governance will determine whether these systems serve as tools for efficiency or as vulnerabilities in complex, interdependent networks.

AI-Driven Threat Detection and Predictive Security

AI has become a critical enabler for real-time anomaly detection in modern supply chains. ML models can continuously monitor large volumes of operational data, including transaction flows, IoT sensor readings, system logs, and API traffic, to identify deviations from expected patterns. Such anomalies can indicate cyber intrusions, fraudulent activity, logistics disruptions, or the introduction of counterfeit components, enabling organizations to respond quickly and limit potential damage (Schroeder and Lodemann, 2021; NeuralTrust, 2025).

Despite these advantages, AI introduces its own risks. Adversarial attacks can manipulate models by injecting poisoned training data or crafting inputs specifically designed to evade detection. These techniques can cause the AI to misclassify threats or overlook suspicious events, creating critical blind spots in security operations (Anthi et al., 2020; Ibitoye et al., 2019).

Integrating predictive security into operational planning further strengthens supply chain resilience. AI models trained on historical and real-time data can forecast likely disruptions such as supplier delays, demand fluctuations, or attack-prone segments of the network. These insights can be used to align procurement strategies, inventory buffers, and logistics contingency plans with evolving risks (Ivanov and Dolgui, 2020; Schroeder and Lodemann, 2021). When paired with business continuity planning, predictive AI enables dynamic adjustments to resources and responses as threats emerge.

AI-driven threat detection and predictive security provide supply chains with unprecedented visibility into vulnerabilities and potential disruptions. To maximize their effectiveness, organizations must implement defenses against adversarial manipulation while ensuring that predictive insights are integrated into day-to-day operational decision making.

Conclusion

The evolution toward Supply Chain 5.0 represents a profound transformation in how organizations design, operate, and secure their global networks. Securing hyperconnected Supply Chain 5.0 demands an integrated approach that unites digital, physical, and human elements into a cohesive security framework. As digital systems intertwine with physical operations, and as intelligent automation reshapes planning and execution, the boundaries between cybersecurity, physical security, and product integrity have dissolved. This book proposes that modern supply chains cannot treat these domains as separate silos. Instead, they require a unified, integrated security architecture that safeguards data, protects physical assets, ensures authenticity, and preserves human oversight in an increasingly automated world.

Across the security domains examined in this book, a consistent pattern emerges. Resilience planning must address both nation state and organized crime threats alongside accidental disruptions. As supply chains become more interdependent and data driven, disruptions can cascade rapidly, blurring the line between cyber and physical risks. The case studies and scenarios presented underscore the need for proactive mitigation, continuous monitoring, and collaboration with partners, regulators, and law enforcement.

Each area of cybersecurity—cargo protection, authentication, AI security, data integrity, and OT defenses—carries its own set of risks, enabling technologies, and mitigation strategies. Yet these components reinforce one another. Zero Trust Architectures and continuous monitoring secure digital perimeters. IoT sensors, geofencing, and AI-enabled video analytics protect goods in transit and storage. Blockchain, DNA taggants, PUFs, and serialization ensure that products remain genuine and traceable throughout their lifecycle. Digital twins and advanced analytics help forecast disruptions, test attack scenarios, and strengthen resilience before failures occur. OT systems including SCADA, robotics, and autonomous equipment require robust segmentation and anomaly detection to prevent cyber-physical catastrophes. And through it all, human oversight remains essential: Governance frameworks, auditability, and training ensure that automation enhances, not replaces, responsible decision-making.

Taken together, the table of security domains presented in this chapter reveals the deeper lesson of Supply Chain 5.0: Security is no longer a set of controls, but an ecosystem of interconnected safeguards. Every node, device, dataset, and human decision contributes to the overall trustworthiness of the system. Organizations that embrace this holistic model will be better equipped to anticipate threats, adapt to disruptions, and maintain continuity in an era of geopolitical uncertainty, accelerating technology, and growing criminal sophistication.

Ultimately, Supply Chain 5.0 is about more than efficiency. It is about building networks that are secure, resilient, transparent, and trustworthy. The companies that thrive will be those that treat security not as an obligation or a cost center but as a strategic capability, one that protects their products, data, operations, and reputation. By integrating layered defenses, ethical automation, continuous monitoring, and rigorous provenance, supply chain leaders can build systems capable of withstanding both today's threats and tomorrow's unknowns.

As the global landscape continues to evolve, the principles outlined in this book provide a roadmap for safeguarding the next generation of supply chains. The future belongs to those who can secure it, and Supply Chain 5.0 offers both the vision and the tools to do so.

KEY TAKEAWAYS

- The future belongs to supply chains that secure themselves by design. They build trust with stakeholders and enhance resilience across operations.
- The line between cyber and physical risks has disappeared. Integrated defense strategies are needed to address vulnerabilities across IT, operational technology, and physical logistics.
- Human oversight remains essential, even in highly automated systems.

- Blockchain enables greater transparency, tamper resistance, and traceability, but only when deployed with secure coding practices, cryptographic controls, and proper auditing.
- Data integrity and provenance are core drivers of trust.
- Building supply chain resilience means addressing both targeted threats and systemic fragility. Simplified network structures, redundancy, and intelligence sharing are essential to mitigate cascading disruptions.
- Zero-trust principles are critical in hyperconnected ecosystems. Every user, device, and transaction must be verified continuously, with no assumptions of inherent trust.
- Ensuring product authenticity is essential to protecting consumer safety, brand value, and supply chain integrity. Multi-layered authentication methods must go beyond simple identification tags.
- Effective security depends on collaboration. Partnerships across industries, regulatory bodies, and law enforcement enhance the ability to detect, prevent, and respond to threats.
- Security must evolve alongside the supply chain. As systems grow more connected and autonomous, security practices must become more adaptive, embedded, and data-driven at every level.

References

3D Printing Industry (2016, May 19) Thieves are using 3D printers. https://3dprintingindustry.com/news/thieves-using-3d-printers-79277/ (archived at https://perma.cc/N3GM-CUJ6)

3Gimbals (2025) Securing global supply chains in an era of heightened risk. https://3gimbals.com/insights/securing-global-supply-chains-in-an-era-of-heightened-risk/ (archived at https://perma.cc/6956-FNGN)

Aanonsen, C. E. (2025) Stuxnet, revisited (again): Producing the strategic relevance of cyber operations. *Journal of Cyber Policy*, 1–17

Abdmeziem, M. R., Sheldon, F. T., and Atif, Y. (2025) Zero trust architectures for IoT and cloud environments: Strategies for mitigating data breaches and unauthorized access. www.researchgate.net/publication/397786472_Zero_Trust_Architectures_for_IoT_and_Cloud_Environments_Strategies_for_Mitigating_Data_Breaches_and_Unauthorized_Access (archived at https://perma.cc/3ZHR-E2U4)

Adexin (2023) Digital twin in supply chain. https://adexin.com/blog/digital-twin-in-supply-chain/ (archived at https://perma.cc/QP43-VLYG)

Ahmad, A., Khan, H. and Das, S. (2022) No privacy in the electronics repair industry. Cornell University, arXiv. https://arxiv.org/abs/2211.05824 (archived at https://perma.cc/NC3V-5J8P)

Airehenbuwa, B., Hasan, T., Sarkar, S. and Guin, U. (2025) Advancing security with digital twins: A comprehensive survey. arXiv. https://arxiv.org/abs/2505.17310 (archived at https://perma.cc/DD9R-EJ9U)

Allianz Commercial (2024) Navigating troubled waters: Risk challenges for shipping in 2024. https://commercial.allianz.com/news-and-insights/expert-risk-articles/shipping-red-sea-impact.html (archived at https://perma.cc/JYQ5-R5AZ)

Anthi, E., Williams, L., Rhode, M., Burnap, P. and Wedgbury, A. (2020) Adversarial attacks on machine learning cybersecurity defences in industrial control systems. arXiv. https://arxiv.org/abs/2004.05005 (archived at https://perma.cc/E74S-PPBS)

Aon (2025) The evolving threat of cargo theft: Five key mitigation strategies. www.aon.com/en/insights/articles/the-evolving-threat-of-cargo-theft-5-key-mitigation-strategies (archived at https://perma.cc/4Z7B-ZSZT)

Aqua Security (2021) SolarWinds attack: Play by play and lessons learned. www.aquasec.com/cloud-native-academy/supply-chain-security/solarwinds-attack/ (archived at https://perma.cc/9ZLX-4DWL)

ASIS International (2020) Criminals eye stalled supply chains for weak links. www.asisonline.org/security-management-magazine/articles/2020/10/criminals-eye-stalled-supply-chains-for-weak-links/ (archived at https://perma.cc/37HU-S8YA)

Balamurugan, M., Shanmugasamy, K. and Balaguru, S. (2025) Humans in the loop, lives on the line: AI in high-risk decision making. *European Journal of Computer Science and Information Technology*.

Batty, D. (2024) Markets and farm shops among targets of organised crime gangs, say experts. *The Guardian*. www.theguardian.com/business/2024/nov/09/markets-farm-shops-rising-food-theft-europe (archived at https://perma.cc/GEH9-AJ83)

BDO (2021) Building a 4.0 digital thread for supply chains. BDO USA. www.bdo.com/insights/industries/manufacturing/building-a-4-0-digital-thread-for-supply-chains (archived at https://perma.cc/6XX2-3B7A)

Benjamina, V., Bracaa, E., Cartera, I., Kanchwalaa, H., Khojasteha, N., Landowa, C., … Heverina, T. (2024, October 28) Systematically analyzing prompt injection vulnerabilities in diverse LLM architectures. arXiv. https://arxiv.org/abs/2410.23308 (archived at https://perma.cc/J77J-GF65)

Biggio, B. and Roli, F. (2018) Wild patterns: Ten years after the rise of adversarial machine learning. *Pattern Recognition*, 84, 317–31. https://doi.org/10.1016/j.patcog.2018.07.023 (archived at https://perma.cc/2G9B-G4R3)

Bode, C. and Wagner, S. M. (2015) Structural drivers of upstream supply chain complexity and the frequency of supply chain disruptions. *Journal of Operations Management*, 36, 215–28. https://doi.org/10.1016/j.jom.2014.12.004 (archived at https://perma.cc/YM9F-NLC7)

Boston Consulting Group (2024) Digital twins in logistics and supply chain optimization. www.bcg.com/publications/2024/digital-twins-in-logistics (archived at https://perma.cc/RUA9-TZLH)

Boyens, Jon, et al. (2022) Cybersecurity supply chain risk management practices for systems and organizations. No. NIST Special Publication (SP) 800-161 Rev. 1 (Withdrawn) National Institute of Standards and Technology,

Boyes, H. (2015) Cybersecurity and cyber-resilient supply chains. *Technology Innovation Management Review*, 5(4), 28–34. https://timreview.ca/article/888 (archived at https://perma.cc/PUL3-PKXP)

Brooks, C. (2023) The Target breach 10 years later. *Security Info Watch*. www.securityinfowatch.com/retail/article/53098895/the-target-breach-10-years-later (archived at https://perma.cc/WPP8-P7JH)

BSI Consulting and TT Club (2025) 2024 Cargo Theft Report: Supply Chain Report April 2025. TT Club, www.ttclub.com/fileadmin/uploads/tt-club/Documents/TT_and_BSI_annual_theft_report/TT_Club_Report_-_Supply_Chain_Report_April_2025.pdf (archived at https://perma.cc/4Q56-NRPA)

BSI Group (2022) Supply chain congestion increases threat of cargo theft. www.bsigroup.com/en-US/insights-and-media/media-center/press-releases/2022/may/supply-chain-congestion-increases-threat-of-cargo-theft/ (archived at https://perma.cc/9HR8-LUZ6)

CargoNet (2024, November 4) 2024 third quarter supply chain risk trends analysis: Organized crime groups drive increase in theft activity. www.cargonet.com/news-and-events/cargonet-in-the-media/2024-q3-theft-trends/ (archived at https://perma.cc/V6P2-XQTZ)

CISA (2021) Supply chain compromise. Cybersecurity and Infrastructure Security Agency. www.cisa.gov/news-events/alerts/2021/01/07/supply-chain-compromise (archived at https://perma.cc/JQ6A-WQVF)

CISA (2023) Analysis of the Colonial Pipeline ransomware attack. US Department of Homeland Security. www.cisa.gov/news-events/analysis-reports (archived at https://perma.cc/9QPP-PWXQ)

Cloud Google Blog (2023) How SolarWinds still affects supply chain threats two years later. Google Cloud. https://cloud.google.com/blog/products/identity-security/how-solarwinds-still-affects-supply-chain-threats-two-years-later (archived at https://perma.cc/QX9P-9PGE)

Collier, Z. A. and Sarkis, J. (2021) The zero trust supply chain: Managing supply chain risk in the absence of trust. *International Journal of Production Research*, 59(11), 3430–45. https://doi.org/10.1080/00207543.2021.1884311 (archived at https://perma.cc/TG52-U4XE)

Collins, S. and McCombie, S. (2012) Stuxnet: the emergence of a new cyber weapon and its implications. *Journal of Policing, Intelligence and Counter Terrorism*, 7(1), 80–91.

Collyer, D. (2024) Case Study: Maersk's response to NotPeyta – how cybersecurity best practices mitigated a major cyberattack. https://sosintel.co.uk/case-study-maersks-response-to-notpetya-how-cybersecurity-best-practices-mitigated-a-major-cyberattack/ (archived at https://perma.cc/X4E8-6GEZ)

Curoe, M. (2023) How has the Colonial Pipeline cyber-attack impacted the logistics industry? Redwood Logistics. www.redwoodlogistics.com/insights/how-has-the-colonial-pipeline-incident-impacted-logistics (archived at https://perma.cc/9JH5-N96A)

Cybersecurity Dive (2024) CrowdStrike outage renews supply chain concerns, federal officials say. www.cybersecuritydive.com/news/crowdstrike-outage-supply-chain/723198/ (archived at https://perma.cc/MCB7-TNPG)

Davies, J. and Wang, Y. (2021) Physically unclonable functions (PUFs): A new frontier in supply chain product and asset tracking. *IEEE Engineering Management Review*, 49(2), 116–25.

DC Velocity Staff (2025) Cargo theft report shows rise in deception and fraud. DC Velocity. www.dcvelocity.com/supply-chain/other-services/safety-security/cargo-theft-report-shows-rise-in-deception-and-fraud (archived at https://perma.cc/JQ7A-SLJP)

Deloitte (2023) Using blockchain to drive supply chain transparency. Deloitte Insights. www.deloitte.com/us/en/services/consulting/articles/blockchain-supply-chain-innovation.html (archived at https://perma.cc/KK2W-H2LX)

Dimensional Research and SailPoint. (2025) AI agents: The new attack surface. A global survey of security, IT professionals and executives. https://docs.sailpoint.com/pdf/en/special-report/SailPoint-The-Rising-Risk-of-AI-Agents-Expanding-the-Attack-Surface-report-SP2648%20.pdf (archived at https://perma.cc/8CYT-BFUF)

EU Commission (2023) Artificial Intelligence Act: Regulatory Framework for High-Risk AI Systems. https://artificialintelligenceact.eu/ (archived at https://perma.cc/5L4V-NU8C)

European Commission (2024) The Artificial Intelligence Act. https://digital-strategy.ec.europa.eu/en/policies/regulatory-framework-ai (archived at https://perma.cc/YW7Z-8XBB)

European Cyber Security Organization (2023) Cybersecurity scenarios and digital twins. https://ecs-org.eu/ecso-uploads/2023/07/ECSO_WG6_DigitalTwin-2.1.pdf (archived at https://perma.cc/3AUH-R36W)

Frenette, J. (2023) Ensuring human oversight in high-performance AI systems: A framework for control and accountability. *World Journal of Advanced Research and Reviews*.

Frontier Enterprise (2025) The 2025 cybersecurity predictions bonanza. www.frontier-enterprise.com/the-2025-cybersecurity-predictions-bonanza (archived at https://perma.cc/SG5S-H5MS)

GAO (2024) Cyber resiliency: CrowdStrike outage highlights challenges. United States Government Accountability Office. www.gao.gov/products/gao-24-107733 (archived at https://perma.cc/V8MD-265V)

Gaushell, D. J. and Darlington, H. T. (1987) Supervisory control and data acquisition. *Proceedings of the IEEE*, 75(12), 1645–58.

Gooch, J., Daniel, B., Abbate, V. and Frascione, N. (2016) Taggant materials in forensic science: a review. *TrAC Trends in Analytical Chemistry*, 83, 49–54

Gray Widder, D. and Wong, R. Y. (2024) Thinking upstream: Ethics and policy opportunities in AI supply chains. arXiv.

Haneef Zaidi, S. A., Khan, S. A. and Chaabane, A. (2024) Unlocking the potential of digital twins in supply chains: A systematic review. *Supply Chain Analytics*, 7, 100075. https://doi.org/10.1016/j.sca.2024.100075 (archived at https://perma.cc/4EA8-MMT5)

He, F., Zhu, T., Ye, D., Liu, B., Zhou, W. and Yu, P. S. (2024) The emerged security and privacy of LLM agent: A survey with case studies. arXiv. https://arxiv.org/abs/2407.19354 (archived at https://perma.cc/MNY4-LLRC)

Herder, C., Yu, M. D., Koushanfar, F. and Devadas, S. (2014) Physical unclonable functions and applications: A tutorial. *Proceedings of the IEEE*, 102(8), 1126–41.

Holloway, M. (2015) Stuxnet worm attack on iranian nuclear facilities. http://large.stanford.edu/courses/2015/ph241/holloway1/ (archived at https://perma.cc/TDR8-HKFN)

Horizon Powered (n.d.) AI video analytics in modern surveillance: Five powerful uses. https://horizonpowered.com/ai-video-analytics-in-modern-surveillance (archived at https://perma.cc/5VMF-C2WS)

IAPP (2024) Human in the loop in AI risk management — not a cure-all approach. https://iapp.org/news/a/-human-in-the-loop-in-ai-risk-management-not-a-cure-all-approach (archived at https://perma.cc/3AUY-RRSF)

Ibitoye, O., Abou-Khamis, R., El Shehaby, M., Matrawy, A. and Shafiq, M. O. (2019) The threat of adversarial attacks on machine learning in network security: A survey. arXiv. https://arxiv.org/abs/1911.02621 (archived at https://perma.cc/2LX9-U57Q)

IEEE (2022) Ethically aligned design: A vision for prioritizing human well-being with autonomous systems. https://ieeexplore.ieee.org/document/9398613 (archived at https://perma.cc/39VF-J6KT)

Interlake Mecalux (n.d.) Nestlé Nescafé production center in Girona, Spain. www.interlakemecalux.com/case-studies/nestle-nescafe-production-center (archived at https://perma.cc/5BDN-4BPH)

ISM. (2024) Navigating the ethical landscape of AI in supply chains. www.ismworld.org/supply-management-news-and-reports/news-publications/inside-supply-management-magazine/blog/2024/2024-08/navigating-the-ethical-landscape-of-ai/ (archived at https://perma.cc/KV4P-TUHX)

iTRACE Technologies, Inc. (2022) Fossil Case Study: Combating product diversion and brand protection in the watch industry. https://itracetech.com/fossil-case-study/ (archived at https://perma.cc/5HRN-VD8M)

Ivanov, D. and Dolgui, A. (2020) Viability of intertwined supply networks: Extending the supply chain resilience angles towards survivability. *International Journal of Production Research*, 58(10), 2904–15. https://doi.org/10.1080/00207543.2020.1750727 (archived at https://perma.cc/PH5M-LF8E)

Ivanov, D., Dolgui, A. and Sokolov, B. (2019) The impact of digital technology and Industry 4.0 on the ripple effect and supply chain risk analytics. *International Journal of Production Research*, 57(3), 829–46. https://doi.org/10.1080/00207543.2018.1488086 (archived at https://perma.cc/PH5M-zzzz)

Ivanov, D., Sokolov, B. and Dolgui, A. (2014). The ripple effect in supply chains: Trade-off 'efficiency-flexibility-resilience' in disruption management. *International Journal of Production Research*, 52(7), 2154–72. https://doi.org/10.1080/00207543.2013.858836 (archived at https://perma.cc/7YGV-3ATD)

Jagielski, M., Oprea, A., Biggio, B., Liu, C., Nita-Rotaru, C. and Li, B. (2018) Manipulating machine learning: Poisoning attacks and countermeasures for regression learning. In *2018 IEEE Symposium on Security and Privacy* (pp. 19–35)

Karamchand, G. (2024) Zero trust and AI: A synergistic approach to next generation cyber threat mitigation. *World Journal of Advanced Research and Reviews*, 24, 3374–87

Khan, R. U., Yin, J. and Mustafa, F. S. (2021) Accident and pollution risk assessment for hazardous cargo in a port environment. *PLoS ONE*, 16(6), e0252732. https://doi.org/10.1371/journal.pone.0252732 (archived at https://perma.cc/QUF7-PAHC)

Kidd C. and Raza M. (2024) *SCADA Systems: What they are & how they work*. Splunk, a Cisco Company

Kim, Y., Sohn, S. G., Kim, K. T., Jeon, H. S., Lee, S. M., Lee, Y. and Kim, J. (2024) Exploring effective zero trust architecture for defense cybersecurity: A study. *KSII Transactions on Internet & Information Systems*, 18(9)

Klepper, D. (2025) Russian military intelligence targets Western logistics firms in cyber campaign. *AP News*. https://apnews.com/article/6308ca3e11c8299470df573e4f422878 (archived at https://perma.cc/7EPT-JFTD)

Knapp, E. D. and Langill, J. T (2015) Industrial Network Security: Securing critical infrastructure networks for smart grid, SCADA, and other industrial control systems. Syngress.

Kohtamäki, M. and Rajala, R. (2023) Security and trust in the circular economy supply chain. *Journal of Business Research*, 155, 113367. https://doi.org/10.1016/j.jbusres.2022.113367 (archived at https://perma.cc/9EM9-GDAQ)

Korolov, C. (2024) Case in point: Taking stock of the CrowdStrike outages. *CIO*. www.cio.com/article/3853689/case-in-point-taking-stock-of-the-crowdstrike-outages.html (archived at https://perma.cc/22VQ-H78Z)

Kushner, D. (2013) The real story of stuxnet. *IEEE Spectrum*, 50(3), 48–53. https://spectrum.ieee.org/the-real-story-of-stuxnet (archived at https://perma.cc/M6DV-AAHS)

Kuzdraliński, A., Miśkiewicz, M., Szczerba, H., Mazurczyk, W., Ociepa, T., Lechowski, M. and Księżopolski, B. (2025) Advancements in DNA tagging and storage: Techniques, applications, and future implications. *Wiley Interdisciplinary Reviews: Computational Molecular Science*, 15(4), e70040

Langner, R. (2011) Stuxnet: Dissecting a cyberwarfare weapon. *IEEE Security & Privacy*.

Loadsure (2025) Embedded insurance delivers essential risk management to the just in time supply chain. www.loadsure.net (archived at https://perma.cc/G69E-9VRD)

Maley, K. (2025) Vendor risk management: Your hidden cybersecurity blind Spot. *Cyber Defense Magazine*. www.cyberdefensemagazine.com/vendor-risk-management-your-hidden-cybersecurity-blind-spot/ (archived at https://perma.cc/2MCW-Z4KP)

Malik, S., Dedeoglu, V., Kanhere, S. and Jurdak, R. (2021) PrivChain: Provenance and privacy preservation in blockchain enabled supply chains. arXiv. https://arxiv.org/abs/2104.13964 (archived at https://perma.cc/PN3V-VKKA)

Mariappa, B. M. and Aithal, P. S. (2023) Critical analysis of container accidents in international logistics. *International Journal of Case Studies in Business IT and Education*, 7(3), 194–204. https://doi.org/10.5281/zenodo.8237866 (archived at https://perma.cc/A8TB-K3BV)

Masood, A. (2025) Hardening your AI: A leader's guide to agent security, challenges and future directions. https://medium.com/@adnanmasood/hardening-your-ai-a-leaders-guide-to-agent-security-security-challenges-and-future-directions-f227003d590c (archived at https://perma.cc/PH5M-zzzz)

Mayer, Roger C., et al. (1995) An integrative model of organizational trust. *The Academy of Management Review*, (20)3, pp. 709–34. JSTOR, https://doi.org/10.2307/258792 (archived at https://perma.cc/8HN2-6ZM7)

McKay, M. H. (2024) Realizing the promise of AI governance involving humans-in-the-loop. *HCI International Conference Proceedings*.

McKinsey & Company (2024) Using digital twins to unlock supply chain growth. www.mckinsey.com/capabilities/quantumblack/our-insights/digital-twins-the-key-to-unlocking-end-to-end-supply-chain-growth (archived at https://perma.cc/7G5Y-C33X)

Moody's Analytics (2025) Human in the loop: Why oversight still matters in AI-driven risk and compliance. www.moodys.com/web/en/us/insights/ai/human-in-the-loop-why-human-oversight-still-matters-in-ai-driven-risk-and-compliance.html (archived at https://perma.cc/GUP4-L8TP)

Munich Re. (2025) Cargo theft tactics and trends report 2025. www.munichre.com/specialty/global-markets-ireland/en/news-and-insights/cargo-theft-tactics-and-trends-report-2025.hsb.html (archived at https://perma.cc/27UD-6AED)

Narajala, V. S. and Narayan, O. (2025) Securing agentic AI: A comprehensive threat model and mitigation framework for generative AI agents. arXiv. https://arxiv.org/abs/2504.19956 (archived at https://perma.cc/E8JC-RWUC)

National Institute of Standards and Technology (NIST) (2023) AI Risk Management Framework (AI RMF 1.0) www.nist.gov/itl/ai-risk-management-framework (archived at https://perma.cc/5T6D-STPF)

NeuralTrust (2025) The critical role of AI in strengthening supply chain security. NeuralTrust Blog. https://neuraltrust.ai/blog/ai-supply-chain-security (archived at https://perma.cc/7VDX-6Y7D)

Newman, L. H. (2021) DarkSide ransomware hit Colonial pipeline and created an unholy mess. *WIRED*. www.wired.com/story/darkside-ransomware-colonial-pipeline-response/ (archived at https://perma.cc/U3QQ-GKQ8)

Nyonyoh, R. (2025) The strategic threat of supply chain attacks: A national security and economic perspective. *Asian Journal of Economics, Business and Accounting*, 25(4), 483–91. https://doi.org/10.9734/ajeba/2025/v25i41765 (archived at https://perma.cc/CNN4-HUPJ)

Oduro-Antwi, M., Nguyen, D. and Sood, K. (2026) Physically unclonable functions (PUF)-based IoT security: Challenges and opportunities. *Internet of Things Security*, 201–217

OECD (2023) Global trade in counterfeit and pirated goods: Trends and impacts.

OECD (2025) Counterfeiting, piracy and the Swiss economy 2025. OECD Publishing, www.oecd.org/en/publications/counterfeiting-piracy-and-the-swiss-economy-2025_6d206067-en/full-report/component-6.html (archived at https://perma.cc/ZGH5-WLUK)

Office of Science and Technology Policy (2022) Blueprint for an AI Bill of Rights. https://bidenwhitehouse.archives.gov/ostp/ai-bill-of-rights/ (archived at https://perma.cc/5FRU-54QG)

OWASP (2025) OWASP Top 10 for LLM Applications: Prompt Injection. https://genai.owasp.org/llmrisk/llm01-prompt-injection (archived at https://perma.cc/E2ET-VMPX)

Palmer, D. (2019) Ransomware: The key lesson Maersk learned from battling the NotPetya attack. *ZD Net*, April 29.

Panjee, P., Kaewchueaknang, V. and Amornsawadwatana, S. (2025) A systematic literature review of cargo loss risks in road transportation: Impacts and future directions. *Safety*, 11(1), 20. https://doi.org/10.3390/safety11010020 (archived at https://perma.cc/3PXH-2JGH)

Peter, O., Pradhan, A., and Mbohwa, C. (2023) Industrial internet of things (IIoT): Opportunities, challenges, and requirements in manufacturing businesses in emerging economies. *Procedia Computer Science*, 217 (2023): 856–65.

ProvisionAI (2023) Digital twins and simulation to enhance supply chains. https://provisionai.com/digital-twins-and-simulation-to-enhance-supply-chains/ (archived at https://perma.cc/3SJ6-GZAW)

Quionero-Candela, J., Sugiyama, M., Schwaighofer, A. and Lawrence, N. D. (2009) *Dataset Shift in Machine Learning*. MIT Press.

Rai, A. (2020) Explainable AI: From black box to glass box. *Journal of the Academy of Marketing Science*, 48(1), 137–41. https://doi.org/10.1007/s11747-019-00710-5 (archived at https://perma.cc/G934-NP59)

Raji, I. D. and Buolamwini, J. (2019) Actionable auditing: Investigating the impact of publicly naming biased performance results of commercial AI products. In *Proceedings of the 2019 AAAI/ACM Conference on AI, Ethics, and Society* (pp. 429–35) https://doi.org/10.1145/3306618.3314244 (archived at https://perma.cc/YNH7-FAZX)

Rivera, J. J. D., Muhammad, A. and Song, W. C. (2024) Securing digital identity in the zero trust architecture: A blockchain approach to privacy-focused multi-factor authentication. *IEEE Open Journal of the Communications Society*, 5, 2792–814.

Rodriguez-Diaz, E., Alcaide, J. I. and Garcia-Llave, R. (2024) Challenges and security risks in the Red Sea: Impact of Houthi attacks on maritime traffic. *Journal of Marine Science and Engineering*, 12(11), 1900. https://doi.org/10.3390/jmse12111900 (archived at https://perma.cc/A2Q9-92FQ)

Rose, S., Borchert, O., Mitchell, S. and Connelly, S. (2020) Zero Trust Architecture. NIST Special Publication 800-207, National Institute of Standards and Technology. https://nvlpubs.nist.gov/nistpubs/specialpublications/NIST.SP.800-207.pdf (archived at https://perma.cc/E24M-RCDF)

Saberi, S., Kouhizadeh, M., Sarkis, J. and Shen, L. (2019) Blockchain technology and its relationships to sustainable supply chain management. *International Journal of Production Research*, 57(7), 2117–35. https://doi.org/10.1080/00207543.2018.1533261 (archived at https://perma.cc/29UG-8ZXN)

Schöning, J. and Kruse, N. (2023) AI-supported assessment of load safety. arXiv. https://arxiv.org/abs/2306.03795 (archived at https://perma.cc/D8FJ-RREQ)

Schroeder, M. and Lodemann, S. (2021) A systematic investigation of the integration of machine learning into supply chain risk management. *Logistics*, 5(3), 62. https://doi.org/10.3390/logistics5030062 (archived at https://perma.cc/F796-X78M)

SecureRedact (2023) Smart video in warehousing: How to reap the rewards while keeping employee data safe. www.secureredact.ai/articles/smart-video-in-warehousing-how-to-reap-the-rewards-while-keeping-employee-data-safe (archived at https://perma.cc/MZ2V-RNTX)

SecuringIndustry.com. (2025, July 28) Two-thirds of cosmetics bought online 'likely fake'. www.securingindustry.com/cosmetics-and-personal-care/two-thirds-of-cosmetics-bought-online-likely-fake-/s106/a17096/ (archived at https://perma.cc/6UX2-TZW3)

Sharief, S. A., Chahal, P. and Alocilja, E. (2021) Application of DNA sequences in anti-counterfeiting: Current progress and challenges. *International Journal of Pharmaceutics*, 602, 120580. https://doi.org/10.1016/j.ijpharm.2021.120580 (archived at https://perma.cc/LEX3-55C8)

Shokri, R., Stronati, M., Song, C. and Shmatikov, V. (2017) Membership inference attacks against machine learning models. In *2017 IEEE Symposium on Security and Privacy* (pp. 3–18) https://doi.org/10.1109/SP.2017.41 (archived at https://perma.cc/X3XK-AQ42)

Stackpole, B. (2024) MIT report details new cybersecurity risks. MIT Management Sloan School. https://mitsloan.mit.edu/ideas-made-to-matter/mit-report-details-new-cybersecurity-risks (archived at https://perma.cc/6QWY-2PMV)

Stanton, D. and Manning, M. (2019, October 17) 5 elements of a successful supply chain provenance strategy. Oracle SCM Blog. https://blogs.oracle.com/scm/5-elements-of-a-successful-supply-chain-provenance-strategy (archived at https://perma.cc/CU6G-M526)

Stouffer, K., et al. (2015) Guide to Industrial Control Systems (ICS) Security. NIST Special Publication 800–82, National Institute of Standards and Technology.

Sui, J., Chu, L. and Bao, H. (2023) An opcode-based vulnerability detection of smart contracts. *Applied Sciences*, 13(13), 7721. https://doi.org/10.3390/app13137721 (archived at https://perma.cc/Z4U4-748H)

Tan, S. F. and Samsudin, A. (2021) Recent technologies, security countermeasure and ongoing challenges of Industrial Internet of Things (IIoT): A survey. *Sensors*, 21(19), 6647.

TAPA Brazil (2024) Brazil annual cargo theft report 2024. Transported Asset Protection Association. https://tapa.memberclicks.net/assets/2025-National-Cargo-Theft-Conferfence/Presentations-for-Sharing/Brazil%20Annual%20Cargo%20Theft%20Report%202024_TAPA.pdf (archived at https://perma.cc/878L-VUVD)

TechTarget (2021) SolarWinds hack explained. www.techtarget.com/whatis/feature/SolarWinds-hack-explained-Everything-you-need-to-know (archived at https://perma.cc/5UAP-7CCL)

Teixeira, A. R., Ferreira, J. V. and Ramos, A. L. (2025) *Intelligent Supply Chain Management: A systematic literature review on AI contributions*. MDPI.

Tramèr, F., Zhang, F., Juels, A., Reiter, M. K. and Ristenpart, T. (2016) Stealing machine learning models via prediction APIs. In *25th USENIX Security Symposium* (pp. 601–18) www.usenix.org/conference/usenixsecurity16/technical-sessions/presentation/tramer (archived at https://perma.cc/GG3M-MRHD)

Transportation Security Administration (TSA) TSA updates, renews cybersecurity requirements for pipeline owners and operators. www.tsa.gov/news/press/releases/2023/07/26/tsa-updates-renews-cybersecurity-requirements-pipeline-owners (archived at https://perma.cc/GH7X-LCFU)

Trend Micro (2025) What is digital twin technology. www.trendmicro.com/en_no/what-is/ai/digital-twin.html (archived at https://perma.cc/DW2D-LFKT)

United States, Department of Justice (2021) Department of Justice seizes $2.3 million in cryptocurrency paid to the ransomware extortionists DarkSide. Office of Public Affairs, 7 June. www.justice.gov/opa/pr/department-justice-seizes-

23-million-cryptocurrency-paid-ransomware-extortionists-darkside (archived at https://perma.cc/LW85-GLST)

Wang, M., Duong, B., Fenniri, H. and Su, M. (2015) Nanomaterial-based barcodes. *Nanoscale*, 7(26), 11240–47.

Wellbrock, W., Malinovska, M. and Ludin, D. (2025) Ethical implications and risks of AI in supply chain management. *Discover Sustainability*, 6(886).

Weller, A. (2019) Transparency: Motivations and challenges. In *Explainable AI: Interpreting, Explaining and Visualizing Deep Learning* (pp. 23–40) Springer. https://doi.org/10.1007/978-3-030-28954-6_2 (archived at https://perma.cc/8GVM-GAGJ)

Wired (2014) How Target made itself a target for hackers. www.wired.com/2014/06/target-hack/ (archived at https://perma.cc/FMQ4-JDRA)

Woode, D. (2024) Gangs hit Christmas lorries delivering high value presents. *The Times*. www.thetimes.co.uk/article/xmas-freight-zl2qwxlgt (archived at https://perma.cc/BE2V-X68E)

World Economic Forum (2025) How digital twin technology can enhance cybersecurity. www.weforum.org/stories/2025/03/how-digital-twin-technology-can-enhance-cyber-security/ (archived at https://perma.cc/TU4S-XXYS)

WorldCargo News (2016) Counterfeit seals used to mask cargo theft via 3D printing. www.worldcargonews.com/safety-security/2016/05/counterfeit-seals (archived at https://perma.cc/S9PN-HYXS)

XM Cyber (2024) How digital twins are revolutionizing threat management. https://xmcyber.com/blog/how-digital-twins-are-revolutionizing-threat-management/ (archived at https://perma.cc/EN9J-6LTL)

Xu, H., Yu, W., Griffith, D. and Golmie, N. (2018) A survey on industrial Internet of Things: A cyber-physical systems perspective. *IEEE access*, 6, 78238–59.

Xu, M., Fan, J., Huang, X., Zhou, C., Kang, J., Niyato, D., Lam, K.-Y. (2025) Forewarned is forearmed: A survey on large language model-based agents in autonomous cyberattacks. arXiv. https://arxiv.org/abs/2505.12786 (archived at https://perma.cc/ZNG2-WMJK)

Yadav, A., Kumar, S. and Singh, J. (2022) A review of physical unclonable functions (PUFs) and its applications in IoT environment. *Ambient Communications and Computer Systems: Proceedings of RACCCS 2021* (2022): 1–13.

Yahoo News (2025, September 4) Apple lost $16M through returns of counterfeit products in large-scale fraud scheme. https://ca.news.yahoo.com/apple-lost-16m-returns-counterfeit-203449270.html (archived at https://perma.cc/6RJX-Z8UG)

Zaidi, M. W., Goudz, A., Noche, B. and Atif, M. (2019) Blockchain technology as a risk mitigation tool in supply chain. *International Journal of Transportation Engineering and Technology*, 5(3), 50–59. https://doi.org/10.11648/j.ijtet.20190503.12 (archived at https://perma.cc/5VEB-E2MK)

15 Overcoming Barriers to Supply Chain 5.0 Adoption

A lot of people want to innovate, as long as it's just doing the same thing we've always done.

DYCI SFREGOLA, NEW GEN ARCHITECTS

Transitioning to Supply Chain 5.0 implies a human-centered, intelligence-driven ecosystem that offers organizations enormous value. Yet even the most forward-thinking companies encounter obstacles that delay or dilute the benefits of these technologies. Understanding these barriers is essential for leaders seeking to turn ambition into measurable outcomes.

This chapter unpacks the organizational, technological, human, financial, and ecosystem-level challenges that complicate adoption, and, more importantly, how to overcome them. Research highlights that barriers such as technological complexity, rigid organizational structures, regulatory uncertainty, and cultural resistance are among the most significant impediments to Supply Chain 5.0 adoption. These challenges stem from the need to integrate advanced technologies like AI, IoT, and robotics into legacy systems while ensuring data security, workforce readiness, and compliance with evolving regulations (Laddha and Agrawal, 2024; Cingöz, 2025; Fares et al., 2025). Moreover, the human-centric nature of Supply Chain 5.0 amplifies cultural and skill-related barriers, requiring organizations to balance automation with human expertise and ethical considerations (Frederico, 2021; Agrawal et al., 2024).

Addressing these issues demands holistic strategies that combine technological innovation with organizational agility, regulatory alignment, and ecosystem collaboration. Although substantial research has been done on technology adoptions since the precedent industrial revolutions, moving the discussion from the Fourth Industrial Revolution to Industry 5.0 fundamentally shifts the core values and priorities, which is exactly why this era of technological adoption is considered different. The difference lies in the value-driven approach of Industry 5.0, contrasting with the technology-driven and efficiency-as-sole-goal focus of Industry 4.0.

Figure 15.1 provides a summary of the fundamental differences in the core values, primary goals, and view of the industrial revolutions related to technology adoptions across industrial revolutions related to technology adoption. In short, Industry 5.0 is different because it represents a deliberate shift in philosophy; it places the welfare of the worker and the health of the planet on equal footing with profitability, ensuring technology serves humanity, rather than the other way around. The next sections of this chapter cover how these technologies and shift related to supply chain context.

Key Barrier: Organizational—Misalignment, Fragmentation, and Legacy Thinking

Many organizations articulate ambitious digital strategies but lack the operational readiness and governance structures to execute them effectively. McKinsey reports that fewer than 30 per cent of digital supply chain initiatives achieve their intended impact, largely due to unclear strategic alignment and fragmented accountability (McKinsey & Company, 2024). Common symptoms include competing priorities across departments, the absence of a single accountable leader for transformation, and limited visibility into ROI or success metrics.

One reason for these challenges is that traditional supply chains were designed for linear, siloed workflows, optimized for predictability rather than agility. In contrast, Supply Chain 5.0 demands interconnected, data-driven processes that enable real-time decision-making and human–machine collaboration (Frederico, 2021; Salwaldamia, et al., 2024). Barriers include rigid planning cycles that cannot adapt to volatility, outdated procurement models focused on cost rather than resilience, and manual workarounds embedded over decades.

What works: Establishing a Supply Chain 5.0 Program Management Office (PMO) with cross-functional authority, outcome-based KPIs, and strong executive sponsorship ensures alignment between strategy and execution. Research emphasizes that rigid organizational structures and lack of governance are among the most critical barriers to Industry 5.0 adoption

Figure 15.1 Value-Driven Approach to Technology Adoption

Human Centricity

Industry 4.0 Focus: Full automation; using technology to replace human labor to maximize efficiency and reduce costs.

Industry 5.0 Focus: Human–Machine Collaboration (Co-Creation); using technologies like Cobots (Collaborative Robots). A.I and VR/AR to augment human skills.

Goal: To allow humans to focus on tasks requiring creativity, critical thinking, problem-solving, and emotional intelligence, while machines handle the repetitive, high-precision, or hazardous work. This ensures worker well-being design consideration, not an afterthought.

Sustainability

Industry 4.0 Focus: Efficiency and resource optimization primarily for cost reduction.

Industry 5.0 Focus: Environmental Responsibility; actively integrating sustainability throughout the entire product lifecycle, from design to disposal.

Goal: To minimize the environmental footprint, promote the circular economy (reuse, repair, recycle), and reduce energy and resource consumption. This moves beyond merely "doing less harm" to making a positive societal contribution.

Resiliency

Industry 4.0 Focus: Lean operations and just-in-time logistics, which can be vulnerable to global shocks.

Industry 5.0 Focus: Robustness and Agility; creating manufacturing processes and supply chains that can quickly adapt to unforeseen disruptions (like pandemics, geopolitical crises, or resource shortages).

Goal: To build systems that are antifragile (able to grow stronger through disruption) through local production, personalized manufacturing, and decentralized, modular production setups.

(Cingöz, 2025; Laddha and Agrawal, 2024). Organizational misalignment and legacy thinking consistently rank among the top barriers to adoption, alongside technological and cultural challenges (Laddha and Agrawal, 2024; Cingöz, 2025). Studies further highlight that rigid structures and limited cross-functional integration significantly hinder the transition to human-centric, intelligence-driven supply chains (Frederico, 2021; Lekamge, 2024).

For example, Maersk overcame fragmentation by replacing legacy platforms with unified digital systems, enabling integrated logistics and real-time visibility across 130 countries (Deloitte, 2025). Also, Unilever redesigned workflows using process mining, digital twins, and shared data lakes, achieving measurable improvements such as a 3 percent increase in overall equipment effectiveness and 8 percent cost reduction across 124 factories (Hargreaves, 2025; Wheeler, 2025).

Key Barrier: Technological—Complexity, Interoperability, and Security

Most global supply chains still rely on ERP systems designed 20–30 years ago (legacy infrastructure), creating significant challenges when integrating advanced technologies such as AI, IoT, and autonomous systems. These legacy platforms were built for structured, transactional processes, not for real-time analytics or ML.

The key challenges include limited API compatibility and lack of modular architecture, inflexible data schemas that hinder interoperability, and/or high technical debt, making modernization costly and risky. Research shows that 73 percent of enterprises pursuing AI integration with ERP systems face compatibility and data standardization issues, with average modernization timelines exceeding two years (Singh, 2025; Mubarik, 2025).

What works: Incremental modernization using cloud-based microservices, middleware, and API orchestration layers enables organizations to decouple legacy systems and integrate advanced capabilities without full system replacement (Adewale, 2025; Ogunwole et al., 2023).

Another key barrier is poor or fragmented data. Data quality remains a critical barrier to Supply Chain 5.0 adoption. Gartner estimates that 80 percent of supply chain data lacks the quality required for advanced analytics and AI-driven decision-making (Lavelle and Ruane, 2024). The report's root causes include disconnected partners and siloed systems, inconsistent master data across regions, and/or absence of robust governance frameworks. What works is when industry leaders advocate for a federated data governance model, combining centralized policy-setting with decentralized execution. This approach ensures data ownership, quality scoring, and lifecycle management while enabling agility across global networks (Meyer, 2025; BCG, 2024).

As seen in the previous chapter, as supply chains become more connected the attack surface expands dramatically. Threats include ransomware targeting logistics hubs, vulnerabilities from OT and IT convergence, and adversarial attacks on AI models. Top risks identified were ransomware and supply chain attacks exploiting third-party vendors, AI model manipulation through adversarial inputs, and/or IoT device vulnerabilities in smart factories.

What works: Studies emphasize that Zero Trust Architecture (ZTA), combined with continuous monitoring and secure-by-design AI development, is essential for mitigating these risks (Kour et al., 2024; Kost, 2025; CISA, 2025). Other implementations include implementing ZTA principles (never trust, always verify), establishing threat intelligence partnerships for proactive defense, and/or using blockchain for data integrity and quantum-resistant cryptography for future resilience (Kiran and Suryawanshi, 2025).

It is important to note that technological complexity and interoperability issues are consistently ranked among the top barriers to Industry 5.0 adoption (Laddha and Agrawal, 2024; Cingöz, 2025), while cybersecurity concerns are amplified in human-centric, AI-driven ecosystems, requiring adaptive security frameworks (Frederico, 2021; Mohammed et al., 2024). Both areas are under current further exploration in academic and industry settings.

Key Barrier: Human and Workforce—Skills, Culture, and Trust

Supply Chain 5.0 requires hybrid talent, meaning professionals who combine expertise in data analytics, automation, cybersecurity, and human-centric design. However, global talent shortages persist, particularly in AI literacy, cybersecurity, and systems engineering. Studies show that the skills gap is one of the most critical barriers to Industry 5.0 adoption, with rigid organizational structures and insufficient reskilling strategies exacerbating the challenge (Brkovic et al., 2023; Modgil et al., 2023; Cingöz, 2025).

Solutions include: skills academies focused on AI, IoT, and data governance; on-the-job upskilling programs leveraging real operational contexts; cross-disciplinary training to bridge technical and managerial competencies; and/or partnerships with universities and technology providers to create future-ready curricula (Samuels and Pelser, 2025).

Resistance to change, an ill-equipped workforce, lack of well-defined goals, and skills shortages remain major obstacles in digital transformation initiatives (Mubarik, 2025). Kewalramani et al (2024) argue that the high failure rate of digital transformation initiatives is often not due to technology or budget issues, but to poor change management, specifically, a failure to manage the people side of change (adoption and utilization).

Effective approaches can include focus on the human and cultural factors that inhibit adoption and utilization of new systems (Mubarik, 2025), transparent communication of the "why" behind transformation, early involvement of frontline workers in design and testing, demonstrating benefits through pilot projects to build trust, and/or aligning incentives with adoption goals, ensuring employees see personal and organizational value (McKinsey & Company, 2025).

Lastly, automation anxiety is real. Liao et al. (2023) confirm that simply installing cobots is not enough; success requires the psychological preparedness of the human. Organizations must focus not just on the robot's technical capabilities, but on job design that enhances the worker's sense of competence (Liao et al., 2023).

Successful companies reframe automation as augmentation, not replacement. Workforce-related barriers such as skills gaps, cultural resistance, and trust are consistently ranked among the top impediments to Industry 5.0 adoption (Laddha and Agrawal, 2024; Rejeb et al., 2025).

For example, DHL's deployment of collaborative robots (cobots) improved productivity while reducing physical strain, leading to higher employee satisfaction and engagement (Supply Chain Digital, 2025). Cobots handle repetitive tasks, freeing workers for higher-value roles such as quality control and process optimization (Garus and Greis, 2025).

Key Barrier: Financial—Cost, ROI Uncertainty, and Risk Aversion

Supply Chain 5.0 technologies, such as AI-driven analytics, IoT-enabled visibility, and collaborative robotics, require substantial upfront capital for infrastructure, integration, and workforce training. Many organizations struggle to justify these costs due to uncertain ROI timelines and intangible benefits like resilience and agility, which are harder to quantify (Laddha and Agrawal, 2024; Cingöz, 2025).

Key challenges include difficulty linking technology investments to measurable financial outcomes, CFO skepticism driven by past failures in digital transformation, and/or pressure to prioritize short-term cost control over long-term strategic gains. Gartner emphasizes that less than 30 percent of digital supply chain initiatives achieve their intended financial impact, primarily due to unclear ROI frameworks and fragmented accountability (Gartner, 2025).

Economic volatility and inflationary pressures often force organizations to defer technology investments in favor of immediate operational needs. Research shows that financial constraints rank among the top barriers to Industry 5.0 adoption, alongside technological and organizational challenges (Nasimi and Vargourani, 2025; Rejeb et al., 2025). Also, executives often perceive advanced technologies as high-risk investments, fearing sunk costs if adoption fails. This perception is amplified in industries with thin margins and volatile demand, where financial resilience is critical (Ali et al., 2025; Agrawal et al., 2024)

Phased investment strategies and proof-of-value pilot programs are emerging as best practices for organizations adopting large-scale, disruptive technologies. Rather than committing to full deployment upfront, successful companies de-risk transformation by validating use cases in controlled phases, generating measurable benefits, and iterating based on real performance outcomes. This approach helps address common barriers such as high investment requirements, uncertainty around return on investment (ROI), and the lack of a clear starting point or roadmap. As Mubarik (2025) notes, phased strategies help organizations manage financial burden, align technology upgrades with strategic goals, and build confidence in long-term modernization efforts. Launch small-scale pilots to demonstrate tangible benefits before scaling (Nasimi and Vargourani, 2025) and use outcome-based KPIs tied to cost savings, revenue growth, or resilience metrics.

Decision-Making Framework for Barriers and Industry 5.0

Leaders face overwhelming complexity and need structured guidance because Supply Chain 5.0 environments involve interconnected technologies with different risks, costs, and maturity levels. A clear framework would help executives cut through complexity, prioritize what matters, and make informed decisions rather than reacting to trends or vendor pressure. Without a structured approach, these pressures lead to stalled pilots, fragmented initiatives, or security gaps.

Adopting Supply Chain 5.0 capabilities such as AI, IoT, digital twins, advanced authentication, and Zero Trust Security requires more than buying technology. Organizations face intersecting financial, organizational, technological, and ecosystem barriers, including high investment requirements, integration complexity, skills shortages, and regulatory uncertainty (Mubarik, 2025; Deral et al., 2024). To help leaders, this section provides a seven-step model for navigating barriers and increases the chances of value-driven choices.

Step 1. Clarify Strategic Intent and Risk Appetite

The starting point is not technology but strategy (Alquraish, 2025; Ghobakhloo et al., 2025). Leaders should define:

- what problems they are solving (e.g., cargo theft, counterfeiting, OT risk, lead-time);
- how these link to broader goals such as resilience, sustainability, and service levels;
- the organization's risk appetite; what level of disruption, cyber exposure, or reputational risk is acceptable.

Step 2. Assess Readiness Using a "TOE+" Lens

The well-established Technology–Organization–Environment (TOE) framework is widely used to understand technology adoption drivers and barriers in supply chains (Chaudhuri et al., 2024; Hadi Almaher et al., 2024; Hwang et al., 2016).

For example, leaders can adapt as a quick diagnostic such as:

- technology—current systems, data quality, integration capability, cybersecurity posture;
- organization—skills, culture, change readiness, governance, leadership support;
- environment—customer expectations, regulatory demands, partner capabilities, competitive pressure.

For Supply Chain 5.0, it is helpful to add a fourth lens:

- human and ethical factors—impacts on workforce, trust, and responsible AI or automation.

Step 3. Identify Barriers and Enablers Explicitly

Research on digital supply chain transformation shows recurrent barriers: Financial constraints, integration complexity, heterogeneous legacy systems, lack of digital skills, interoperability issues, and unclear ROI (Mubarik, 2025; Deral et al., 2024).

Leaders should map:

- barriers—e.g., budget limits, fragmented data, OT/IT silos, weak vendor risk management;
- enablers—e.g., strong executive sponsorship, existing IoT footprint, solid cybersecurity team, regulatory tailwinds.

This barrier–enabler map provides a realistic baseline and informs which initiatives are feasible now and which require capability-building first.

Step 4. Prioritize Use Cases, Not Technologies

Rather than starting with "AI" or "blockchain," high-performing firms prioritize concrete use cases that have clear value and feasible implementation paths, such as:

- reducing cargo theft and diversion in high-risk corridors;
- preventing counterfeit components in critical product lines;
- strengthening OT security in key factories or distribution hubs;
- improving visibility and exception management for time-critical shipments.

Studies of Supply Chain 4.0/5.0 adoption show that focusing on targeted, high-impact use cases accelerates value realization and supports resilience (Huang et al., 2023; McKinsey & Company, 2016; Islam et al., 2025; Salim and Sakhri, 2025).

Step 5. Design Phased Investments and Proof-of-Value Pilots

Given high capital requirements and uncertainty around ROI, phased investment and proof-of-value pilots are emerging as best practice (Mubarik, 2025; Kesici and Coban, 2025).

Key principles:

- start with small, well-bounded pilots in a specific lane, site, or product category;
- use pilots to validate technology fit, integration effort, security implications, and real financial impact;
- scale only when you have evidence on cost, benefit, and operational impact—not just vendor claims.

This approach directly addresses common barriers such as unclear ROI, "where do we start?" and fear of disruption, while limiting downside risk.

Step 6. Define Multi-Dimensional Success Metrics

Digital and security investments often fail because only narrow financial metrics are tracked. A more balanced view should include:

- operational metrics—on-time delivery, order fill rate, dwell time, incident rates, inventory accuracy;
- security metrics—number of security incidents, mean time to detect/respond, counterfeit detection rates, cargo theft losses;
- resilience metrics—time to recover from disruption, supply diversification, visibility coverage;
- human/ethical metrics—workforce safety, decision transparency, AI override rates.

These indicators allow leaders to judge whether a given Supply Chain 5.0 initiative is strengthening the system, not just adding complexity.

Step 7. Embed Governance and Learn Continuously

Recent work on digital supply chain transformation emphasizes that governance and learning are as important as technology (Alquraish, 2025; Ghobakhloo et al., 2025).

Core elements:

- a cross-functional steering group that includes supply chain, IT, cybersecurity, finance, and risk;
- regular post-implementation reviews of pilots and scaled deployments to update risk registers and roadmaps;

- clear ownership for ongoing model monitoring (e.g., AI drift), vendor risk, and control testing;
- continuous training and communication to keep people aligned as the technology landscape evolves.

The long-term goal is that this approach transforms the framework into a dynamic, continuous process rather than a one-time initiative. To measure progress and ensure alignment with Industry 5.0 principles, organizations should track metrics across three core pillars:

- Human: Employee satisfaction, skill development rate, and retention levels.
- Sustainability: Reduction in energy consumption, waste minimization, and improvements in circularity scores.
- Resilience: Time to recover from disruptions (TTR), supply chain visibility index, and reduction of single points of failure.
- Feedback loop: Leverage data generated by digital tools such as IoT sensors and AI-driven analytics to continuously refine strategic priorities, operational processes, and technology deployments. This iterative feedback mechanism ensures that the transformation remains adaptive and value-driven.

Navigating the Human Side of Digital Supply Chain Transformation

Technological change in supply chains often involves more than just deploying new tools. It also reshapes workflows, decision-making structures, and daily routines. As a result, transformation efforts are as much about people as they are about systems.

One framework frequently used to support clarity during these transitions is the RACI matrix. This tool helps organizations define and communicate roles in a structured way:

- Responsible: The individuals or teams who carry out specific tasks or deliverables. They are directly involved in the execution of the work.
- Accountable: The person ultimately answerable for the completion and quality of the outcome. This role often holds decision-making authority.

- Consulted: Stakeholders who provide input, expertise, or feedback. Communication is two-way, and their opinions can influence how tasks are executed.
- Informed: Individuals or groups who need to be kept updated on progress or decisions. They are not actively involved but are affected by the outcomes.

Using a RACI matrix allows organizations to reduce ambiguity and support smoother collaboration, particularly in cross-functional or distributed teams.

Digital transformation initiatives also tend to involve shifts in how employees interact with technology. In one example, a tablet-based system introduced in a warehouse environment was designed with a user-friendly interface that mirrored familiar consumer applications. This approach lowered resistance and made the new system easier to adopt. Many workers reported feeling more engaged and capable, contributing to reduced turnover and higher morale.

Organizations undertaking large-scale digital changes often find that incremental rollouts are more manageable than wholesale shifts. Gradual implementation gives teams time to learn, adjust, and offer feedback. It also enables leaders to identify and resolve early challenges before broader deployment.

Rather than displacing human roles, many digital systems are designed to enhance and support them. When tools are intuitive and designed around user needs, they tend to be perceived less as threats and more as enablers. Workers often respond positively to technologies that reduce friction, simplify complex tasks, or improve visibility across the supply chain.

Overall, digital transformation is most effective when technology and people evolve together. The process works best when it acknowledges existing expertise, respects operational realities, and supports gradual adaptation over time.

REAL-WORLD EXAMPLE Overcoming Strategic Implementation Barriers at Siemens

One of the most persistent barriers to adopting modern supply chain strategies is the misalignment between long-term planning and rapidly changing market conditions. Siemens, a global industrial leader, encountered this challenge amid a series of global disruptions, including the COVID-19 pandemic, geopolitical instability, and increasing environmental regulations. These pressures revealed the limitations of traditional supply chain strategies, which were often too rigid and internally focused to remain effective in a volatile environment.

To address this challenge, Siemens developed a new strategic framework known as the Strategic Diamond. This model is designed to keep strategies aligned with real-world conditions by connecting internal objectives with external market signals in a structured and adaptable way. It also directly integrates principles from Dynamic Capabilities Theory (DCT), which emphasizes an organization's ability to sense, seize, and reconfigure in response to change.

The Strategic Diamond consists of five interrelated components: Trends and triggers, focus areas, strategic activities, strategic fields, and strategic key elements. These elements work together to help Siemens continuously interpret changes in the market, prioritize actions, and keep the overall strategy aligned with evolving demands. Unlike static frameworks that focus primarily on risk mitigation after disruptions occur, the Strategic Diamond enables proactive adaptation by embedding continuous feedback loops into the strategy development and execution process.

A core strength of the framework is its focus on maintaining both transparency and adaptability. Siemens ensures that every strategic activity is clearly connected to broader business goals and external developments, enabling decision-makers to act with clarity and confidence. The framework also improves alignment across the organization by making the impacts of operational activities on strategic outcomes visible and actionable.

One example of this approach in practice is Siemens' response to evolving environmental standards. When new ISO norms related to sustainability were identified as strategic triggers, Siemens aligned them with its long-term goal of achieving net-zero carbon emissions. These were consolidated into an established focus area, then translated into a strategic initiative for end-to-end carbon footprint tracking. This initiative was not implemented in isolation, but instead linked directly to competitive objectives and customer value creation, maintaining strategic coherence while responding to external demands.

Siemens' experience illustrates how overcoming barriers to strategy adoption requires more than just better execution. It demands a strategic framework that is inherently connected, flexible, and built for resilience. By combining the structured logic of the Strategic Diamond with the adaptive thinking of DCT, Siemens has created a supply chain strategy that remains relevant, actionable, and aligned with both business and market realities.

REAL-WORLD EXAMPLE Overcoming Barriers to Integrated Business Planning Adoption

A global consumer healthcare organization faced significant challenges in transforming its supply chain and financial planning processes. The implementation of Integrated Business Planning (IBP) revealed complex barriers across technological, cultural, and organizational dimensions.

Technological barriers included fragmented systems across multiple markets, inconsistent demand planning processes, and initial data reliability issues. The organization addressed these challenges by standardizing enterprise resource planning systems, implementing concurrent financial technologies, and creating a centralized planning approach.

Cultural resistance emerged as a critical obstacle. Commercial teams were initially reluctant to expose performance gaps and trust new planning methodologies. Leadership overcame this by establishing a collaborative culture that emphasized transparency and collective problem-solving. Key strategies included securing top-level executive sponsorship, creating a unified "we're in this together" mindset, and implementing regular cross-functional leadership meetings.

Resource constraints posed another significant challenge. The organization mitigated this by:

- engaging an external consulting firm to accelerate implementation
- selecting top internal talent for the rollout
- prioritizing larger markets with more flexible resources
- accepting initial performance uncertainties as part of the transformation process

Change management became a critical success factor. The organization invested heavily in continuous training, governance processes, and organizational alignment. By establishing an objectives and key results (OKRs) framework, they created a unified approach to strategic planning.

The implementation journey demonstrated that successful business transformation requires more than technological investment. It demands a holistic approach that integrates systems, processes, and organizational culture. The organization's patient, collaborative approach ultimately created a more agile and intelligent operational model.

Key lessons learned include the importance of:

- executive sponsorship
- transparent communication
- continuous learning
- collaborative problem-solving
- systemic approach to organizational change

REAL-WORLD EXAMPLE Natural Fiber Welding: Scaling Circular Materials for a Regenerative Future

Natural Fiber Welding (NFW) has been one of the most visible innovators in circular and regenerative materials over the past decade, helping redefine what sustainable supply chains might look like. Founded by chemist Luke Haverhals in 2014, the company gained attention for replacing petrochemical-based textiles with high-performance, plant-based alternatives engineered for circularity. Using a patented ionic-liquid process to bond natural cellulose fibers at the molecular level, without plastics or toxic additives, NFW developed a portfolio of materials that perform like synthetics but are fully biodegradable, recyclable, and free from microplastics.

NFW's flagship materials include MIRUM, a plant-based leather alternative; CLARUS, a high-performance textile made from natural and recycled fibers; PLIANT, a rubber-free outsole material; and TUNERA, a bio-based foam. These products promised substantial environmental benefits compared to traditional leather, plastics, and foams, such as dramatically lower emissions, reduced water and energy use, and the ability to integrate with regenerative agriculture supply chains. These innovations fueled widespread interest across the fashion, footwear, automotive, and outdoor industries. Major brands such as Patagonia, Allbirds, BMW, Reformation, and Stella McCartney adopted NFW materials, and the company reached a global audience through a high-profile partnership with Ralph Lauren for the 2024 Olympic Games.

However, despite its rapid ascent and prominent partnerships, NFW experienced a major setback after investing heavily in a large contract opportunity that ultimately fell through. Having placed most of its strategic and financial resources into this single deal, the company suffered a significant blow when it did not materialize. As a result, NFW, once seen as a leading example of regenerative supply chain innovation, now faces an uncertain future at the time of this writing. Its trajectory underscores both the promise and the vulnerability of breakthrough materials companies operating in capital-intensive, highly competitive industries, and highlights the importance of diversified customer portfolios in scaling next-generation sustainable technologies.

Conclusion

In the evolving landscape of global supply chain management, organizations face unprecedented challenges in technological transformation. Traditional supply chain models, characterized by rigid planning cycles and resistance to change, are being disrupted by advanced predictive technologies and data-driven strategies.

The journey begins with recognizing the fundamental barriers: Financial skepticism, technological complexity, and deeply entrenched operational mindsets. Leadership often views sophisticated technological investments as unnecessary expenses, preferring familiar, incremental approaches. However, innovative organizations are discovering that true competitive advantage lies in building adaptive, intelligent supply chain ecosystems.

By developing secure, private data environments that integrate internal operational data with external market insights, companies can create predictive models that transform decision-making. These advanced systems go beyond traditional analytics, offering real-time forecasting of potential disruptions, optimizing delivery schedules, and even predicting consumer behavior with remarkable accuracy.

The implementation of such technologies is not merely a technical exercise but a strategic transformation. One global consumer goods company demonstrated this by creating AI-driven models that generated a 12 percent sales increase through sophisticated inventory management and dramatically reduced resource consumption. The key was not just technological implementation, but a holistic approach that aligned technological capabilities with strategic business objectives.

Successful adoption requires more than sophisticated algorithms; it demands a cultural shift. Organizations must build a narrative that connects technological investment to tangible business outcomes, showing how flexibility and predictive capabilities directly translate to competitive advantage. By demonstrating clear financial returns, mitigating risks, and gradually transforming operational culture, companies can overcome institutional inertia and embrace a more dynamic, intelligent approach to supply chain management.

The future of supply chains is not about eliminating human involvement, but about empowering human decision-makers with unprecedented insights and adaptive capabilities. As technologies continue to evolve, the most successful organizations will be those that can seamlessly integrate human creativity with technological intelligence.

KEY TAKEAWAYS

- Successful adoption of Supply Chain 5.0 requires addressing organizational misalignment and legacy thinking that prevent strategy from translating into execution.
- Legacy technologies and rigid ERP architectures remain major blockers, making interoperability, data governance, and cybersecurity foundational prerequisites for progress.
- Human-centricity in Supply Chain 5.0 demands a workforce with hybrid skills in data, automation, systems thinking, and change management, which most organizations currently lack.
- Cultural resistance, fear of automation, and weak change-management practices often undermine digital transformation more than the technologies themselves.
- Financial constraints, unclear ROI, and risk aversion remain major barriers, especially when long-term resilience and flexibility are undervalued compared to short-term cost savings.
- Phased investments and proof-of-value pilots are essential tools for reducing financial uncertainty and building organizational confidence in disruptive technologies.
- Cybersecurity risks increase dramatically in AI-enabled, hyper-connected supply chains, requiring Zero Trust Architectures and secure-by-design practices.
- Holistic decision-making frameworks such as TOE+, Dynamic Capabilities Theory, and phased adoption models help leaders prioritize high-value use cases over chasing technologies.

- Overcoming workforce-related barriers requires transparent communication, involvement of frontline teams, and job designs that frame automation as augmentation rather than replacement.
- Supply Chain 5.0 transformation succeeds when organizations integrate technology, people, strategy, and governance into a continuous learning system rather than a one-time initiative.

References

Adewale, T. (2025) API-driven microservices for seamless integration across global supply networks. www.researchgate.net/publication/387823066_API-Driven_Microservices_for_Seamless_Integration_Across_Global_Supply_Networks (archived at https://perma.cc/3WGP-RR2A)

Agrawal, S., et al. (2024) Can Industry 5.0 technologies overcome supply chain disruptions? *Operations Management Research*. https://doi.org/10.1007/s12063-023-00410-y (archived at https://perma.cc/3SCM-LAJP)

Ali, I., Nguyen, K. and Oh, I. (2025) Systematic literature review on Industry 5.0: Current status and future research directions with insights for the Asia Pacific countries. *Asia Pacific Business Review*, 1–28.

Alquraish, M. (2025) Digital transformation, supply chain resilience, and sustainability: A comprehensive review with implications for Saudi Arabian manufacturing. *Sustainability*, 17(10), 4495.

BCG (2024) Federated Data Governance Model. Boston Consulting Group Insights. https://media-publications.bcg.com/Federated-Data-Governance-Model.pdf (archived at https://perma.cc/KG2S-JALH)

Brkovic, M., Ćulibrk, J., Rikalovic, A., Tasić, N. and Bajić, B. (2023) Industry 5.0 and the skills gap: Strategies for developing a future-ready workforce. In *19th International Scientific Conference on Industrial Systems*. https://doi.org/10.24867/is-2023-t6 (archived at https://perma.cc/YZP2-TMG3)

Chaudhuri, R., Singh, B., Agrawal, A. K., Chatterjee, S., Gupta, S. and Mangla, S. K. (2024) A TOE-DCV approach to green supply chain adoption for sustainable operations in the semiconductor industry. *International Journal of Production Economics*, 275, 109327.

Cingöz, K. (2025) Prioritizing the barriers to the implementation of Industry 5.0 in the supply chain with AHP. *International Journal of Business Management and Technology*. www.theijbmt.com/archive/0968/534469609.pdf (archived at https://perma.cc/ATA7-GF9V)

CISA (2025) Zero trust architecture dynamically secures users, devices, and resources, moving beyond static perimeter defenses. Cybersecurity &

Infrastructure Security Agency. www.cisa.gov/topics/cybersecurity-best-practices/zero-trust (archived at https://perma.cc/TS98-CYSB)

Deloitte (2025) Digital transformation reshapes Maersk from shipping giant to global logistics integrator. www.deloitte.com/dk/en/services/consulting/perspectives/digital-transformation-reshapes-maersk-from-shipping-giant-to-global-logistics-integrator.html (archived at https://perma.cc/2YL2-EWCQ)

Deral, D., Köse, Ş. G. and Kazançoğlu, İ. (2024) Barriers to digital supply chain management: A qualitative research. *Yildiz Social Science Review*, 10(1), 28–42.

Fares, N., Anass, C., Shardeo, V. and Garza-Reyes, J. A. (2025) Supply chain management in the Industry 5.0 era: Strategic implications. *Benchmarking: An International Journal*, 1–29.

Frederico, G. F. (2021) From Supply Chain 4.0 to Supply Chain 5.0: Findings from a systematic literature review and research directions. *Logistics*, 5(3), 49. https://doi.org/10.3390/logistics5030049 (archived at https://perma.cc/YL5G-59VD)

Gartner (2025) Overcome resistance for successful supply chain digital transformation. www.gartner.com/en/documents/7215430 (archived at https://perma.cc/UJU6-WRE8)

Garus, C. and Greis, D. (2025) Beyond efficiency: Rethinking the psychosocial and long-term impacts of collaborative robots in the workplace. Online Journal of Robotics & Automation Technology. https://irispublishers.com/ojrat/fulltext/beyond-efficiency-rethinking-the-psychosocial.ID.000563.php (archived at https://perma.cc/Q6B4-V9NL)

Ghobakhloo, M., Iranmanesh, M., Foroughi, B., Tseng, M. L., Nikbin, D. and Khanfar, A. A. (2025) Industry 4.0 digital transformation and opportunities for supply chain resilience: a comprehensive review and a strategic roadmap. *Production Planning & Control*, 36(1), 61–91.

Hadi Almaher, M. A., Thiruchelvam, S. A. L., Bin Mat Isa, A. A. (2024) A conceptual model for blockchain adoption intentions: A T-O-E framework perspective. *Journal of Infrastructure, Policy and Development*. 8(6): 4685. https://doi.org/10.24294/jipd.v8i6.4685 (archived at https://perma.cc/P6CA-HJWY)

Hargreaves, L. (2025, April 11) How Unilever's digital system sharpens the supply chain. *Supply Chain Digital*. https://supplychaindigital.com/digital-supply-chain/unilever-using-new-digital-tools-boost-productivity (archived at https://perma.cc/5AT7-ULWZ)

Huang, K., Wang, K., Lee, P. K. and Yeung, A. C. (2023) The impact of industry 4.0 on supply chain capability and supply chain resilience: A dynamic resource-based view. *International Journal of Production Economics*, 262, 108913.

Hwang, B. N., Huang, C. Y. and Wu, C. H. (2016) A TOE approach to establish a green supply chain adoption decision model in the semiconductor industry. *Sustainability*, 8(2), 168.

Islam, M. T., Sepanloo, K., Woo, S., Woo, S. H. and Son, Y. J. (2025) A review of the industry 4.0 to 5.0 transition: Exploring the intersection, challenges, and opportunities of technology and human–machine collaboration. *Machines*, 13(4), 267.

Kesici, B. and Coban, A. (2025) A decision-making framework for struggling with digital supply chain barriers through Industry 5.0 technologies. *Journal of Decisions & Operations Research*, 10(2).

Kewalramani, C., Mehta, R. and Koilakonda, R. (2024) Establishing a change management center of excellence (COE) for digital transformations. *International Research Journal of Economics and Management Studies IRJEMS*, 3(6).

Kiran, U. and Suryawanshi, S. (2025) Navigating cybersecurity in Industry 5.0: From risks to solutions. In *Industry 5.0: Key Technologies and Drivers* (pp. 237–63) Cham: Springer Nature Switzerland.

Kost, E. (2025) Zero trust as a defence against supply chain attacks. UpGuard Research. www.upguard.com/blog/prevent-supply-chain-attacks-with-zero-trust-architecture (archived at https://perma.cc/7ESK-DQSU)

Kour, R., Karim, R., Dersin, P. and Venkatesh, N. (2024) Cybersecurity for Industry 5.0: trends and gaps. *Frontiers in Computer Science*, 6, 1434436.

Laddha, S. and Agrawal, A. (2024) Unveiling barriers to Industry 5.0 adoption in supply chains: A DEMATEL approach. *RAUSP Management Journal*. https://doi.org/10.1108/RAUSP-08-2023-0146 (archived at https://perma.cc/8JN8-C9X5)

Lavelle, J. and Ruane, R. (2024) Gartner identifies top trends in supply chain technology for 2024. Gartner. www.gartner.com/en/newsroom/press-releases/2024-03-20-gartner-identifies-top-trends-in-supply-chain-technology-for-2024 (archived at https://perma.cc/GW7N-GPZU)

Lekamge, D. (2024) Challenges and motivators associated with transition from Industry 4.0 to Industry 5.0 in supply chain management functions of the Finnish manufacturing sector. https://lutpub.lut.fi/bitstream/handle/10024/168653/1/master%20thesis_ovite_lekamlage_dinuka.pdf (archived at https://perma.cc/L7QS-PZM7)

Liao, S., Lin, L. and Chen, Q. (2023) Research on the acceptance of collaborative robots for the industry 5.0 era—The mediating effect of perceived competence and the moderating effect of robot use self-efficacy. *International Journal of Industrial Ergonomics*, 95, 103455.

McKinsey & Company (2016) Supply Chain 4.0 – The next generation digital supply chain. *McKinsey Insights*. www.mckinsey.com/capabilities/operations/our-insights/supply-chain-40--the-next-generation-digital-supply-chain?utm_source=chatgpt.com#/ (archived at https://perma.cc/P79T-MPGZ)

McKinsey & Company (2024) Tech-enabled transformations: Three supply chain success stories. *McKinsey Insights*. www.mckinsey.com/capabilities/operations/our-insights/tech-enabled-transformations-three-supply-chain-success-stories (archived at https://perma.cc/QK2D-9RCB)

McKinsey & Company (2025) Change is changing: How to meet the challenge of radical reinvention. *McKinsey Insights*. www.mckinsey.com/capabilities/people-and-organizational-performance/our-insights/change-is-changing-how-to-meet-the-challenge-of-radical-reinvention (archived at https://perma.cc/3MQQ-DKED)

Meyer, M. (2025) Federated data governance explained: A framework for scalable control. *Alation*. www.alation.com/blog/federated-data-governance-explained/ (archived at https://perma.cc/ZU4K-HM55)

Modgil, S., Singh, R. K. and Agrawal, S. (2025) Developing human capabilities for supply chains: An Industry 5.0 perspective. *Annals of Operations Research*, 348(3), 2075–2105.

Mohammed, A., Sundararajan, S. and Kumar, S. (2024) Enhancing human-centered security in Industry 4.0: Navigating challenges and seizing opportunities. In *Artificial Intelligence Solutions for Cyber-Physical Systems* (pp. 214–35) Auerbach Publications.

Mubarik, M. S. (2025) Overcoming barriers to digital transformation: Challenges of implementing innovative digital technologies in supply chains. In *Technological Innovations and Industry 5.0* (pp. 19–36) Elsevier.

Nasimi, M. A. and Vargourani, F. N. (2025) Examining the barriers to adopting Industry 5.0 in supply chains. *Journal of Governance Studies & Development Management*. www.jgsdm.ir/article_223202_340746f546d1b3194bfdb27ecc62d93b.pdf?lang=en (archived at https://perma.cc/Y8U9-EM4L)

Ogunwole, O., Onukwulu, E. C., Joel, M. O., Adaga, E. M. and Ibeh, A. I. (2023) Modernizing legacy systems: A scalable approach to next-generation data architectures and seamless integration. *International Journal of Multidisciplinary Research and Growth Evaluation*, 4(1), 901–09.

Rejeb, A., Rejeb, K., Zrelli, I. and Süle, E. (2025) Industry 5.0 as seen through its academic literature: An investigation using co-word analysis. *Discover Sustainability*, 6(1), 307.

Salim, M. and Sakhri, A. (2025) Revolutionizing supply chain management: Emerging trends and strategies for the future. SSRN 5223075.

Salwaldamia, B., Hafida, B. and Ghoujdam, M. E. K. (2024) Supply Chain 5.0: A comprehensive literature review on implications, applications and challenges. *International Journal of Innovative Science and Research Technology*. https://doi.org/10.38124/ijisrt/ijisrt24apr034 (archived at https://perma.cc/TFA8-Y65N)

Samuels, A. B. and Pelser, A. M. (2025) Transitioning from Industry 4.0 to 5.0: Sustainable supply chain management and talent management insights. *SA Journal of Human Resource Management*, 23, 2874.

Singh, M. (2025) Integrating artificial intelligence with legacy systems: A systematic analysis of challenges and strategic considerations. *European J. Comput. Sci. Inform. Technol*, 13(32), 38–45.

Supply Chain Digital (2025) DHL Supply Chain introducing first cobots to Latin America. https://supplychaindigital.com/news/dhl-supply-chain-introducing-first-cobots-to-latin-america (archived at https://perma.cc/RAM2-H52W)

Wheeler, K. (2025, January 22) How Unilever uses AI & digital twins for sustainability. *Technology Magazine*. https://technologymagazine.com/articles/how-unilever-uses-ai-digital-twins-for-sustainability (archived at https://perma.cc/XJH9-VBQV)

Conclusion

Shaping What's Next: The Road Ahead for Supply Chain 5.0

The best product leaders do not just execute roadmaps. They reshape possibility.

VIJAY SANKARARAMAN

Supply Chain 5.0 is not a model to adopt but a dynamic convergence of global needs and technological capabilities. It redefines supply chains as adaptive, human-centered ecosystems designed to balance resilience, sustainability, and profitability in a volatile world.

In this changing landscape, supply chain professionals are not simply implementing predetermined processes; they play an active role in shaping outcomes. Whether managing sourcing strategies, designing distribution networks, or deploying digital technologies, professionals are at the forefront of driving innovation and organizational change. The future of supply chains depends on our decisions.

Force Multipliers: Shaping What Comes Next

One of the most important insights to emerge from our interviews with supply chain and technology leaders is that the future of supply chains will not be shaped by technology alone. Tools and platforms matter, but the greatest impact comes from the people who know how to use them in ways that amplify effectiveness across the system. These individuals act as force multipliers.

A force multiplier is not a single skill, tool, or decision. It is a combination of factors that significantly increases the effectiveness of a team or organization. In high-performing supply chains, force multipliers take many forms. They include leaders who build trust across functions, who bring clarity to complexity, and who help teams stay focused on outcomes rather than activity. They are the ones who ask, "Are we solving the right problem?" and "Is this a real signal, or just noise?"

As Vijay Sankararaman put it, the real unlock is not in the tech stack or the roadmap, but in "the effect of the force multiplier" (Sankararaman, 2025). These are the people who bring out the best in others. They influence without controlling. They help teams move faster not by pushing harder, but by removing friction, clarifying direction, and aligning incentives.

This insight applies directly to the transformation agenda of Supply Chain 5.0. Building systems that are adaptive, sustainable, and human-centered requires more than capital investment. It requires leadership that multiplies the capacity of others. This does not mean doing more. It means enabling more. It means creating the conditions where people, processes, and technologies work together with greater impact than any one element could achieve alone.

In the end, the organizations that scale are not just the ones that adopt new tools. They are the ones where product and supply chain leadership becomes the pulse of transformation.

From Experience to Action: 10 Lessons

As we close this book, it is worth pausing to reflect on the voices that shaped it. The insights gathered here come from respected supply chain and technology leaders from around the world. Their experiences span industries, regions, and technologies, yet they converge on challenges, opportunities, and trends that are strikingly universal. We are deeply grateful to each of them for sharing their perspectives so openly.

From these conversations, 10 key insights emerged. They are not meant to be a rigid framework, but they capture patterns that cut across geographies and business models. Together, they offer a practical lens on what matters most as organizations navigate the shift from Industry 4.0 to Supply Chain 5.0. These insights speak to both the strategic decisions at the boardroom level and the everyday choices made on factory floors, in logistics hubs, and across digital networks.

1. Design Supply Chains That Amplify Human Capability

Supply Chain 5.0 is fundamentally about designing systems where people and technology complement one another. Instead of using automation to replace human work, leading organizations focus on using digital tools to enhance human judgment, creativity, and problem-solving. This approach reframes technology as augmentation rather than substitution, creating a dynamic where both people and machines achieve outcomes neither could deliver alone.

When technology supports decision-making rather than displacing it, adoption improves and resilience increases. Employees feel empowered rather than threatened, which leads to higher engagement and faster learning curves. In interviews, leaders consistently reported that this human-centric design mindset leads to stronger operational performance and a more adaptive workforce during times of disruption.

2. *Build Trust and Shared Value with Partners Before Deploying Technology*

Advanced technologies and digital networks cannot succeed in the absence of trust. Supply Chain 5.0 requires seamless data exchange and coordinated decision-making, but these capabilities are meaningless if partners do not believe their interests are protected. Leaders emphasized that technology must be built on top of aligned incentives and transparent governance.

Organizations that invest in trust-building see higher adoption rates and greater collaboration across their networks. Clear agreements on how data is shared, how risks are managed, and how benefits are distributed ensure that every participant sees tangible value. This shared value model turns technology from a tool into the backbone of a resilient ecosystem, making collaboration sustainable over the long term.

3. *Adopt Distributed, Modular Networks to Strengthen Resilience*

Traditional centralized supply chains were designed for efficiency, but they have repeatedly shown their fragility in the face of disruption. Supply Chain 5.0 favors modular, distributed networks that can adapt dynamically to shocks. Regionalized production, micro-factories, and diversified supplier bases allow capacity to shift closer to demand and available inputs when disruptions occur.

This approach is not only about risk mitigation; it also opens up opportunities for speed and customization. Distributed networks can respond more quickly to localized changes in demand, support shorter lead times, and enable more sustainable logistics models. In this way, resilience and agility reinforce each other, turning flexibility into a competitive advantage.

4. Integrate Training into the Flow of Daily Work

Lasting transformation does not come from isolated classroom sessions but from embedding learning directly into operations. Training "in the flow of work" allows employees to practice new skills and tools under real conditions, which accelerates both competence and confidence. This approach also reinforces safety by letting workers learn procedures in the environments where they will actually be applied.

Organizations that adopt this model find that cultural change takes deeper root. Because learning is tied to live operational outcomes, new behaviors become part of the normal rhythm of work rather than a separate initiative. Over time, this creates a workforce that is not only skilled in new technologies but also more adaptable to ongoing change.

5. Use Bottom-Up Data and Customer Feedback to Drive Decisions

Supply Chain 5.0 depends on real-time, granular data captured at the edges of the network. Information from warehouse floors, supplier tiers, and customer touchpoints provides a more accurate foundation for decision-making than top-down models alone. Combined with active customer feedback loops, this bottom-up approach creates systems that respond dynamically to actual conditions and human needs.

High-quality edge data also becomes the fuel for advanced analytics and AI systems. When organizations integrate operational data with customer insights, they create a feedback-rich environment where supply chains can continuously tune themselves for better alignment, less waste, and higher value creation. This blend of technology and human input is what makes 5.0 truly adaptive.

6. Plan for Disruption and Design for Antifragility

Modern supply chains operate in an environment defined by volatility and uncertainty. Resilience is no longer about absorbing small fluctuations; it is about preparing for scenarios that stretch well beyond expected ranges. Scenario planning that challenges core assumptions helps organizations identify structural vulnerabilities before they are exposed by real-world events.

Antifragility goes further by turning disruption into a source of strength. Modular design, rapid feedback loops, and adaptive processes allow supply chains not only to survive shocks but to emerge stronger because of them. Leaders who embrace this mindset view disruption as a catalyst for innovation and competitive advantage rather than merely a threat to manage.

7. *Build Workforce Trust to Accelerate Technology Adoption*

Even the most sophisticated systems fail if the workforce sees them as complex, opaque, or threatening. Supply Chain 5.0 initiatives succeed when organizations prioritize transparency, intuitive design, and communication that addresses fears early. When employees understand how technology supports their roles and why data is being collected, resistance turns into engagement.

Aligned incentives are equally critical. Rewarding employees who contribute to adoption—whether by training peers or providing data for AI systems—signals that their efforts matter. Over time, this trust-based approach creates a culture where technology is seen as a partner in success rather than a disruptor of stability.

8. *Align Sustainability Goals with Profitability*

Sustainability often enters the supply chain conversation through regulatory requirements. Initiatives such as emissions reporting and responsible sourcing standards can provide a necessary baseline and move entire industries in the right direction. Regulations create a floor of compliance that forces organizations to measure, report, and account for environmental and social impacts. They also establish common language and benchmarks, which can accelerate collective progress and ensure that environmental stewardship is not optional.

However, leaders emphasized that Supply Chain 5.0 requires going beyond compliance to achieve true transformation. The most successful organizations use regulations as a starting point, then innovate well past the minimum standards in search of breakthroughs that align sustainability with profitability. By rethinking materials, redesigning processes, or creating circular systems, they uncover cost savings, new revenue streams, and competitive advantages that compliance alone cannot deliver. This is where sustainability becomes not just an option but a driver of innovation and a source of long-term strategic value.

9. Create Governance Models that Balance Control and Agility

AI-enabled and digitally integrated supply chains demand governance structures that can move at the speed of data. Traditional hierarchical decision-making often slows response times, making organizations less adaptable. Supply Chain 5.0 requires governance that empowers operational teams to make rapid, informed decisions while maintaining strategic oversight at higher levels.

This balance between control and agility allows organizations to act decisively during disruptions without losing alignment with long-term objectives. Clear roles, transparent metrics, and defined decision rights become critical enablers of both speed and accountability in a complex, interconnected network.

10. Treat Transformation as a Continuous Capability

Supply Chain 5.0 is not a one-time initiative but an ongoing capability that must evolve alongside technology, regulation, and customer expectations. Organizations that succeed in this era approach transformation as a living process rather than a fixed destination. They embed experimentation, pilot testing, and reassessment into their culture to stay aligned with a constantly shifting environment.

However, true impact comes from more than running pilots. Leading companies build clear pathways to rapidly scale successful projects across the entire supply network. They move beyond isolated experiments and create repeatable mechanisms for turning proven ideas into enterprise-wide capabilities. This requires deliberate governance, cross-functional coordination, and investment in change management to ensure that innovation spreads quickly and effectively. By combining continuous experimentation with the ability to scale breakthroughs, organizations make adaptability a permanent strength and keep their supply chains relevant in an unpredictable world.

Anticipating the Next Wave of Innovation

A new generation of innovations is poised to redefine how supply chains are designed, operated, and managed. What once seemed experimental is moving rapidly into mainstream practice, and the coming decade will see these technologies shift from isolated pilots to enterprise-wide capabilities. The challenge for leaders is not only to adopt these tools but also to anticipate how they will converge and reshape entire supply networks.

One of the most transformative developments is the rise of autonomous decision-making systems powered by AI, ML, and advanced analytics. These systems are advancing beyond early pilots into platforms capable of monitoring disruptions, interpreting real-time demand signals, and dynamically adjusting inventory and logistics flows with minimal human intervention. This evolution does not eliminate the role of people but redefines it. As routine tasks are automated, supply chain professionals are focusing less on daily operational control and more on strategic orchestration, exception management, and long-term network design. The next stage of progress will connect these AI systems across multiple organizations to create self-optimizing networks that can respond in real time to global conditions.

At the material level, innovation is reshaping the physical foundation of supply chains. Companies are developing bio-based materials, regenerative inputs, and closed-loop production systems that reduce dependence on finite resources. Packaging made from agricultural waste or algae and industrial inputs derived from captured emissions are early examples of a deeper transformation. Supply chains are beginning to integrate circular economy principles at scale, moving toward a future where operations not only minimize harm but also restore resources and ecosystems. Regenerative logistics is becoming an operational necessity rather than simply a sustainability initiative.

The evolving relationship between humans and intelligent machines is equally critical. The next wave of innovation is defined not by full automation but by a model of human and AI working together. Machines excel at processing large volumes of data and managing routine tasks at speed, while humans bring contextual understanding, ethical judgment, and strategic insight. Organizations that build systems around this partnership and prepare their workforce to manage networks rather than individual tasks will turn AI into a source of greater creativity, resilience, and adaptability.

These innovations will not arrive at the same pace across every industry. Adoption will depend on factors such as supply chain complexity, regulatory pressures, and organizational culture. High-technology industries may integrate autonomous systems quickly, while sectors facing material constraints may prioritize regenerative practices. To navigate this uneven landscape, leaders must establish structured frameworks for experimentation and create processes that allow successful projects to scale rapidly across the entire network. Innovation that remains trapped in pilots cannot transform the supply chain.

Together, these trends represent a fundamental shift from supply chains as linear pipelines to supply networks as dynamic and adaptive ecosystems. Anticipating the next wave of innovation requires more than observing technology mature. It calls for deliberate preparation, integrated strategies, and the development of workforce capabilities that can thrive in hybrid human and machine environments. Organizations that move beyond experimentation and learn to scale breakthroughs quickly will not only participate in the next wave of innovation but will define it.

Supply Chain 5.0 Readiness Checklist

Before moving forward, it helps to pause and ask an important question: How ready are we to bring Supply Chain 5.0 to life? The principles in these pages are not abstract concepts. They require action, alignment, and commitment across technology, people, and purpose.

This self-assessment in Table 16.1 is designed to help you take an honest look at where your organization stands today. It is not meant to serve as a pass or fail scorecard. Instead, it offers a way to understand your starting point and identify the areas that need the most focus. For each statement, rate your agreement on a scale from 1 (Not at all) to 5 (Fully achieved).

- 40–50: You're well on your way to Supply Chain 5.0. Focus on scaling and sharing best practices.
- 25–39: Solid foundation, but room for alignment across strategy, culture, and technology.
- Below 25: Time to revisit your supply chain strategy with 5.0 principles in mind. Start small, but start now.

Table 16.1 Supply Chain 5.0 Readiness Checklist

Statement	Rating (1–5)
We have a clear sustainability strategy embedded in our supply chain operations.	
Our supply chain uses technology to support human decision-making, not replace it.	
We actively invest in workforce upskilling to prepare employees for AI and digital tools.	
Our supply chain metrics include social and environmental impact, not just cost and speed.	
We have contingency plans and redundancies that support adaptive, resilient operations.	
Cross-functional teams collaborate to integrate ESG, risk, and innovation into supply strategy.	
We maintain visibility into multi-tier supplier networks, including ESG performance.	
We've adopted or piloted technologies like digital twins, blockchain, and AI for transparency.	
Our executive leadership is committed to inclusive, purpose-driven supply chain transformation.	
We continuously evaluate our supply chain's impact on customers, communities, and the planet.	

From Vision to Execution: Turning Supply Chain 5.0 Into Practice

While Supply Chain 5.0 offers a compelling vision of digitally integrated, human-centered, and sustainable supply networks, turning that vision into operational reality is a complex undertaking. Success depends not on adopting a single technology or following a prescriptive roadmap, but on carefully navigating a process of strategic execution that reflects the unique characteristics, capabilities, and constraints of each organization.

The process typically begins with an honest and structured assessment of current-state capabilities. Tools such as the SCOR DS from the Association for Supply Chain Management and the European Commission's Industry 5.0 framework offer methodologies that help organizations evaluate their digital infrastructure, workforce skills, process maturity, and sustainability practices. These frameworks do more than provide scorecards. They encourage companies to reflect critically on where they stand relative to industry peers, where the gaps in their supply chain competencies exist, and what steps are most likely to deliver strategic value. For some organizations, this assessment may reveal a need to invest in foundational technologies such as integrated data systems or real-time visibility tools. For others, the priority may be workforce development or embedding sustainability criteria into supplier selection processes.

Once strategic gaps are identified, the next challenge is prioritization. Here, targeted experimentation often proves more effective than large-scale transformation attempts. Pilot programs allow companies to test new technologies, processes, and business models in controlled environments. By focusing on a single product line, geographic region, or operational function, organizations can evaluate the practical effectiveness of innovations, collect operational data, and identify potential risks before committing to broader implementation. For instance, when Unilever explored blockchain technology for traceability, it initially applied the solution to a single commodity supply chain, monitoring performance and learning operational lessons before extending the technology across other business units. This phased approach reduces the risk of disruption, builds organizational learning, and helps secure internal buy-in through demonstrated results.

However, piloting alone is insufficient. Scaling innovations from isolated projects to enterprise-wide transformation requires deliberate planning and sustained organizational commitment. Technology upgrades are necessary, but they are rarely sufficient. Human factors—including workforce skills, organizational culture, and leadership alignment—play a decisive role in determining whether innovations take root or stall. Employee reskilling initiatives help equip staff with the digital fluency and problem-solving skills needed to operate and manage more automated and data-driven supply chains. Cross-functional collaboration, breaking down silos between procurement, operations, IT, and sustainability teams, ensures that changes are coordinated and strategically aligned. Transparent communication from leadership, explaining the rationale for change and the expected benefits, helps build trust and reduce resistance to new technologies and processes.

Governance structures must also evolve. Traditional hierarchical decision-making may hinder the responsiveness required in digitally enabled supply chains. Organizations may need to adopt more agile governance models that empower operational teams to make faster, data-informed decisions while maintaining oversight and strategic direction at higher levels. This shift requires clarity of roles, performance metrics, and accountability structures that support both control and flexibility.

Ultimately, implementing Supply Chain 5.0 is not a one-time project but an ongoing process of learning, adaptation, and refinement. Technologies will continue to evolve. Regulatory landscapes will shift. Customer expectations will change. Organizations that embed flexibility and continuous improvement into their supply chain strategies will be better equipped to adapt to emerging challenges and capitalize on new opportunities. Periodic reassessment, guided by frameworks like SCOR DS or Industry 5.0, allows organizations to recalibrate their strategies as conditions evolve.

Rather than viewing transformation as a linear journey from a defined starting point to a fixed endpoint, supply chain leaders must treat Supply Chain 5.0 as a dynamic capability to be cultivated over time. The goal is not simply to digitize or automate existing processes, but to build a supply chain ecosystem that is adaptable, resilient, and responsive to both current needs and future possibilities. Organizations that understand this distinction and approach transformation as a continuous strategic endeavor will be better positioned to thrive in an increasingly complex and uncertain global environment.

Agency and Responsibility in Shaping Supply Chain 5.0

Supply Chain 5.0 is not a fixed endpoint or a single, uniform model to be implemented in the same way across all industries. It is better understood as an evolving framework of possibilities that will take shape differently across organizations, sectors, and regions. Whether future supply chains become more autonomous, more sustainable, or more responsive will depend not on technology alone, but on the cumulative decisions made by supply chain professionals within their unique operating environments. The adoption, adaptation, or rejection of emerging technologies and practices will be driven by strategic choices, not predetermined trends.

Professionals working in this space must recognize that they are not simply inheriting a set of best practices; they are actively shaping the future of supply chain management through every choice they make, from supplier engagement and technology investment to workforce development and sustainability initiatives. Understanding industry standards, regulatory frameworks, and available technologies provides a necessary foundation for strategic planning. Yet this foundation is only part of the equation. Equally important is the ability to assess operational realities, weigh risks, and prioritize actions that align with both immediate goals and long-term organizational strategy.

The future architecture and performance of global supply chains will not emerge from any single decision or innovation. Rather, it will reflect the cumulative outcomes of countless actions taken by professionals across industries and regions. Whether supply chains primarily serve the goals of economic growth, environmental sustainability, social equity, or a balanced combination of these outcomes will be determined by how companies and their leaders respond to the forces shaping the landscape today.

Supply Chain 5.0 can be understood as the convergence of what is needed with what is now possible. On one side are pressing global needs: Greater transparency, environmental stewardship, operational resilience, and ethical business practices. On the other side are the expanding technological and organizational capabilities that can address these needs. Supply chain professionals stand at the intersection of this convergence. The strategic decisions they make, and the operational actions they take, will shape supply chains that influence not only company performance, but also broader economic systems, environmental resources, and social well-being.

It is important to recognize that many of the forces shaping supply chains lie beyond the direct influence of supply chain professionals. Geopolitical volatility, climate change, disruptive technologies, and shifting consumer demands are external realities that organizations must navigate. However, while professionals may not control these forces, how they prepare for and respond to them will play a decisive role in determining the future of their supply networks. Agility, resilience, and adaptability will become defining traits for supply chains that succeed in this complex environment.

The future of supply chain management is not a foregone conclusion. It will be constructed through the collective strategies, judgments, and leadership decisions made by professionals like you. The systems that emerge over the coming years will reflect how today's leaders choose to adapt, invest, innovate, and collaborate in response to challenges and opportunities.

Reaching the end of this book signals more than a completed reading journey. It marks a point of readiness. By engaging with the concepts, frameworks, and examples presented here, you have gained the perspective and understanding needed to navigate this changing landscape. But acquiring knowledge is only the beginning. The true impact will come from how you apply that knowledge in practice. Supply chains are not theoretical constructs. They are real systems, influencing people, communities, businesses, and environments every day.

The future of supply chains will not be shaped by technology alone, nor by strategic planning in isolation. It will be shaped by professionals who are willing to think critically, act decisively, and lead with both expertise and responsibility. The challenges we face are significant. But so too is our collective potential to build supply chains that strengthen businesses, support healthier societies, enable more resilient economies, and create a more sustainable world.

The work ahead is ours. The next step belongs to us.

What We Learned Writing This Book

When we first sat down to write this book, we believed we were writing about the future. As we dug deeper, we realized something that surprised us: Supply Chain 5.0 is not a vision of what is coming next. It is already here. What we thought would be a roadmap for the next decade turned out to be a snapshot of the present. We are seeing the goals of Supply Chain 5.0 woven into the innovations and transformations happening in real supply chains right now. This is happening even though Industry 4.0 is not fully realized and technologies like fusion power and quantum computing are still just on the edge of commercialization.

One of the biggest lessons we took away from this work is that sustainability, resilience, and human-centricity cannot stand apart from traditional business goals such as efficiency and profitability. They must be integrated. It is easy to think of Supply Chain 5.0 as a matter of technology adoption, but what we found is that real transformation depends just as much on strong business judgment. You have to know how to align these ambitious goals with the day-to-day realities of running a business. We learned that pragmatism and ambition are not opposites; they have to live side by side if you want change to last.

Another insight that stood out to us was how much Supply Chain 5.0 depends on people and machines learning to work together in new ways. We went into the research thinking that this shift would require everyone to become more technical, maybe even to learn programming. What we found was almost the opposite. One of the most important enablers of Supply Chain 5.0 is the rise of intuitive human–machine interfaces that make working with AI and robotics feel more natural and more human-centered. This aligns perfectly with the human-centric goal of Supply Chain 5.0. What matters most is understanding the moving line between what people do best and what computers do best, and being willing to adjust as that line shifts over time. If we fail to do that, we risk giving the wrong work to the wrong hands, or being left behind with processes and configurations that no longer fit the world around us.

A theme that came up again and again in our research was the shift from optimization to orchestration. For decades, supply chain leaders have been taught to search for the single right answer, the one perfect design. What we learned is that there is no single right answer. Supply chains are living, adaptive systems operating in a world that is volatile, uncertain, complex, and ambiguous. Instead of optimizing for one imagined future, we need to design for a range of possibilities. That means treating historical data with more humility. The past tells us about probabilities, but only within the context in which that data was created. We came to think of it like driving. The rear window is clear. The side windows are cloudy but still give us useful context. The front window, the view of the future, is opaque. Yet we are slowly learning ways to see through it, sometimes in surprising ways, like using social media activity as a leading indicator of demand.

Perhaps the biggest takeaway is that Supply Chain 5.0 is not optional. At first glance, its goals can appear lofty or even idealistic. But when you look at the forces driving them, you realize they are inevitable. The planet is under pressure in ways that threaten its ability to sustain us unless supply chains become part of the solution. A growing population and a turbulent environment make resilience essential. Human-centricity is being demanded by employees, customers, regulators, and society as a whole. COVID made it painfully clear just how fragile our current systems are. We also came to see how many of today's problems trace back to the way we built and managed supply chains through the last four industrial revolutions. Industry 5.0 feels like the moment when we have to pay that debt and find ways to bring people, technology, and the planet back into balance.

Along the way, one of the richest sources of learning came from the executives we interviewed. We are deeply grateful for their willingness to share their time, experience, and wisdom with us. Their openness and candor were a reminder of how much collective knowledge exists within the supply chain community and how generous people can be when invited to shape a bigger conversation. Their willingness to invest in us, and many of the stories they shared, give us real reason to be optimistic about the future. They reminded us that while Supply Chain 5.0 is about technology, it is ultimately about people. Again and again, we saw evidence that when people are given the chance, they can and do use these tools to build something better.

We also came to appreciate the gray areas. There are times when profitability and the goals of Supply Chain 5.0 reinforce each other, and throughout the book we shared examples of companies finding that sweet spot. But there are also times when the tradeoffs are real. One thing Supply Chain 5.0 leaders will need is the ability to make decisions in those gray areas with confidence, clarity, and context. That is why we believe these goals must be embedded in how we train and measure supply chain professionals going forward.

Perhaps the most humbling realization we had while writing is how quickly the future is approaching. The changes we are talking about are not just for our children or grandchildren to experience. The next five, ten, and twenty years will reshape supply chains and the world around them in profound ways. To meet that pace, we need to create structures and incentives that allow companies and leaders to think further ahead, whether that comes from regulation, market forces, investors, or customer expectations.

By the end of this journey, we stopped thinking of Supply Chain 5.0 as a technology or a checklist. We began to see it as a mindset. It is about building a system where business success, human well-being, and the health of the planet are not competing priorities but interconnected goals. And the most exciting part is that this shift is not something we have to wait for. As we discovered while writing this book, it is already underway.

Reference

Sankararaman, V. (2025, July 22). Force Multiplier | Unsung anthem in product leadership [LinkedIn post]. www.linkedin.com/pulse/force-multiplier-unsung-anthem-product-leadership-vijay-sankararaman-z3zne/?trackingId=Zj%2B3InyHRga%2BXHgd6dNjQg%3D%3D (archived at https://perma.cc/F2EE-EM5M)

APPENDIX

Table A.1 Actionable Principles for PLAN in Supply Chain 5.0

Principle	Plan-Order	Plan-Source	Plan-Transform	Plan-Fulfill	Plan-Return	Plan-Orchestrate
1. Integrate Strategic, Tactical, and Operational Planning	Align order fulfillment policies with business goals	Link sourcing strategy to long-term supply resilience	Connect production scheduling to strategic capacity plans	Ensure delivery models match customer service vision	Align reverse logistics with brand and sustainability strategy	Synchronize all planning levels across functions and geographies
2. Adopt Predictive, Data-Driven Forecasting	Use AI to anticipate order volumes and timing	Forecast supplier capacity and raw material needs	Predict production demand and resource constraints	Forecast delivery demand and transport capacity	Predict return volumes and disposition needs	Share predictive insights across all domains for unified action
3. Embed Sustainability Metrics in All Plans	Prioritize low-carbon shipping modes for orders	Source from suppliers meeting ESG standards	Plan production to minimize waste and energy use	Optimize delivery routes for emissions reduction	Integrate refurbish/recycle goals into return plans	Apply ESG metrics as a shared orchestration KPI
4. Leverage Scenario Planning and Digital Twins	Model seasonal peaks or demand shocks	Simulate supplier disruptions or shortages	Test production line changes or new product introductions	Simulate delivery delays or last-mile failures	Model regulatory shifts or return surges	Run cross-domain scenarios for resilience testing

5. Balance Automation with Human Oversight	AI suggests order allocations; humans approve exceptions	Automated sourcing decisions; buyers handle strategic negotiations	Machines optimize scheduling; humans adjust for ethics and safety	Routing AI optimizes delivery; humans address customer-specific needs	Automated returns sorting; humans decide on reuse/refurbishment	Orchestration AI coordinates plans; leaders validate strategy
6. Plan Across the End-to-End Value Network	Share demand plans with upstream suppliers	Collaborate with tier-1 and tier-2 suppliers on capacity	Coordinate with manufacturing partners on output targets	Align with carriers and 3PLs for delivery readiness	Share return forecasts with refurbishment partners	Ensure all nodes in the value chain operate to a common plan
7. Optimize for Agility as well as Efficiency	Build flexibility for rush orders or shifts in demand	Allow rapid reallocation to alternative suppliers	Enable fast changeovers in production lines	Adjust delivery resources in real time to meet shifts	Reallocate processing capacity to handle sudden return spikes	Rapidly shift resources across domains when disruptions occur

(*continued*)

Table A.1 (Continued)

Principle	Plan-Order	Plan-Source	Plan-Transform	Plan-Fulfill	Plan-Return	Plan-Orchestrate
8. Integrate Circular Economy Principles	Plan order policies to encourage eco-friendly delivery options	Source materials with end-of-life recovery potential	Incorporate remanufacturing in production planning	Include reusable packaging in delivery plans	Maximize refurbish, recycle, and resale channels	Align all planning with circular economy KPIs
9. Use Control Towers for Real-Time Visibility	Track live order status to adjust priorities	Monitor supplier performance and inventory in real time	View production KPIs and bottlenecks instantly	Track carrier and delivery milestones	Monitor return flows and processing times	Oversee the entire supply chain from a single data platform
10. Continuously Measure, Learn, and Improve	Review fulfillment lead times and customer feedback	Track sourcing cost, quality, and compliance metrics	Monitor production efficiency and quality outcomes	Measure delivery accuracy, speed, and cost	Assess return processing speed and asset recovery rate	Implement process, policy, technology, or behavioral changes that enhance supplier's value.

INDEX

NB: page numbers in *italic* indicate figures or tables.